Houses and the Hearth Tax:
the later Stuart house and society

Houses and the Hearth Tax:
the later Stuart house and society

Edited by
P S Barnwell and Malcolm Airs

The British Acadamy Hearth Tax Project, Roehampton University
Oxford University Department for Continuing Education
Vernacular Architecture Group

CBA Research Report 150
Council for British Archaeology
2006

Published 2006 by the Council for British Archaeology
St Mary's House, 66 Bootham, York YO30 7BZ

Copyright © 2006 Authors, English Heritage and Council for British Archaeology (English Heritage copyright applies to Chapters 5, 14 and 18)

ISBN 1 902771 65 6

British Library Cataloguing in Publication Data
A catalogue for this book is available from the British Library

Cover designed by BP Design, York

Typeset by Archetype IT Ltd, www.archetype-it.com

Printed by Pennine Printing Services
part of the Jarvis Print Group

The publisher acknowledges with gratitude a grant from
English Heritage towards the cost of publication

Front cover illustration: Cottons Farmhouse, Staplehurst, Kent © S Pearson

Back cover illustration: Wickens, Charing, Kent © S Pearson

Contents

List of illustrations vi
List of tables ix
List of abbreviations x
Acknowledgements xi
Summaries – English, French and German xii

Part 1: The Hearth Tax 1

    1 Introduction *David Hey* 3
    2 Understanding the Hearth Tax Returns: Historical
       and Interpretative Problems *Elizabeth Parkinson* 7
    3 Understanding Exemption from the Hearth Tax *Tom Arkell* 18
    4 Chimneys, Wood and Coal *Margaret Spufford* 22

Part 2: Regional Studies 33

   The South and East 33

    5 London's Suburbs, House Size and the Hearth Tax *Peter Guillery* 35
    6 Kent: History, Houses and the Hearth Tax *Sarah Pearson* 46
    7 Some Highways and Byeways on the Essex Hearth Tax Trail *Pat Ryan* 55
    8 The Hearth Tax and Historic Housing Stocks: A Case Study from Norfolk *Adam Longcroft*. . . . 62
    9 The Houses of the Dorset Hearth Tax *R Machin* 74
  10 Bristol: The Hearth Tax as a Decodable Street Directory *R H Leech* 83

   The Midlands. 95

  11 The Taxable Chimneys of Huntingdonshire in Cambridgeshire *E M Davis*. 96
  12 The Hearth Tax in Warwickshire *N W Alcock* 106

   The North. 121

  13 The East Riding of Yorkshire *Susan and David Neave* 122
  14 The West Riding Hearth Tax Returns of 1672 and the Great Rebuilding *Colum Giles*. 132
  15 The Durham Hearth Tax: Community, Politics and Social Relations *Adrian Green* 144
  16 Northumberland, Newcastle upon Tyne, Berwick upon Tweed and North Durham:
      One County *Grace McCombie*. 155
  17 The Hearth Tax and Housing in Westmorland *Colin Phillips* 164

Part 3: Conclusion 175
  18 Houses, Hearths and Historical Inquiry *P S Barnwell*. 177

Bibliography 184
Index 191

List of Illustrations

2.1	Extract from the Exchequer duplicate for Gloucestershire for 1662M (TNA E179/116/554). © Crown Copyright.	9
2.2	Extract from the Exchequer duplicate for Lancashire for 1664L (TNA E179/250/11). © Crown Copyright	10
2.3	Extract from the Exchequer duplicate for Cambridgeshire 1664M–1665M (TNA E179/84/437). © Crown Copyright.	12
2.4	Extract from the Exchequer duplicate for Glamorgan for 1666L (TNA E179/221/297). © Crown Copyright.	13
2.5	Extract from the Exchequer duplicate for Glamorgan for 1670M (TNA E179/221/294). © Crown Copyright.	14
2.6	Church Farm, Porthkerry, Glamorgan. © Copyright R T Parkinson.	15
2.7	Extract from the Exchequer duplicate for Devon for 1672M–1673L (TNA E179/245/19). © Crown Copyright	16
4.1	Price of underwood in pence per acre, 1250–1720 (after Rackham 2003). Reproduced with permission	22
4.2	Coalfields and some settlements where coal was used or which were short of fuel in the 17th century (after Hatcher 1993). Reproduced with permission	26
4.3	Price of fuel supplied to Westminster School, 1590–1640 (after Hatcher 1993). Reproduced with permission	27
4.4	Shipments of coal from Newcastle and Sunderland, 1508–1700 (after Hatcher 1993). Reproduced with permission	28
5.1	London in 1662–66, mean dwelling size by number of hearths. After Power 1986	36
5.2	The area north of Whitechapel Road in 1674–75.	40
5.3	Nos 22 and 24 Cannon Street Road, east of Whitechapel, London. © English Heritage. NMR	41
5.4	The Fossan Estate, Spitalfields, London, in 1674–75.	42
5.5	Front-staircase 'weavers' houses' of the 1670s, Virginia Road, north of Spitalfields, London. © London Borough of Hackney Archives Department	42
5.6	Part of southern Clerkenwell in 1674–75.	43
5.7	Peter's Lane, Clerkenwell, London. © English Heritage. NMR	43
5.8	A building on Blackboy Alley, near the Fleet Ditch, London. © City of London, LMA	44
6.1	The geographical regions of Kent. Reproduced from Harrington et al 2000. © British Record Society.	47
6.2	Number of hearths per 1000 acres (400 ha). Reproduced from Harrington *et al* 2000. © British Record Society.	48
6.3	Shurland House, Sheppey, Kent. Reproduced by kind permission of TNA	49
6.4	Wickens, Charing, Kent. © S Pearson.	50
6.5	Old Well House, East Peckham, Kent. © Crown Copyright. NMR.	51
6.6	Bishops Farmhouse, Boughton Monchelsea, Kent. © S Pearson	53
6.7	113 High Street, Wingham, Kent. © S Pearson	53
7.1	Density of households per 1000 acres (400 ha) in the hundreds of Essex. © P Ryan	55
7.2	Moyns Park, Steeple Bumpstead, mansion, *c* 1580. © P Ryan	56
7.3	Appletree Farm Cottage, Cressing, Essex. © P Ryan	57
7.4	Potter Row House, Ingatestone, Essex. © P Ryan	57
7.5	Beaumont Otes, Writtle, Essex. © P Ryan	58
7.6	The Bell, Woodham Walter, Essex. © P Ryan	58
8.1	Proportion of households in Norfolk taxed on one hearth 1664/66. © A Longcroft	65
8.2	Soils in Norfolk. Reproduced by kind permission of T Williamson.	66
8.3	Proportion of households in Norfolk taxed on two hearths. © A Longcroft	66
8.4	Proportion of households in Norfolk taxed on one or two hearths. © A Longcroft.	67
8.5	One- and two-cell plans in Norfolk: surviving houses of 16th- and 17th-century date in Stiffkey. © A Longcroft.	68
8.6	Proportion of households in Norfolk taxed on three to six hearths. © A Longcroft	69
8.7	Three-cell plans in Norfolk: surviving houses of 16th- and 17th-century date in south Norfolk. © A Longcroft	69

List of Illustrations   vii

8.8	Proportion of households in Norfolk taxed on ten hearths or more. © A Longcroft	70
8.9	The great estates of Norfolk in the 19th century. Reproduced by kind permission of S Wade Martins	70
8.10	Distribution of pre-*c* 1730 vernacular buildings in Norfolk. Reproduced by kind permission of P Tolhurst.	71
9.1	Three-unit central hall hearth passage house, Melbury Osmund, Dorset. © R Machin	76
9.2	Three-unit unheated central room type, Plush, Dorset. © R Machin	77
9.3	Two-unit Hart's Cottage type, Edmondsham, Dorset. © R Machin	78
9.4	Two-unit Virginia house type dated 1573, Puddletown, Dorset. © R Machin	79
9.5	Chetnole Farm, Chetnole, Dorset. © R Machin	80
9.6	Iles Farm, Leigh, Dorset. © R Machin.	81
10.1	20 Small Street, Bristol. Plan by Dollman and Jobbins, 1863	86
10.2	57 Castle Street, Bristol. Reproduced by permission of Bristol City Reference Library	88
10.3	57 and 70 Castle Street, Bristol. Schematic section. © R H Leech.	89
10.4	Gilbert Moore's garden house on St Michael's Hill, Bristol. Bristol City Museum and Art Gallery. Reproduced by kind permission	91
10.5	Extract from Millerd's map of 1673 showing the garden houses of Thomas Jennings and Thomas Wells	92
10.6	Garden house of Thomas Wells, Bristol. Bristol City Library, Loxton drawings. Reproduced by kind permission	93
11.1	Map of Huntingdonshire. © English Heritage. NMR.	97
11.2	Hearth Tax return 1664 for Huntingdonshire and Cambridgeshire. Kirby and Oosthuizen 2000. Reproduced with permission.	98
11.3	Spaldwick Manor, Huntingdonshire. © E M Davis	99
11.4	Plans of Pepys House, Brampton, Huntingdonshire. © E M Davis	100
11.5	Brook End Farmhouse, Great Catworth, Huntingdonshire. © E M Davis.	101
11.6	Bunyan Cottage, Wornditch, Kimbolton, Huntingdomshire. © E M Davis	103
11.7	Highbury, Great Staughton, Huntingdonshire. © E M Davis	104
11.8	Photograph, demolition in 1936 of Hail Weston farmhouse. Reproduced by permission of the County Record Office Huntingdon	105
12.1	Administrative divisions of 17th-century Warwickshire. © N W Alcock.	106
12.2	Mapping of Hearth Tax statistics for Warwickshire. Reproduced with permission of T Slater.	108
12.3	Mapping of Hearth Tax data for gentry and great houses in Warwickshire. Reproduced with permission of T Slater	110
12.4	Building materials in Warwickshire. Reproduced with permission of T Slater	111
12.5	The parish of Chilvers Coton, Warwickshire, in the 17th century. © N W Alcock.	112
12.6	Arbury Hall, Warwickshire. Reproduced with permission of Birmingham City Archives	113
12.7	Chilvers Coton village (Warwickshire) in 1684, area A. Reproduced with permission of WCRO	114
12.8	Chilvers Coton village (Warwickshire) in 1684, area B. Reproduced with permission of WCRO	115
12.9	Manor Farm, Stoneleigh, Warwickshire. © N W Alcock	116
12.10	11–12 Coventry Road, Stoneleigh, Warwickshire. © N W Alcock.	116
12.11	Ivy Farm, Canley, with two hearths in 1674. © N W Alcock	117
12.12	Warwickshire houses with one hearth. © N W Alcock	117
13.1	Maps of Watton, East Riding of Yorkshire, showing decrease in housing. East Riding Archive Office. Reproduced with permission	123
13.2	Oak Cottage, South Dalton, East Riding of Yorkshire. © D Neave	124
13.3	Cottage at Wheldrake, Vale of York. Private collection.	125
13.4	East Riding townships where 75% or more of the houses had only one hearth in 1672.	126
13.5	Elmswell Old Hall, East Riding of Yorkshire. University of Hull Photographic Service	128
13.6	Wilberforce House, Hull. © D Neave	129
13.7	Knedlington Old Hall, East Riding of Yorkshire. © D Neave.	130
14.1	Wood Lane Hall, Sowerby, West Yorkshire. © Crown Copyright.	132
14.2	The open housebody at Birks, Slaithwaite, West Yorkshire. © Crown Copyright	135
14.3	Green Top, Marsden, West Yorkshire. © Crown Copyright.	136
14.4	Ryecroft, Tong, West Yorkshire. © Crown Copyright	138
14.5	Peel House, Warley, West Yorkshire. © Crown Copyright	139
14.6	Fireplace and overmantel at Lower Old Hall, Norland, West Yorkshire. © Crown Copyright	141
14.7	The remains of High Bentley, Shelf, West Yorkshire. © Crown Copyright.	142
15.1	Terrain map of County Durham. © B K Roberts	145
15.2	Map of one-hearth households in 1666 in County Durham. © British Record Society	147

15.3	Old Queen's Head, Wolsingham, Weardale. © A Green	148
15.4	Westernhopeburn Farmhouse, Eastgate, Weardale. © A Green	149
15.5	Slashpool Farm, Hett village, County Durham. © A Green	149
15.6	East Oakley House, West Auckland, County Durham. © A Green	151
16.1	Map of Northumberland and the Bishoprick of Durham from Michael Drayton's *Poly-Olbion*, 1622. Reproduced by permission of Newcastle City Library	156
16.2	Edlingham Castle, Northumberland. © G McCombie	157
16.3	Chipchase Castle, Northumberland. © G McCombie	157
16.4	Belsay Castle, Northumberland. © G McCombie	158
16.5	Elsdon Tower, Northumberland. © G McCombie	159
16.6	Hole Bastle, Northumberland. © G McCombie	160
16.7	Denton Hall, Northumberland. © G McCombie	161
16.8	John Speed's map of Newcastle, 1610. © G McCombie	161
16.9	41–46 Sandhill, Newcastle upon Tyne. © G McCombie	162
16.10	Alderman Fenwick's House, Newcastle upon Tyne. © G McCombie	163
17.1	Sketch map of Westmorland jurisdictions and surrounding areas. Adapted from Phillips 1973, 45	165
17.2	A one-hearth house of shortly before 1670 in Rydal. From Armitt 1916	168
17.3	Lowther Hall, Westmorland in the 1680s. Reproduced by kind permission of the Chapter of Carlisle Cathedral	170
17.4	Part of north-east side of Stricklandgate, Kendal, 1898 Ordnance Survey 6-inch map	172
18.1	Timber chimneys. © English Heritage. NMR	178

List of Tables

2.1	The Hearth Tax 1662–89.	7
4.1	The domestic use of coal in Kent, 1600–1749	24
4.2	The domestic use of coal in Kent and Cornwall, 1600–1749	25
5.1	London's suburbs: some comparative Hearth Tax statistics	37
7.1	Timber hoods and brick chimney stacks on the Walker maps of Essex (1586–1616)	59
7.2	Percentage of households in Hearth Tax Project categories in 1671 for Essex	59
8.1	Exempted persons as a proportion of those paying the hearth tax, Norfolk, Michaelmas 1664	63
8.2	Numbers of hearths in the houses of husbandmen and yeomen.	68
9.1	Dorset Hearth Tax 1662–64.	74
10.1	Small Street, Bristol, in 1662	85
10.2	The south side of Castle Street, Bristol, in 1664–65	87
10.3	Extract from the Hearth Tax return of 1662 for the parish of St Michael, Bristol	90
10.4	Extract from the Hearth Tax return of 1664–65 for the ward of St Michael, Bristol	91
10.5	Extract from the Hearth Tax return for 1664–65 for the ward of St Thomas, Bristol: properties with ten or more hearths	93
12.1	Household of Sir Richard Newdigate	113
12.2	Households of Henry Baker, John Parker, Thomas Abbotts, Ann White and William Randle	115
12.3	Correlation of 1674 hearths and rooms in Stoneleigh probate inventories	118
13.1	East Riding of Yorkshire: households and hearths by wapentake 1672	127
17.1	Westmorland: households by numbers of hearths, 1669 and 1674/75	166
17.2	Westmorland: rural gross probate values and numbers of hearths	167
17.3	Westmorland: households with three and three-plus hearths	168
17.4	Kendal: occupiers of part of the east side of the north end of Stricklandgate, 1669–95.	171

Abbreviations

BIA	Borthwick Institute for Archives, University of York
BRO	Bristol Record Office
CROC	Cumbria Record Office, Carlisle
CROH	County Record Office, Huntingdon
CROK	Cumbria Record Office, Kendal
DRO	Durham Record Office
DUA	Durham University Archive
ERO	Essex Record Office
LMA	London Metropolitan Arhives
LRO	Lancashire Record Office, Preston
NMR	National Monuments Record
RCHME	Royal Commission on the Historical Monuments of England
TNA	The National Archives
VCH	Victoria History of the Counties of England
WCRO	Warwickshire County Record Office

Acknowledgements

This volume contains a revised and edited version of the papers presented at a conference held at Rewley House, Oxford, in October 2004 with additional chapters contributed by David Hey and Paul Barnwell. The conference was part of an annual series hosted by Oxford University Department for Continuing Education with the general aim of exploring new approaches to the study of vernacular buildings. The programme was planned in association with the Vernacular Architecture Group and the British Academy Hearth Tax Project at Roehampton University.

The impetus for the theme of the conference came from Margaret Spufford and the editors are deeply indebted to her vision and her determination to bring together scholars from a wide variety of disciplines and geographical locations to engage in fruitful debate. She played a key role in planning the detailed programme and identifying the appropriate contributors, and she was instrumental in pressing for the publication of the proceedings. In a very real sense, this volume is a testament to her belief in the interdisciplinary potential of Hearth Tax studies.

Many of the contributors are working on the county volumes which are in the process of being published by the British Record Society. We are grateful to them for sharing their interim findings with us, and to all the contributors for responding to the tight deadline imposed by the editors in order to ensure prompt publication. The scholarly debts that they incurred in preparing their papers are duly acknowledged in the individual chapters. We also gratefully acknowledge Allan T Adams of English Heritage for assisting with the preparation of the illustrations.

Two previous volumes from the series have been published by the Council for British Archaeology (*Vernacular Buildings in a Changing World,* ed Sarah Pearson and Bob Meeson, CBA Research Report **126**, 2001 and *The Vernacular Workshop: From Craft to Industry, 1400–1900,* ed P S Barnwell, Marilyn Palmer and Malcolm Airs, CBA Research Report **140**, 2004). We are immensely gratified at its continued support in disseminating the proceedings to a larger audience than was able to attend the conference. Similarly, as with the two preceding volumes, publication would not have been possible without the generous financial support of English Heritage and we gratefully acknowledge its important contribution to this area of scholarship.

Summary

The Hearth Tax was a national tax levied in England and Wales between 1662 and 1689. It was a property tax, assumed to approximate to the householders' wealth, measured by the number of fireplaces their houses possessed. It was collected in two annual instalments of one shilling per hearth. The main surviving returns for the taxes date from 1662–66 and 1670–74, and include partial lists of those who were exempt from the tax. It is the only national listing of people between the medieval poll taxes and the census returns of the 19th century, and has the potential to present an overview of the country's wealth, population, and social structure in the later 17th century. Some of the returns have been published in the past by scholars working on particular counties or regions, but there has been no consistency of approach or attempt to view the material on a national scale. This omission is now being addressed by the British Academy Hearth Tax Project at Roehampton University, which aims to ensure publication of the most complete return for each county for which reliable documents are available, each volume presented in a uniform way with consistent analytical tables and maps. It is an ambitious project which will take many years to bring to fruition, and the Oxford conference provided an opportunity for early discussion both of the contribution the Hearth Tax can make to the study of buildings in the 17th century and on the significance of buildings for understanding the Hearth Tax.

This volume presents the outcome of that discussion and offers an important summary account of housing and society in that period based on both physical and documentary research. It is divided into three parts with an introductory section setting out the central importance of the hearth and the potential and the difficulties of using the tax as a tool for historical research. This is followed by detailed regional studies with a geographical spread from the southern part of the country through the midlands to the north. Although each study takes an individual approach, common themes include the difficulties of interpreting houses rated on a single hearth in both town and country, the relative status of their owners, the evolution of heated upper storeys and the adoption of chimney stacks built in permanent materials, and the relationship between statistics derived from the documents and the physical evidence visible on the ground. Of particular note are the regional differences in plan forms and size of houses as a reflection of local distinctiveness in traditional architecture. The various strands are brought together in a concluding section which draws on the information presented in the individual chapters and poses questions for further research. The dialogue between understanding of surviving structures and interpretation of the tax and other documentary sources on a regional basis makes this an important book which as well as providing a synthesis of current knowledge will act as a catalyst for further research. It will appeal to local and general historians as well as students of vernacular buildings.

Résumé

L'impôt sur les cheminées [Hearth Tax] était un impôt national perçu en Angleterre et au pays de Galles entre 1662 et 1689. C'était un impôt sur la propriété, qui était censé représenter une approximation de la fortune du propriétaire, et qui était mesuré en fonction du nombre de cheminées dont jouissait sa demeure. Cet impôt était perçu deux fois par an au taux de un shilling par cheminée. Les principales déclarations d'impôts qui restent encore sont datées de 1662 à 1666 et de 1670 à 1674, et comprennent des listes partielles de ceux qui étaient exemptés de cet impôt. C'est la seule liste nationale de personnes entre la capitation du Moyen-Âge et les relevés de recensement du 19ème siècle, et cette liste offre éventuellement la possibilité de présenter une vue d'ensemble de la richesse du pays, de sa population et de sa structure sociale à la fin du 17ème siècle. Certaines déclarations ont déjà été publiées auparavant par des spécialistes qui travaillaient sur des comtés ou des régions précises, mais il n'y a eu ni approche uniforme concernant ce matériel ni effort d'appréciation à l'échelle nationale. Le Projet sur l'impôt sur les cheminées [Hearth Tax Project] de la British Academy à l'université de Roehampton s'occupe à l'heure actuelle de remédier à cette omission, dans l'intention de publier la déclaration la plus complète pour chaque comté pour laquelle sont disponibles des documents fiables, chaque volume étant présenté de manière uniforme avec des cartes et des tableaux analytiques cohérents. Il s'agit là d'un projet fort ambitieux dont la réalisation va prendre de nombreuses années, et le congrès d'Oxford a donné l'occasion de discuter dès le début à la fois de la contribution que peut faire l'impôt sur les cheminées à l'étude des bâtiments au 17ème siècle et de la signification des bâtiments pour une meilleure compréhension de l'impôt sur les cheminées.

Ce volume présente les résultats de cette discussion et offre un important compte-rendu résumé du logement et de la société à cette époque, sur la base de recherches à la fois matérielles et documentaires. Il est divisé en trois parties avec une introduction qui explique l'importance fondamentale de la cheminée et la difficulté d'utiliser l'impôt comme instrument de recherche historique. Cette introduction est suivie d'études régionales détaillées dont l'envergure géographique s'étend de la partie Sud du pays, à travers le centre et jusqu'au Nord. Bien que chaque étude adopte une approche individuelle, les thèmes communs couvrent les difficultés liées à l'interprétation de maisons évaluées à une seule cheminée, à la fois à la ville et dans les campagnes, le standing relatif de leurs propriétaires, l'évolution des étages supérieurs chauffés et l'adoption de souches de cheminées construites en matériaux permanents, et les rapports entre les statistiques dérivées des documents et les indices matériels visibles sur le terrain. Il convient de noter tout particulièrement les différences régionales entre les formes de plans et entre les dimensions des maisons car ces différences reflètent les particularités locales au sein de l'architecture traditionnelle. Les divers fils sont regroupés dans une conclusion qui se base sur l'information présentée dans les chapitres séparés et pose certaines questions nécessitant des recherches plus poussées. Le dialogue entre la compréhension de structures restant encore et l'interprétation de l'impôt et d'autres sources documentaires sur une base régionale font de ce volume un travail important qui non seulement fournit une synthèse des connaissances actuelles mais qui servira également de catalyseur pour des recherches plus poussées. Il sera apprécié des historiens locaux et généraux ainsi des étudiants de bâtiments d'architecture locale.

Übersicht

Die sogenannte Kaminsteuer war eine staatliche Abgabe, die in ganz England und Wales in der Zeit von 1662 bis 1689 erhoben wurde. Es war eine Art Grundsteuer, die in Beziehung zum Vermögen der Grundbesitzer stand, und an der Anzahl der Kamine, die ein Haus besaß gemessen wurde. Diese Steuer wurde zweimal im Jahr eingenommen und betrug einen Schilling pro Kamin. Die am besten überlieferten Steuerberichte aus den Jahren 1662–74 enthalten zum Teil auch Listen von den Personen, die von dieser Steuer befreit waren. Es ist das einzige staatliche Verzeichnis, das die Zeit zwischen der mittelalterlichen Kopfsteuer und der Volkszählung des 19. Jahrhunderts überbrückt und somit über die Bevölkerung in dieser Zeit Aufschluss gibt. Es bietet eine einzigartige Möglichkeit einen Überblick über den Wohlstand, die Einwohnerzahl und die soziale Struktur der Bevölkerung im späten 17. Jahrhundert zu erhalten. Einige dieser Verzeichnisse wurden schon damals von Gelehrten veröffentlicht, die in bestimmten Grafschaften oder Regionen Forschung betrieben, aber es gibt keinen systematischen Ansatz diese Material landesweit zusammenzutragen. Das Kaminsteuerprojekt, unterstützt von der „British Academy" und von der Universität Roehampten durchgeführt, soll diese Wissenslücke schließen.

Das Projekt hat zum Ziel ein komplettes Verzeichnis für jede Grafschaft zu veröffentlichen, für die zuverlässige Quellen verfügbar sind. Jeder Band wird in einem einheitlichen Format zusammengestellt und soll vergleichbare analytische Tabellen und Karten enthalten. Es ist ein sehr ehrgeiziges Projekt, zu dessen Verwirklichung viele Jahre benötigt werden. Die Oxforder Konferenz bietet die Möglichkeit eines frühen Meinungsaustauschs, um den Beitrag, den die Kaminsteuer zur Studie von Gebäuden im 17. Jahrhundert machen kann, zu bewerten, und in welchem Ausmaß die Studie von Gebäuden zum Verständnis der Kaminsteuer beitragen kann.

Dieser Band fasst die Ergebnisse dieser Diskussion zusammen und verkörpert einen wichtigen zusammenfassenden Bericht über den Zustand von Wohnungen und der allgemeinen Gesellschaft in dieser Zeit und der sich auf Untersuchungen des Baustils und Quellenstudien beruft. Er ist in drei Teile unterteilt, in der Einleitung wird die zentrale Bedeutung des Kamins behandelt und es werden die Möglichkeiten und Grenzen die diese Steuer für die historische Forschung bietet, erörtert. Im Hauptteil sind detaillierte regionale Studien geographisch von Süden nach Norden geordnet. Obwohl jede Studie individuell angelegt ist, werden gemeinsame Themen angesprochen, wie zum Beispiel die Schwierigkeit Stadtwohnungen mit einem Kamin mit denen auf dem Land zu vergleichen, der relative gesellschaftliche Rang der Besitzer, die Entwicklung von beheizten oberen Stockwerken, die Einführung von Schornsteinen aus dauerhaften Material und das Verhältnis zwischen Quellenstatistiken und den realen Verhältnissen an Ort und Stelle. Von besonderem Interesse sind die regionalen Unterschiede in der Bauweise und der Größe der Häuser, die die örtlichen Besonderheiten und traditionelle Architektur widerspiegeln. Die diversen Themen aus den verschiedenen Kapiteln werden im Schlussteil zusammengeführt und Fragen für zukünftige Forschung entworfen. Der in diesem Band entfachte Dialog zwischen dem Verständnis von überlebenden Hausstrukturen und der Interpretation der Steuerberichte und anderen Quellen macht dies zu einem bedeutenden Buch, das sowohl den bisherigen Wissenstand zusammenfasst und auch zu weiterführenden und vertiefenden Studien anregen wird. Es ist vor allem für Historiker und Studenten einheimischer Architekturformen von Interesse.

PART 1: THE HEARTH TAX

1 Introduction *by David Hey*

The tax that was levied on every householder's hearths twice a year between 1662 and 1689 was the chief source of the government's revenue during the reigns of Charles II and James II. Fireplaces and elaborate chimney stacks had become a matter of pride in larger houses and were readily identified, and by this time even the humblest houses were usually fitted with a chimney. Hearths had become an obvious target for tax, 'it being easy to tell the number of hearths, which remove not as heads or polls do'. But, like most taxes, the Hearth Tax was unpopular and it was abolished after the Glorious Revolution. The returns for each county are now kept in The National Archives under E179.

Meekings, of what was then the Public Record Office, published the first edition of a county's returns, as *Surrey Hearth Tax 1664*, an alphabetical list of entries in the record (Meekings 1940). His introduction to a subsequent volume of *Dorset Hearth Tax Assessments, 1662–64* (Meekings 1951) long remained the standard guide. At first, Hearth Tax returns were used mainly by social and economic historians to estimate population totals for individual parishes or townships and to reconstruct the social structure of local communities. The methods used to interpret the returns in these ways are outlined in the contributions to Schürer and Arkell's *Surveying the People: The Interpretation and Use of Document Sources for the Study of Population in the Later 17th Century* (Schürer and Arkell 1992). In recent years, Hearth Tax returns have also become widely used by family historians and for the study of surname distributions (eg Hey and Redmonds 2002). They are particularly useful in this respect for they date from half-way between the period of surname formation and the present day.

Hoskins recognised the potential of the returns for the study of vernacular architecture. In *Local History in England* he wrote,

> These records ... were not made for the purpose of telling us what houses looked like in the second half of the 17th century, but we can derive a certain amount of information from them about the size of houses and the number of fireplaces in them. The great majority of people lived in houses with only one fireplace, but they must not be dismissed simply as the rural proletariat, as some writers have done.... Obviously, the Hearth Tax assessments are of very limited value for the study of vernacular building in the 17th century and they must be used with great caution; but they should not be entirely ignored (Hoskins 1959, 189).

Later, in the final chapter of his *The Midland Peasant*, headed 'An Excursus on Peasant Houses and Interiors, 1400–1800', he wrote: 'The Hearth-Tax assessment of 1670 is a useful guide to the variety of houses-sizes in the Midland village at a given point of time', particularly as the list of householders included those who were exempt from payment (Hoskins 1965, 299–300). He went on to provide a detailed analysis of the return for Wigston Magna in Leicestershire.

Nevertheless, Hearth Tax returns were ignored entirely by Barley in his seminal study of *The English Farmhouse and Cottage*, a work that combined surveying and recording standing structures with documentary research, especially on probate inventories (Barley 1961). He made amends later when he contributed a section on 'Nottinghamshire Houses' to the introduction to the edition of the records of the Nottinghamshire Hearth Tax (Barley 1988), and in his *Houses and History* he noted that

> The returns have not been studied systematically or in a uniform manner as evidence for housing, but a few regional studies show that surviving houses are not a random sample of those then standing: they represent the largest and the best built. Most small and middling farmers had only one hearth, in the hall; only houses with more than two hearths are likely to have had one or more of them in a chamber (Barley 1986, 245).

As he was writing, three important studies of northern houses were in the process of being published. First, Harrison and Hutton wrote *Vernacular Houses in North Yorkshire and Cleveland* (1984). Based on surveys of some 770 houses, the early chapters concentrated on plans, construction methods, building materials, etc, but then a section entitled 'Rural Housing and Society' examined the available documentary sources, starting with the 1672–73 Hearth Tax returns for North Yorkshire, as a useful, comprehensive 'index of comparative prosperity'. They built on this base by using all the registered wills and probate inventories.

A year later, Pearson's Royal Commission study of *Rural Houses of the Lancashire Pennines* used the 1664 returns to estimate population levels and to provide 'a picture of the number of hearths within each house'. She observed that 'It is often extremely difficult to assess the number of original hearths in 17th-century houses from the physical remains alone, since it is not always possible to tell whether a fireplace was later inserted or was merely altered at a later date. The Hearth Tax can therefore provide us with evidence which we cannot obtain from buildings' (RCHME 1985, 108).

Another Royal Commission study, by Giles, *Rural Houses of West Yorkshire*, went much further in using Hearth Tax returns alongside probate inventories to reveal 'striking local differences even within the building zones. This is a timely corrective to the tendency to think of one area as uniformly wealthy and another as uniformly poor'. He chose three areas of approximately equal size, but with different economies and settlement patterns, to compare the distribution of wealth, noting that 'the assumption underlying the analysis of the Hearth Tax Returns is that, despite evasion and omission, the source reflects reasonably accurately the distribution of wealth at the time of assessment' (RCHME 1986, 121–22).

Students of vernacular architecture had therefore accepted the value of using Hearth Tax returns in constructing a broad picture of their regions and in making comparisons with other parts of the country. In particular, it was felt that the timing of the returns meant that they could be used to test Hoskins's concept of 'the great rebuilding' (Hoskins 1953) up and down the land. But comparative studies (in the field of social and economic history as well as vernacular architecture) were hampered by the lack of scholarly editions and transcripts of returns for many of the counties of England and Wales. It was with this in mind that Margaret Spufford began the 'Roehampton Project' at Roehampton University, which aims to ensure that every county has at least one return in print, with full scholarly apparatus. The resulting volumes will include statistical analyses of the returns and maps that present the results in a vivid and easily accessible form. The project was enthusiastically endorsed by The National Archives and got off the ground with a successful Heritage Lottery Fund bid in 2000. The huge task of microfilming the returns was completed in May 2001 and free copies of all relevant films were sent to each County Record Office. A team of volunteer transcribers started work under the direction of staff at Roehampton, and editors and contributors were recruited for the county volumes. The British Record Society has taken the lead in publishing volumes, in association with county record societies or other appropriate local bodies. In 2000, even before the award of the grant, two volumes had appeared, one on Kent (Harrington *et al* 2000), the other on Cambridgeshire (Evans and Rose 2000). The next in line are volumes on County Durham and the West Riding of Yorkshire.

The tables and maps that will demonstrate the distribution of wealth across the country are an essential part of the scholarly analysis of the returns. It has become clear, however, that precise comparisons between different counties will have to be hedged with qualifications. First, the taxable units were not always parishes or townships; they often included subdivisions such as 'quarters' or hamlets. In the West Riding, for example, Haworth had two quarters, Ecclesfield had four, and Huddersfield had five; the seven townships of the Graveship of Holme were gathered together under 'Holmfirth'; and the returns for the parish of Dent were listed under six 'bills' with no district names attached.

Second, to overcome the problem that parishes or townships varied enormously in size, tables showing the number of hearths per 1000 acres (400 ha) have been constructed as indicators of wealth. However, Pennine townships include thousands of hectares of barren, uninhabited moorland, so they appear comparatively poor by this measure, even though the surviving housing stock, especially in the Upper Calder Valley, shows that these townships had some of the finest vernacular buildings in the land. The lack of contemporary maps means that the extent of the wastes in moorland townships cannot be measured and then deducted from the total size. In very many cases township boundaries cannot be drawn accurately for any period before the 19th century, by which time some of the administrative units that were used for collecting the Hearth Tax had been absorbed into others. These problems do not make the mapping and tabulation exercises worthless, but the qualifications need to be kept in mind when making comparisons between different parts of the country.

The third problem with tables arranged on a county basis is that counties are not necessarily the best basis for comparison. Each county contains a variety of sub-regions with marked differences in wealth and the quality and appearance of the vernacular architecture. Nor were the sub-regions themselves uniformly wealthy or poor. Moreover, even in the richest districts, the quality of housing varied from place to place. Some of the outlying townships in the Upper Calder Valley, for instance, display none of the substantial yeomen houses for which the district is deservedly famous. Thinking needs to be cast in terms of different 'countries', a word that the English once used to mean the same as the French *pays*.

As the essays in this volume show, a major problem in interpreting the distribution of wealth is in determining what might be meant by a one-hearth house. Such was overwhelmingly the most common type and in some counties these comprised over 70% of the housing stock. Houses of this kind clearly included a wide variety of forms. Hoskins had pondered over this problem long ago in *The Midland Peasant*. His analysis of the 1670 assessment for Wigston Magna showed that 'out of the 161 houses, no fewer than 120 had one hearth only: that is, three houses in every four'. He concluded that

> it would be a mistake to equate all the one-hearth houses with cottages, the homes of a rural proletariat. We might assume this from the 47 who were exempted from the tax, but even here at least nineteen were widows, some of them of good peasant standing, and some were old men of good stock ending their days in decent quiet. They cannot be described as a proletariat or as paupers. Among the one-hearth houses that were taxed, several were the houses of small or middling farmers, or of craftsmen or tradesmen... The one-hearth house generally denoted a two-roomed house, but

sometimes it was a house of three rooms and occasionally still larger (Hoksins 1965, 299).

He identified several householders who were taxed on two hearths in local probate records: 'Among the two-hearthed houses which can be certainly identified in the inventories that of William Johnson had six rooms', others had four, five or six; 'all were described as yeomen in their wills'. He concluded that

> The number of hearths cannot be related to the number of rooms except in a rough and ready way. If we may generalise, a one-hearth house usually implied two or three rooms; a two-hearth house five or six rooms; three or four hearths imply seven to nine rooms. Above four hearths there is no definite relationship (Hoskins 1965, 299).

In her contribution to the recent Kent Hearth Tax volume, Pearson concludes that, although we can accept a general correlation between wealth and the size of houses, the owners of houses with three or four hearths might not necessarily have been wealthier than those with one or two. What needs to be considered is not so much style, or even plan form, as the age of a building and the form and physical structure of its hearths and chimney stacks which influenced the number of fireplaces a building might have. She observes that 'The 1664 Hearth Tax reflects standards of heating at a single moment during a period of transition' (Harrington *et al* 2000, c–ci). Whereas the newer houses, such as those in the expanding dockyard towns, were well equipped, the occupiers of older buildings were often slow to upgrade them, preferring instead to adapt and add to their properties. She adds the intriguing suggestion that the levying of the Hearth Tax might have inhibited the introduction of new fireplaces and queries whether the term 'great rebuilding' helps to clarify what actually took place, or tends to mask the real situation. Perhaps with the publication of the present volume, where Hoskins's ideas are examined in different parts of the country, the concept can finally be abandoned?

At the opposite end of the social scale to the owners of substantial houses who still managed with only one or two hearths were those who were exempted from payment of the Hearth Tax. The Roehampton Project has attracted funding to enable the transcription of the little-known bundles of exemption certificates in class E179 at The National Archives and, as part of the same series as the Kent and Cambridgeshire volumes, in 2001 the British Record Society published an edition of *Norfolk Hearth Tax Exemption Certificates 1670–1674* (Seaman *et al* 2001). Thousands of new names have come to light, but the problem remains that exemption certificates do not survive for many parishes or townships. As the proportion of the householders who were exempt from payment of the tax varies considerably from place to place, even when a complete list survives, it is not possible to be certain that the record is complete.

Who were the exempt? It is certain that not all were in receipt of parish poor relief (see chapter 3). They also included those who paid less than 20s rent a year on their properties. A clear distinction between the two groups was made in the West Riding township of Hutton Wandesley on 7 October 1672, where five people were said to 'receive relief out of the poor man's box' and another five householders were listed as paying rents under £1 but 'do not receive relief'. In other cases, too, the distinction is clear. At Rawcliffe, in 1671, 39 householders were 'Discharged by certificate' and another eighteen were 'Omitted by reason of poverty', while at Snaith eighteen were 'Omitted by reason of poverty' and certificates were issued for another three. But in most cases the terms are ambiguous. Exemption certificates often state that they are for poor people, without explaining what is meant by 'poor'. There is no way of arriving at overall figures to distinguish paupers from those who were exempted because of the low rents that they paid, but it is clear that all the exempt were considered to be poor by the standards of the time, even if they were not paupers in receipt of parish relief. For example, a petition from the churchwardens and other leading figures in Tadcaster to the Lord Mayor of York supported the case of 'a poor man' who should not have been taxed because of the low rent that he paid. It reads:

> At the request of the bearer hereof Anthony Wisse of the East Part of Tadcaster for certifying the true value of what he farmeth: we do humbly certify that he is a poor man and that the poor cottage he lives in which is all that ever he farms in all the world is but six shillings eight pence per annum; and being of late charged with the duty of Hearth money: contrary to the Act in that behalf he humbly begs your lordships best help and assistance for acquitting him hereof and he will as in duty bound ever to pray for you: to the truth hereof we set to our hands this sixth of December [16]71.

It seems that it is possible to speak of 'the exempted poor in the Hearth Tax returns' as long as it is made clear that they are not equated with parish paupers.

Finally, as with all taxation documents, consideration needs to be given as to whether some people managed to avoid payment of the tax. Local studies suggest that the returns are reasonably comprehensive. The tax collectors and constables were authorised to enter houses in order to check the number of hearths and it is unlikely that they missed many households. It is noticeable, however, that in some townships the constable who attested the accuracy of the return did not appear in the list of taxpayers.

Unwin (2002) has noted that of the 71 Hallamshire Cutlers' Company masters who took apprentices in 1671 and 1672 only nine did not appear in the Lady Day 1672 Hearth Tax return, where they were easy to spot because their smithies were recorded. But when she looked at the names of the 176 cutlers who completed an apprenticeship in 1671 or 1672 she found that only 110 became freemen immediately, and that another 23 became freemen several years later. In other words, 43 never became freemen but presumably worked as journeymen or at another job. It is unlikely that many of them left Hallamshire, for there were few opportunities to practise their craft elsewhere, but only three were householders in the Lady Day 1672 return. Were they lodgers, or were they living with parents? This might help to explain why the central township of Sheffield had large numbers of households with more than one domestic hearth. It has clear implications for other parts of the country.

Interpreting the Hearth Tax returns is not a straightforward task and any conclusions must be hedged with qualifications, but the Roehampton Project, when complete, will offer substantial documentary evidence that has only just begun to be analysed. Hearth Tax returns do not offer the rich detail of probate inventories or estate surveys, but they have become an essential additional source of information for the study of vernacular architecture. The following essays attempt to absorb this material at a regional level and show how it can aid an understanding of domestic buildings in the two decades after the Restoration in all parts of the land. They also show how study of the buildings is vital to refine interpretation of the Hearth Tax returns.

2 Understanding the Hearth Tax Returns: Historical and Interpretative Problems

by Elizabeth Parkinson

Introduction

The importance of the 17th-century Hearth Tax to vernacular architecture lies in the county returns produced by the tax administrators recording names of householders with the number of their fire hearths. The information appears simple, but there are many pitfalls to be overcome in attributing numbers of fireplaces to specific buildings. Generally the number of hearths represents a single building, but sometimes it refers to part of a subdivided house or even to hearths in several buildings. Secondly, the name usually refers to the occupier, but sometimes it may be the owner. Finally, there may be errors or omissions in the list because both the recording of individuals and the way in which they were recorded depended not only on the diligence of the compiler but also on changes in the law and their timing. In this paper sample extracts from several different county tax returns will be used in order to illustrate the variations during the life of the tax.

A summary of the history of the tax

The Hearth Tax has a complicated history which is summarised in Table 2.1. As noted in the heading, the tax was levied from 1662 to 1689. During this time four acts of parliament were passed, the initial one imposing the tax in 1662, two further acts in close succession, and the final repealing act in 1689.[1] The need for the passing of three acts within two years is indicative of problems of legal interpretation and organisation, and laid a somewhat shaky foundation for the management of the tax. The collections were made twice yearly at Michaelmas (29 September) [M] and Lady Day (25 March) [L]. During the 27 years of the tax several different management systems were tried, some more than once (Meekings 1940; Meekings 1951). Such frequent changes were typical at a time of fiscal experimentation by a government very short of money. Those periods of administration which have been highlighted in bold in Table 2.1 represent the dates when copies of the Hearth Tax documents had to be returned to the Exchequer. Some are now preserved at The National Archives; in addition, some of the records retained locally may have survived in Quarter Sessions material at local county record offices or in estate papers. For 1662M to 1666L and 1670M to 1689L about eight different lists were compiled for each county, but their survival is patchy. Warwickshire now has a rich collection with eight for some divisions of the county whereas most counties have about two and Berkshire has only one. All is not lost for Berkshire, however, for it has some interesting subsidiary lists (Gibson 1985).

Table 2.1 The Hearth Tax 1662–89

THE LAW

19 May 1662	An act for establishing an additional revenue ...
27 July 1663	An additional act for the better ordering ...
17 May 1664	An act for collecting the duty ... by officers to be appointed by His Majesty
24 April 1689	An act for the taking away the revenue arising by Hearth-Money

THE ADMINISTRATIONS

Collections	Officials	Net yield per annum
1662M–1664L	**Sheriffs**	**£115,000**
1664M–1665M	Receivers	
1666L	**Receivers/Farmers**	**£112,500**
1666M–1669L	Farmers	£103,000
1669M–1674L	**Receivers**	**£145,000**
1674M–1679L	Farmers	£144,500
1679M–1684L	Farmers	£157,000
1684M–1688L	Commission	£216,000

The anticipated annual yield in 1662 was £300,000, which was the total by which the royal revenue was deficient.

The yield of the tax

The need for changes in the administration of the tax was driven by the necessity to increase its yield. In 1662 it was expected that the tax would make up a shortfall in the King's revenue of £300,000. Table 2.1 shows that at no time during its life did the proceeds of the tax reach this target (Chandaman 1975, 77–109).[2] The first receivers were overburdened by the collection of the sheriffs' arrears. Under the first farmers, the yield fell even more, partly because of increased hostility to the tax as householders had now to open their doors to strangers searching for hearths and collecting the money rather than to known local officials. The introduction of the second receivers, with their increasingly efficient management, was a change for the better as the yield began to increase. The highest return of the tax was obtained in the years before it was repealed (Chandaman 1975, 76–109; Braddick 1994, 241–70).

The differing administrations

The sheriffs' administration 1662M to 1664L

To return to 1662, the terms of the initial act stated that 'every dwelling and other House and Edifice ... shall be chargeable ... for every Fire hearth and Stove ... the sum of Two shillings by the year and every year'. The money was to be paid in two equal instalments and was to be paid by the occupier or, if the house was empty, by the owner according to a list of named householders with the number of their hearths. Exemption from payment was allowed for occupants already excused from paying church and poor rates due to the smallness of their estate, and for those living in properties with a rental not greater than 20s a year. A third miscellaneous group of hearths was also exempted, which included those in private hospitals and almshouses other than the very rich ones, those in 'any blowing house and stamp furnace or kiln', and any private ovens. The details of exemption are complex, partly on account of the different set of officials who managed it, and are discussed in chapter 3.

Initially, assessment and collection of the tax was administered by the ordinary county machinery of local government — the petty constables, high constables and sheriffs. The lowest official, the petty constable, was responsible for notifying the householders within his jurisdiction that they had to provide an assessment of the number of hearths in their occupation. From the self-assessments the petty constable had to compile a list of all the liable hearths with the names of the occupiers or owners of the houses in which they were, and deliver it to the next meeting of the Quarter Sessions. The clerk of the peace was then responsible for collating all the constables' returns into a single county list to be inspected by three justices and enrolled in duplicate.

One copy was to be returned to the Exchequer within a month of the Quarter Sessions meeting as the record for collection. The other was retained locally for the sheriff and served as a check on the amount of money to be collected. Provision was also made for the recording and enrolment of any changes in hearth numbers in the subsequent collections.

A sample illustration of one of these early 1662 lists is given in Figure 2.1. It records the householders for Clifton in the Gloucestershire hundred of Kingsbarton. As it was a county record drawn up by local government officials it was compiled according to hundreds and constabularies or tithings which may or may not be coterminous with parishes. William Morris, the constable, recorded the occupiers of the tithing together with the number of hearths. He stated that they were all rateable to the church or poor and that he could find no stoves.[3] The document illustrated is a copy of Morris's work which, like the returns of his fellow petty constables, was amalgamated into a single county list and signed by three justices at the Quarter Sessions on 14 August 1662 before being returned to the Exchequer in London. The fact that it is a copy is important because all the county lists were reproductions of previous or earlier records and may therefore contain copying and clerking errors, a difficulty to which further reference will be made.

Across the country as a whole, most of the 1662 assessments were returned to London by 3 October 1662. This was no mean feat considering that the petty constables had to interpret an unfamiliar law and complete the work alongside their myriad routine duties such as organising muster parades, collecting money for roads and bridges, and supervising watch and ward. Inevitably there were errors and omissions as some made their own interpretations of liability, some listed everyone, and some did nothing at all. It is very important to understand the range of ability because the 1662 list was used again as a basis for a later return. The justices were also feeling their way as to the exact interpretation of the act, as revealed by queries and deliberations in some of their surviving notebooks (Parkinson 2001, 153–80).

Within six days of 29 September 1662 the constable, if he was still in office, had to collect the money according to his list and hand it over to his high constable together with the names of the payers and those who had refused. The high constables passed everything on to the sheriff, who was responsible for returning the money from his county to the Exchequer. Refusal to pay was met by distraint (seizure of goods) or noted as an arrear for which a stipulated time for recovery was allowed. Expenses were granted for each official involved in the collection and time limits were imposed for each stage of the assessment and collection process. All this sounds fairly straightforward but it must be remembered that the annual appointment of the sheriff and of some petty constables meant that the official compiling the assessment might have

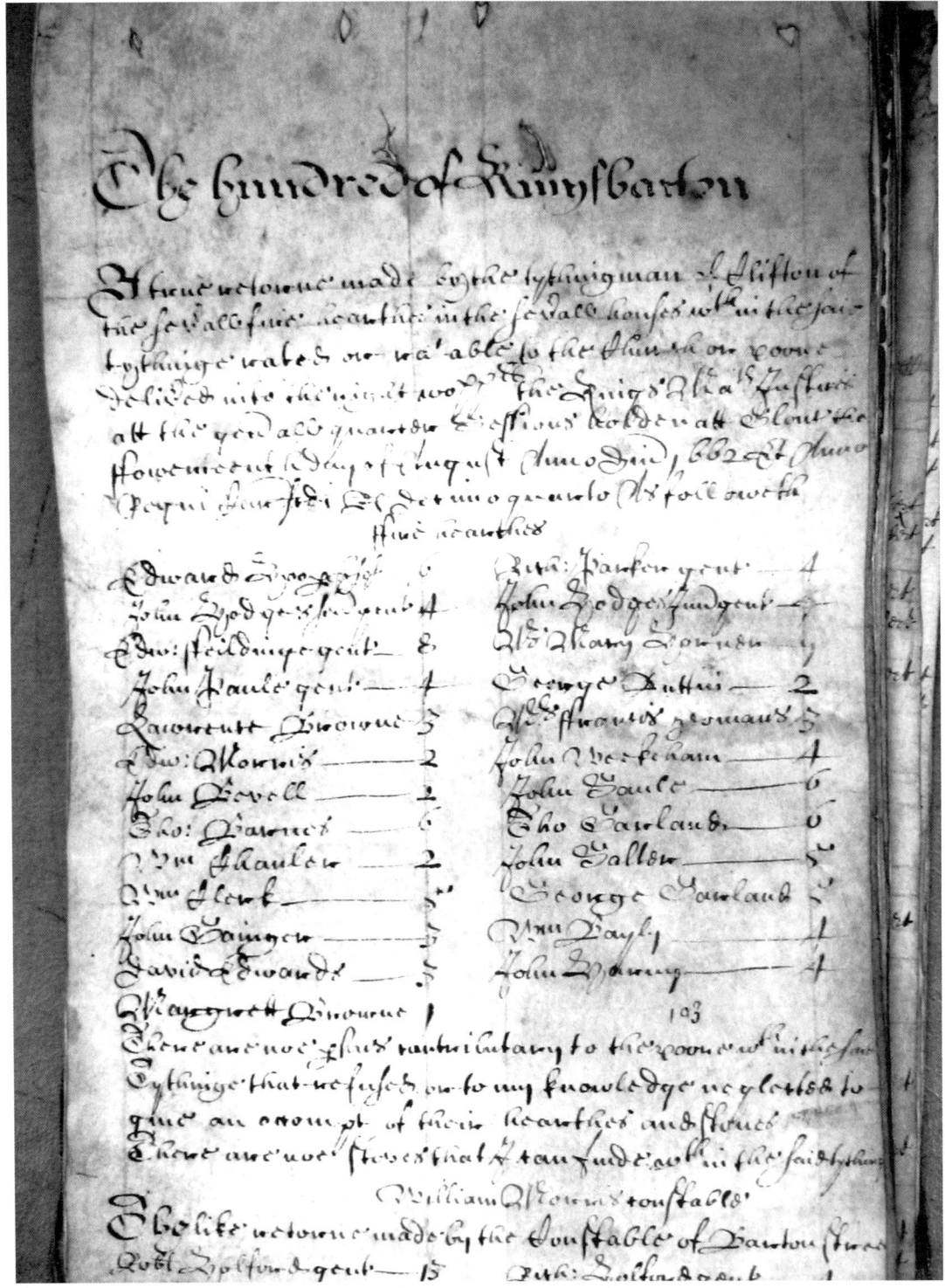

Fig 2.1 Extract from the Exchequer duplicate for Gloucestershire for 1662M. (The National Archives: E179/116/554). © Crown Copyright

been replaced by the time the money was collected. High constables generally served for longer periods but changeovers occurred for them also, with the attendant problems of handing over half-finished collections with the accompanying paperwork.

The difficulties posed by the changeover of officials were eased by the first Revising Act of 1663 which made the outgoing official responsible for the collection of the levy due during his term of office. A stricter assessment procedure was also introduced because the House of Commons thought, wrongly, that the slow return of money to the Exchequer was due to slack assessment. Now all houses, both occupied and empty, had to be searched to check the accuracy of the number of their hearths. All hearths and householders, both chargeable and non-chargeable, had to be listed together with changes in liability since the first assessment. By recording every hearth the government hoped that omissions in future lists could be traced. In practice the task hugely increased the

10 Part 1: The Hearth Tax

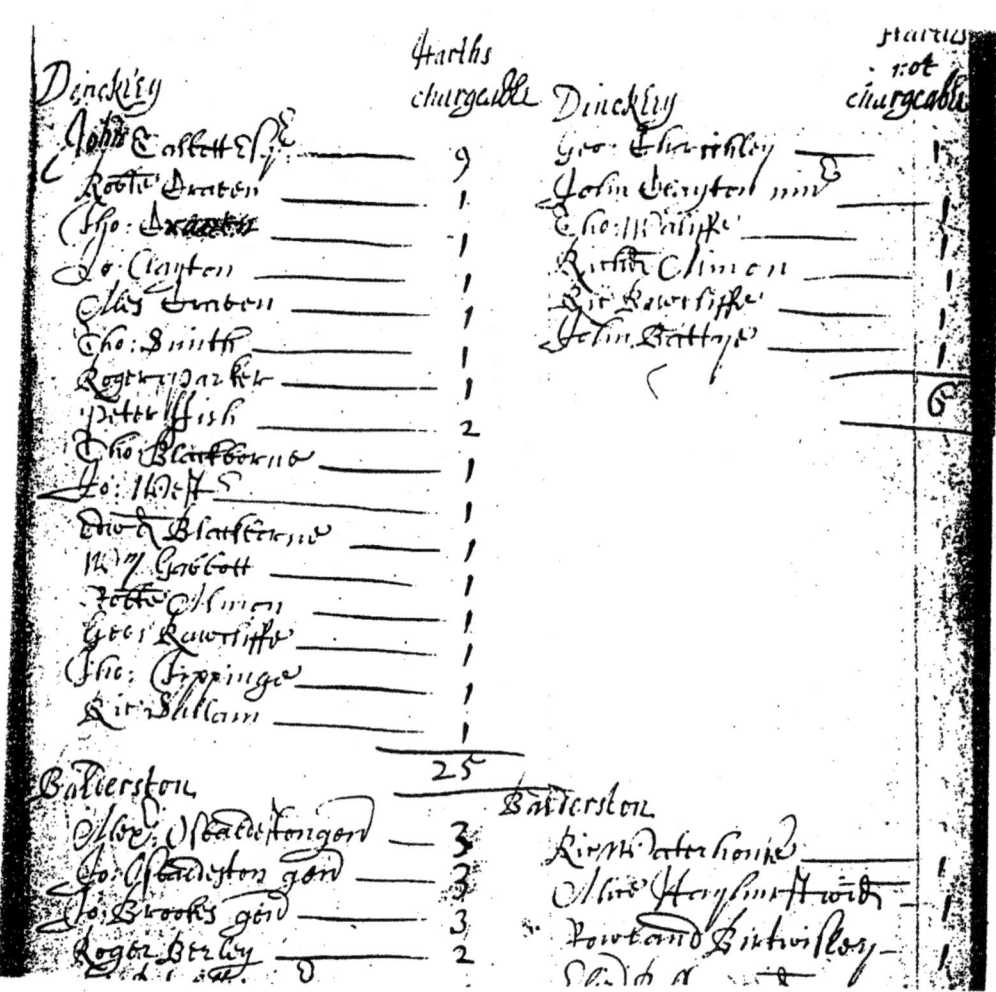

Fig 2.2 Extract from the Exchequer duplicate for Lancashire for 1664L. (The National Archives: E179/250/11). © Crown Copyright

workload of the constables. In Kingston, Surrey, it meant recording an additional 600 names of those exempted from the levy. The petty constable's return was also subject to an additional check at the high constable level, and further examination by two justices. These changes generally took effect for the 1664L collection, but in some cases the lists were not returned until September or October 1664, so it is doubtful if they were ever used (Meekings 1940; Meekings 1962). By May 1664 more drastic changes were afoot.

The list for that collection chosen for illustration is that for Dinckley, a township in the Lancashire hundred of Blackburne (Fig 2.2). The duplicate of which this is a part was enrolled at the Quarter Sessions in April 1664, as the Lady Day collection was being made. It follows the layout required by law in recording the householders in two columns, one for chargeable hearths, and the other for non-chargeable ones. The choice of Blackburne hundred is deliberate because it is well represented in the section of the document which records those hearths walled up since the last assessment. In Dinckley,

three of the chargeable occupiers had each walled up one hearth — Thomas Blackburne, Roger Parker and Thomas Smith. We do not know quite why this was done. In another township, Trawdon, over 90% of the householders are recorded with one or more walled-up hearth, which looks suspiciously like an avoidance tactic. The county list of the same date for Nottinghamshire does not distinguish the walled-up hearths, but the variable incidence of repetition of names in the chargeable and non-chargeable columns, ranging from 0 to 24%, suggests that some occupiers actively recorded some of their hearths as no longer liable so as to evade payment (Parkinson 2001, 158). Evasion probably occurred to varying degrees on a national scale, because the stricter assessment procedure of 1664L did not result in the identification of a higher number of liable hearths. In fact, the number of chargeable hearths listed fell by around 200,000 between 1662M and 1664L. In practice, parliament's attempt with the first Revising Act to produce more accurate assessments actually resulted in a lower number of hearths assessed as liable.

The first receivers' administration 1664M to 1665M

It has already been mentioned that even greater changes were afoot at the time of the 1664L collection. They resulted from the second Revising Act, passed in May 1664, which removed the organisation of the tax from local government officials and handed it over to receivers appointed by the king for each area, and to their sub-collectors or chimney men, who were in fact professional tax collectors. The timing of these changes was crucial. Just as the 1664L collection should have been underway the recently appointed sheriffs were aware that their Hearth Tax duties were about to be removed. Not surprisingly, some did not bother to become involved and left the work to their successors as arrears. Arrears are notoriously difficult to collect, and therefore added to the difficulties faced by the receivers. A further timing problem was that although the receivers were appointed in the summer of 1664, their teams of sub-collectors did not start work until the spring of 1665, by which time the 1664M collection was overdue. As a result, the lists are in effect a combined assessment and return of those who had or had not paid, covering one or more collections.

The implementation of this act with the centrally appointed receivers, who had to provide sureties, tightened the Exchequer's control. There was also a streamlining of the administrative areas by amalgamating the smaller counties, so reducing the number of officials with whom the Exchequer had to deal. Two aspects of liability were tightened at the same time. In future, neither a dwelling which was previously assessed as chargeable nor one with more than two hearths could be exempted unless it became ruinous. In addition, those landlords who subdivided properties after 1663 so as to reduce the rental value to below the threshold for exemption were themselves made liable for the tax. As for the assessment procedure, the act did not stipulate the making of a new survey, but the instructions that followed insisted instead on the amending of an earlier one. Each receiver was to be given a copy of the Lady Day 1664 list, together with a manual and a specimen form showing how to update the list. Unfortunately, because the 1664L lists were not returned to the Exchequer in time, copies of the 1662 assessment were issued instead: they omitted the exempt and so did not match the instructions, and also required many more alterations to be made (Arkell 1992, 51–64).

An example of the county lists is shown in Figure 2.3. It is an extract from a part of Doddington parish in the Cambridgeshire hundred of Witchford. The layout conforms to that required by the specimen form, with the central section representing the copied 1662M assessment and the extreme left-hand column recording the arrears. The next left-hand column gives the duty payable at 1664M, and the extreme right-hand column the changes since 1662. The annotations on the right-hand side follow the instructions. 'Ex' is an abbreviation for *examinatur*, which was to be written against every entry where there was no change from the previous assessment. In the subsequent entry, the name of the new occupier (Henry Motley) has been noted. The following two entries were clearly entered in error in 1662. Henry Bowler's property was empty, so the owner Nathaniel Nevett is recorded. Thomas Morris underestimated his hearth number in 1662 because the collector found that in 1664 he had two hearths not one. At the end is a list of new entries. The last eight are clearly not liable because they do not pay poor rates. We have no information about the first seven entries. Perhaps they were simply omitted from the previous list (Evans and Rose 2000, 100).

To understand the intricacies of this record it is important to note that it was not enrolled at the Quarter Sessions until 11 January 1667, over two years after the 1664M collection, and nearly one year after the receivers had left office. Reading further into the document, although the heading of the left-hand column relates to the duty for the half year 1664M, the comments in the extreme right-hand column may refer to any or all of the three collections 1664M to 1665M. The inconsistent use of the arrears column and the variable phrasing of the comments reflect the origin of the record as an amalgam of the work of several people for three collections. This Cambridgeshire list follows the instructions to a degree, but does not conform with the 1663 act which required that the chargeable and non-chargeable households should be listed in two separate columns.

For other counties, unlike Cambridgeshire, duplicates with varying layouts were compiled for each of the three collections from 1664M to 1665M. The three lists for Herefordshire contain very few references to the non-chargeable and only a few annotations recording stopped-up or defaced hearths. The surviving Hampshire duplicate for 1665M has no annotations but does record the non-chargeable by name in a separate column.[4] Trying to conform with the confused instructions issued in 1664 whilst also complying with the two-column layout required in 1663 and recording for a retrospective collection was very onerous and time-consuming for the officials. The resulting diversity of format is therefore no surprise.

The first farm 1666M to 1669L

The receivers were hastily removed from office in the spring of 1666 and replaced by farmers. The government was so short of money that it decided at short notice to contract out the management of the tax from 1666M to a consortium of London merchants who paid the government in advance for the privilege. They managed the London area themselves but sub-farmed the remainder of the country. The contract was due to start with the 1666M collection, but the farmers agreed to complete the 1666L collection already begun by some receivers, and deliver the money and documentation to the Exchequer. This

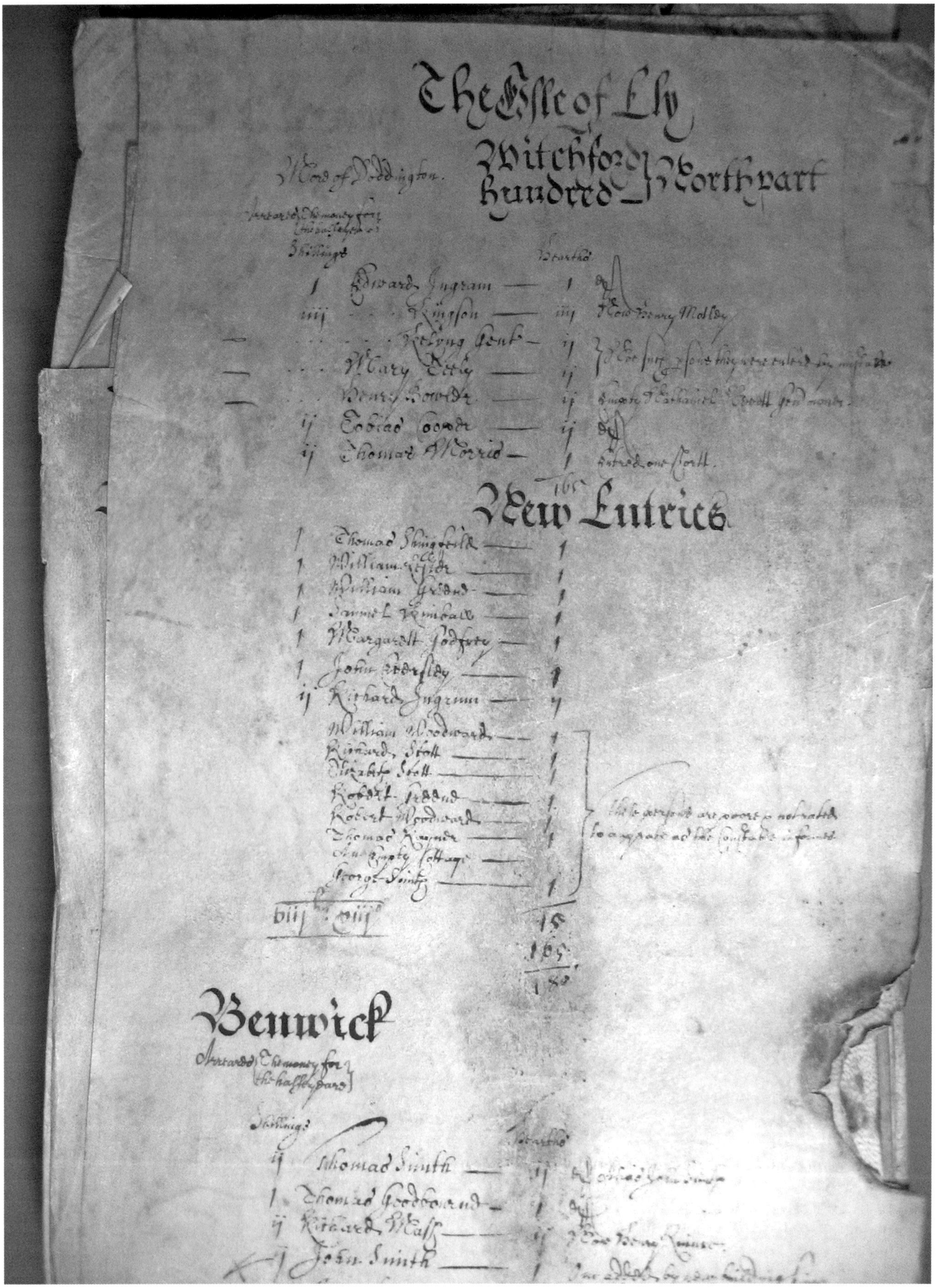

The Isle of Ely

Witchford hundred — Northpart

Edward Ingram

Mary Kelly

Thomas Morris

New Entries

Margarett Godfrey

Richard Ingram

William Woodward

Richard Stott

Elizabeth Stott

Robert Woodward

George Smith

Benwick

Thomas Smith

John Smith

Fig 2.3 Extract from the Exchequer duplicate for Cambridgeshire. 1664M–1665M (The National Archives: E179/84/437). © Crown Copyright

Understanding Hearth Tax Returns   13

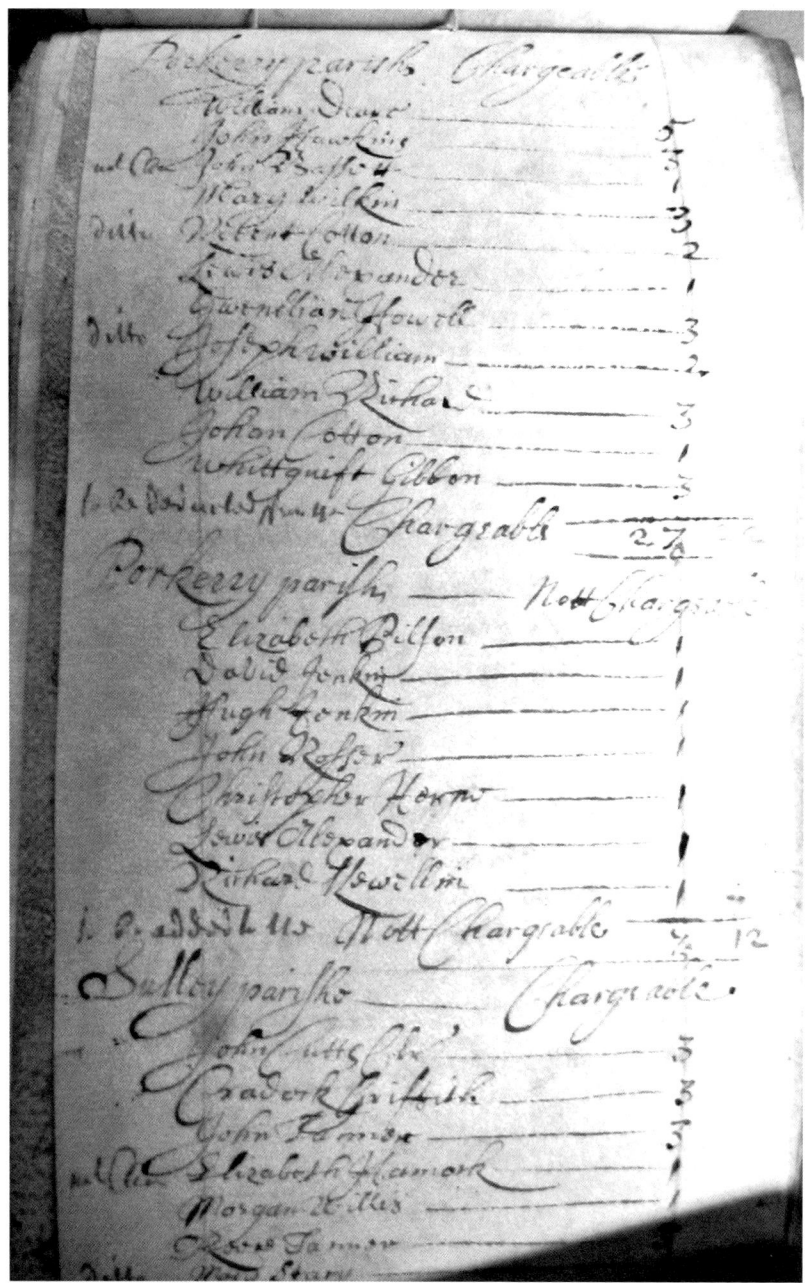

Fig 2.4   Extract from the Exchequer duplicate for Glamorgan for 1666L. (The National Archives: E179/221/297). © Crown Copyright

was necessary because the Exchequer had to repay loans granted on the proceeds of this collection. The returns for the collection exhibit certain particular characteristics. Some show no evidence of enrolment, no doubt a time-saving measure so that the arrears could be collected; others are in the form of paper books showing which official had collected what.

The illustration for the 1666L collection is Figure 2.4. It records the householders in Porthkerry in the Glamorgan hundred of Dinas Powys. This particular document bears no evidence of enrolment, and the spelling of some of the placenames hints at a hand unfamiliar with the Welsh language (Parkinson 1990, 8,14, 99). As well as listing seven households separately as non-chargeable, this document also notes that three of the eleven chargeable house-holds had become exempt. Perhaps such entries record those households where no money could be collected and noting them in this way meant that the officials could not be chased for arrears. There is possible corroboration of this in several other Welsh county lists, in which, as here, a significant number of the additional non-chargeable hearths adds up to a multiple of five, as here, suggesting the possibility that this money was syphoned off.[5]

The second receivers' administration 1669M to 1674L

The farmers were only required to return documents to the Exchequer for the 1666L collection, so there is

14   Part 1: The Hearth Tax

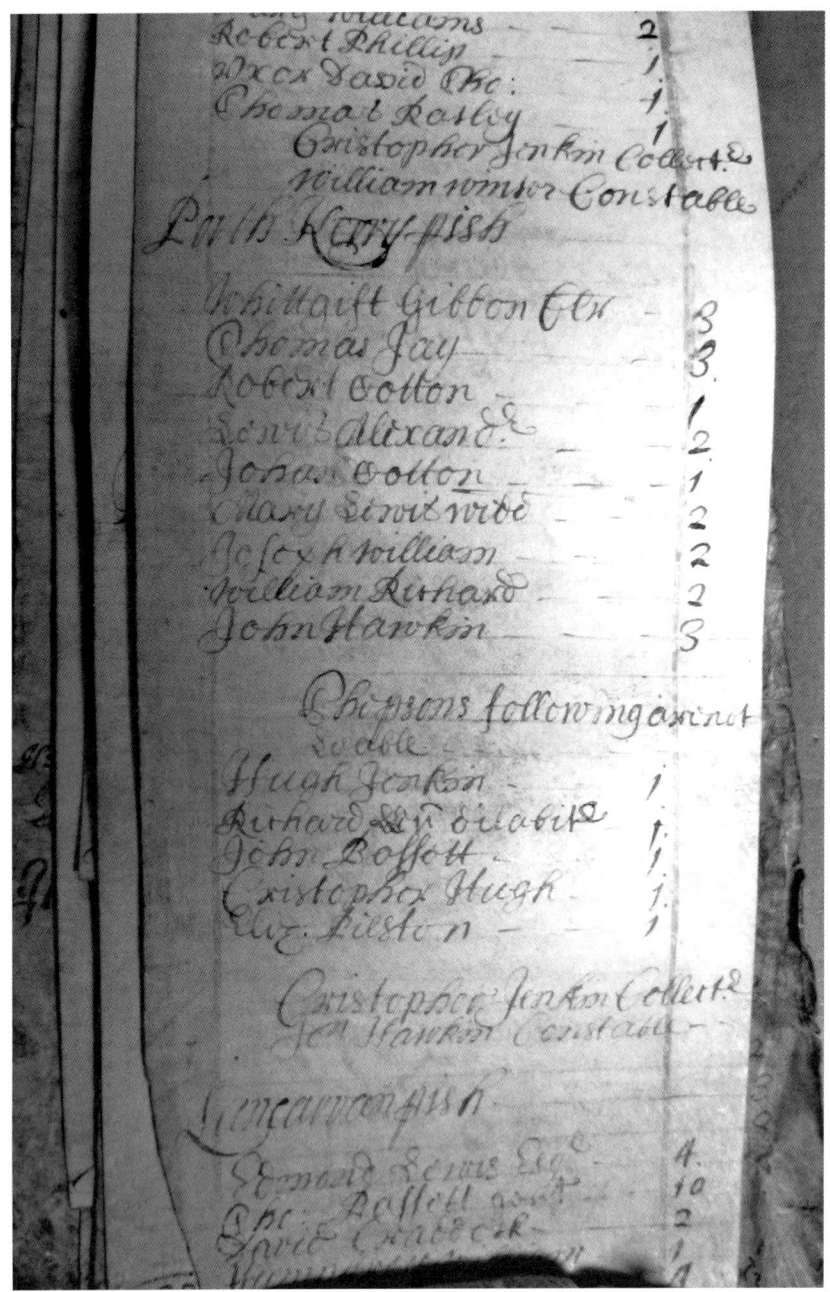

Fig 2.5   Extract from the Exchequer duplicate for Glamorgan for 1670M. (The National Archives: E179/221/294). © Crown Copyright

a three-year gap in the surviving records while they were in total control. In November 1668 the farmers gave notice that they would revoke their contract after the 1669L collection, but parliament took over a year to decide what to do next. Eventually, in the spring of 1670, a second receivers' administration was set up. Unlike the first receivers, the new ones were managed by a central Hearth Tax office although they were still answerable to the Exchequer. Further streamlining occurred with a reduction in the number of administrative areas and the introduction of a system of graded payments for expenses. Instructions were again issued as to how to compile the lists, but unfortunately no copy has survived. Because of the late start made by the officials, their returns covered the three collections 1669M to 1670M, the first two collections being made retrospectively. The illustrated example (Fig 2.5) is again that of Porthkerry in Glamorgan. The non-liable are listed separately, with the number of hearths aligned differently from the chargeable. Overall, only nine chargeable households are listed, with eighteen hearths, and only five non-chargeable, suggesting further evasions and omissions since 1666. Throughout the document there are a few scattered comments referring to one or other of the collections (Parkinson 1994).

Porthkerry was chosen for the last two examples because it is clearly represented in both surviving legible lists, so allowing a comparison. In 1670, the

Fig 2.6 Church Farm, Porthkerry, Glamorgan.
© *Copyright R T Parkinson*

minister Whittgift Gibbon heads the list but he is at the end in 1666. It was quite common for locally compiled lists to follow the order in rating lists, in which those paying most are listed first. The 1666 list compiled by non-local tax collectors had no such need to follow tradition. The additional designation in 1670 of 'clr' for *clericus* allows us to identify Gibbon as the minister. Armed with this and other information we can identify his house which in its present form is shown in Figure 2.6 (Griffiths 1979). The building would appear to be little altered, the three chimneys representing the three hearths. Reading beyond Gibbon, the order of householders is very different, suggesting that a new survey was made. Over time the tax administrators introduced a system of topographical listing, thus making it easier for them and us to identify individual properties. The first name in the 1666L list is that of William Deare, assessed for five hearths in 1666. He is absent from the 1670 list. We know from his will that he lived in a hamlet outside the village, and in 1670 was recorded in the neighbouring parish of Penmark. Thus different officials might record householders in a different place. Then there are the spelling variations — Christopher Hearne appears thus in 1666, but as Christopher Hugh, the more likely Welsh spelling in 1670; Elizabeth Pilson appears as Pilston in 1670. These are no doubt copying errors. It is also interesting that women often headed households both chargeable and exempt; some were widows though they are not always designated as such.

As to the numbers of entries in both lists, eighteen households were recorded in 1666 compared with fourteen in 1670. Lewis Alexander appears twice in 1666 with two one-hearth entries, one chargeable, one not. In a small hamlet, even in Wales, it is likely that these two entries refer to the same individual, but whether the two hearths refer to a single property or two is unknown. By 1670M Alexander was paying for both hearths, but again it is not known whether either of the hearths was let. Having accounted for both William Deare and Lewis Alexander, the total number of householders listed in 1666 has been reduced to sixteen, closer to the fourteen recorded in 1670. Examining the hearth numbers, there were 34 hearths in 1666 and 24 in 1670. The addition of William Deare's five hearths brings the total hearth number in 1670 up to 29. This is still five hearths fewer than in 1666, but with no additional information on lettings it is impossible to equate the remaining 1666 entries with their equivalent in 1670. This comparison of just one small village illustrates the inconsistencies between records of different dates, and shows how it is only by comparison with other documents that some of the problems can be teased out.

In some counties receivers for the 1671 collections produced only a schedule of variations recording the changes since the previous list. Between 1671 and 1674 each county or administrative area produced a varying number of duplicates of generally similar format, although the recording of the non-liable varies and may even change within a county. Where the exempt are noted they appear under a variety of headings, such as discharged by legal certificate, under the value and poor, not liable, paupers, non-solvent, receiver of alms of the parish or take collection. Some may also be noted in numerical terms, often as those receiving alms. The illustration for this date (Fig 2.7) is the beginning of the 1672–73 survey for Tiverton town in the Devon hundred of Tiverton. The chargeable hearth numbers for the two collections of 1672M and 1673L are listed in separate columns. The non-chargeable under the heading paupers are listed only once since the exemption certificate was valid for both collections. The first chargeable entry is that for George Clarke Esquire, who, in May 1670, was appointed the receiver for Cornwall, Devon and Exeter. A feature of many urban lists, although not evident in this Tiverton sample due to its small size, is the relatively large number of entries with hearth numbers ranging from ten to twenty. Many of these refer to inns. Where such entries can be linked to identifiable inns their position in the list can be used to trace the routes of the sub-collectors, as Hoskins found in Exeter (Hoskins 1957).

The second and third farm and the commission

The reversion to farming at 1674M was due to the personal choice of Lord Treasurer Danby who favoured such privatisation as a means of obtaining credit. Two successive five-year contracts were negotiated with different bankers at different rents. Unlike the first farm, there was no sub-farming, all farmers being managed centrally and with a proviso that the records were made available to the govern-

16 Part 1: The Hearth Tax

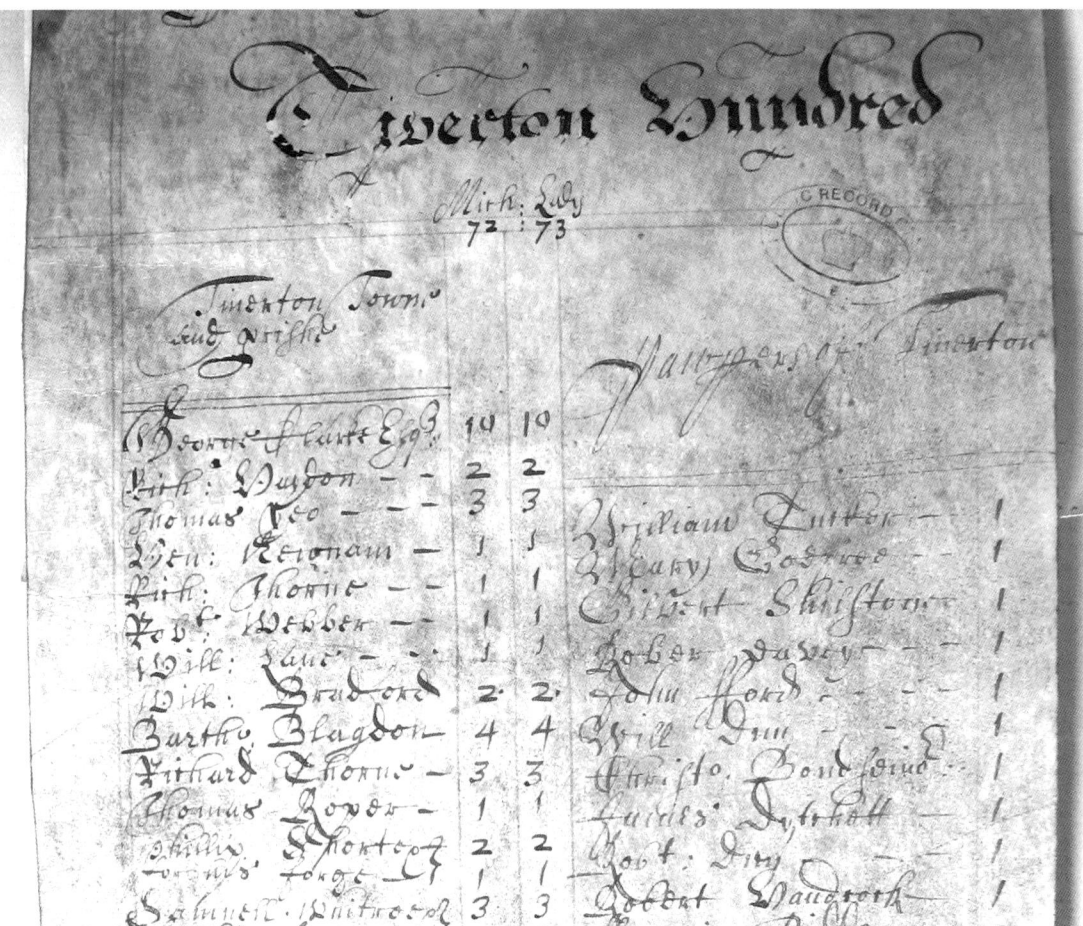

Fig 2.7 Extract from the Exchequer duplicate for Devon for 1672M–1673L (The National Archives: E179/245/19). © Crown Copyright

ment. In 1684, after it was discovered that the third farm had raised much more money than it paid to the Exchequer, the administration was handed over to salaried commissioners who also managed the excise. The tax was abolished in 1689 by the newly crowned William and Mary in order to gain popularity.

Conclusion

The six sample extracts have provided a platform from which to discuss the diversity of the Hearth Tax lists and to indicate some of the problems of interpretation. The rapid changeover of officials, together with their varying interpretation of the law and the instructions, has meant that no single dated list can be viewed as an exemplar in terms of comprehensiveness of information. Furthermore, even within a county the quality of information may vary depending upon the assiduousness of the original compiler or the copier. Each list is a snapshot of taxpayers and, sometimes, the non-payers, for a variable number of collections. There is no single way of testing the completeness of a list, but comparisons with other lists or with parochial records of the same date can throw light on the differences. In spite of these reservations

such an important source of national data has been used and will continue to be used as an indicator of house size, wealth and population across England and Wales, and one which is valuable for the study of vernacular architecture. The county analyses instigated by Margaret Spufford at Roehampton are beginning to reveal national contrasts (Evans and Rose 2000; Harrington *et al* 2000; Spufford 2000b). Some of the problems and possibilities arising from these county studies will be discussed in the ensuing chapters.

Chapter 2: Notes

1   The details of the acts of parliament can be found in Statutes of the Realm (1810–28). The specific references are: the 1662 act, 14 Car. II, c. 10 (extracts are printed in the Appendix to chapter 3 of this volume); the 1663 act, 15 Car. II, c. 13; the 1664 act, 16 Car. II, c. 3; the repealing act, 1 Wm and Mary, c. 10.
2   Chandaman (1975) gives no figures for the yields of the last two collections probably because the information nationwide is not readily available.
3   The original instruction issued to the constables for compiling their lists of liable household-ers was 'None to be charged by this act that is

exempted from the usual taxes, payments and contributions towards the church and poor' (TNA E179/360 and Arkell 2003). This explains the wording used in the Gloucestershire duplicates. In other county lists, such as those for Middlesex and Nottinghamshire (TNA E179/253/16 and TNA E179/254/27), the information is much briefer, only recording the names of the householders, the number of hearths, and the sum due in shillings. In these instances it is difficult to tell exactly who is included.

4 The majority of Hearth Tax documents can be found in The National Archives under the E179 number. The catalogue can be examined on line at www.nationalarchives.gov.uk. The references for the Herefordshire documents are TNA E179/119/485/4; E179/485/3 and E179/119/486. The Hampshire document is E179/176/565. A published transcription of the latter can be found in Hughes and White 1991.

5 This phenomenon occurs in the Breconshire list TNA E179/219/63; in Carmarthenshire TNA E179/264/22, and in Radnorshire TNA E179/224/593.

3 Understanding Exemption from the Hearth Tax
by Tom Arkell

Exemption from the Hearth Tax was created by three hastily worded amendments that were tacked on to the original Hearth Tax Act as it passed through parliament in March 1662 (it was given royal assent in May). The first excused properties that were already exempt from paying the local taxes to church and poor, the second those with a rental value of 20s (£1) a year or less, while the third was an apparent ragbag that covered private ovens, kilns, hearths for working metal ore, and most almshouses (see Appendix A). During the next two years exemption was restricted further to properties that were already exempt and to those with no more than two hearths, while all the non-chargeable properties were required to be listed in the Hearth Tax returns along with the chargeable. The effect was to set exemption from the Hearth Tax at a much higher level than exemption from the poll tax of 1660 – only the recipients of alms or poor relief were excused the latter.

At first the Hearth Tax was administered by local government and parish personnel, who knew their local inhabitants well enough to implement the first exemption clause. All this changed from 1664 when receivers were appointed as specialist tax collectors, but it was not until they were replaced by farmers in 1666 that the government began to face up to the difficulties of administering exemption from the Hearth Tax. Now, the ignorant and suspicious strangers who were responsible for assessing and collecting the Hearth Tax required solid proof of entitlement to exemption for all the exempt. The only way in which this could be done legally was with the exemption certificates that had been devised originally to identify those who qualified solely under the second exemption clause, but not the first. Therefore, from the time when the second receivers were installed from 1670 onwards, the government pursued a relentless campaign to drop the first exemption clause and to make the 20s rental clause the only criterion for exemption, backed up by appropriately worded printed exemption certifications, which had to be endorsed by the local minister, at least one churchwarden or overseer of the poor, and two local JPs.

Many officials were understandably quite confused by this new interpretation, especially since their original instructions in 1662 had simply stated: 'None to be charged by this act that is exempted from the usual taxes, payments and contributions towards the church and poor'. Now the sole criterion was infinitely more complex and derived from the certified 'belief that the house wherein any person doth inhabit is not of greater value than of 20 shillings per annum, upon the full improved rent'.

Unfortunately, no copy of the instructions issued in 1670 has survived, but the reference to the need for annual certificates in the relevant clause from 1684 was clearly based upon the earlier one (Appendix B). This spells out how the new policy for entitlement to exemption from the Hearth Tax from 1670 onwards derived solely from a strict interpretation of the 20s rental clause.

During the next few years it also became apparent that some JPs and other officials were engaged deliberately in a rearguard action against this change of tack, because the central government's attempt to impose greater control on the local officers deprived them of their discretionary powers and forced some obviously needy households into paying the Hearth Tax. Cumulative evidence of such resistance is provided by some missives from the Treasury lords to the archbishops, complaining of many 'undue' certificates being signed by the clergy, and to various JPs accused of deliberately endorsing certificates that still exempted householders who were excused from the usual payments to the church and poor (Appendix C). Further evidence of such opposition is provided by the wording of numerous exemption certificates (Appendix D). In Hertford, for example, it was claimed that many of those who received alms lived in houses with rents of over 20s, while the one for Putney and Roehampton specifically stated that they were not certifying the rents of those who were named, and another from Westmorland that they had included (wrongly) the debts of their exempt in their calculations for the value of their possessions.

It is often claimed that exemption from the Hearth Tax was granted 'upon grounds of poverty' and that all the exempt were paupers or just poor, without any further definition or explanation. Such statements, however, are potentially very misleading. The notion that people were exempt by reason of poverty stems from a widespread misreading of the badly worded first exemption clause, which was intended to excuse only an occupier who was exempt from his local rates 'by reason of his poverty or the smallness of his estate', and not for other reasons such as that his landlord paid his rates or that the tenant performed a recognised service for the parish and so was excused from paying its rates. This would have been made much clearer if the first exemption clause had been redrafted as, for example: 'no person who is exempted from the usual taxes, payments and contributions toward the church and poor *by reason of his poverty or the smallness of his estate* shall be charged or chargeable with any duties by this act imposed'. Students who do not appreciate that the meaning of the word 'pauper' was not confined until a century later to those who received alms are also misled by phrases such as 'certified paupers'. In fact pauper was used interchangeably with 'poor' in the 17th century and was commonly applied to those who paid no rates. Thus, when the exempt are described as poor, it must be understood in terms of the 'labouring poor' or 'meaner sort' without reference to the poor law. Similarly, 'poverty' was sometimes used as shorthand for exemption from the local taxes and/or the Hearth Tax and so explains why, when the Surrey JPs allowed the certificate for Putney and Roehampton 'as to the poverty, but not the rents of the above named persons', they meant that their properties were excused from paying the local taxes, but without confirming the level of their rental values.

Attempts to estimate what proportion of households were exempt from the Hearth Tax are unavoidably problematic because the various Hearth Tax documents did not record them consistently. Many returns omitted some or even most of the not chargeable and one cannot even assume that all exemption certificates included every household that was dependent on charity. For instance, eight names were added in a different hand to the 1671 certificate for Gresham in Norfolk, with the following comment: 'these eight take collection which we supposed were needless to have been put in at first before the signing of this certificate'. Thus the most reassuring lists specifically mention those householders who received different categories of poor relief, although when they record more than a few in numbers without their names, they can rarely be trusted. On the other hand, lists sometimes included among their exempt (either deliberately or through ignorance) households that should have paid with the result that significantly different proportions of exempt can be detected for some places at different times. Thus 50% were recorded as exempt in the city of Hereford in 1664 and only 23% in 1671, while in Birmingham the proportion rose from 37% in 1673 to 47% a year later.

Overall proportions of the exempt taken from the more reliable lists ranged from over 80% to under 20% in individual communities, with the norm or median for most rural areas appearing to be around 35% and somewhere between 40% and 45% for towns. As a crude general rule one would expect to discover that a very approximate half of these households received some form of charitable assistance, with most getting no more than an occasional dole at Christmas or Easter or some other time, or practical relief in kind such as clothes or food. In most parishes regular pensions were paid to no more than 2–3% of all households, although this proportion could rise to around 10% in some towns and 'open' communities. The non-pauper exempt ranged from ill-paid and semi-employed cottagers and labourers who made shift to survive with various strategies, to those with regular employment and productive gardens, of whom a few even had smallholdings or owned possessions worth over £10 when they died, although many who survived to old age turned eventually to their parish for assistance. The exempt from the Hearth Tax therefore covered a much wider spectrum than is usually credited: if we classify all the exempt in modern terms as paupers living in poverty, we present a distorted picture that is far from the reality.

Chapter 3 Appendices

(Spelling has been modernised and emphases added)

Appendix A
The Hearth Tax Act 1662: Statutes of the Realm (1810–28), 14 Car. II c. 10

16. Provided always, that *no person who by reason of his poverty or the smallness of his estate is exempted from the usual taxes, payments and contributions toward the church and poor shall be charged* or chargeable *with any the duties by this act imposed*.
17. Provided always, and be it hereby enacted, that *if the churchwardens and overseers of the poor* of the parish together *with the minister* of the same or any two of them (whereof the minister to be one) shall in writing under their hands *yearly certify their belief that the house wherein any person doth inhabit is not of greater value than of twenty shillings per annum, upon the full improved rent*; and that neither the person so inhabiting, nor any other using the same messuage, hath, useth or occupieth any lands or tenements of their own or others of the yearly value of twenty shillings per annum, nor hath any lands, tenements, goods or chattels of the value of ten pounds in their own possession, or in the possession of any other in trust for them; that then in such case upon such certificate made to the two next justices of peace, and allowed (for which certificate and allowance no fee shall be paid) *the person on whose behalf such certificate is made, shall not be returned* by the constable or other officer *and the said house is hereby for that year discharged* of and from all the duties by this act imposed.
19. Provided that this act or anything herein contained shall not extend to charge any blowing house and stamp furnace or kiln or any private oven within any of the houses hereby charged nor any hearth or stove within the site of any hospital or almshouse for the relief of poor people whose endowment and revenue doth not exceed in true value the sum of one hundred pounds by the year.

Appendix B
The 1684 Instructions for the Officers managing the Hearth money

4. That if the churchwardens and overseers of the poor of the parish and the minister of the same, or

any two of them (whereof the minister is to be one), shall in writing under their hands certify their belief that the house wherein any person doth inhabit is not of greater value than of 20s per annum, upon the full improved rent, and that neither the person so inhabiting nor any other using the same messuage, hath, useth, or occupieth any lands or tenements of their own or others of the yearly value of 20s per annum, nor hath any lands, tenements, goods or chattels of the value of £10 in their own possession or in the possession of any other in trust for them, that then upon such Certificate made to the two next Justices of the Peace and allowed by them, the person on whose behalf such certificate is made, and the house, is discharged from the duty for that year only wherein the certificate is made. That is to say *a Certificate made in the year 1669 cannot discharge the duty due in the year 1670*, but if the house wherein the party certified for doth inhabit be of greater value than 20s a year upon the full improved rent; Or that the person so inhabiting or any other using the same, hath, useth, or occupieth, any lands or tenements of their own or others, of the yearly value of 20s, or hath any lands, tenements, goods or chattels of the value of £10 in their own possession, or in the possession of any other in trust for them; Or if the said Certificate be not signed by the minister of the parish and by one or more of the churchwardens or overseers of the poor, and allowed under the hands of two Justices of the Peace, it is illegal and void, and cannot bind up or hinder you or your deputies from levying his Majesty's duty.

5. That in case a Certificate be made for any person or persons disagreeing with or contrary unto any of the particular requisites mentioned in the 4th Instruction immediately foregoing, you or your deputy, is to acquaint the Justices of the Peace or one of them that allowed the same, and also the Officers of the parish or some of them that signed it, with the illegality thereof, and desire redress, and in case of their refusal, you are to acquaint the Lords Commissioners of his Majesty's Treasury, or the Lord High Treasurer for the time being therewith.
[TNA T54/9 (Warrants not Relating to Money), **9**, 445–54]

Appendix C
Treasury books

1670 June 29: Letter to two Justices of the Peace for Herefordshire and similar to two in Hertfordshire

We have seen a certificate allowed and signed by you for the Exemption of several persons in the parish of King's Walden in your county from payment of the Hearth duty to his Majesty because they are by reason of their poverty and smallness of estate not taxed to the usual rates towards the church and poor: which certificate we do not find by the Act that either the minister, churchwardens and overseers of the poor have power to make or the Justices of the Peace to allow. There is indeed in the last Act a clause which empowers the making and allowing certificates; and to prevent for the future the trouble and inconvenience which irregular certificates have heretofore occasioned, his Majesty's officer is furnished with a printed form drawn by good advice and exactly according to the law, which hath been tendered to you, but refused and instead thereof these made which the law does not justify.

1674 November 4: Manual to the Archbishops of Canterbury and York severally

We are informed that either through the ignorance of some persons in the law or by partiality and favour great number of undue certificates are from time to time signed in all places of the kingdom by ministers, vicars, curates, churchwardens and overseers for persons not qualified as above: to the great diminishing of the said revenue. You are forthwith to write to the Bishops of the several dioceses to strictly charge all ministers, vicars, curates and churchwardens to use all possible circumspection in the signing of any certificates and that they be well assured that persons certified for be qualified as above: and that they certify no other.

1683/4 March 4: to Thomas Farrier, Justice of the Peace for Buckinghamshire

The Hearth money Commissioners have complained to the Treasury Lords of several abuses in the illegality and unfairness in the granting of certificates in your neighbourhood. I enclose you the information as you are named in it. As your neighbour and friend I ... advise you to take speedy care ... and so regulate your certificates as that every person that by law ought not to be certified for may pay the King's duty.
[The one for Wendover certified] 'that the several poor persons hereunder named are either Collectioners or such as by Reason of their Poverty or Smallness of Estate are not any ways taxed or assessed to the usual Payments or Contributions towards the Church and Poor, neither have they or any of them more than two chimneys'.
[*Calendar of Treasury Books* (1904–57), **3**, 605–06; **4**, 604; **7**, 1064–65]

Appendix D
Exemption certificates

1. 1670 Dyke in Bourne (Lincs)

[Written on the back of printed certificate] 'The King's Majesty in his Proclamation is pleased to take notice of the many illegal and undue certificates. Therefore you are to take care that you insert no names but what to your knowledge are truly comprehended in the terms of this certificate upon pain of his Majesty's high displeasure and of being rendered as persons ill affected.'

2. 1670 Oxhill (Warwicks)

[Printed certificate with sixteen names, signed by the Rector, two officers and two JPs, but with nine names annotated by the receiver asserting their liability]
[Undated printed certificate with eight names written by the receiver, unsigned, but annotated:] *'The Minister refuseth to sign this Certificate'*
[and on the back:] 'Pray send this again'

3. 1671 Gresham (Norfolk)

[Printed certificate with 25 names, with eight added in a different hand followed by:] *'These eight take collection which we supposed were needless to have been put in at first before the signing of the certificate.'*
'We allow of this certificate containing 25 names' [and then added in MS:]
'until cause be shown to the contrary.'

4. 1672 Putney and Roehampton (Surrey)

[Printed certificate for 50 names]
'We allow of this certificate containing 50 names' [and then added in MS:]
'as to the Poverty, but not the rents of the above named Persons' [signed by four JPs]

5. 1672 All Saints, Hertford

[MS certificate] 'These whose names are underwritten usually were exempted from the duty of hearth money by reason of their poverty; but very few or none in our Corporation of Hertford but do pay above twenty shillings a year, but these pay nothing to church nor poor, but most take alms of the parish:' [64 names]

6. 1673 Newbystones in Morland (Westmorland)

[MS certificate] 'These are to certify whom it may concern that all those persons whose [20] names are underwritten are not any of them really worth 20s per annum or £10 in goods or money debtless, and therefore freed from paying the duty of Hearth money by the Act.'
[TNA E179/334; 347; 338/491; 346; 331/1; 348]

4 Chimneys, Wood and Coal *by Margaret Spufford*

The central importance of the domestic hearth is well attested in many countries, and none more so than the thickly forested and mountainous terrain of Japan. Lacking substantial reserves of coal, its forests have always been vital both for timber buildings and for firewood. The Japanese author Nobumasa made the point quite specifically in 1660, when he wrote:

> ... the hearth is central to the person. Whether one be high or low, when one lacks wood, one lacks fire and cannot exist. One must take care that wood be abundant. To assure that wood not become scarce, one cherishes the mountains. And thus, because they are the foundation of the hearth, which nurtures the lives of all people, the mountains are to be treasured (Totman 1989, 77).

The same conviction that 'when one lacks wood, one lacks fire and cannot exist' is equally applicable to England.

The general background to the 16th and 17th centuries in England is well known. The population rose steeply until the 1650s, and the price of basic grains rocketed, especially in times of dearth. What is not so widely known, perhaps, is that there was a sharp cooling period in late 16th- and late 17th-century western Europe (Grove 2004, **1**, 400–02; **2**, 629–31, 638). In every decade from the 1530s onwards, there were at least two winters, sometimes three, which were recorded as 'severe', 'very severe', or 'extremely severe'. In the 17th century there were more decades with three such winters (Jones *et al* 2001, 112). The Cam, and even the Ouse, froze during both centuries; even the port of King's Lynn was unusable during some winters because it had frozen. In Switzerland, the large lakes froze hard enough to carry men and cargoes (Frenzel 1994, 209–11). There is no question that river and even sea navigation would have been impossible during some winters,

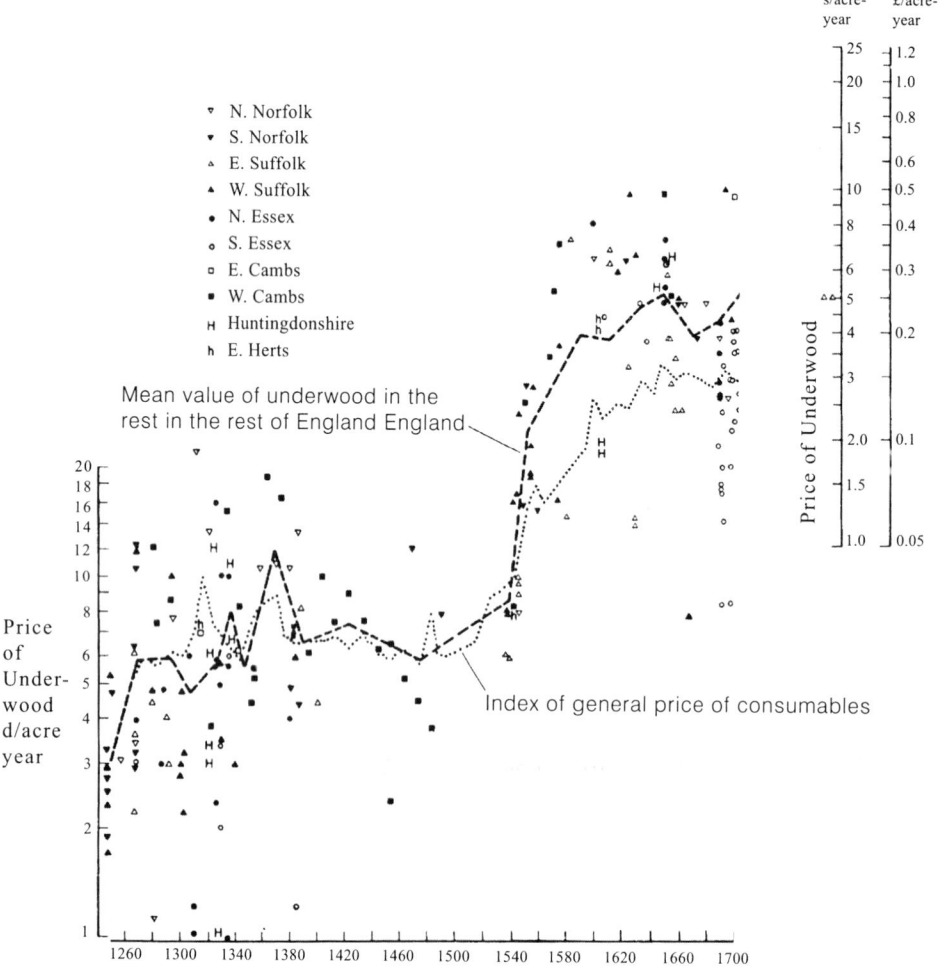

Fig 4.1 Price of underwood in pence per acre, 1250–1720 (after Rackham 2003). Reproduced with permission

and there would also have been an increasing need for fuel. At the same time as this cooling period, the demand for firewood rose. Not only was there an increased demand for domestic fuel, but also a very large increase in industrial activity, demanding huge resources of wood to sustain it. The graph of wholesale prices of underwood per acre shows a dizzying rise in a dramatic crescendo in the 1530s and 1540s (Fig 4.1; Rackham 2003), at the same time as the prices of other ordinary consumables rose. The most important point is that the price of wood rose faster than food, as it did in Sussex (Perlin 1989, 179–80). The pace slackened in the 1590s, but prices went on rising to a peak in the 1640s. It is tempting to suggest that this rise in the price of fuel was driven not only by the population rise, and the growth of industry, but also by the cold winters. Indeed, can the need to keep warm have been one factor in the increased number of chimneys? Certainly historians have not thought nearly as much of dearth of fuel to cope with the cold as of dearth of food. William Harrison's *Description of England* of 1587 is well known to all those concerned with the Hearth Tax. Despite his expansive title, Harrison was really describing the environs of his own village of Radwinter in Essex with a parish boundary that nearly touched on Saffron Walden. Moreover, he was describing the 'memories of the old men yet dwelling' in Radwinter, and the three things they saw remarkably changed in their lifetimes. One of them was 'the multitude of chimneys lately erected, whereas in their young days there were not above two or three, if so many, in most uplandish towns [villages] of the realm' (Harrison 1587, 201). For all scholars of the Hearth Tax, this is a well-known text. Indeed, it seems likely that it was the very conspicuous nature of such a multitude of chimneys appearing that later led to the notion of taxing them. Was it increasing cold weather that led to the rise in numbers of hearths and chimneys? There is another passage in Harrison's book, however, that is not nearly so well known. He wrote of the 'great sales yearly made of wood, whereby an infinite quantity hath been destroyed within these few years' (Harrison 1587, 280). Despite noting as well that 'there is a good store of great wood or timber here and there even now in some places of England' (Harrison 1587, 276), pessimism prevailed, from what he saw around him, and he continued:

> ... thus much I dare affirm, that if woods go so fast to decay in the next hundred years of grace, as they have done and are like to do in this ... it is to be feared that the fenny bote, [such as] broom, turf, gale, heath, firze, brakes, whins, ling, dies, hassocks, flags, straw, sedge, reed, rush, and also sea coal will be good merchandise even in the city of London (Harrison 1587, 280–81).

In fact, everything burnable, right down to reeds and straw, was in demand to keep those hearths, so treasured by the Japanese, alight in the Saffron Walden area. The fuel graph shows that the few figures for underwood obtainable for north Essex and west Suffolk were even higher than the already very high price of fuel in the late 16th and early 17th century.

There is some confirmation of the shortage of wood to burn from other writers. Arthur Standish wrote in the 1613 edition of his *New Directions of Experience to the Commons Complaint*: '40 years ago the poorest sort scorned to eat a peace of meat roasted with sea coal, which now the best magistrates are constrained to do' (cited in Hatcher 1993, 33). He even wrote of his fears that the supply of coal might run out near the coasts. In the 1616 edition, when he referred to the want of wood through the entire kingdom, he added, 'especially in London, Cambridge and Oxford'.

The dating of this observation fits well with Harrison's *Description*. Harrison's 'old men' of the late 1570s who had seen great changes in their lifetimes would have been remembering a period at least ten years earlier. Standish's reference to the 'poorest sort' being unwilling to eat meat roasted with sea coal also refers to the 1570s. There is here an indication that in the 1560s and 1570s there was a turning point when coal became much more commonly used in vernacular houses. This indication can be given precise point by looking at Pearson's recent work on the port of Sandwich. Her lists of probate inventories which refer to fuels in store, and of items connected with coal fires in Sandwich between 1564 and 1600, chronicle the swing from wood to coal in a little seaport admirably placed to receive coal coming down the coast from Newcastle. From the beginning of her lists, the appraisers normally noted both wood and coal in store. The first man only to have coal listed among his goods died in 1587. The people of Sandwich had no word for 'grate'. There was a 'cradle for coal' in the hall of Thomas Silbeck, and in 1598 comes reference to 'two irons to burn coals' in the hall. The *Oxford English Dictionary* gives the first use of 'grate' in this sense as occurring in 1605, with the quotation that 'a grate shall be laid wherein the coals of fire must lie'. There was a new situation emerging in Sandwich, which would necessitate its own language. But few of the appraisers had to deal with a man as thoroughly adapted to the new environment as Thomas Silbeck, whose goods were worth over £200 in 1597. Quite apart from the 'cradle for coal' in his hall, there was a 'coal back' in his parlour, and he was the only man before 1600 in Sandwich who had an outhouse actually called a 'coal house'. It contained no less than £6 worth of 'sea coal'.

This search for new vocabulary for a piece of equipment for the fire fits precisely with William Harrison and Arthur Standish's record of the appearance of domestic coal. In examining both wills and inventories for hearth equipment solely concerned with coal, 'grates' proved the most reliable indicator. Take, for example, the inventory of John Taylor alias Parishe, of Nethercote, husbandman, in the peculiar of Banbury, taken in July 1612, which carefully notes 'One iron grate, to burn coal' in his kitchen. The first

Part 1: The Hearth Tax

Table 4.1 The domestic use of coal in Kent, 1600–1749 (based on Overton et al 2004)

	1600–49 No with coal	1600–49 Total inventories	1600–49 % with coal	1650–99 No with coal	1650–99 Total inventories	1650–99 % with coal	1700–49 No with coal	1700–49 Total inventories	1700–49 % with coal
Benenden	4	82	4.9	12	81	14.8	3	31	9.7
Biddenden	4	111	3.6	12	65	18.5	4	33	12.1
Bridge	1	18	5.6	1	15	6.7	1	12	8.3
Burmarsh	1	16	6.3		21	0.0		8	0.0
Canterbury	11	92	12.0	19	78	24.4	14	20	70.0
Chartham	2	65	3.1	2	63	3.2	2	17	11.8
Ebony		27	0.0	1	11	9.1	1	7	14.3
Elham	3	77	3.9	3	67	4.5	2	31	6.5
Elmsted	1	35	2.9		26	0.0	1	15	6.7
Folkestone	14	83	16.9	15	40	37.5	39	62	62.9
Goudhurst	9	103	8.7	7	84	8.3	2	30	6.7
Headcorn	1	41	2.4	2	52	3.8	2	27	7.4
Iwade		26	0.0	3	10	30.0	4	13	30.8
Lenham	5	73	6.8	5	57	8.8	7	39	17.9
Milton	22	68	32.4	38	65	58.5	27	33	81.8
Minster	12	83	14.5	15	45	33.3	8	14	57.1
Newington	5	57	8.8	11	54	20.4	7	15	46.7
Orlestone		19	0.0	4	16	25.0	2	7	28.6
River	1	20	5.0		13	0.0		4	0.0
Ruckinge		56	0.0	2	36	5.6	1	21	4.8
Sheldrich		6	0.0		1	0.0	2	14	14.3
Smarden	2	112	1.8	8	79	10.1	5	46	10.9
Stelling		35	0.0		18	0.0		7	0.0
Ulcombe		39	0.0		43	0.0	3	16	18.8
Walmer	4	31	12.9	4	22	18.2	5	10	50.0
Waltham		16	0.0	2	22	9.1	2	9	22.2
Westbere	1	24	4.2	1	13	7.7		3	0.0
Wye	3	107	2.8	5	79	6.3	4	35	11.4

Banbury reference to coal in the inventories comes in 1592 (Brinkworth et al 1985, no. 9).

Two different phenomena have launched this enquiry. Between them, William Harrison and Arthur Standish have drawn attention to the increasing use of domestic coal and the paucity of timber. There is a huge literature on the exploitation and possible denudation of wood, particularly in the 17th century, and unfortunately the protagonists do not by any means always agree. On the other hand, Hatcher's definitive study of the late 16th- and 17th-century exploitation of coal makes that part of the enquiry relatively easy (Hatcher 1993).

Because of the rising price of wood and its diminishing supply, questions need to be asked about the design of chimneys and the materials of which they were constructed. Did the greater use of brick and stone result from the gradual increase in coal as a fuel, particularly as coal gave out a much greater intensity of heat than wood? Or was the spread of brick related to the 'need' for more hearths upstairs, and to the 'fashion' or 'need' for more heated rooms in a house? There may have been a genuine requirement for more warmth in these winters of the Little Ice Age. When Smith wrote on the Hertfordshire evidence in 1992, he was very clear about the functions and capacities of timber chimney stacks. Timber chimney stacks, he wrote,

> could serve one fireplace, or two back-to-back, but not, apparently, fireplaces on different floors ... So far as is known, no chimney stack with more complex flues than two set back-to-back was ever built in timber, and this was a pressing motive for the adoption of brick chimneys. In the late 17th century, upstairs rooms either came to be used as bedrooms for the first time, or a higher standard of comfort in general was demanded; whichever of these two factors caused the change, there was a demand for fireplaces. This is when, and why,

Table 4.2 The domestic use of coal in Kent and Cornwall, 1600–1749 (based on Overton *et al* 2004)

	Kent			Cornwall		
	Total inventories	Inventories with coal	% with coal	Total inventories	Inventories with coal	% with coal
1600–09	233	10	4.3	184	3	1.6
1610–19	371	16	4.3	273	3	1.1
1620–29	339	31	9.1	280	4	1.4
1630–39	358	33	9.2	195	2	1.0
1640–49	253	16	6.3	211	2	1.0
1650–59	23	4	17.4	22	0	0.0
1660–69	304	32	10.5	276	1	0.4
1670–79	333	51	15.3	293	4	1.4
1680–89	325	47	14.5	307	6	2.0
1690–99	223	39	17.5	294	0	0.0
1700–09	192	41	21.4	229	2	0.9
1710–19	176	46	26.1	198	1	0.5
1720–29	122	31	25.4	173	2	1.2
1730–39	66	20	30.3	148	1	0.7
1740–49	24	10	41.7	139	5	3.6

'Coal' refers to: coal irons, coal, range, and grate, excluding coal associated with industrial use.

brick chimney stacks were introduced into the vernacular buildings of Hertfordshire on a large scale (Smith 1992, 185–86).

He goes on to comment that 'about the middle of the 17th century considerable improvement in design, *perhaps connected with the kind of fuel used,* led to the adoption of grates' (Smith 1992, 186).

These considerations for Hertfordshire need to be addressed by building experts in other regions. Was there a swing from timber to brick or stone chimneys in particular areas, and, if so, when? Was there a change or improvement in design, and, if so, when? Did it connect with a change in fuel? If not, what trends in increased prosperity, and economic and social change, did it represent? Why were more people using rooms upstairs to sleep in? Are the increase in the number of hearths and the increased use of coal as a fuel connected causally, or do the two just happen to coincide?

Unfortunately, very little work has been done on fuel. Historians have not generally peered into the contents of people's woodsheds and yards given in the probate inventories. The shining exception is Overton, whose book *Production and Consumption, 1600–1750* has recently appeared (Overton *et al* 2004). He uses Kent and Cornwall as case studies. We know, of course, of the Port of Sandwich's import of sea coal. Overton shows (Table 4.1) from the Kent inventories that there was a dramatic increase in the proportion of inventories which mention coal between the first and second halves of the 17th century. This was inevitably highest in the ports, or near towns like Canterbury. But coal travelled inland too, as far as the market town of Lenham. It even got, surprisingly, into the thickly wooded areas of the Weald. People in three parishes round Cranbrook used coal, and one yeoman of Benenden was owed as much as £20 in 1677 for the 'carriage of coal'. This was a very considerable sum: one 'servant' of Banbury was paid 3s 6d when 'he went to the cole pitt', 48km (30 miles) away, in 1614 (Brinkworth *et al* 1985, no. 162).

These major changes in fuel supply and the design of chimneys to accommodate them had a knock-on effect on hearth furniture and even on cooking-pots. Overton points out that cauldrons, which were hung over the fire from a fire-crane, were disappearing from parishes where coal was much used, and that they were replaced by a wider range of pots and pans, including saucepans.

Cornwall, the second of Overton's case studies, presents a complete contrast to wealthy, coal-using Kent (Table 4.2). This is not for lack of information: the Cornish inventories, decade by decade, produce very satisfying totals. But even at the end of the 17th century, in the decade 1680–89, only six of the 307 surviving inventories mentioned coal. That is 2%. People in Cornwall simply did not use coal. Even if brick or stone was in common use for chimney construction, the products of what would be known as the South Wales coalfield were not used (Fig 4.2).

In the present state of fragmentary knowledge it is not possible to survey each county systematically to understand the relationship between the information derived from probate inventories and the physical evidence in the field in terms of chimney innovation.

The extent of the disappearance of timber and destruction of woodland in the 16th and 17th centuries has been much debated. On the one hand, a Venetian ambassador in the reign of Henry VIII

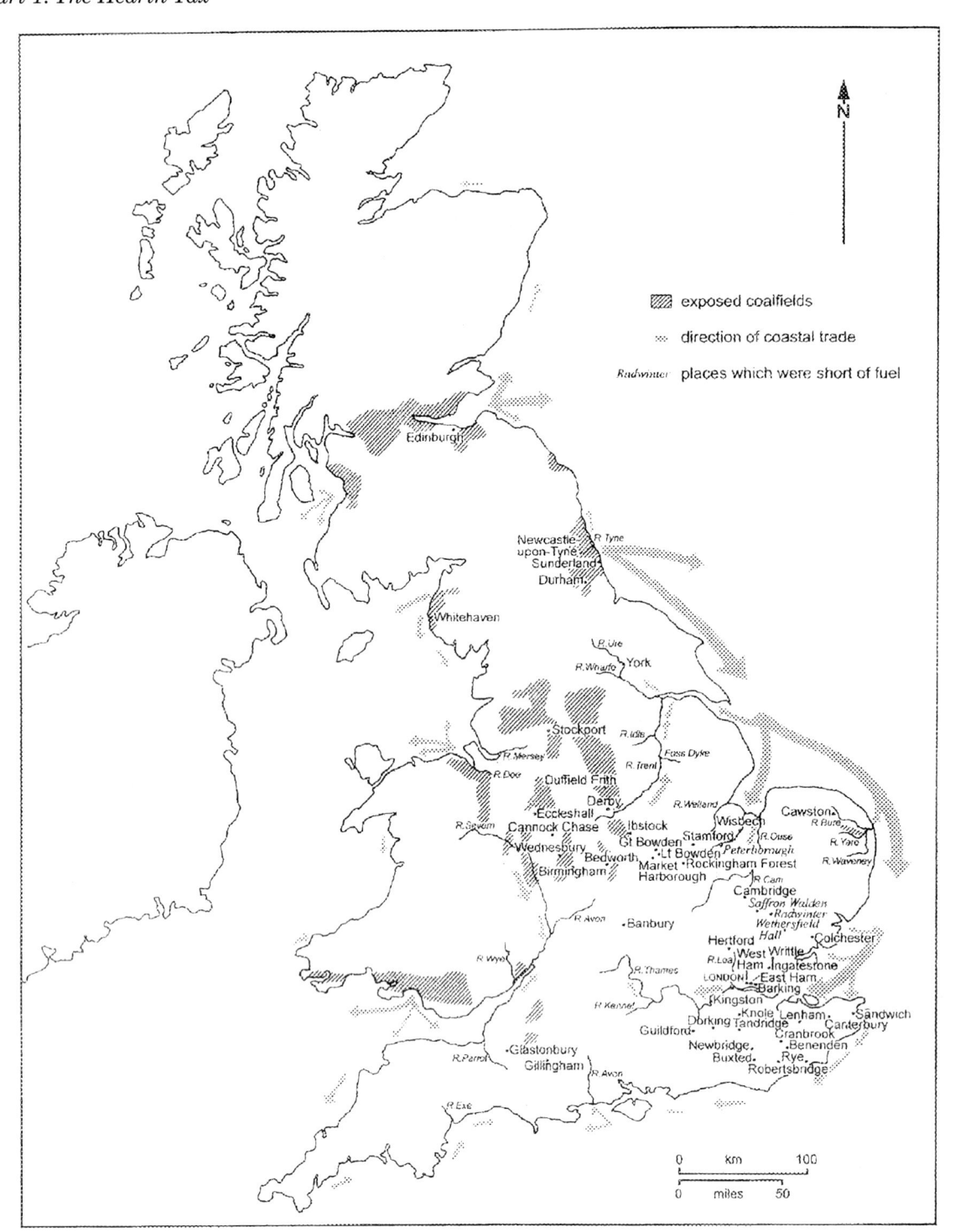

Fig 4.2 Coalfields and some settlements where coal was used or which were short of fuel in the 17th century (after Hatcher 1993). Reproduced with permission

(1509–47) admired the abundance of wood in the country, which was so great that it was a common export. Six hundred shiploads a year were exported to Calais. English wood was in such demand in non-English France that a merchant reported he had seen 37 hoys (small boats) go out of Rye in Sussex on one tide. Fishermen from Dunkirk successfully begged the king for a licence to import Sussex firewood to cure their herrings. In spite of Harrison's comments, Essex itself grew timber for export (Perlin 1989, 163–64).

England was industrially extremely backward at this period. Essentials like iron, dyes, and glass were imported, and Henry VIII relied mainly on munitions workers around Antwerp for his armaments. While England imported these items, which demanded great quantities of wood in their manufacture, its own forests remained more or less intact. Then a change of alliances caused a reversal of policy. The widespread fear of invasion by the French meant that England could no longer depend on the Continent for its supplies. Most of Henry VIII's revenue from

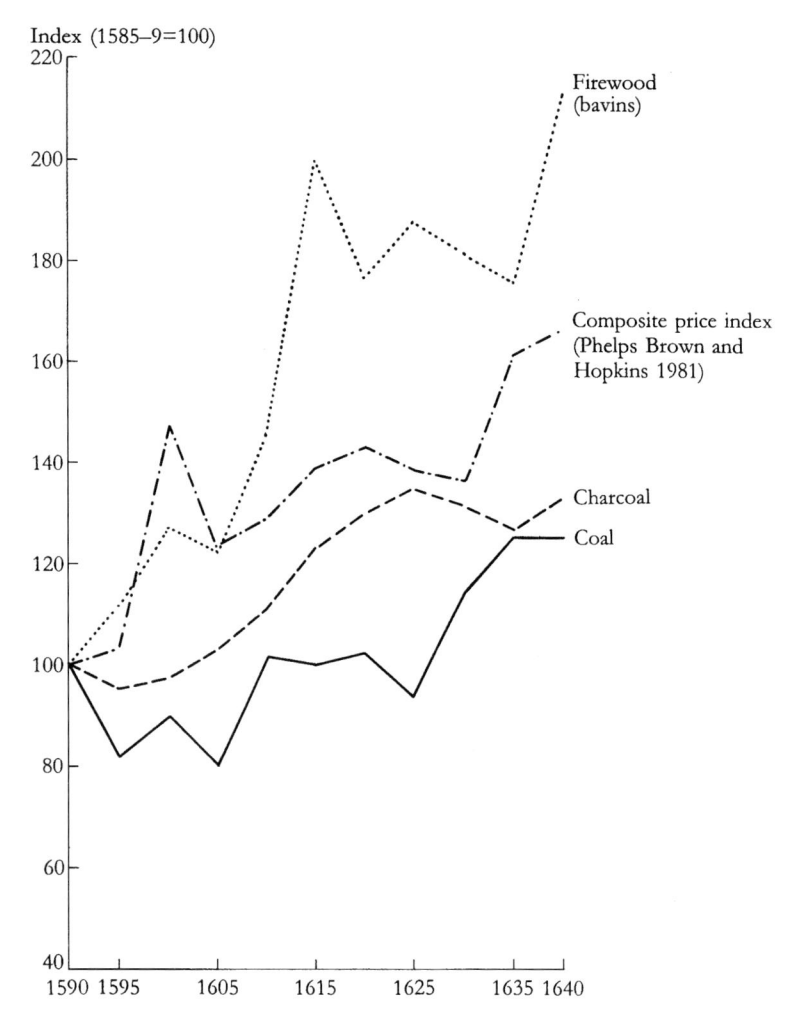

Fig 4.3 Price of fuel supplied to Westminster School, 1590–1640 (after Hatcher 1993). Reproduced with permission

the suppression of the monasteries went into his new coastal defences against French invasion. Since he needed British armaments, he patronised the three ironmasters and gunfounders who started their enterprise in 1543 in Sussex, which was 'a grand nursery of oak and beech' (Perlin 1989, 166). And that, according to one school of thought, was the beginning of the decline of English forests. Sir William Sidney, grandfather of Sir Phillip, bought the iron-rich land of Robertsbridge upon the surrender of Robertsbridge Abbey. He had a blast furnace and a forge built. It took 53 woodcutters to keep the Robertsbridge furnace supplied with wood for its charcoal. By 1549 there were 53 forges and furnaces operating in Sussex, and England was in the forefront of the arms race. Local people saw the destruction of the forests as 'their utter undoing' since wood was a basic necessity to build and heat their homes, cook their meals, and make their tools and fishing boats. But nothing was done by Government. There was a flurry of bills to protect wood, and even hedges, but they all failed. Two ironmasters in Surrey converted over 2000 oak, ash and beech trees into fuel for their works in one year of operation. The ironworks increased in number from around 53 in 1549 to over 100 in 1577. Crossley has produced a useful map showing the coincidence of the woods on the Sussex uplands and the sites of furnaces and forges (Crossley 1999, 62–63). There has been so much interest in the rise of the new industries in England that no one has really focused on the continuing plight of the poor, without wood to cook, keep warm, and heat their water in a time of increasingly cold and severe winters (see Fig 4.1).

It is no wonder that one of the factors in popular riots became the shortage of wood for fuel. A century later, in the 1690s, Gregory King estimated there were only 1,214,083 ha (3,000,000 acres) of cultivated woodland left, or only 8% of the kingdom, together with a similar area of forests, parks and commons (Thomas 1983, 194–95, 370 n 6; Thirsk and Cooper 1972, 779).

By the early 17th century coal was replacing charcoal as the fuel in the manufacture of glass (Spufford and Spufford 1964, 28), lead and copper, and in brick making, brewing and pottery making. There were difficulties in using coal as a replacement for charcoal in iron smelting: the coal gave off sulphurous fumes which contaminated the metal. In 1686 Robert Plot, in *The Natural History of Staf-*

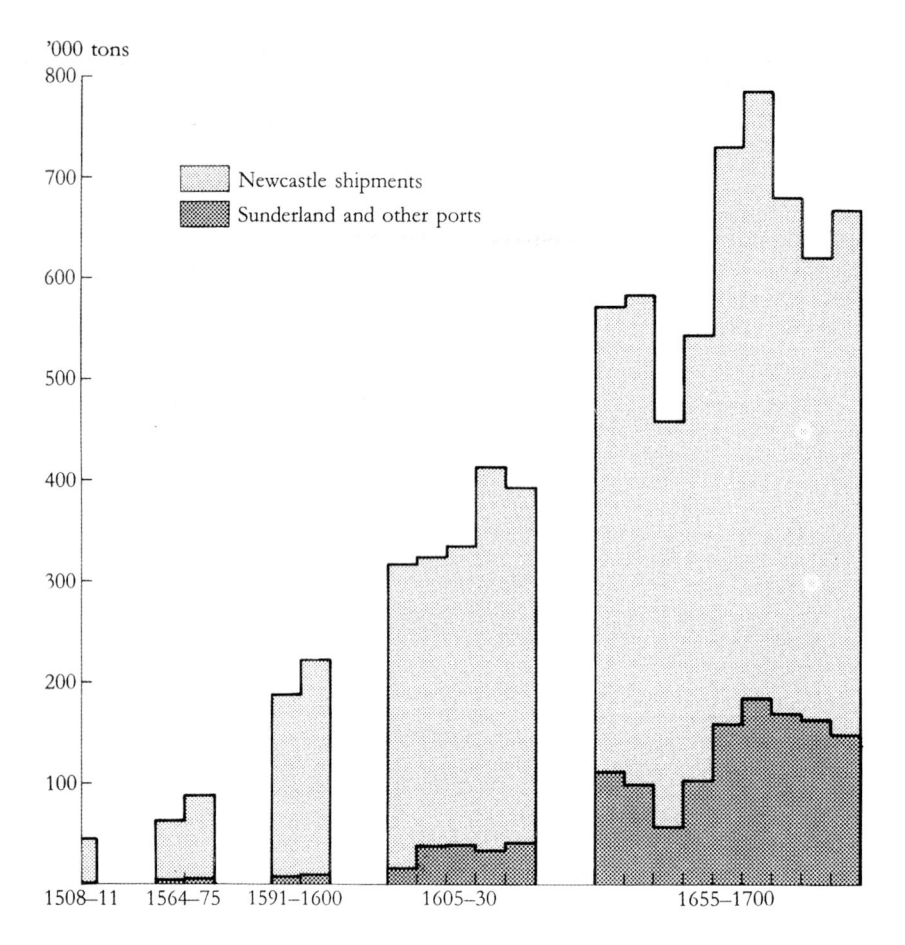

Fig 4.4 Shipments of coal from Newcastle and Sunderland, 1508–1700 (after Hatcher 1993). Reproduced with permission

fordshire, gave an excellent description of coal, including the industries for which it was, and was not, suitable. He is specific about its unsuitability for working with iron (Plot 1686, 310). The problem was overcome in the early 18th century, when coke was successfully used for smelting iron (Richards 2003; Thirsk and Cooper 1972, 307–13). Apart from this major problem, coal was increasingly in demand, for both industry and domestic purposes.

A great deal is known about the late 16th- and 17th-century exploitation of coal, thanks to Hatcher's definitive study of the coal industry (Hatcher 1993). In making a graph of the price of fuel purchased by Westminster School to 1640 (Fig 4.3), he took as his start date the half-decade 1585–90 – just the period when Harrison was lamenting the sale of virtually anything that would burn, and the Utopian time when Standish's 'poorest sort' scorned to eat food cooked over sea coal. The price for firewood paid by Westminster College, however, reveals that the schoolboys there were already being forced to get accustomed to this strange taste. The price of firewood rose dramatically in the 1590s. When Arthur Standish wrote, between 1611 and 1616, it is known from Rackham's work (see Fig 4.1) that firewood prices were literally soaring, and even the price of coal was being pushed up, no doubt reflecting demand. If the shipments of coal from Newcastle and other ports on the Sunderland-Durham coalfield are examined (Fig 4.4) the 17th-century rise in output is shown to have been staggering. The rise in shipments really took off in the 1590s, just when the schoolboys of Westminster were paying through the nose for their firewood – but it continued in the most dramatic fashion right through to the second half of the 17th century. There is no doubt at all of the increasing importance of coal as a fuel in the domestic economy. But there is a *caveat*: coal is a heavy, awkward commodity and not really suitable for distribution by road. Hatcher thought its distribution was likely to be either coastal, or up navigable rivers. He therefore mapped his 17th-century coalfields along with such rivers: if an inland town or area was not near a navigable river, coal was a good deal less likely to fuel its fireplaces or its industry. The biggest of all rivers was the Thames. From the beginning of the 16th century the prosperous were, in their wills, making provision of coal for the poor in London. A goldsmith in 1503 left 12 quarters of coal to be distributed to the poor. In 1532 a fletcher left 24 quarters of coal to be distributed annually to the poor three weeks before Christmas.[1] In 1619 a minister of Kingston requested the bailiffs to build a brick storehouse and distribute the profits of the wharf there on the north side of Kingston Bridge to the poor in coal.[2] But coal was not only distributed on Thames-side. Testators in Dorking and Guildford bequeathed it, and the practice also reached smaller settlements in Surrey. In 1560 Paul Coke, who farmed 7.25 ha (18 acres) in Tandridge, a village between Godstone and Oxsted, provided for his wife by leaving her the house for life, a place next the barn 'to lay her coals in' and two bushels of barley malt, two bushels of oats malt, three bushels of wheat every quarter, eight pounds of cheese, and three pounds of butter a year, and a load of coals a year, with 6s 8d.[3] Coal was a familiar fuel in Surrey, not only along the riverside, but much more widely in the countryside in the first half of the 16th century.

Such was the predominance of coal in London that in 1661 John Evelyn was moved to write of the thick cloud that obscured the city:

> If this goodly City justly challenges what is her due and merits all that can be said to reinforce her Praises and give her Title; she is to be reliev'd from that which renders her less healthy, really offends her, and which darkens and eclipses all her other Attributes. And what is all this but that Hellish and dismal Cloud of SEA-COAL? which is not onely perpetually imminent over her head ... but so universally mixed with the otherwise wholsome and excellent Air, that her Inhabitants breathe nothing but an impure and thick Mist accompanied with a fuliginous and filthy vapour ... corrupting the Lungs ... so that Catarrhs, Phthisicks, Coughs and Consumptions rage more in this one City than in the whole Earth Besides.

John Evelyn blamed the brewers, dyers, lime-burners, and soapboilers rather than domestic fires for this smog (Evelyn 1661, 5–6).

It has been possible, with the help of many local informants, to add to Hatcher's picture of the 17th-century use and distribution of coal. It was not all sea coal, shipped coastally and used mainly near the coasts (see Fig 4.2). Nor was it all distributed by the rivers, which sometimes froze in the winter. The widespread use of coal inland is quite surprising. Where a settlement actually lay in a coal mining area, like Duffield Frith in Derbyshire, the use of coal was to be expected. The coal mines within the parish were valued at £30 a year in 1650, a higher sum than any other mines in the county. Despite that, a very small proportion of inventories from Duffield specifically mention wood, coal, or other fuel. There had been extensive woods in the Frith, and there were common rights within it. But a very substantial clue, which does much to explain the absence of coal from inventories, is given by the will of Thomas Wild of Hazelwood of 1643. There was no coal in his own inventory, but he bequeathed a horse to his son, with the instruction that he shall carry out errands for his mother, including 'fetching her every fortnight a load of Coal till Michaelmas next, she paying for them at the pits [damaged] one shilling'. If householders in Duffield all fetched their coal regularly like this, it is not surprising that appraisers found so little coal in the yards. Banbury in Oxfordshire is not the sort of market town which lies on the edge of any industrial zone. Yet there were 28 inventories recording coal in the first published volume of wills and inventories for the peculiar of Banbury, beginning with one in the inventory of a skinner of 1592. The editors of the volume refer to the use of sea coal throughout the Thames Valley in Elizabeth's reign. But all the coal in northern Oxfordshire did not necessarily come from the sea, even though it was commonly referred to as sea coal. In 1620 Thomas Taylor of Neithrop left his wife Alice the 'room next to the gatehouse standing on the west end of my house with the chamber over the same, and my executors shall build her a sufficient chimney in the same room'. They were also 'yearly to fetch my wife Alice one load of sea coals, she paying for them at the *pit*' (my italics). The appraisers who took the inventory of Thomas Wisse, a husbandman of Nethercote, were even more helpful. They listed some 'Bedworth coals' amongst his goods. Bedworth coal pit lay just under 48km (30 miles) away, between Coventry and Nuneaton. The vicar of Cropredy leased his 'privy tithes' in 1612, and the lessees were to fetch him three loads of coals yearly to the vicarage 'from Bedworthe or some other convenient place where sea coals or pit coals are to be sold'. By 1630, this had been changed to two loads a year from Wednesbury in Staffordshire. Wednesbury is 77km (43 miles) away (again by crow, not packhorse or wagon) and it sounds as if this was six days' carrying service. So Banbury people were accustomed to coal fetched from Warwickshire and Staffordshire. Not only the more prosperous people in Banbury burnt coal: by 1603, coal was regularly bought for the poor out of the town's Poor's Stock during the summer when it was cheaper, and sold in the winter to the poor at a price which did not diminish the stock (Brinkworth *et al* 1985, nos 9, 224 and 143). In the light of this evidence, it is legitimate to wonder whether people in market towns, surely places which sucked in the fuel from the surrounding countryside, also used coal from the end of the 16th century, *if they were within reach of a coal pit.*

Market Harborough, in Leicestershire, was just such a place. It lay south-east of Leicester and by 1614 its inhabitants were using coal. The fuel could have come from the Ibstock area which later became known as 'Coalville', 40km (25 miles) away. Elizabeth Hill, widow, had 3s 4d worth of coal to burn in her grate that year. References become more common, although the first 'coal house' did not appear until 1634. Shoe makers and plumbers had grates. The largest quantities of coal seemed to be kept, not unsurprisingly, by victuallers. By the 1660s most inventories listed coal. It is difficult to estimate the quantities from the values given, but in 1661, 2.25 tonnes (45 cwt) were valued at £2 5s, so coal was then 1s a hundredweight. The people of the nearby village of Great Bowden were slower to use coal and, when they did, the first men to do so in abundance were the blacksmiths. John Moore, who died in 1639, had coal worth £7 4s. By the end of the 17th century almost every person in the village, including labourers, was dependent on coal. Little Bowden was less dependent, but coal was still getting there.

Further evidence for the need to adjust ideas on the common use of coal inland before the Civil War comes from Lancashire. The *Stockport Probate Records* (Phillips and Gibson 1985) comprise 118 wills and inventories between 1578 and 1619 containing 21 references to coal, 8 to coal and coal carts, 1 to a coalwain, and 19 to grates. Stockport was, of course, in the immediate vicinity of the Lancashire coalfield. Nevertheless, it is necessary to be cautious. The key phrase may be 'using coal if they were within reach of a coal pit'. A study of the wills and inventories of weavers from parishes bordering on the Solway and in the area south-west of Carlisle from 1660 onwards, shows people there were dependent on peat for their fuel. Their peat spades were in the inventories, and there was only one single reference to coal, in 1682.

Radwinter, where William Harrison lamented the scarcity of fuel in the 1580s, lay practically adjacent to the market town of Saffron Walden. This was precisely the sort of town where a scarcity of fuel might be expected, and where supplies might be sought from the surrounding countryside. Saffron Walden lay 32km (20 miles) from Cambridge, which was further inland. We know from Standish that Cambridge itself suffered a great scarcity of fuel, and its inhabitants had even imported wood from Essex, according to Harrison (1587, 67). It also lay 48km (30 miles) from Colchester, which was in quite a different situation: in 1570, the widow Ann Barrington of St Giles, Colchester, left a bequest of half her 'shells' and coals lying at the New Hythe of Colchester, so Colchester did have coal, or access to coal. In all the research for this project, however, it has not been possible to discover whether the trade of 'retail coal merchant' had yet developed. It is not clear if the fuel-starved inhabitants of north-east Essex could go to Colchester – a town about 136km (85 miles) from the nearest inland pit – and buy coal. Ryan has found seven probate inventories from the Archdeaconry of Colchester in the bundles of letters of administration for 1683–90.[4] All but three come from the main part of the archdeaconry over towards the east and the sea. All references to coal are in them. Only three come from the north-east corner of the county where Radwinter and Saffron Walden lay, and all three, including one from Saffron Walden itself, refer only to wood as fuel.

Hedge breaking was a particular misdemeanour of the poor. It normally meant the searching of hedges for fuel but could be, and has been, confused by historians with the deliberate breaking of new hedges as a protest against enclosure. Tenants who took sub-tenants who might practise hedge breaking in search of fuel could be fined, as they were at Wethersfield Hall in Essex, not 10 miles from Radwinter, in 1561 (Hindle 2004, 43–48; McIntosh 1998, 84–88).

It is even more to the point that the jurors of the court of Saffron Walden itself ordered in 1554 that no one should break hedges under penalty of a shilling fine, to be paid by the main tenant of the dwelling in which the breaker lived. This was on the assumption that the culprit would not be able to pay the fine. The penalty rose to 2s for a second offence, and expulsion for frequent misdemeanours. This regulation was inadequate, for in 1557 a new byelaw was passed, stating that anyone who broke hedges should sit in the stocks for three hours for each time he or she was caught, and the landlord should pay 1s for each offence (McIntosh 1998, 87). This may not sound vivid, but consider the desperation of the very poor, dependent on fuel for warmth in this colder period, and to heat water or cook food. At Ingatestone in Essex hedge stealers were whipped until they 'bleed well' in the 1590s and 1600s (Rackham 2003, 168). All the admittedly tiny fragments of evidence it has been possible to gather to check Harrison's alarming assessment of the scarcity of fuel in the 1570s in the north-west corner of Essex, seem to show he was right for his own area.

Ryan has also searched twelve volumes of wills (Emmison 1982–2000) covering Elizabeth's reign, and found 98 bequests of firewood, three of charcoal, and fifteen of coal. All those of coal were either associated with blacksmiths, or gifts to the poor of Barking, and East and West Ham, all of which lay on the Thames estuary. The earliest reference to coal in the inventories of the peculiar of Writtle is as late as 1672 (Steer 1950).[5] It therefore seems that the houses of Essex were heated by wood, though coal was used industrially in smithies. Yet in the 16th century most farmhouses and houses in the towns and larger villages had one or more chimney of brick, from the evidence of the Walker maps (see p.56). In the 17th century all new farmhouses were built with brick chimneys, often with several flues in one stack. French has also investigated the use of wood and coal in Essex, heavily handicapped by the small number of Essex probate inventories, at least until after the Restoration. He thinks that coal and wood were both used in Essex and Suffolk, but that coal was not used commonly until the 1630s except by smiths. Coal was only used widely after the River Stour was made navigable in the early 18th century. Here, then, in one easy move, the suggestion that brick chimneys may have been built with the new fuel in mind collapses. It is possible that there is confusion between poverty and prosperity in Essex, an area where the fuel was wood, which remained affordable to those farmers who chose to build brick chimneys.

The plight of the poor in Saffron Walden and Radwinter is mirrored in Peterborough, another inland town, but on the River Nene, which ran out through the port of Wisbech. Wisbech is tidal, and was accessible to sea-going vessels, but the port was in constant difficulty, and only really began to prosper in the 19th century.[6] Peterborough is particularly interesting because the information is directly comparable with that for 16th-century Sandwich. The Sandwich data is dated 1565–1600; that for Peterborough 1575–99. It has been complied by Briston, who is editing extracts from the rolls of the Courts of the Dean and Chapter of Peterborough Cathedral for their manor of Peterborough. She has examined a group of presentments of various tenants of properties of the Dean and Chapter in the centre of Peterborough, from which she has identified not only the social status of the tenants but also the position of the houses they were sub-letting in the city centre. The houses lay on the main residential street, Priestgate, and round the Marketstead, the open space to the west of the main west gate of the Abbey. There were also houses and cottages on Highgate, which was really Hythe-gate, the street leading south to the Nene itself, and its wharf, which suggests some river traffic.

The point of these presentments is that they were all for 'keeping a fire in a certain dwelling where there is not a chimney to the great danger of the neighbours and against ancient ordinance of the court'. Twenty-nine people were presented for this offence between 1575 and 1599, including the tenants of the Guildhall. As well as those with no chimney, another eight had 'inadequate' or 'not reliable' or 'not efficient' chimneys, where they 'kept fire to the great danger of their neighbours'. So 37 people with tenements in the centre of Peterborough had 'no chimney' or an 'insufficient' one in the late 16th century – and for some reason, their lord, the Dean and Chapter of Peterborough, had got very worried about it. On top of that, this group of tenants were sub-letting to sub-tenants about whom there was considerable anxiety. Twenty-three sub-tenants of cottages, tenements, or rooms were presented in the Marketstead and the Highgate, or Hythegate, in October 1570 (the month is probably revealing) because they had not collected sufficient fuel for winter, as had been ordered by the court. There was a further wave of more substantial fines in 1577 against those who 'accepted tenants who had insufficient firewood' and who, in winter, broke the hedges of the lords' tenants and carried away wood.

So in late 16th-century Peterborough, unlike late 16th-century Sandwich, the barges bringing coal upriver from Wisbech had definitely not yet arrived. There seems to have been a fuel famine. And no one was yet searching for the word 'grate'. Instead, a very large number of the houses in the centre of the city had no chimney at all, although some had 'insufficient' ones. Perhaps there had recently been a fire, judging by the degree of anxiety being expressed. Whatever the reason, the two towns, Sandwich and Peterborough, have to be held in mind as contrasting settlements. The Newcastle colliers had not yet turned far enough into the Wash, and the descriptions of Peterborough make it sound as if their barges would be very welcome when they got there. It is necessary to think of a huge variety of conditions subsisting side by side in 16th- and 17th-century England, as wood became more scarce in some places, and the Durham miners in their 'hovels' laboured to supply the new need. Local pits were also opened up inland to satisfy demand. Different situations pertained in different areas: in Hertfordshire and south Essex people made their houses more comfortable by heating their bedrooms; in Saffron Walden and Peterborough the poor sub-tenants, out of reach of an inland coal pit, would have recognised the truth of the Japanese author who wrote in 1660 that 'when one lacks wood, one lacks fire, and cannot exist'.

Acknowledgements

I have drawn heavily on the expertise of geographers. Dick and Richard Grove, Professor Michael Chisholm, and Dr Paul Richards have all given me help and information.

Joan Thirsk, and other local historians, and Sarah Pearson, and other building historians, have all given me information. Nat Alcock gave me information about Bedworth in Warwickshire. Mrs Pam Ancott went through the probate inventories for Market Harborough and Great and Little Bowdon and tabulated the use of coal for me. Miss Briston, who is editing the manor court rolls of the Dean and Chapter of Peterborough, sent me her dramatic findings on the lack of both chimneys and fuel, and is still looking for the 'ancient ordinance' of the court, prescribing the use of a chimney there. Mrs Heather Falvey, working on her PhD at Warwick, sent me her jewel of a finding on the arrangement for fetching coal for a widow in Duffield. Jeremy Gibson provided me, as ever, with a bonanza of information about Banbury. Tom Jackson sent me information on peat in the Solway area. Anthony Poole made a special trip to his record office to copy the account he had noticed which recorded that a yeoman was owed £20 for carting coal. Pat Ryan searched exhaustively through the Elizabethan and later wills of Essex and also found unknown probate inventories amongst bundles of letters of administration for me. Henry French added his opinions on Essex fuel. Cliff Webb searched all the Surrey wills in his database for references to coal. I am very grateful indeed to all these people.

My essential graphs and map have been adapted with permission from Rackham 2003 and Hatcher 1993. Mark Overton made his data on the domestic use of coal in Kent and Cornwall available to me long before the appearance of his book (Overton *et al* 2004). Without these fundamental pieces of information this work would have been impossible.

Chapter 4: Notes

1 LMA DW/PA/7/3 ff 203v–204v.
2 LMA DW/PA/7/10 f 75r.
3 LMA DW/PA/5/1562/84.

4 ERO D/ACWG 46. I cannot thank Mrs Ryan enough for all the help she has given me in this work.
5 Mrs Ryan also searched Steer 1950 for me. She tells me that brick chimneys became more common in the 16th century in Essex, and there were houses with more hearths in southern Essex, towards London.
6 In 1566, thirteen keels and other vessels of 3–10 tonnes used the port (*VCH* 1953, 207–08). The colliers that travelled down the coast were usually of only about 35 tonnes, although vessels in the overseas coal trade were much larger. These boats were used for the corn and coal trades, but only employed twelve watermen. There was no real remedy until Vermuyden constructed a sluice in 1631, but even then there was continuous trouble, and the port of Wisbech only really began to prosper in the early 19th century. See Davis 1962, and *VCH* 1953, 263–64; cf Willan 1976, 17–18 and 44 n 48.

PART 2: REGIONAL STUDIES

THE SOUTH AND EAST

5 London's Suburbs, House Size and the Hearth Tax
by Peter Guillery

Introduction

This chapter attempts to use the Hearth Tax to get at questions of architectural form and housing in late 17th-century London's humbler domestic buildings, not in the City of London, either before or after the Fire, but in its burgeoning and unburnt suburbs. Some basic reminders about London's social geography will set the scene. Metropolitan population grew from about 200,000 in 1600 to about 400,000 in 1650, and on to about 575,000 in 1700 when the capital's housing stock was about 60,000 to 70,000 houses. This suggests that there were then about eight to ten people per house, if not household, on which distinction there is significant vagueness. London was a huge centre of industry, with about half its workforce in 1700 engaged in manufacturing. Rapid growth and the prevalence of humble, if not poor, working people meant great density, and many small new houses. In terms of the balance of population, the suburbs overtook the City in the early 17th century, accounting for more than 400,000 people by the 1670s (Finlay and Shearer 1986, 47; Spence 2000, 63–65; Guillery 2004, 7–8).

After population, the next crucial starting point is Power's important and unsurpassed analysis of London Hearth Tax returns from the 1660s (Fig 5.1; Power 1986). It is notable that in mapping the comparative size of properties by the number of hearths in 1662–66 he used the word 'dwellings' as opposed to either house or household. What follows here is not about the suburbs to the west where the mean was five or more hearths — that is, not about Covent Garden, St Giles, or about Nicholas Barbon and the late 17th-century standardisation or industrialisation of speculative building for a 'middling sort' market that ended up producing houses that typically had eight to ten hearths each (McKellar 1999; Summerson 1945). Instead, the focus is on suburbs to the east and north, from Whitechapel, round to Spitalfields, Shoreditch and the southern more built-up parts of Clerkenwell, in all of which places dwellings had on average four or fewer hearths. The inhabitants of these suburbs were overwhelmingly working people, artisans and labourers. This was also true south of the river, not otherwise considered here. These people were not necessarily impoverished, but affluence was exceptional. Their suburbs were newly built, part of London's 17th-century expansion. From small beginnings around 1600 the parishes without the walls and the northern and eastern districts beyond grew to have a population of more than 200,000 by the 1670s, making them on their own about ten times more populous than England's next biggest cities, Norwich and Bristol (Wrigley 1990, 42). The 20,000 or more houses in which they lived were therefore relatively new, and essentially urban. Available visual evidence suggests that they were neither rural nor polite in character, and anything but standardised. Analysis of Hearth Tax returns for these peripheral urban areas may be particularly worthwhile precisely because few of the houses were very old. As ever, there are plenty of ambiguities in attempting to use Hearth Tax evidence for architectural history, not least the house versus household question, but the problems are perhaps somewhat fewer than when dealing with areas where the housing stock would have been a more indeterminate mix of old and new.

Map concordance, households and houses

The heart of this analysis is a comparison of a particular Hearth Tax roll, the Middlesex survey or assessment of 1674–75,[1] with John Ogilby and William Morgan's map of the City of London of 1676, which extended to many of the extramural suburbs that appear in the Middlesex assessment. The survey work for these parts of this map was probably done in 1674–75, so it can be taken as being contemporary with the assessment. In his introduction to the London Topographical Society's reprint of the map as the *A to Z of Restoration London*, Hyde judged Ogilby and Morgan to be largely accurate in the articulation of houses along streets, though somewhat less so in the depiction of separate houses in courts and alleys (Hyde 1992). The map thus seemed, *a priori*, likely to be a valuable fix. And so it has proved; it does hold together with the assessment remarkably well, the two documents seeming to prove each other's reliability and completeness. The assessment includes exempt dwellings, marked 'r', which probably stands for 'returned exempt' (see below). The names of the exempt are interspersed with those of the liable, comparison with the map indicating a topographical sequence. Empty houses are also recorded, as well as the names of those (very few) whose homes had no hearths. The assessment could thus be used as a directory, though that approach is not pursued here (cf chapter 10). The map and the Hearth Tax assessment together begin to give places embryonic shape, which it is occasionally possible to enhance through pictorial evidence relating to particular buildings. There are, however, undeniable ambiguities. A complete transcription or count from the assessment, not attempted here, might penetrate some of these, as might comparative research using other late 17th-century records

36 Part 2: Regional Studies

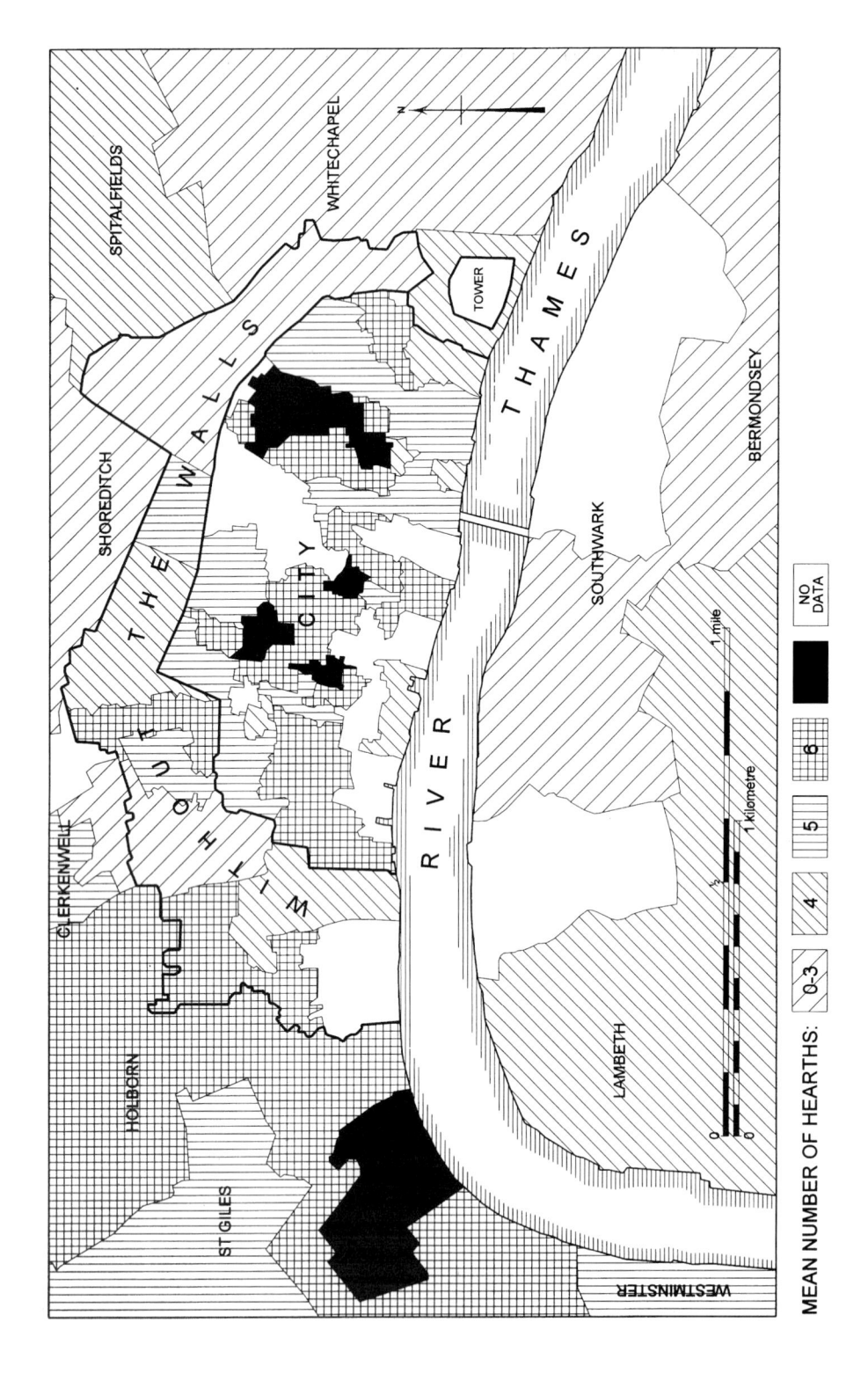

Fig 5.1 London in 1662–66, mean dwelling size by number of hearths. After Power 1986

London's Suburbs, House Size and the Hearth Tax 37

Table 5.1 London's suburbs: some comparative Hearth Tax statistics

	assessed h'holds/houses			hearths			mean			exempt (%)		
	1664	1674/75	change	1664	1674/75	change	1664	1674/75	change	1664	1674/75	change
WHITECHAPEL	2,482	2,304	−7.2%	5,897	6,433	+9.1%	2.4	2.8	+16.7%	1,740 (70.1%)	889 (38.6%)	−48.9%
RATCLIFF	1,121	1,110	−1%	3,389	3,767	+11.2%	2.9	3.4	+17.2%	544 (48.5%)	275 (24.8%)	−49.4%
SPITALFIELDS	948	1,329	+40.2%	3,062	4,687	+53.1%	3.2	3.5	+9.4%	427 (45%)	120 (9%)	−71.9%
BETHNAL GREEN	217	274	+26.3%	621	1,002	+61.4%	2.8	3.7	+32.1%	113 (18.2%)	–	–
CLERKENWELL*	2,692**	2,424	−10%	8,145*	7,896	−3.1%	3.0*	3.3	+10%	–	965 (39.8%)	–

Number of hearths in houses (liable and exempt)

1674/75	0	1	2	3	4	5	6 or more	of which exempt
WHITECHAPEL	0.5%	24.4%	24%	25.9%	8.9%	4.5%	11.8%	38.6%
SPITALFIELDS	0%	1.4%	16.7%	39.1%	19.9%	9.5%	13.5%	9%
CLERKENWELL	0%	32.1%	20.9%	20.9%	8.5%	4.6%	13%	40.5%

*includes St Sepulchre and St Botolph Aldersgate without

** = 1662–66 (1662–66 figures derived from Michael Power, as tabulated in Power 1972, 252 and as cited in Champion 1995, 106; 1674/75 figures from TNA E179/143/370)

such as the poll tax, also beyond the scope of the present study.[2]

The extent of the concordance between the map and the assessment raises the possibility that the assessed properties might in this instance, and unusually, have been what we would now define as houses rather than households. It is, of course, clear that the Hearth Tax was to be charged to occupiers, not to landlords, making the basic unit of taxation the household not the house. The act of 1664 tried to prevent landlords escaping the Hearth Tax by dividing houses into tenements. It is also difficult to be sure just what 'house' or 'household' meant in the late 17th century. But where a Middlesex assessment of 1664 occasionally mentions both 'empty houses' and 'empty rooms',[3] the assessment of 1674–75 only ever says 'empty'.[4] Even in localities where multiple occupation might be expected there appears to be no separate enumeration of households as opposed to houses.

Some numerical comparison supports this interpretation, and sheds other light on the matter (Table 5.1). Power's analysis shows that by 1664 Whitechapel had 2482 households or dwellings and 5897 hearths, giving a mean of 2.4 hearths per household. The 1674–75 assessment lists 2304 Whitechapel properties with 6433 hearths, giving a mean of 2.8. That indicates that in ten years there was an increase of more than 500 in the number of hearths in Whitechapel, and a decrease of nearly 200 in the unit of assessment. Contemporary 'Returns of New Buildings' suggest that 423 new houses were built in Whitechapel in the period 1656 to 1677 (George 1925, 413). While not closely reliable, this figure is probably broadly indicative. About half these houses, say 200, could be supposed to have gone up between 1664 and 1674, though perhaps rather fewer, as it should not be forgotten that after the Fire, when the City was being rebuilt, builders were more than usually hard to come by elsewhere in London. The new buildings in Whitechapel might, in principle, have been improving redevelopment, that is the replacement of 400 one-hearth households by 200 four- to five-hearth households. However, there are few substantial groups of such large properties in Whitechapel in the assessment of 1674–75. Indeed, there were only 580 with four or more hearths; it is unlikely that a third of these would have been ten years old or less, and that numbers of smaller houses had not also been built. Perhaps, instead, these statistics help to confirm that the later assessment does list houses rather than households. About 200 or somewhat fewer new houses would thus easily explain the increase of about 500 hearths, without the need to posit major clearance. This would mean that in 1664 Whitechapel would have had about 2100 houses for its 2482 households, which would generate a constant 2.8 mean for hearths across the period. A comparable decrease in the numbers of assessed properties with an increase in the mean number of hearths in the riverside hamlet of Ratcliff might be similarly explained. In Spitalfields (see below) and Bethnal Green the sheer volume of new building in this period makes an equivalent comparison more difficult. Similarly, the Clerkenwell numbers (see below) include extramural parishes that were affected by the Fire, introducing a significant loss factor. However, these complications do not seem to undermine the analysis.

This interpretation also suggests that if Whitechapel in 1664 had 2482 households in about 2100 houses, then up to, but no more than, 18% of the houses were multiply occupied, which percentage corresponds roughly to the percentage increase in the mean number of hearths per unit of assessment. If some houses were divided into three or more households, the percentage of houses multiply occupied would be so much less. This level of multiple occupation would be consistent with other evidence. 'Returns of Divided Houses' in 1637 showed that about 15% of houses in and around the City were multiply occupied, rather more in parts of the periphery than in the centre (Harding 2001, 132; Baer 2000, 22). Further out to the east, multiple occupation was rare in newly built-up Shadwell in the 1650s, but rose to be present in about 25% of the district's houses by the 1690s (Power 1972; Spence 2000, 101–02). It should be recalled here that multiple occupation might not have been openly admitted, as attempts to limit, even prevent, suburban expansion up to an act of 1657 'for preventing the multiplicity of Buildings in and about the Suburbs of London' had tried to forbid the division of houses, which came to be seen as a contributing factor to the spread of both plague and fire (Champion 1995). An aversion to openness on the point of divided occupancy might help to explain why the assessor in 1674–75 might not have listed households, but it is not sufficient explanation. Suburban London would have presented those responsible for collecting the Hearth Tax with larger problems. Dealing with somewhat shadowy multiple occupation would anyway have been tricky, but it would have been made all the more difficult by great mobility. Tenancies could be very short, and immigration, exacerbated by the knock-on effect of displacement by the Fire, made for an exceptionally fluid population. It would have been enormously troublesome to catch up with every tenancy. In Wapping, a rough riverside neighbourhood, about half the properties assessed in 1674–75 were marked 's', which probably means surveyed from the outside only, and not entered. In most of the other suburban Middlesex parishes to London's east and north around a fifth to a quarter of assessed properties with three or more hearths were marked 's'.[5] Further, there was a large amount of new building, some of which would have been unlet or part-let. All these factors perhaps tended to make it easier to list and place responsibility for the tax on landlords or housekeepers, rather than on tenants. If the assessor was recording houses, the listed names were presumably those of the principal, that is ground-floor, tenants who would generally have been housekeepers if not landlords.

The concordance of the assessment with the map thus seems to bring forward the locations and numbers of many small, that is one- to four-hearth, houses, 17th-century buildings about which we otherwise know very little. No doubt, there would have been lots of jiggery-pokery, and the returns should not be thought of as inherently reliable, but even allowing for some avoidance through the bricking up or simple concealment of hearths, the prevalence of small numbers is striking. Unheated rooms must, of course, be taken into account. Determining their extent is always a problem with attempts to translate Hearth Tax assessments into architecture. The Treswell surveys that were made in the years up to 1612 show that unheated rooms in one-room layouts were then widespread in and around the City. Fleet Lane on the west side of the City, leading up to the Fleet Ditch (that is the River Fleet), had numerous one-room plan houses, some little more than 3m (10ft) square (Schofield 1987, 79). Six of nine houses in a row along Fleet Lane had unheated chambers, suggesting that each had three rooms in two storeys and garrets with only a single ground-floor hearth. Even in such small properties there was some multiple occupation, this group including many one-room tenancies. This might suggest that the Hearth Tax in London can say rather little about house size. However, it should be borne in mind that many of the houses shown on the Treswell plans were already old by 1600, so not necessarily indicative of up-to-date building practice.

There are reasons for believing that somewhat greater certainty is possible when dealing with London houses known to have been built after 1600. By the mid-17th century newly built houses on the edges of the town appear to have had few unheated rooms, other than basements, which were anyway rare, garrets and rear wash-house outshuts. Turning again to Power, his study of Shadwell, which was built up in the second quarter of the century, generated a mean of 3.7 rooms for houses that averaged 2.7 hearths in 1664 (Power 1978). It is unlikely that other new suburbs would have been significantly less well appointed. An analogy can be drawn with council houses of the 1950s, built with central heating before higher-status older houses had it installed. From another angle, a degree of over-specification is not unusual in a speculative-building context where the status of actual occupants often fell below that intended. If it is accepted that the 1674–75 assessment does list houses, it is probably a passable rule of thumb for 17th-century suburbs that the number of hearths plus one represents the number of rooms. So one-hearth houses might be understood as generally likely to have been a single room with an unheated garret, as was true elsewhere (Harrington et al 2000, xcvi). Power's study of Shadwell in 1650 also showed that about 70% of its houses had three or fewer rooms, with about 45% having only two rooms (Power 1978). But Shadwell was not overcrowded. It just had small houses. Across east London Power estimated an average of 1.7 persons per hearth in the 1660s (Power 1972).

These are not Dickensian living conditions, and seem even less so when unheated rooms are remembered.

Whitechapel

The concordance between the Hearth Tax assessment of 1674–75 and Ogilby and Morgan's map can be illustrated through several suburbs, relating the findings to other evidence of particular buildings. This is done here by working round from east to west, starting in Whitechapel. Already by 1600 Whitechapel Road was, as John Stow had it, 'pestered with Cottages and Allies' (Stow 1603, **2**, 72). But more substantial side streets and greater growth came later (Fig 5.2). Castle Street, which survives as Old Castle Street, lay to the north of Whitechapel Road, principally accessible from Wentworth (Wentford) Street, which was not laid out until c 1640 (Sheppard 1957, 238). Castle Street appears to have been fairly regularly, and not insubstantially, built, definitely a street rather than an alley. The map shows 56 properties, the Hearth Tax assessment lists 57, all but four with three or fewer hearths, with a mean of 2.4.[6] A high proportion (23) were marked as exempt, so this seems unlikely to have been the sort of place that would have been above subdivision. Yet, even if there had been multiple occupancy in only 10% of the houses a significant difference between the map and the assessment would result if the latter had been recording households. This point has perhaps been laboured; from here on the assessment of 1674–75 will be taken to be listing houses in the usual sense of the word. Katherine Wheel Alley to the east (e89 on the map) had 70 houses in the assessment, just as it appears to on the map, though alleys and courts are trickier to count. It was more mixed, with 23 one- or two-hearth houses (20 marked as exempt), and seventeen with five or more hearths. There were even two nine-hearth houses, perhaps those on the west side with the formal gardens.

None of Whitechapel's two- and three-hearth 17th-century houses appears to have survived long enough to have been drawn or photographed. However, if the net is cast a bit beyond the parish boundary towards Wapping, Shadwell, Bethnal Green and Limehouse, a picture of variety does emerge (Guillery 2004, 41–55). The one-room layout of from 3.6 to 5.1m (12 to 17ft) square was widespread in small two-storey speculations (Fig 5.3), built in pairs and in short rows, of timber or brick, sometimes with chimney stacks that suggest two hearths and unheated garrets, sometimes as what appear to have been three-hearth houses with heated garrets. Staircases were commonly at the front near the entrance in houses of this size in these 17th-century suburbs, this layout being well suited to multiple occupation as access to upper storeys did not compromise the ground-floor space. Other multiple-occupation building types of the period, from almshouses to legal chambers and Oxbridge colleges, are similarly

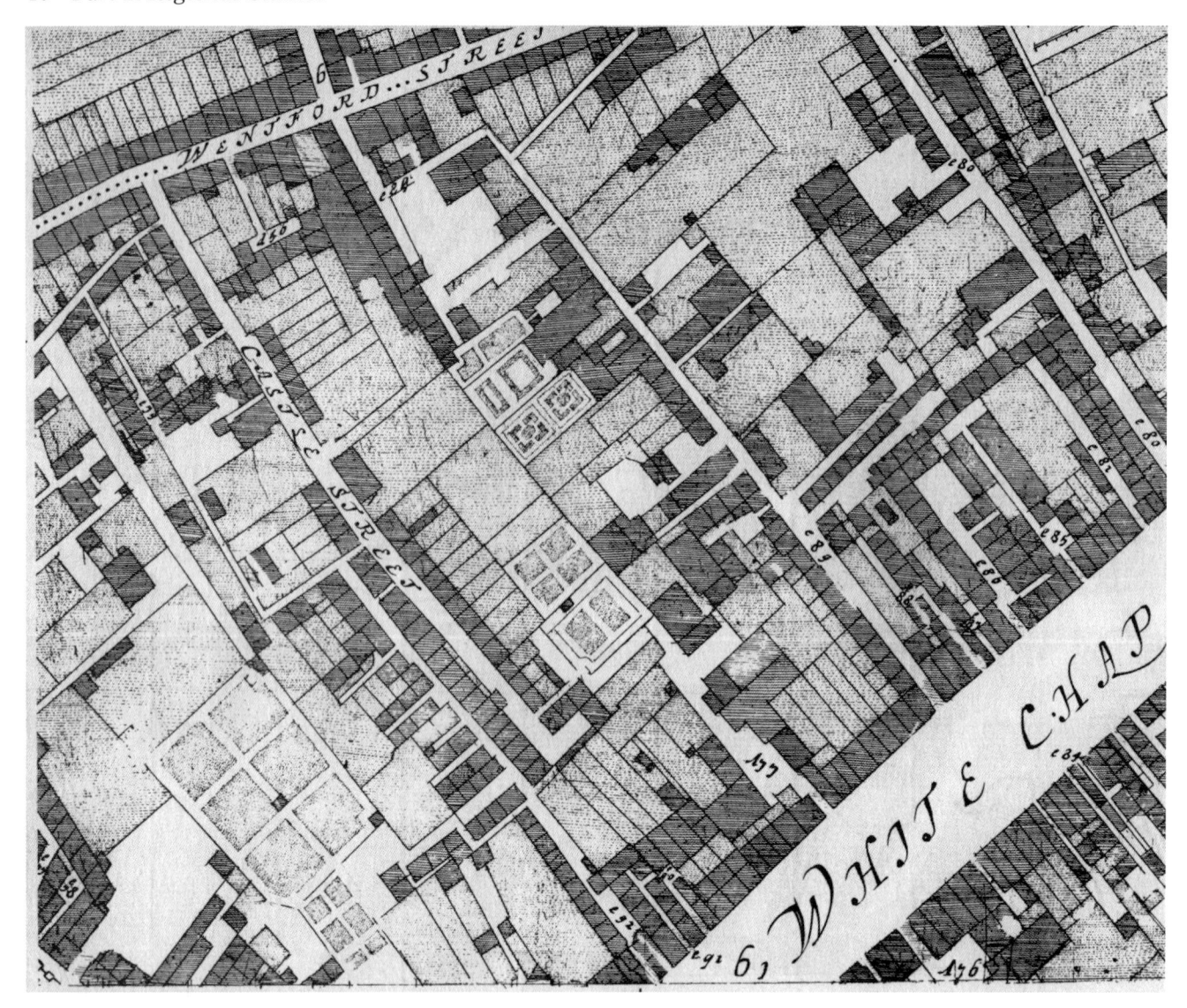

Fig 5.2 The area north of Whitechapel Road, London, in 1674–75. Ogilby and Morgan 1676

arranged (Guillery 2004, 57–58, 95). Front staircases are characteristically lit by small windows that made the front elevations highly irregular; this makes it possible to detect the layout in views and photographs (see Figs 5.5 and 5.8).

Spitalfields

Spitalfields, to the north of Whitechapel, was largely developed in association with the silk industry. It saw enormous growth in the third quarter of the 17th century, the number of hearths rising from 3062 in 1664 to 4687 in 1674–75, 53% up in ten years, the household mean in 1664 being 3.2, the house mean in 1674–75 being 3.5 (Table 5.1). Though complicated by the sheer extent of new building, this seems not unlike the relationship analysed for Whitechapel, again tending to suggest multiple occupancy in 10–15% of houses. However, there were significant differences in the housing stocks of these two districts. Only 1% of Spitalfields's houses had one hearth, compared to 24% in Whitechapel. Correspondingly, only 9% were exempt in Spitalfields, these concentrated to the south near Whitechapel, where 39% were exempt. Yet the means were not greatly different, as only 13% of Spitalfields houses had more than five hearths, comparable to 12% in Whitechapel. In the late 1650s the Fossan Estate, near Whitechapel and just north of Castle Street, was laid out with a regular grid of streets, its houses largely built of brick (Fig 5.4). On Dean and Flower Street building plots were granted in 1656–57 (Sheppard 1957, 245–46). By 1675 62 houses could be mapped; 61 were assessed for Hearth Tax. Here there were three-storey houses, 50 of which had only three or four hearths. Looking at their outline on the map it seems clear that they were only one room deep. Thrall Street, which was built *c* 1658, was at least part timber. The map and the assessment agree that it had 27 houses, the north side having a row of ten three-hearth houses. Along Rose Lane 40 of the 50 houses assessed (the map shows 52) had three hearths or fewer. No views of these buildings are known.

A bit further north, White Lion Yard, on the site of

Fig 5.3 22 and 24 Cannon Street Road, just east of Whitechapel, London, chimneypots suggesting a pair of two-hearth houses, possibly of the late 17th century, number 24 having been refronted. Photographed in 1928. Demolished. © English Heritage. NMR

what is now Folgate Street, off Bishopsgate, was at least part-occupied by silk weavers and throwsters (fibre twisters) (Sheppard 1957, 73). The map shows 62 properties, the assessment listing 60, of which 27 were marked as exempt; there were 26 with one hearth, 24 with three hearths, and none with more than four, giving a mean of only 2.1. The site was wholly redeveloped with better-quality houses in the early 18th century. Again, no evidence has come to light to indicate what it looked like before then. Nearby, Black Eagle Street on the Wheler estate was laid out and built up in the 1660s and 1670s (Sheppard 1957, 98–99). It too has disappeared, displaced by Truman's Brewery. Its assessment cannot be usefully compared with the map as it extended beyond its edge, but it provides further evidence for the relatively small size of houses in even the better new parts of this district. In a 1671 Hearth Tax assessment there were only seventeen houses, twelve having three hearths. By 1675 there were 28 houses, all bar two with three or four

hearths, most (17) having three. The mean for the street is 3.4, about average for Spitalfields.[7] There are suggestive comparisons for the likely appearance of these buildings from the north end of the silk district, where a number of late 17th-century buildings survived to be recorded, often having three heated rooms each, stacked vertically, with 'weaving' windows, and front staircases (Fig 5.5; Guillery 2004, 79–115).

Clerkenwell

The widespread existence of houses of a similar scale can be documented in suburbs further west, where metalworking trades were concentrated. In many households the same hearth may well have served both industrial and domestic purposes, and the 1674–75 assessment appears not to refer anywhere to 'industrial hearths' as exempt or otherwise. St Giles Cripplegate without the walls (north of the Barbican) had a mean of 3.3 hearths per house, as did Clerkenwell where 53% of the houses had only one or two hearths, and the spread of house sizes was more like in Whitechapel than in Spitalfields (Table 5.1). There were, however, local differences. On the relatively desirable open space of Clerkenwell Green only nineteen of 61 houses had fewer than four hearths, while the adjoining, and less salubrious, Hockley in the Hole, leading towards Holborn, had 82 houses, of which only 23 had more than two hearths, more than half the total being marked as exempt. Into Holborn, the poorer eastern division of which had a mean of 3.6 hearths per house, Liquor Pond Street (now obliterated by Clerkenwell Road) was largely made up of two-, three-, and four-hearth houses. Many of these were new; of 61 properties seventeen were empty. Portpoole Lane, which survives, but without early buildings, did have some larger houses, along with a row of twelve three-hearth houses. Back across Saffron Hill, Strangeway Street ran down to the River Fleet, and in 1674–75 had fourteen houses (fifteen on the map) of which eleven had four hearths.[8]

Looping back eastwards to a more southerly part of Clerkenwell leads to Peter's Lane (c58 on the map), near Smithfield, linking St John Street to Cow Cross (Street) (Figs 5.6 and 5.7). Here there were 34 assessed houses of which 27 had three hearths or fewer. These included a row of six three-hearth houses part of which survived into the era of photography. These tall timber houses were only one room deep, that is about 4.5m (15ft) square on plan. Either the garrets or ground-floor shops must have been unheated.

Further south, and on the parish boundary near the Fleet Ditch, Blackboy Alley ran off Chick Lane with 25 houses. Here the checking of concordance with the map breaks down, as it is not possible to be sure where one alley ends and the other begins. Of these houses thirteen had three hearths, only one had four, none more. In the 1840s Thomas Hosmer

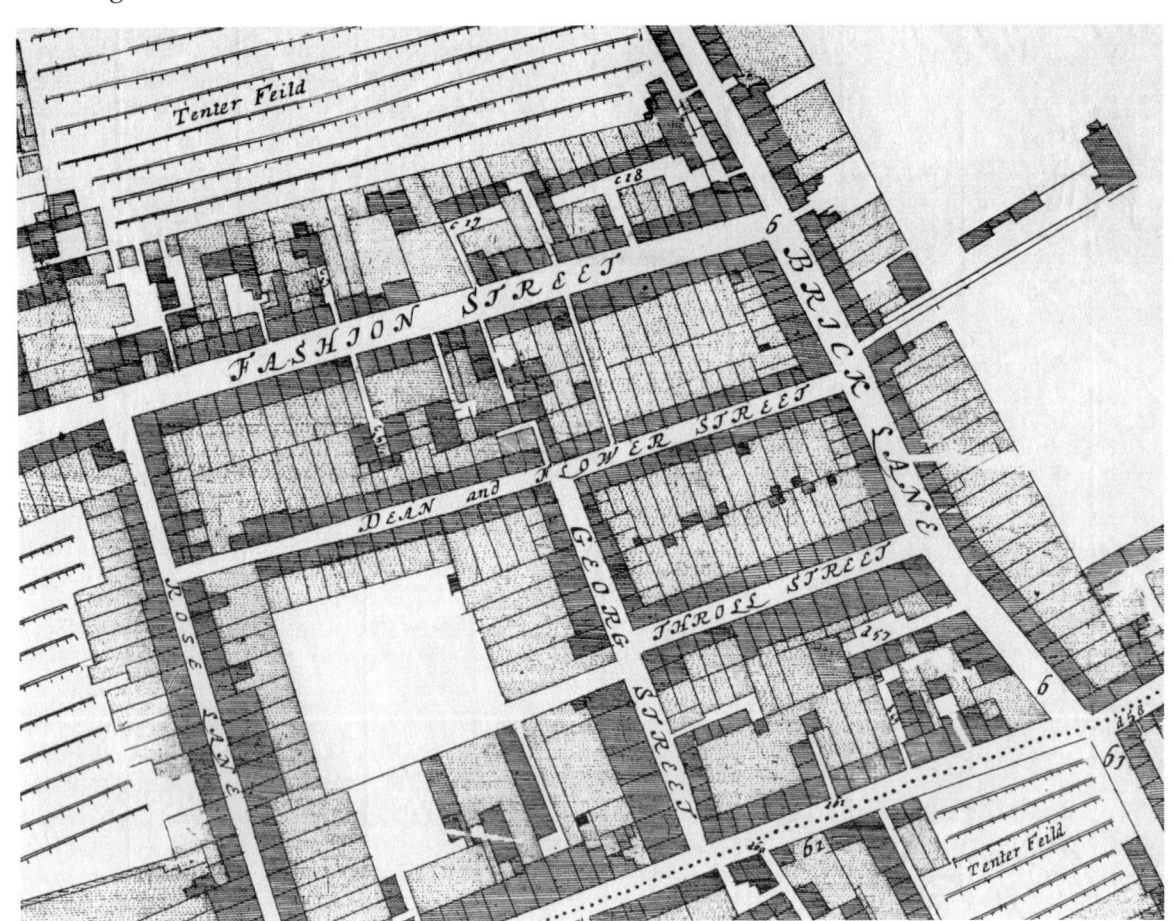

Fig 5.4 The Fossan Estate, Spitalfields, London, in 1674–75; this area was developed in the late 1650s. Ogilby and Morgan 1676

Fig 5.5 Front-staircase 'weavers' houses' of the 1670s, Virginia Road, just north of Spitalfields, London. Demolished. Watercolour by J. Appleton, 1890. © London Borough of Hackney Archives Department

Fig 5.6 (above) Part of southern Clerkenwell, London, in 1674–75. Ogilby and Morgan 1676

Fig 5.7 (left) Peter's Lane, Clerkenwell, London, one-room-plan houses, probably built in the early 17th century. Demolished. Photographed c 1867. © English Heritage. NMR

Shepherd drew a part timber-framed building on Blackboy Alley (Fig 5.8), then described as a 'thieves' lodging house', perhaps the model for Fagin's, as it was just here that Dickens set much of *Oliver Twist*. This building was very probably standing in the 1670s, but it appears to have had at least four hearths, maybe six to judge by the chimney stack. Perhaps it was built as a pair of three-hearth houses, possibly with front staircases, as the small windows imply, maybe with multiple occupation in mind.

Rents, exemptions and politics

The concordance between the assessment and the map leads to more questions than answers. The

Fig 5.8 A building on Blackboy Alley, near the Fleet Ditch, London, perhaps a 17th-century pair of tenements. Demolished. Watercolour of the 1840s by Thomas Hosmer Shepherd. © City of London, LMA

study of rents from the Four Shilling aid assessments of 1693–94 brings out again the contrast between the low-rent east and the high-rent west (Spence 2000, 71). However, even in the eastern suburbs only 40% of household rents were then less than £5 a year, which sum would rarely have stretched to pay for three rooms in London. William Baer's study of the post-fire city, where rents were relatively high, has shown that what he calls the 'upper end of the mechanick class' (Baer 2000), that is artisans who could depend on continuous work, could afford rents of from £6 to £9 a year, enough to pay for three or four rooms, or a small house, even in the City. Such are the houses that have been encountered in eastern and northern suburbs. Power's analysis of trades in relation to the Hearth Tax in the 1660s is consistent with this, concluding that City 'craftsmen' averaged about four hearths each, semi-skilled workers about three (Power 1986). It was about 200 years before the Yorkshire artisan caught up (cf chapter 14).

For the families of journeymen and labourers housing options would have been less good, one or two rooms in divided houses, or the smallest houses.

The rent for two rooms might have been about £4 or more a year. In the less salubrious parts of Covent Garden, around Drury Lane, inhabitants of two-room tenements with rents of about £3 a year paid poor relief (Smuts 1991, 129, 137). They were not themselves the poor. Single-room tenancies were common in 17th-century London, but the rent for even one room in all but the very poorest districts was more than £1 a year (Spence 2000, 68; Baer 2000; Guillery 2004, 35). Thus, and here is the point, few rents were below the threshold for exemption from the Hearth Tax. Yet Power found a 70% exemption rate in Whitechapel (Table 5.1), and a 51% exemption rate across the whole of East London in 1664 (Power 1972, 252). Continuing high rates of exemption in 1674–75 have been mentioned in passing in relation to particular streets, but the total numbers of those exempt were nothing like as high as a decade previously (Table 5.1). The proportion of exemptions in Whitechapel had nearly halved, more than can readily be explained by a shift in the unit of assessment from household to house. In Spitalfields the proportion of exemptions was down by 72%. Exemption certificates from the 1670s relating to the parishes examined here have not been found. However, those for other East London hamlets and other Middlesex parishes indicate that all those marked 'r' in the 1674–75 assessment were certified as exempt. A substantial number of other names that do not appear in the assessment are also certified as exempt. These may be tenants rather than landlords, people who would have been assessed in the 1660s but were not in 1674–75.[9] Returning to the deduction that the assessment of 1674–75 takes houses rather than households as its unit suggests that the assessor was not necessarily assessing household rent anyway. Some of the lowest rents would have been in divided houses of three or more hearths, none of which is marked as exempt.

These seeming anomalies are perhaps showing deliberate, even systematic, underassessment, substantial in the 1660s and hauled back somewhat in the 1670s (cf chapters 3 and 15). Underassessment through excessive exemption was a known problem: 'We are informed that either through the ignorance of some persons in the law or by partiality and favour great number of undue certificates are from time to time signed in all places of the kingdom'.[10] London's working suburbs had been on the losing side at the Restoration, which was widely resented. People on both sides had been scarred by confrontation and conflict, and stability in East London mattered a great deal in the 1660s. Underassessment for the Hearth Tax might have been both politic and overlooked.

Conclusions

Whatever motivations may have lain behind the configuration of the assessment of 1674–75 its concordance with Ogilby and Morgan's map has seemed to show that there were many 17th-century houses in London's suburbs with four hearths or fewer. What looks like reliable quantification of what is almost known is seductive. However, given the possibility of deliberate underassessment and wider evidence of the untrustworthiness of Hearth Tax lists, it is probably unsafe to assume that every hearth was recorded (cf chapter 10). Against the unreliability of Hearth Tax returns it is known that many of suburban London's varied and vernacular 17th-century houses were built for humble artisan occupancy, not in long and uniform rows or terraces, but in small and irregular groups with huge architectural variability, alternately timber and brick, one-room layouts being so widespread as to be almost universal.[11] Much remains hidden. There are no pictures of one-hearth houses, or of the rents or alleys in which some people lived in converted sheds. London was not Paris or Edinburgh where limitations to outward urban growth produced high-density tenemental living as the rule. Multiple occupation was not uncommon, but it was not the norm. London sprawled, but growth was so fast that it cannot be described as low density. That said, the frequency with which the front-staircase layout is encountered, and its survival through the 18th century in the silk district where tenemental living certainly was the rule, does hint at a design vocabulary in late 17th-century London that was highly suited to, if not actually devised for, multiple occupation. This is a vexed and fascinating topic that needs further research. All their shortcomings and ambivalence notwithstanding, Hearth Tax returns used alongside other sources may be a key.

The prevalence of small 'vernacular' houses in early modern London is easily forgotten, because it is difficult to get a handle on what they were like. Looking back through the prism of the 18th century and what is known so well about London's standardised or industrialised house-building culture, the enormous variety of London's 17th-century houses is obscure. There are no easy interpretative routes from the Hearth Tax to architectural history. Nevertheless Hearth Tax records could be a powerful if problematic reminder of the extent and variety of vernacular architecture in early modern London.

Chapter 5: Notes

1 TNA E179/143/370. I am grateful to Elizabeth Parkinson for sharing her thoughts on the interpretation of this Middlesex Hearth Tax roll of 1674–75.
2 Such an approach is being employed by the current Centre for Metropolitan History project, 'People in Place: families, households and housing in early modern London', set for completion in 2006.
3 TNA E179/143/406; see also Power 1972, 254
4 TNA E179/143/370.
5 Ibid.
6 Ibid.
7 Ibid.
8 Ibid.
9 Ibid and TNA E179/143/367.
10 'Manual to the Archbishops of Canterbury and York severally', 4 November 1674, as transcribed by Tom Arkell in chapter 3, Appendix C.
11 See, for example, LMA 'Plans of City Lands and Bridge House Properties', two volumes, c 1680 to c 1720; and British Library, Crace Collection, Plans of City Properties.

6   Kent: Heating, Houses and the Hearth Tax
by Sarah Pearson

Introduction

Kent was a wealthy county in national terms. In comparison with many counties in the north and west of England, the number of taxable hearths overall, and the proportion of those taxed on dwellings with three or more hearths, was high: 27,077 entries were listed in the return used here, and the number of hearths was 72,077, giving an average of 2.7 hearths per household, which is higher than for most counties.[1] Likewise, the proportion of those listed as exempt was 32%, which is considerably lower than for much of the country (cf chapters 2 and 3). This implies a high level of wealth within the county, and creates a presumption that large numbers of well-heated 17th-century or earlier houses will have survived. The following account shows that this is partly true, but also that the situation is more complex than the overall figures might imply.

The only Hearth Tax return for Kent which survives on anything like a county-wide basis is the Quarter Sessions, or county, assessment for Lady Day 1664. However, even this is incomplete, since it does not include the city of Canterbury, the Cinque Ports, or about half of Romney Marsh. The unit of assessment in Kent was the hundred, which in turn was divided into boroughs. These were ancient units of taxation that in many places bore no relation to ecclesiastical parishes, something which makes mapping and the use of Hearth Tax data extremely difficult.

Bearing in mind that the figures in the 1664 return do not cover all areas, or include all those who did not pay, the number of hearths per household over the county as a whole, breaks down as follows:

Households with 10 or more hearths	2%
Households with 5–9 hearths	11%
Households with 3–4 hearths	22%
Households with 2 hearths	29%
Households with 1 hearth	36%

Figure 6.1 illustrates the geographical regions of Kent. They lie in clearly defined east–west bands between the sea and the Thames estuary in the north, and the high weald along the Sussex border. The agriculture and economy of Kent reflect its geology and geography, with, for example, fruit and arable crops grown on the good soils to the north of the downs, and woodland and pasture for animal husbandry lying in the weald and marshes to the south (Chalklin 1965, 74). But the quality of the soils within the bands varies considerably from east to west, and the distribution of population and of hearth numbers in the county break down into wide swathes running north–south across the geographical regions (Fig 6.2). These show a high density of both people and hearths in the centre of the county, taking in the important towns of Maidstone and Rochester, but also including large tracts of countryside around them. The numbers clearly diminish in stages as one moves eastwards across the map; but the western picture is to some extent deceptive on account of the proximity of London. On this map, as on others not reproduced here, the towns of Deptford, Greenwich, Woolwich, Dartford, and Gravesend (indicated in Fig 6.1) have all been absorbed into their hundreds, unfortunately masking the distinction between the coastal towns and ports which have high household and hearth numbers, and their more sparsely populated and ill-heated rural hinterlands.

The medieval legacy

The story of Kent's 17th-century hearths and houses begins in the Middle Ages since many of its medieval buildings not only survived into the 17th century, but are still there today. This is particularly true of rural parishes in the middle swathe of the county where hearth numbers were high. In the large central parish of Charing, at least 26 medieval houses still remain, and these must have been included among the 170 households that were listed in the parish in 1664, suggesting that a minimum of 15% of the houses in the late 17th century, and probably many more, were medieval (Harrington *et al* 2000, lxxi). In the northern parish of Borden, between Rochester and Faversham, sixteen surviving medieval houses accounted for 22% of the 73 households listed in 1664 (Pearson 1994, 162; Harrington *et al* 2000, 472). However, to the east and west of the county the survival of rural medieval buildings is very much lower, often between 4–6%. On the western edge, only five medieval houses remain in Sundridge which had 115 entries in the Hearth Tax. In the east, there were probably 106 households in the large parish of Ash, near Sandwich, but only six medieval houses have been identified, while in the far smaller parish of Goodnestone in the eastern downs, where 60 households were listed, only three medieval houses remain (Harrington *et al* 2000, lxxxviii–lxxxix, 463, 482; Pearson 1994, 162). The pattern across the county shown in Figure 6.2, with a greater density of hearths in the central area, in fact mirrors the survival pattern of medieval buildings (Pearson 1994, fig 139). The situation in the towns was a little different, for, particularly along the edge of the Thames and the London fringes, most of the housing stock was new, a consequence of the

Kent: Heating, Houses and the Hearth Tax   47

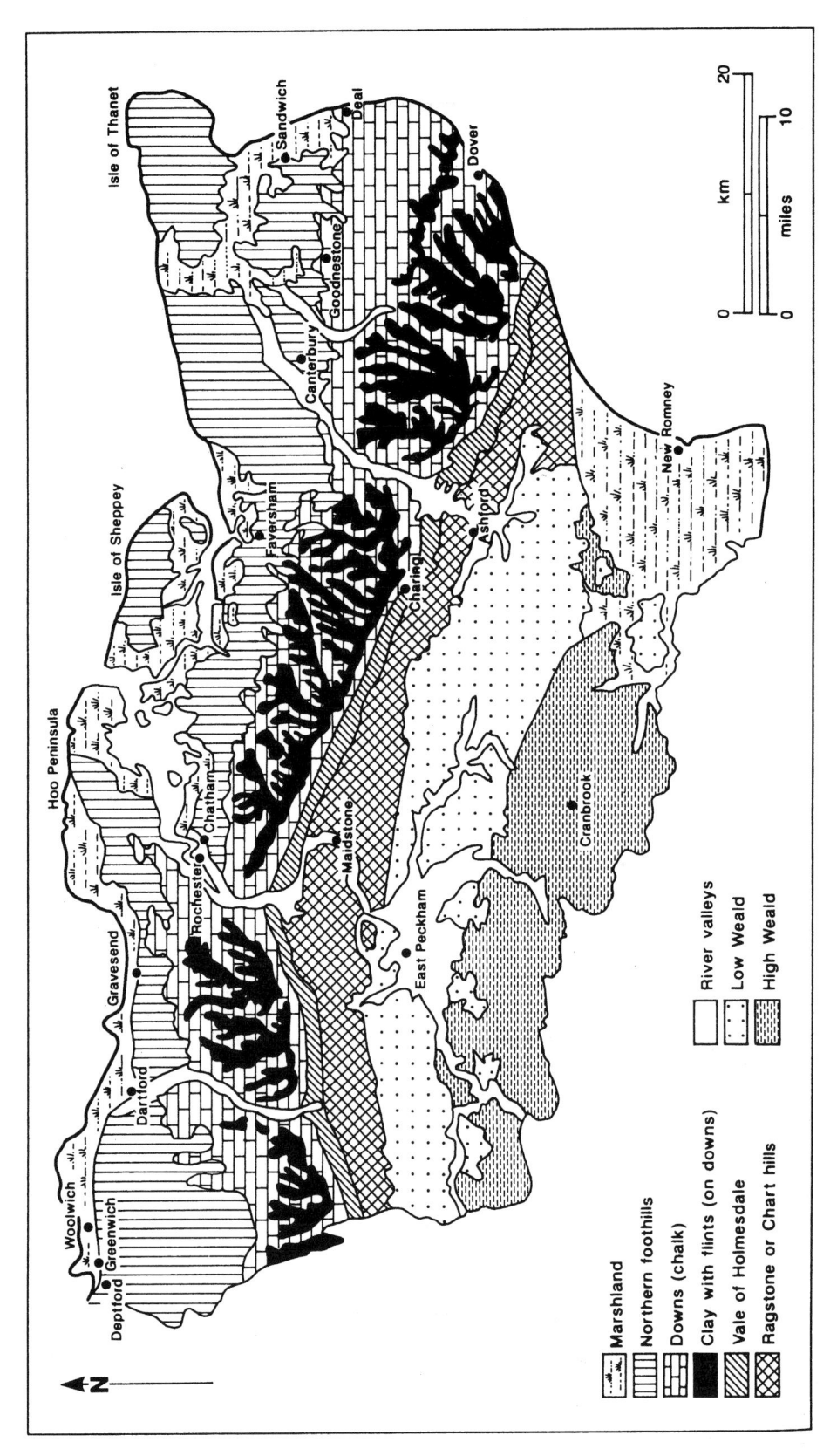

Fig 6.1 *The geographical regions of Kent, showing the main places mentioned in the text. Reproduced from Harrington et al 2000, xxvii, map 2.* © *British Record Society*

48 Part 2: Regional Studies

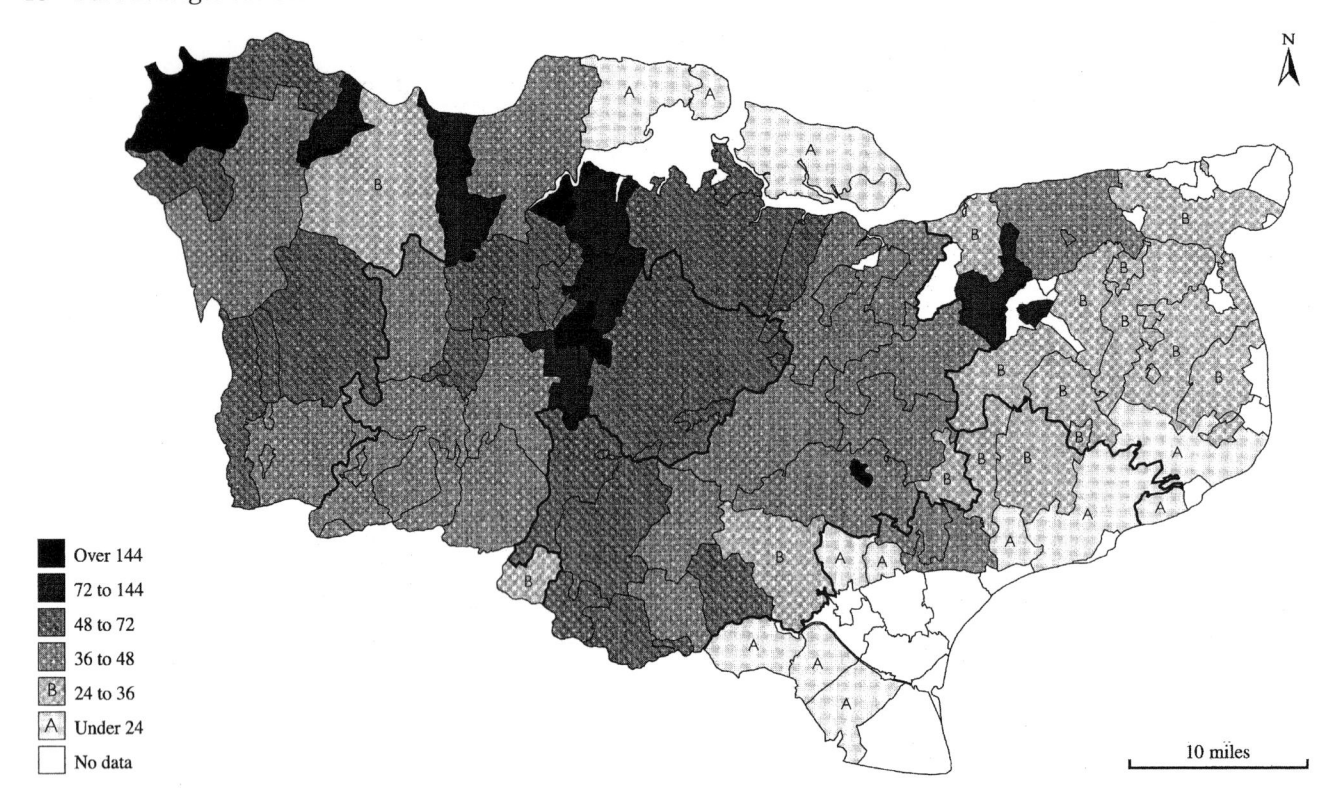

Legend:
- Over 144
- 72 to 144
- 48 to 72
- 36 to 48
- 24 to 36
- Under 24
- No data

Fig 6.2 Number of hearths per 1000 acres (400 ha) in Kent. Reproduced from Harrington et al 2000, xxxiv, map 4. © British Record Society

growing importance of the ports, docks and other towns serving the capital. These facts need to be taken into account when considering houses and their hearths in relation to the Hearth Tax.

The development of heating in earlier houses

In the Middle Ages, all houses had fireplaces in open halls, and none but the very largest had second fireplaces, except possibly another open hearth in a detached kitchen. In time, all but the poorest houses were provided with additional hearths, and the first question which needs to be addressed is when this change took place. There are two aspects to this. The first is when the open hearth was replaced by one within an enclosed flue above. Roberts, writing on Hampshire houses, has graphically illustrated the changes which took place there in the late 15th and the 16th century. Using a sample of firmly dated buildings, he has shown that the first new halls of two storeys with enclosed fireplaces were built around 1460, with the numbers increasing during the first half of the 16th century, that floors (and enclosed fireplaces) began to be inserted into earlier open halls from the 1520s, and that open-hall houses ceased to be built altogether between 1560 and 1580 (Roberts 2003, 148–58, fig 7.1). It is likely that the situation in Kent was not dissimilar, with major changes taking place between 1520 and 1580. However, this only addresses the demise of the open hall or open hearth and the introduction of floored halls and enclosed fireplaces. It does not indicate when extra hearths started to be introduced.

At all but the highest social levels in Kent, the first enclosed fireplaces were built with smoke bays or timber chimneys which had flues of timber and plaster (Barnwell and Adams 1994, 126–35; Pearson 1994, 108–15). While this funnelled the smoke away from the hall and allowed an extra chamber to be built on the upper floor, it did not in itself lead to extra fireplaces, since timber flues normally only served a single fireplace. Only very seldom, and so far never in Kent, has evidence been found for an additional timber flue and upper fireplace, and, although it was presumably possible to have another flue serving a second ground-floor fireplace, this seems to have been a rarity. The decisive factor was when flues began to be constructed of stone or brick, a change which took place slowly during the later 16th and 17th centuries.

The bird's-eye view of Shurland House, Sheppey (Fig 6.3), was painted in 1572, and illustrates the medieval house after it had been updated by Sir Thomas Cheney, possibly before 1532 (Howard 1987, 69–72, 208). It is shown with an open hall, the louvre of the open hearth being clearly visible, and four chimney stacks, one located in what was probably the kitchen at the rear, the others in a new brick lodging range in the base court. However, by the time of the 1664 Hearth Tax, the then owner of the house, James Herbert Esq, was charged on 24 hearths (Harrington et al 2000, 289). The change could have taken place in the late 16th century, as occurred at Roydon Hall, East Peckham, home of the Twysden family, which has several late 16th-century decorated stacks remaining (30 hearths in 1664), but it may well have been the work of Philip

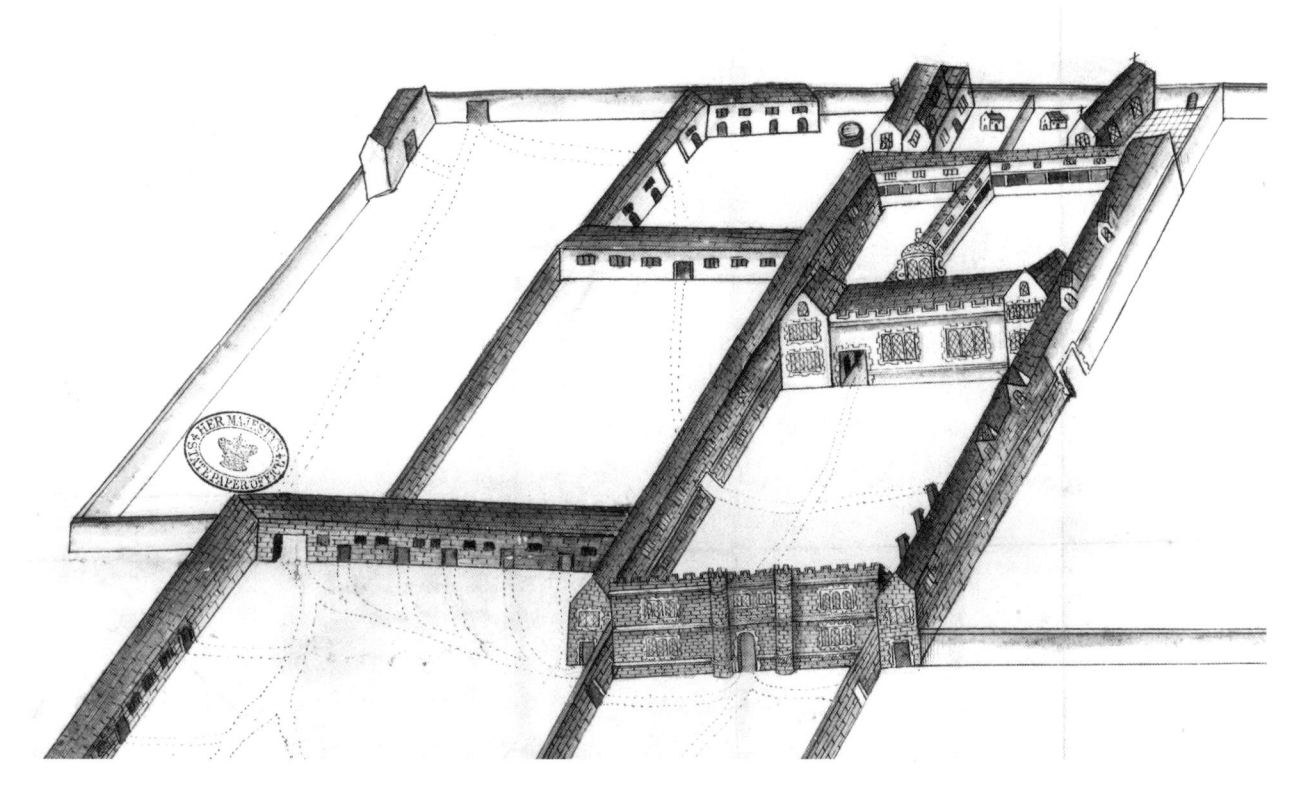

Fig 6.3 Shurland House, Sheppey, Kent. Detail of a bird's-eye view of 1572. The house then had an open hall and four chimney stacks. It was charged on 24 hearths in 1664. The National Archives: MPF1/272. Reproduced by kind permission of The National Archives

Herbert, who was granted Shurland by James I *c* 1605 (Hasted 1797–1801, **6**, 248–50). By the second quarter of the 17th century, large new gentry houses, such as Broome Park, Barham, built by Sir Basil Dixwell in 1635–38 (20 hearths in 1664), were well equipped with fireplaces. The Hearth Tax data indicate that large houses with numerous hearths were distributed across the whole county. However, there was a marked cluster in the north-west, particularly in Blackheath hundred, around Greenwich and Woolwich, where many wealthy London gentry had property; there was also a concentration in and around Maidstone, reflecting its importance as a county town; and a third group with high numbers of hearths was spread across the downs from west to east (see Fig 6.1), since this was where many of the gentry estates were situated (Everitt 1966, 32–34).

Below this social level most parishes had one or more houses with five to nine hearths, although there were higher numbers along the north coast. Many of these were the homes of minor gentry. Wickens in Charing (Fig 6.4) was built in the late 16th century by a younger branch of the important Dering family. It had five hearths served by six flues when built, with the kitchen fireplace served by two flues, an arrangement which was not uncommon. By 1664 an extra fireplace had been added in the chamber over the kitchen, although when this occurred is not easy to say. Other gentry houses had owners or occupiers whose names have no obvious local affiliations, and well-endowed rectories and vicarages might likewise have anything from five to twelve hearths. Many houses with this number of hearths were earlier houses upgraded like Wickens, although a few were no doubt recently built in 1664.

At farmhouse level the introduction of extra hearths almost always seems to have been deferred until the 17th century. In Charing parish, where 75 probate inventories for the period 1565–1698 provide information on hearths, chamber fireplaces became common only during the second quarter of the 17th century:

1565–1625   0/21 inventories had chamber fireplaces = 0%
1625–1664   10/23 inventories had chamber fireplaces = 43%
1664–1698   15/31 inventories had chamber fireplaces = 48%

Probate inventories are not wholly reliable witnesses in this respect, since it is known that they consistently under-record fireplaces, but the difference between the pre- and post-1625 inventories is striking, and suggests that there was a significant change in the second quarter of the century (Spufford 1990, 14–15; Harrington *et al* 2000, lxxi–lxxii).

Turning to the farmhouses themselves, the evidence also suggests the change from timber to brick stacks took place during the 17th century. Several large medieval farmhouses, updated in the 16th century by the insertion of smoke bays or timber chimneys, have brick fireplaces or chimneys inscribed with dates in the first four decades of the 17th century. Examples in central and west Kent

Fig 6.4 Wickens, Charing, Kent. A late 16th-century minor gentry house, built with five fireplaces, but charged on six hearths in 1664. © S Pearson

are The Blue House, East Sutton, 1610, Swallows, Boughton Monchelsea, 1616, and The Old Manor House, Chiddingstone, 1638. All of these have three or four fireplaces in the new stack. In others, the change seems to have occurred later. At Stone Hall and Old Forge Cottage, Sellindge, towards the east end of the county, the open hall had also had a smoke bay inserted in the 16th century, but it seems likely that the change to a brick stack there can be dated as late as 1657 when a new gabled window was built to light the chamber over the hall, the room being heated by a fireplace in the new stack. In some sizeable medieval houses brick stacks were introduced even later. A case in point is Old Well House, East Peckham, which had an open hall into which a smoke bay had been built during the 16th century (Fig 6.5). In 1660 Richard Hatch took up a lease on the house and 17.5 ha (43 acres) of land. He was charged on one hearth in 1664, and when he died in 1671 his inventory mentions only one fireplace. Yet his goods were valued at £179, indicating that he was by no means a poor man. Only later in the century, perhaps in connection with updating the property for a new tenant, was a brick stack with four fireplaces built (Barnwell and Adams 1994, 142–43; Harrington *et al* 2000, lxxx).

The farmhouses so far cited are all large, four-bay dwellings. It is more difficult to obtain information about what occurred in smaller houses. White Cottage, Boughton Monchelsea, was a three-bay 16th-century house with a smoke bay against the gable wall of the hall; the inserted stone and brick stack seems to have been built in 1670, the date being scratched on the rear of the new stack, suggesting that in 1664 the house would still have had only a single hearth (Pearson 2001, 389). That many well-built houses had only one hearth is clear from the Hearth Tax profile of the borough of Stockenbury in East Peckham parish, where Old Well House lies. There, 70, or 67%, of the 105 households were charged on one hearth in 1664, 33 were charged on two, and only one person had three hearths. Several medieval houses survive, and some of them, like Old Well House, were sizeable four-bay buildings. When their 17th-century occupiers died, they left inventory goods valued between £136 and £548, yet they had only one or two hearths in 1664. However, one or two smaller medieval houses also survive, such as 23 Smithers Lane, which seems to have had a small open hall with two rooms at one end. Deeds suggest that in 1691 it 'was now or late in the occupation of Stephen Cheeseman', who was exempted from payment on one hearth in 1664 (Harrington *et al* 2000, lxxix–lxxxiii).

In east Kent there are fewer medieval houses left than in the centre of the county, and most of them are low in height and smaller in overall floor area than those lying further west (Pearson 1994, 123–25, 137). Examples are Old Kent Cottage, Newington near Folkestone, and Ashby Cottage, Westbere, just east of Canterbury. Nothing is known about their 17th-century occupants, but they certainly had only one hearth in 1664 and may not yet have had brick stacks. At Dormer Cottage, Petham, in the eastern

Kent: Heating, Houses and the Hearth Tax 51

a

b

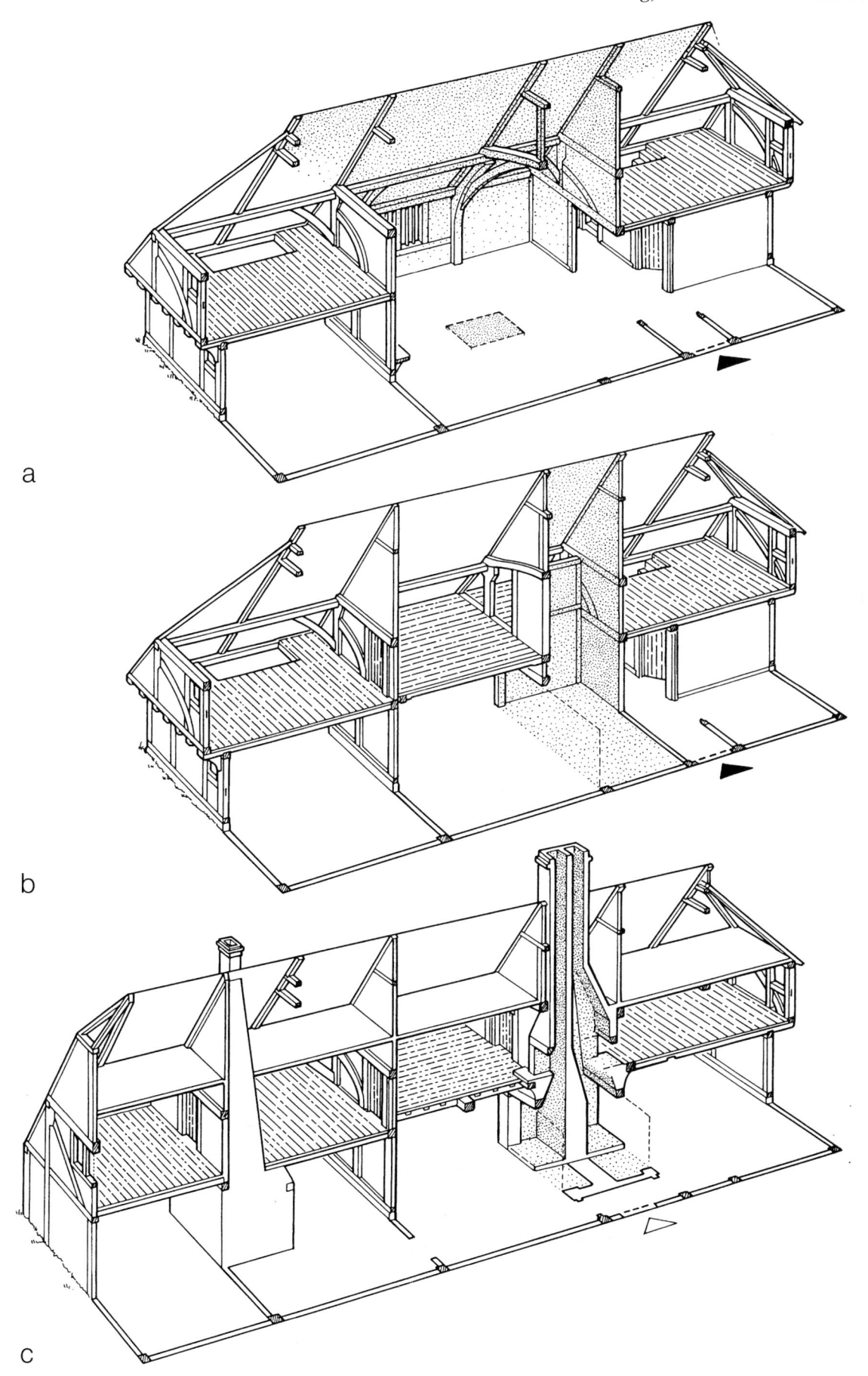

c

Fig 6.5 Old Well House, East Peckham, Kent, illustrating the medieval open hall, the 16th-century smoke bay, and the late 17th-century chimney stack with four fireplaces. From Barnwell and Adams 1994, 142–43.
© Crown Copyright. NMR

downs, a timber stack still serves the modern flue in a former open hall. The details of the hall ceiling and fireplace surround suggest the change from open to floored hall only took place during the 17th century and, although one half of the house has been rebuilt, the survival of the timber stack and the small size of the building make it likely that in 1664 this was a one-hearth house.

New rural houses of the 17th century

So far, it is mostly earlier buildings which have been considered, suggesting that many were upgraded with brick or stone stacks during the course of the 17th century, sometimes before, sometimes after, the 1664 Hearth Tax. But what of new-built houses? In fact, Kent is not a county noted for its 17th-century rural buildings (Rigold 1969, 198). Of course there are examples, but apart from a few exceptional areas, they are relatively scarce until the very end of the century. Boughton Monchelsea in central Kent may serve as an example of a parish with few new 17th-century houses. At least 37 houses built before 1700 survive. Of these twelve are medieval, most of the others were built during the 16th century, and only four are likely to date to the 17th century (Pearson 2001). The new buildings were well heated from the start. Bishops Farmhouse of the mid-17th century has two storeys and attics with an up-to-date lobby-entry plan (Fig 6.6). The main rooms on both the ground and the first floor are heated by four fireplaces served by the central stack, with unheated service rooms and chambers in a wing to the rear. The smaller but more or less contemporary Fir Tree Cottage also has a lobby-entry plan, but is of only two bays and two storeys, with no sign of a rear wing. Nonetheless, the two rooms below, and one of the chambers above, were heated by fireplaces from the start.

In east Kent, in line with the poor survival and small size of their medieval predecessors, new 17th-century houses were also small and poor. A survey of the parish of Goodnestone in the eastern downs (see Fig 6.1) revealed only three surviving buildings that were certainly medieval, together with two dating to the 16th century, and two later ones that may also pre-date 1664 (Harrington *et al* 2000, lxxxiii–xci). The latter pair is of one storey with attics set partly in the roof. Despite their small size, each had two fireplaces, suggesting that the number of hearths sometimes increased even when the houses were small and simple. Between 1680 and the mid-18th century, many timber farmhouses in east Kent were totally rebuilt in brick. Whatever motivated the rebuilding at that time, it implies that the earlier houses were too poor to keep. An idea of what one of the better timber houses of the third quarter of the 17th century looked like can be seen at 113 High Street, Wingham, just east of Goodnestone (Fig 6.7). Despite its small size, single hearth, and first floor set within the roof, the builder of this house in 1667 was proud enough of what he had erected to place his initials and the date in the gables of the attic windows. This is a far cry from the kind of house which might be expected in central Kent by this time, and graphically illustrates why the maps show so few hearths towards the east side of the county.

Town houses

Kent is usually thought of as a rural county, and in the Middle Ages this was largely true, despite the presence of important towns such as Canterbury, Rochester, Maidstone and the Cinque Ports. But by the 17th century the situation had changed as the dominance of the Cinque Ports had given way to the ports, docks and naval bases along the Thames and around the Medway estuary. It has been reckoned that by this time around a third of the population of the county was urban (Chalklin 1995, 206). Town buildings divide into two categories. On the one hand many of the buildings in the older towns were still medieval. On the other hand a huge amount of new building was taking place in the ports and dockyard towns.

Then as now, the mere fact that an urban building was in good repair was no guarantee of its survival. The continuing expansion of the north Kent towns both during the 17th century and since has seen most early urban buildings disappear. The most significant survivals are in the Cinque Ports and their limbs, towns that were already experiencing economic decline by the 17th century, which almost certainly affected the number of new hearths inserted into older buildings. Thus 39 Strand Street, Sandwich, a three-storey 14th-century house with twelve rooms and a very fine 16th-century fireplace in the formerly open hall, probably had only four fireplaces by 1664. The same is true of 82–84 Abbey Street, Faversham, which was a very well-appointed house of the late 16th century with thirteen rooms and highly decorative fireplaces. An inventory of 1601 and a recent survey of the house again suggest there may have been no more than four fireplaces in the late 17th century.

However, it would be wrong to imply that older towns had no well-heated houses. In Maidstone and Rochester about 21% of all houses had five or more hearths, which is in fact a higher proportion than are listed in towns around the Thames estuary such as Deptford (17%), Dartford (15.5%), Gravesend (20%) or Chatham (19%). Maidstone as a county town, and Rochester as a cathedral city, obviously attracted a sizeable number of county families and professional men concerned with administration, and their numbers clearly matched the wealthy officers and gentlemen who formed the upper social strata of the northern towns. But there is generally less sign of wealth in the older inland market towns such as Ashford and Sevenoaks, where only 13% of houses had five or more hearths. In Cranbrook, which had declined from its status as an important

*Fig 6.6   Bishops Farmhouse, Boughton Monchelsea, Kent. A mid-17th-century house with four hearths.
© S Pearson*

Fig 6.7   113 High Street, Wingham, Kent. A small timber-framed house in east Kent, dated 1667. It clearly had a single hearth. © S Pearson

cloth centre, the situation was even bleaker, with only 9% of houses having more than five hearths (Harrington *et al* 2000, table 1).

The differences between old and new towns were also manifested at a lower social level and can be illustrated better from the figures than the actual buildings. Whereas the timber-framed and jettied houses of the 16th century or earlier had to have stacks inserted in order to provide more heat, new houses, both of timber and brick, were being built which had integral stacks and several fireplaces from the start. In the old towns, the number of single-hearth households tended to be above 20%, and in Cranbrook rose to 47%, reflecting the large number of poor people struggling to make a living from the declining cloth trade; but in the new towns, the proportion was far lower. At Chatham it was 10%, at Deptford 11.5%, and at Dartford 19%. Instead, these towns had very high proportions of people charged on two hearths (Gravesend, 41%; Chatham and Dartford, 40%), and fairly high numbers of those charged on three. On the ground the difference can be illustrated by comparing 38 King Street, Sandwich, with 150 High Street, Deptford. The former is a medieval house which retained its open hall, and had seven rooms on two floors, the open hall, a room behind and chamber over that being heated by fireplaces served by the single inserted stack, providing three fireplaces in all. The Deptford house was part of a terrace of brick houses built around 1680 by a potter. Number 150 is the one surviving dwelling. It is a single-cell building of two full storeys plus attic and cellar, and the three upper rooms were probably all served by fireplaces (Guillery and Herman 1999; Guillery pers. comm.). Thus the seven-room Sandwich house and the four-room Deptford house may both, if they were in single occupation, have shown up in the Hearth Tax as three-hearth houses. One- and two-cell houses of late 17th-century date with fireplaces in nearly every room have also been found in Deal and Folkestone. Among the larger examples in Deal is 10 Chapel Street which has two rooms on each of two floors plus cellar and attic; all but the attic rooms were heated, providing six fireplaces in an eight-room house. The smaller examples may be illustrated by several single-cell houses in North Street, Folkestone, recorded before demolition in the 1940s. These had two storeys and attics, the two main rooms both being heated (O'Neil 1949; Harrington *et al* 2000, xcvii–xcviii). The question of how these new houses were occupied is crucial for interpreting the Hearth Tax in towns. If they were in single occupation they will, despite their small size, have been charged on several hearths. But if they were in multiple occupancy they may have been listed as one- or two-hearth households. In Kent no evidence for multiple occupancy has been found so far, but the issue is discussed by Peter Guillery in relation to London houses elsewhere in this volume (chapter 5; cf chapter 7).

Conclusion

Overall the high numbers of hearths taxed in Kent can easily mask significant regional variations. The most striking among these are the wealth of the central part of the county, largely inhabited by the independent and legendary 'yeomen of Kent'; the high hearth numbers in the far north-west, due to the proximity and influence of London; and the poverty of hearths and houses in the east, which was almost certainly a reflection of both the arable nature of the area, with wealthy landlords and a poor peasant workforce, and the distance from London – east Kent is further from London than is Southampton. While these factors led to regional differences, it should be borne in mind that the Hearth Tax was imposed at a time when considerable change was under way. It highlights the state of affairs at a single point in time. A few years later and the picture would have changed. The modernisation of heating in the larger medieval houses in central Kent would have been be completed, many of the small farmhouses in east Kent would have been totally rebuilt, and the urbanisation of the north-west would have continued unabated. Nonetheless, it is worth pointing out the likelihood that these changes would simply have led to more substantial houses and more fireplaces in all areas, not to a completely new pattern of distribution.

One of the most interesting facts to emerge from an analysis of the Hearth Tax and its associated houses is how remarkably similar the pattern of distribution is to that revealed by studying medieval buildings across the county. The London influence in the north-west is greater, but the marked wealth of the north–south swathe across central Kent, and the relative poverty of the east are repeated. The fact that an analysis of medieval houses produced approximately the same pattern of distribution as the one revealed by the Hearth Tax figures, suggests that the regions had continuing identities formed by the geographical characteristics provided by the land and the sea, the agriculture and industry these gave rise to, and the society thus created. The Hearth Tax provides a much-needed snapshot of housing and society half way between the taxation records of the Middle Ages and the modern era.

Chapter 6: Notes

1   This essay is largely based on work undertaken for the introduction to the British Record Society volume on the Kent Hearth Tax for Lady Day 1664 (Harrington *et al* 2000). A fuller discussion of both the background and the buildings, and further references for much of the material, will be found there.

7 Some Highways and Byeways on the Essex Hearth Tax Trail *by Pat Ryan, in collaboration with Dave Stenning and David Andrews*

Summary

The houses of Essex are described as they were at the time of the Hearth Tax. Evidence from surviving buildings, inventories and the Walker maps (see p.56) provide clues as to their appearance, plan forms, and how they were used and heated. Information from an in-depth study of the parishes of Cressing, Roxwell and Ingatestone is used to illustrate how Hearth Tax entries reflect the houses and the households that occupied them.

The Essex Hearth Tax assessment list of 1671[1]

The 1671 list is the most complete surviving Hearth Tax assessment list for the county of Essex. It consists of the names of the householders, followed by the number of hearths on which they were assessed, and is organised by hundred. Each hundred is subdivided into parishes, and the lists are further subdivided into those who had to pay the tax and those who had exemption certificates. In some parishes, the Latin heading to the exemption section states the number of those who were in receipt of alms from the parish, while in others this information is not given. Because of the uncertainty as to whether those in receipt of alms are included amongst the exempt, it is not possible to be sure whether all households in a parish were included. This results in a problem when compiling statistics and drawing distribution maps. However, taking into account the uncertain accuracy of the statistics, the lowest density of households, with fewer than twenty per 1000 acres (400 ha), occurred in the hundreds with marshy, malaria-ridden, coastal parishes, historically notorious for their unhealthy climate (Fig

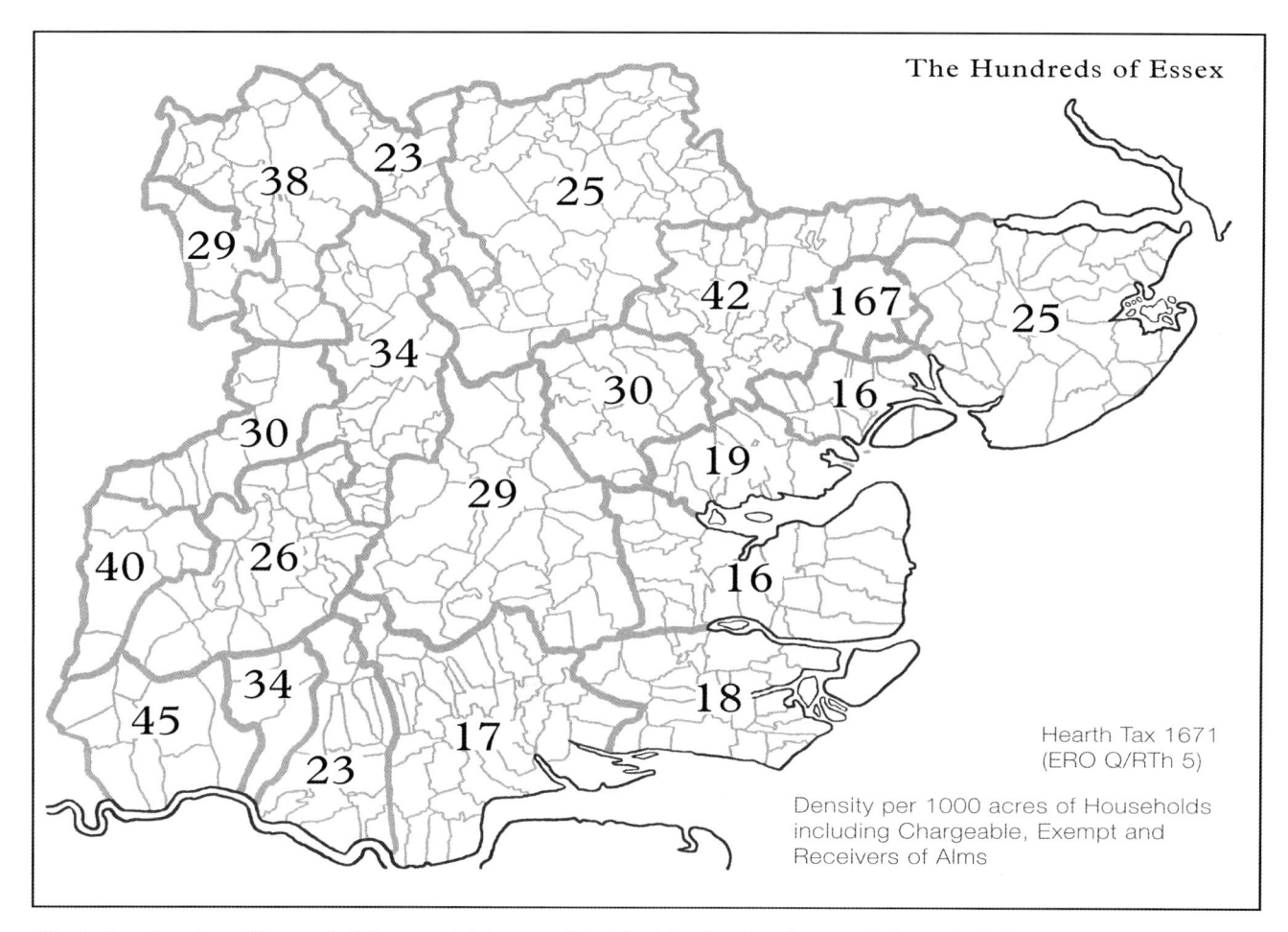

Fig 7.1 Density of households per 1000 acres (400 ha) in the hundreds of Essex. © P Ryan

Fig 7.2 Moyns Park, Steeple Bumpstead, Essex, mansion, c 1580. © P Ryan

7.1). The urban half hundred of Colchester was the most densely populated, with 167 households per 1000 acres. It was followed by the neighbouring hundred of Lexden and the hundreds that were closest to London which had over 40 households per 1000 acres. The remainder of the county fell between these two extremes.

What were the houses like?

According to the list of buildings of special architectural and historic interest, Essex has over 5100 houses that survive from the time of the Hearth Tax. They range from large courtyard mansions, often built of brick and with many hearths, like Moyns Park, Steeple Bumpstead (Fig 7.2), and Ingatestone Hall, to small in-line timber-framed cottages such as Appletree Farm Cottage in Cressing (Fig 7.3), which only had one or at most two hearths. Some are medieval in date, originally with open halls (Fig 7.4), others are late 16th- or 17th-century lobby-entry houses, built with chimney stacks and floored throughout (Fig 7.5). They include 16th-century transitional houses which have a variety of plans but were all built with smoke bays or chimneys, either timber-framed or brick, and almost all with an upper floor throughout (Fig 7.6).

Ten maps, which were made by the Walker family of West Hanningfield between 1586 and 1616, include accurate representations of the buildings, and so give some idea of the housing stock of the county as it was in the late 16th and early 17th centuries (Edwards and Newton 1984). The maps cover about 2% of the county and, although mainly concentrated in mid-Essex, include an estate in the south and another in the north-east of the county. Approximately 64% of the houses are in-line single-storey or one-and-a-half-storey buildings; a quarter of these probably had only one room on the ground floor, for only one window is shown; half may have had two rooms, as they have two windows; and the remainder had at least three rooms. Nearly 12% of the total houses depicted have a hall block and one cross-wing; about 8% have a hall and two cross-wings. The remaining 16% are at least two-storeyed throughout; some are relatively small, but others very large.

By the time of the Hearth Tax, the majority of the older houses had been modernised, either by the installation of a chimney and the insertion of a floor over the hall or by the replacement of the hall with a new two-storey range similar to that of Horseshoes in Cressing or Little Dukes in Roxwell. Innovations usually begin at the wealthiest and most influential levels of society. Brick chimneys were being installed in the lodges in Pleshey Castle deer parks in the mid-15th century when Pleshey was part of the jointure of the queens of England.[2] In the late 15th century a brick chimney replaced the open hearth in the hall of a timber-framed house in the precinct of Beeleigh Abbey, near Maldon, and a possible timber-framed chimney was added to the parlour (Brooks 2004). By 1520, the abbot of Beeleigh agreed with a tenant both to rebuild his farmhouse in Stowe Maries and that it should have a 'new chimney'.[3] The house was two storeys high and it is thought that the original chimney was timber-framed. By the time of the tax it had three hearths and all were constructed with brick. Willow Farm at Great Leighs was built with a timber chimney in the mid-16th century, but that was soon replaced with a brick one. New almshouses built by Sir William Petre in Ingatestone were described in 1566 as 'made all of brick, every house a chimney'.[4] In 1565 an agreement with a carpenter to floor over the hall of a relatively modest house in Ingatestone was recorded in the manor court rolls.[5] The provision of an upper floor almost certainly implies the existence of a chimney. In 1577 William Harrison, parson of Radwinter in

Fig 7.3   Appletree Farm Cottage, Cressing, Essex. Remodelled medieval house. © P Ryan

Fig 7.4   Potter Row House, Ingatestone, Essex. Remodelled medieval house. © P Ryan

north Essex, wrote that the old men of his village commented on the increase in the numbers of chimneys since their youth (Harrison 1587, 201).

The Walker maps, where brick chimneys are T-shaped and painted red, and timber hoods are square and painted brown, also demonstrate the decline in the number of timber hoods and the increase in brick chimneys by the early 17th century (Table 7.1).

How were the houses used and which rooms were heated?

Essex has very few inventories but a collection found in a church chest for the mid-Essex parishes of Roxwell and Writtle are a useful source of information about how the houses were used and which rooms were heated (Steer 1950). It should be remembered, however, that such inventories do not include those of the poorest members of the community. Of the 76 inventories dated between 1662 and 1682 in which the goods are listed under room headings, all refer to a hall. Nearly all also had a parlour, a buttery and at least one chamber. About half had a kitchen, which may have been in a detached building (kitchens are frequently listed after the hall, parlour, buttery and chambers). About twenty of the largest houses had two butteries, one for small beer and one for strong beer, and thirteen had a brewhouse. Most of the chambers were on the upper floor: more than half the inventories listed a chamber over the hall, an indication that there must have been a chimney of some sort in order to allow the smoke to escape from the hall; two-thirds had a chamber over the parlour; a quarter had a chamber over the buttery; and just under a fifth had one over the kitchen.

58 *Part 2: Regional Studies*

Fig 7.5   Benedict Otes, Writtle, Essex. A lobby-entry house built in 1644. © P Ryan

Fig 7.6   The Bell, Woodham Walter, Essex. A transitional house of the late 16th century. © P Ryan

Halls were the main living rooms. They were furnished with tables, chairs, forms, etc, and all had a hearth. Except in the largest houses, the fireplaces were equipped not only with the usual firedogs, andirons, pokers, bellows, and shovels, but also with trammels (adjustable pot hooks) and spits for cooking.

The furnishings of 71% of the parlours included a bed, often the best bed in the house. Only seven had hearth furniture. However, it is possible that

Table 7.1 Timber hoods and brick chimney stacks on the Walker maps of Essex (1586–1616)

Date	Parish	Timber hoods	Brick chimney stacks
1586	Boxted	16%	84%
1591	Chelmsford (rural)	40%	60%
1591	Moulsham	32%	68%
1597	Terling	50%	50%
1598	West Horndon	8%	92%
1601	Ingatestone	5%	95%
1605	Ingatestone and Mountnessing	5%	95%
1615	East Hanningfield	2%	98%
1616	Stock and Buttsbury	0%	100%
1616	Springfield	0%	100%

fireside equipment was often only kept beside hearths which were in regular use. In nearly every case where inventories can be linked to Hearth Tax entries, fewer rooms are listed as having hearth furniture than the number of hearths given in the assessment list.

Buteries were used for the storage of beer and household equipment. Kneading troughs, wash tubs, pots and pans, and dishes were sometimes kept there. None had a hearth. Many of the farmhouses had an unheated milkhouse or dairy, used mainly for butter and cheese making.

In houses which had a brewhouse, the kitchen was usually furnished with tables, chairs, and forms, and its hearth was fitted with trammels and spits for cooking. Where there was no brewhouse, the kitchen seems to have been reserved for the major household tasks of brewing, baking, and washing clothes, because only brewing vessels, kneading troughs, and wash tubs were listed there, and the cooking equipment is found in the hall.

Chambers were used both for sleeping and storing wool, grain, malt, cheese, and equipment like spinning wheels, scales, rakes, and shovels. Nine had hearth furniture.

What fuel was used?

Archaeological evidence suggests coal was available in coastal areas from the 14th century, but its use was probably very limited in scale. Evidence from Elizabethan wills demonstrates that wood was more common as a fuel than coal in Essex in the later 16th century. In most cases bequests of coal were connected with blacksmiths or with merchants importing coal through one of the county's ports (Emmison 1978; Emmison 1982–2000). In the 17th century, inventory evidence gives much the same picture. In addition to its use by blacksmiths, coal only appears amongst the belongings of the wealthier members of the community in the later 17th century, the earliest reference to its use in a domestic situation being in 1672. The port books of Maldon also reflect an increase in the importation of coal at this time.[6]

How do the Hearth Tax entries reflect the different types of houses and the households who lived in them?

The parishes of Cressing, Ingatestone, and Roxwell were studied in detail in order to discover how the entries in the assessment lists reflect the different types of houses and the households who lived in them. For the purposes of the Hearth Tax Project, households are divided into several bands: ten or more hearths, five to nine, three to four, one to two, and exempt. The houses of the largest households in a parish are usually the easiest to identify and the one- and two-hearth households the most difficult.

Households with ten or more hearths

Two per cent of the households in the county had ten or more hearths (Table 7.2). Sixty-six parishes out of a total of 410 had a household with twenty or more hearths, most of them belonging to members of the aristocracy. Many of their houses were built of brick like Leighs Priory, New Hall, Boreham, and Ingatestone Hall. They had suites of rooms for family members and guests, lodging rooms for domestic and farm servants, and a wide range of service rooms. It should be noted that the Hearth Tax entries for these households may also include hearths in other houses on the estate. Lord Albemarle of New Hall was assessed on 140 hearths but an addition to the entry records the fact that they were 'in four houses'. Sir Thomas Davis paid for twenty hearths at Cressing in 1671, but information from earlier

Table 7.2 Percentage of households in Hearth Tax Project categories in 1671 for Essex (ERO Q/RTh 5)

10 hearths and over	2%
5 to 9 hearths	13%
3 to 4 hearths	22%
1 to 2 hearths	63%

lists suggests that six of these were in the occupation of the farm bailiff.

Over half the parishes in the county had one or more households assessed on ten to nineteen hearths. Many of them were the households of gentlemen or were inns. An inventory survives for Sir Henry Clerk's thirteen-hearth household in Pleshey.[7] It names 26 rooms. The hall, great parlour, little parlour, dining room, and drawing room were all heated, and six of the twelve chambers had fireside equipment. The kitchen had a 'range'. There were several garrets and three cellars, in addition to a dairy and a larder. John Wallhead, innkeeper at the Crown in Ingatestone, was assessed on twelve hearths. His inn is shown on the Walker map as a two-storeyed building with two brick chimneys; each one probably served six hearths, two of which may have been in the attics.

Households with five to nine hearths

About 13% of the households had from five to nine hearths. Very few parishes had no households at all in this category. In the three parishes studied in depth they were either those of gentlemen or substantial farmers. Their houses were generally of two storeys at least. Some of the larger farmhouses were remodellings of earlier buildings, such as Cressing Temple farmhouse and Hungry Hall, Cressing, tree-ring dated c 1618 and c 1626–50 respectively. Some were newly built lobby-entry houses with their hearths mostly contained in a central stack which could conveniently heat the principal rooms. Examples are New House (alias Cresleys), Cressing, tree-ring dated to 1633, and Benedict Otes, Writtle, which has a six-flue stack with a plaque bearing the date 1644 (Andrews *et al* 1997). Dukes in Roxwell, owned by Thomas Crush, who was charged for six hearths, was built in the 16th century with a floored hall and two cross-wings. It had attics and cellars. The hall, parlour, parlour chamber, and kitchen were all equipped with fireside implements. Either some of the nine chimneys were dummies or some fireplaces may have been served by two chimneys.

Households with three to four hearths

Twenty-two per cent of the households had three to four hearths. The evidence from the surviving buildings suggests many of them occupied old houses which had been extensively remodelled, whilst some lived in new houses.

Households with one and two hearths

Although 63% of the people of Essex lived in households with only one or two hearths, their houses are the most difficult to identify. Where Hearth Tax entries can be linked to houses quite often only remnants of the original building survive. In Cressing, Tudor Cottage, Red Lion Cottages, and Appletree Farm Cottage were occupied by one or two-hearth households. Only a cross-wing survives in the case of the first two. Appletree Farm Cottage, originally a medieval two-room, open-hall house, was extended in the 16th century, and had floors over the hall and parlour inserted in the 17th century. Although four one-hearth households can be linked to houses depicted on the Walker maps in the rural part of parish of Ingatestone, only one still exists, considerably altered. Two are shown as three-cell in-line buildings with a brick chimney in the vicinity of the cross-passage. The other two are hall-and-one-cross-wing houses. Each of these has a brick stack near the cross-passage. In Roxwell, four inventories, valued between £21 and £59, can be linked to one-hearth entries. All included a hall, a parlour, and a buttery. One only listed ground-floor rooms; the second had a chamber over the parlour; the third had chambers over both the parlour and the hall; and the fourth had chambers over all three ground-floor rooms.

Households in shared buildings

Lady Petre was assessed on 30 hearths at Ingatestone Hall. Her relative, Mr Walgrave, paid for fifteen, but the large house he occupied cannot be identified. Earlier in the 17th century, an inventory was made listing all the furniture in the part of the Hall which was set aside for the use of the heir and his wife so that they might gain experience in the 'government' of the house 'the better to enable them to undertake and perform such a charge'.[8] Mr Walgrave may have been living in part of the Hall.

Small households also shared houses. Three families lived in Little Dukes in Roxwell, a relatively modest house which has a medieval two-storey cross-wing and a 17th-century two-storeyed hall and service range, very similar to Horseshoes in Cressing. Two of the households each had one hearth and were exempt from paying the tax, the third family paid for two hearths. In Writtle, Gamaliel Wrathbone, who paid for one hearth, probably lived in part of a house. His inventory only lists goods in the 'old chamber' and the 'best chamber' where he had hearth furniture and pots and pans. Widows were often left the use of part of the family house. Sometimes they were to have access to the hall fire. In other cases it is noted that one of their rooms had a chimney or a new one was to be built.

Further questions

Work on the Essex Hearth Tax has prompted many questions about the houses of Essex as they were towards the end of the 17th century. When did hearths in open halls give way to chimneys? When were timber chimneys replaced with brick ones? When did the detached kitchen become a brewhouse/bakehouse/wash-house and the kitchen become a room in the house? Is the style of chimney stacks and fireplaces a datable feature? When did coal become a common fuel and had it any influence on the materials or form of chimneys? How do the Hearth Tax entries reflect the different types of houses and how were the houses used? What were one-hearth houses like? The answers to some of these questions have been found but others remain to be answered.

Chapter 7: Notes

1. ERO Q/RTh/5.
2. TNA DL 29/74/1477.
3. TNA SC 6 Hen VII/952.
4. ERO D/DP M186.
5. ERO D/DP M8.
6. I am grateful to Bronwen Cook for this information.
7. ERO D/DSp F7.
8. ERO D/DP F215.

8 The Hearth Tax and Historic Housing Stocks: A Case Study from Norfolk *by Adam Longcroft*

Introduction

Traditional approaches to the study of historic housing stocks have been dominated by the study of historic houses, those which still stand in the modern landscape. However, as Currie has argued, it is dangerous to assume that the surviving houses of a given area are truly representative (Currie 1988, 6). The city of Norwich supported a population larger than that of York during the Middle Ages, but only 214 pre-1700 buildings survive, and they are mostly larger structures associated with a tiny social elite. Here, it is only excavation that has produced evidence of the smaller buildings in the medieval City (Smith and Carter 1983, 5). It is important, therefore, in any investigation of historic housing stocks, to seek other sources of evidence which might shed light on them. This is where documentary sources have been invaluable, often providing profound insights into earlier patterns of building. This essay will draw on surviving Hearth Tax assessments for the county of Norfolk. The text will be supported by illustrations of surviving buildings where they help to clarify salient points.

The Hearth Tax

Most counties have surviving Hearth Tax assessments, and some are fortunate enough to have had individual assessments published in one form or another, making them accessible to a wider readership. Norfolk is particularly fortunate in having three published volumes of Hearth Tax assessments. The first two relate to Michaelmas 1664 and Lady Day 1666 (Frankel and Seaman 1983; Seaman 1988). These two volumes provide the data on which the current study is based. The third, more recent, focuses on exemption certificates for the four main urban centres in the county (Seaman *et al* 2001).

Although, the Hearth Tax has been described as 'an unrivalled source of information about the later 17th century' (Webster 1988, xlii), using the Hearth Tax as the basis for an analytical study is not without its problems. The nature of these limitations has been rehearsed on a number of occasions by other historians and this is not the place in which to do so again. However, it is important to draw attention to key aspects of the Norfolk assessments.

First, despite the fact that Norfolk was one of the richest and most densely populated counties in England in the 17th century, the Hearth Tax returns are, as Spufford has eloquently put it 'frankly disappointing' (Seaman *et al* 2001, ix). Neither of the published assessments, for 1664 and 1666, is complete, and although the two assessments dovetail well – missing fragments in one can often be made good by referring to the other – this is not always the case. No returns survive at all, for example, for the hundreds of Blofield, South Walsham, West Flegg and East Flegg in east Norfolk. The 1666 Lady Day assessment is particularly patchy and lacks assessments for fifteen hundreds.

Secondly, the reliability of the tax is often undermined by the failure on the part of the assessors to record those households exempted from payment. Lists of exempted persons are included in the Norfolk assessment for Michaelmas 1664, but only for a small group of 37 parishes. Within this select group exempted persons account for between 9.5% and 48.1% of the total number of households, and a mean of roughly a third (32.6%; Table 8.1). The latter figure is significantly lower than in some other counties, such as Warwickshire, for example, where the average was found to be 35%, and counties such as Cornwall, Cumberland and Durham, where research by Arkell has shown that the exempt accounted for 38%, 47% and 50% of households respectively. It is higher, however, than the figure for Kent (32%), Derbyshire (28%), Cambridgeshire (25%) and Huntingdonshire (23%). Arkell arrives at a mean figure of 41% for Norfolk as a whole in 1664, significantly higher than the figure for its East Anglian neighbours Suffolk (36%) and Essex (35%) (Arkell 2003). The comparatively high proportion of exempted households in Norfolk probably reflects the fact that the county possessed a smaller area of 'wood-pasture' clayland than its neighbours: it was a distinctive landscape given over largely to a pasture-orientated economy which supported a relatively egalitarian social structure in the 17th century. Unfortunately, the distribution of parishes with 1664 lists of exempted persons is heavily weighted towards the north-east of the county. It should not be assumed, therefore, that this sample is truly representative. Nonetheless, it provides us with a rough guide to contemporary levels of poverty in what was one of the more affluent areas of Norfolk. The number of exempted persons appears to have been proportionally higher in towns than in villages. Over 45% of the population of North Walsham was unable to contribute to the tax (the second highest figure in this sample) and Thetford was not far behind at 37.4%. Worstead, no longer the great manufacturing town it had once been in the Middle Ages, also had a higher than average proportion of its population (35.3%) exempted. Of the exempt, the overwhelming majority possessed

Table 8.1 Exempted persons as a proportion of those paying the hearth tax, Norfolk, Michaelmas 1664. Based on data from Frankel and Seaman 1983

Location	Taxed No	(%)	Exempt No	(%)	Exempted households taxed on a single hearth No	(%)	Total
Ashmanaugh	15	68.1	7	31.8	7	100	22
Bacton	52	73.2	19	26.7	19	100	71
Barton Turf	15	75	5	25	5	100	20
Beeston St Lawrence	9	69.2	4	30.7	4	100	13
Bradenham East	36	81.8	8	18.1	7	87.5	44
Bradenham West	35	60.3	23	39.6	22	95.6	58
Caston	28	66.6	14	33.3	12	85.7	42
Dilham	33	80.4	8	19.5	8	100	41
Edingthorpe	20	74	7	26	7	100	27
Little Ellingham	20	68.9	9	31	?	?	29
Felmingham	35	61.4	22	38.5	22	100	57
Foulden	48	64.8	26	35.1	25	96.1	74
Holme Hale	30	88.2	4	11.7	4	100	34
Honing	51	73.9	18	26	18	100	69
Horning	43	68.2	20	31.7	20	100	63
Hoveton St John	21	84	4	16	4	100	25
Hoveton St Peter	12	60	8	40	8	100	20
Irstead	19	90.4	2	9.5	2	100	21
Neatishead	51	77.2	15	22.7	15	100	66
Necton	65	76.4	20	23.5	19	95	85
Ovington	27	81.8	6	18.1	6	100	33
Paston	38	80.8	9	19.1	9	100	47
North Pickenham	25	69.4	11	30.5	11	100	36
South Pickenham	17	70.8	7	29.1	6	85.7	24
Riddlington	28	77.7	8	22.2	8	100	36
Rockland St Peter	23	71.8	9	28.1	8	88.8	32
Saham Toney	47	68.1	22	31.8	22	100	69
Sco Ruston	14	51.8	13	48.1	13	100	27
Sloley	22	70.9	9	29	9	100	31
Smallburgh	34	73.9	12	26	12	100	46
Swafield	15	68.1	7	31.8	7	100	22
Thetford	164	62.5	98	37.4	92	93.8	262
Tunstead	52	67.5	25	32.4	25	100	77
North Walsham	163	54.8	134	45.1	134	100	297
Watton	60	58.2	43	41.7	38	88.3	103
Witton	27	65.8	14	34.1	14	100	41
Worstead	73	64.6	40	35.3	40	100	113
Total	1,467		710				2,177

only a single hearth. For an exempted individual to have two hearths was an extreme rarity and for him or her to have three hearths was unknown. Although the Hearth Tax was collected twice a year, collections were based on assessments less regularly made. Errors and inaccuracies were, therefore, often perpetuated. Consequently, the number of hearths upon which a person was assessed may not be accurate. Moreover, it cannot be assumed that the number of hearths recorded is a true reflection of a person's wealth. Spufford provides us with two instructive illustrations of this, Richard London of Hinxton and Thomas Amey of Harston, both in Cambridgeshire. Both men were husbandmen, yet

London, who had only £34 to his name when he died, was taxed on five hearths, whilst Amey, who was relatively prosperous and who left £120 in his will, appears to have lived in a two-roomed cottage with only a single hearth (Spufford 1974, 41). Similar inconsistencies could arise at parish level, as illustrated by the case of Chippenham, Cambridgeshire. Whilst Spufford found that the Hearth Tax assessment revealed that 'Chippenham had cottages fit for labourers in abundance, and very few husbandmen', few houses with either three, or four or more hearths are recorded. This surprised Spufford, for Chippenham had emerged from her investigations as the parish which provided 'the most definite and striking evidence of the early emergence of the large yeoman. Chippenham was a paradise for the engrosser' (Spufford 1974, 45). Spufford was forced to conclude that:

> the Hearth Tax can be used as an economic guide, and also as a social guide in the sense that all persons with three or more hearths are likely to be yeomen, just as labourers are very unlikely to occupy a house with more than one hearth. But the extent of economic and social overlap shown by the inventories, and the blurring of economic and social divisions caused by inheritance and personal preference, mean that although the tax may be used as a guide to status and wealth in general, it may not safely be used in any individual example (Spufford 1974, 41).

There are other subtle but equally important distinctions to be considered. The assessment for Michaelmas 1664 was levied and collected by sub-collectors acting for professional receivers. That of Lady Day 1666, however, was put into the hands of a London consortium, which immediately farmed out the responsibility for collecting the tax for an immediate recompense to the Crown of £250,000. The farmers of the tax administered the tax in London but outside the capital left its collection to a group of sub-farmers. The latter were required to act as receivers for the Crown and returned their assessments to the Exchequer (see chapter 2). Since the farmers of the tax were only concerned with profit, the emphasis was on the amount raised in each parish and in each hundred, rather than on the number of persons and hearths. Fortunately, the sub-farmers in Norfolk seem to have done a relatively thorough job, but such was not always the case.

Tax evasion is known to have existed in the 17th century, but the extent of the phenomenon has been the subject of considerable debate. Some historians have suggested that the under-registration of households may have been as high as 40% (Webster 1988, xix). William Fenery of Badwell Ash, Suffolk, refused to pay the tax of 2s on his two hearths in 1662 because it was 'un-conscionable high', but it is not possible to be sure how many of his neighbours followed his example (Colman 1971, 173). As Arkell has shown, evasion in some areas appears to have been rife. For example, in Kineton hundred in Westmorland, the number of houses taxed on three or more hearths rose by 30% between 1664 and 1666, and by a further 36% by 1674, suggesting that many had avoided payment on at least some of their hearths in the first assessment (Arkell 2003, 159).

These factors combine to ensure that the true value of the Hearth Tax assessments lies not so much in the insights they offer into the houses of individuals or individual communities, but, instead, in the opportunity they provide to investigate historical patterns over a wider area. By examining larger areas and larger quantities of assessments, the impact of any anomalies or inconsistencies is minimised.

Mapping the Hearth Tax

Mapping Hearth Tax assessments is also problematic. In the production of the distribution maps which underpin this study it has been necessary to combine data from the 1664 and 1666 assessments. Although this is not without difficulties, it allows a cross-county insight into the 17th-century housing stock. The percentages are based solely on those who paid the tax; exempted persons, by necessity, have been omitted from the calculations. This means that the maps reveal variations in the housing stock of all but those poorest members of society who had insufficient wherewithal to be liable for payment of the tax.

Spufford was one of the first historians to realise the potential of mapping Hearth Tax assessments. In her seminal book *Contrasting Communities*, she used the assessments for Cambridgeshire to explore variations in the rural economy. By plotting the Cambridgeshire assessments in map form she identified, amongst other things, a small group of parishes bordering on the fens in the north of the county which had 'clearly developed differently, economically, from those in the rest of the county . . .' and possessed 'an abnormally high proportion of the middlingly-prosperous . . .' (Spufford 1974, 44).

Since the 1970s, Hearth Tax assessments have been plotted and analysed in similar ways in other areas. Pound, for example, has shown that wealth in Norwich (as reflected in the Hearth Tax) was concentrated within particular wards, such as Middle Wymer ward and St Peter's ward, where the proportion of houses with six hearths or more was largest. In poorer wards, such as South Conesford (centred around King Street), households taxed on a single hearth accounted for nearly three-quarters of the total (Pound 1988, 44). Colman has revealed similarly stark contrasts within the hundred of Blackbourne in Suffolk (Colman 1971, 171), while Giles has discovered considerable variation within the Calder Valley in West Yorkshire (RCHME 1986, 121–25). Working

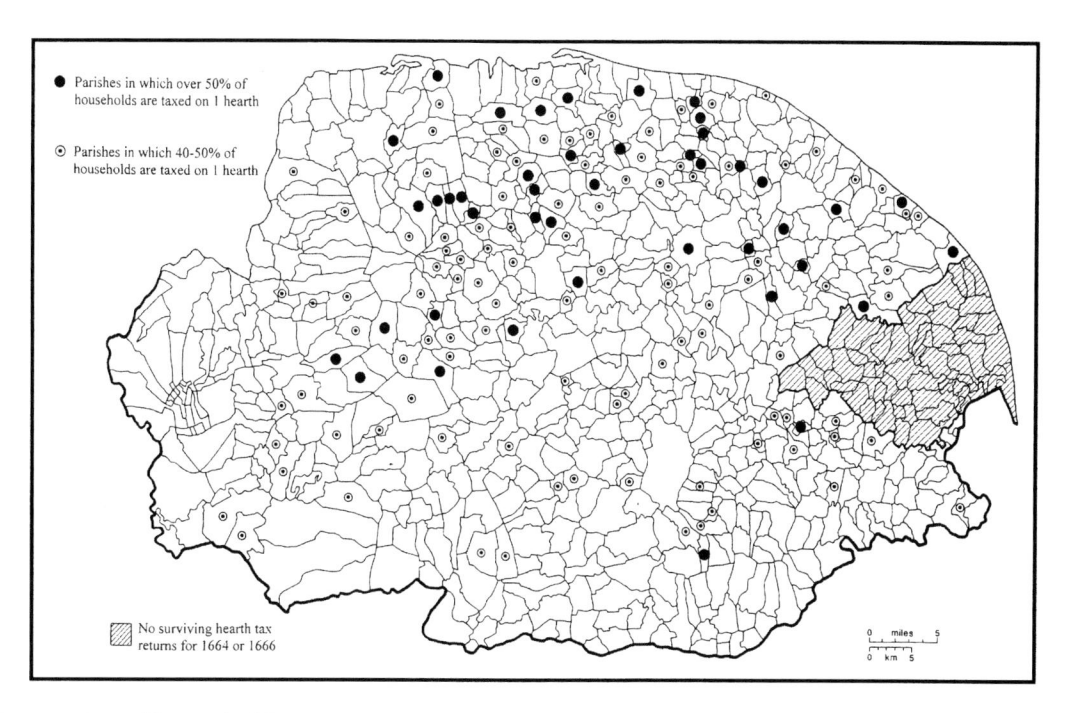

Fig 8.1 Proportion of households in Norfolk taxed on one hearth 1664/66. © A Longcroft

in the Midlands, Alcock found 'notable differences ... between different parts of Warwickshire in the number of hearths and by implication in the size of houses'. He argues that these variations – especially the number of those exempted from the tax – reflect economic diversity: 'a dependence on mining led to a high proportion of cottagers, while pastoral farming (in the Arden) had the opposite result' (Alcock 1993, 201). When Webster compared the number of hearths with the number of taxpayers in Nottinghamshire he came to a similar conclusion: 'The lowest mean values were in the north of the county, the centre-east and south-east and the west. Those areas would seem to have been areas of poorer housing, and presumably of less wealth, which suggests that while the density of taxpayers was greatest along the arable clayland belt, it was not matched by wealth since this was a relatively poor area' (Webster 1988, xxviii). In the Lancashire Pennines, Pearson discovered an interesting link between the survival of houses and the number of hearths listed: 'most of the identifiable [surviving] houses fall within the top 17% and half of them are in the top 9% of houses assessed in the area' (RCHME 1985, 105). In a more recent study of the Hearth Tax assessments for Kent, she has shown that the distribution of hearths largely failed to correspond with the main soil divisions in the county; the distribution of hearths reveals, instead, a series of bands aligned in a north–south fashion which cut across the east–west aligned soil divisions which reflect the underlying geology of the county (Harrington *et al* 2000, xxxiii–xxxv).

When the Norfolk Hearth Tax returns of 1664 and 1666 are statistically analysed and the information they contain is plotted in map form, distribution patterns emerge which strongly imply regional variations in the quality of the contemporary housing stock. It is evident, for example, that households taxed on only one hearth are concentrated in north Norfolk (Fig 8.1), suggesting that householders living in small cottages formed a relatively large proportion of the tax-paying population here. If this distribution is related to soil divisions by looking at a simple soil map of the county (Fig 8.2), it immediately becomes apparent that these smaller houses were clustered in areas characterised by light soils – areas associated, in turn, with a 'sheep-corn' economy in which open-field agriculture was combined with the grazing of large flocks of sheep. The distribution of households taxed on two hearths (Fig 8.3) is also biased towards north Norfolk, and the north-east of the county in particular. In both maps the paucity of instances in central and southern parts of the county is very noticeable.

If these two groups are combined and households taxed on one *or* two hearths are considered, the pattern becomes, if anything, even clearer (Fig 8.4). Parishes in which 60% or more of listed households are taxed on one to two hearths are clearly focused in a broad belt across north Norfolk – an area characterised, as has already been noted, by light soils and sheep-corn husbandry. It should also be noted, however, that these were areas where large estates were beginning to emerge in the 1600s (Williamson 1993, 18). The existence of strong lordship here facilitated, from the 1530s, the creation of vast sheep walks, usually at the expense of the grazing rights of smaller farmers, and occasionally via the deliberate depopulation of village communities (Yaxley 1995, 311–14). This

66 *Part 2: Regional Studies*

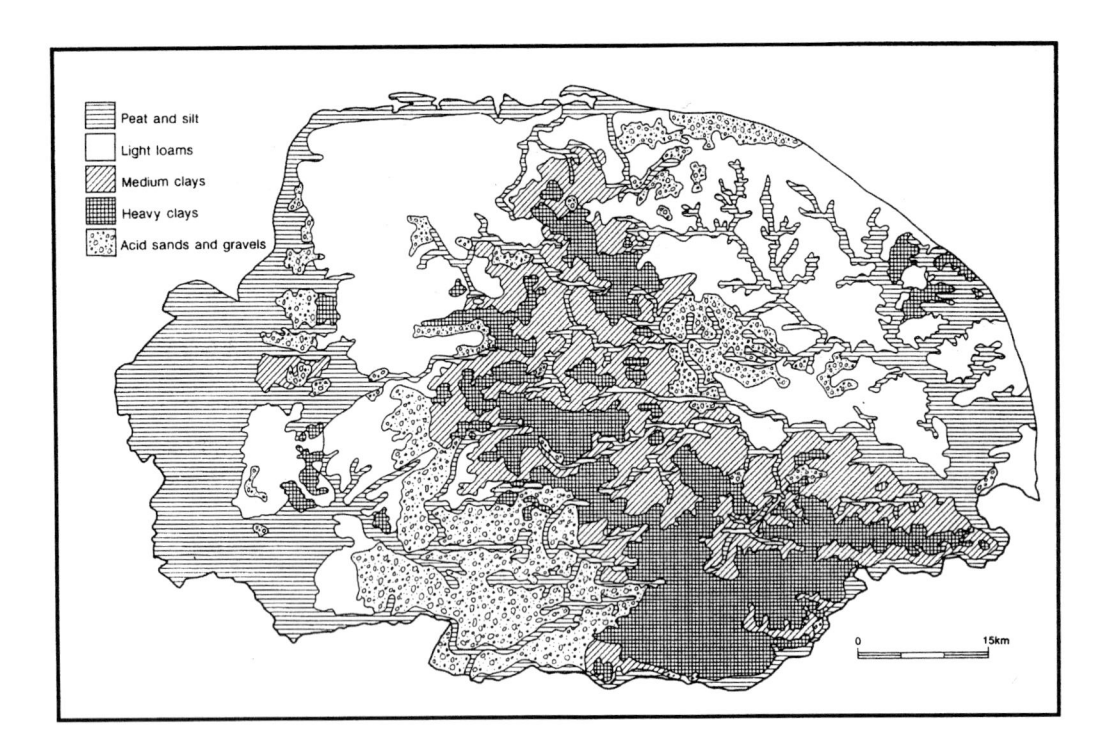

Fig 8.2   Soils in Norfolk. Source: Williamson 1993. Reproduced by kind permission of the author

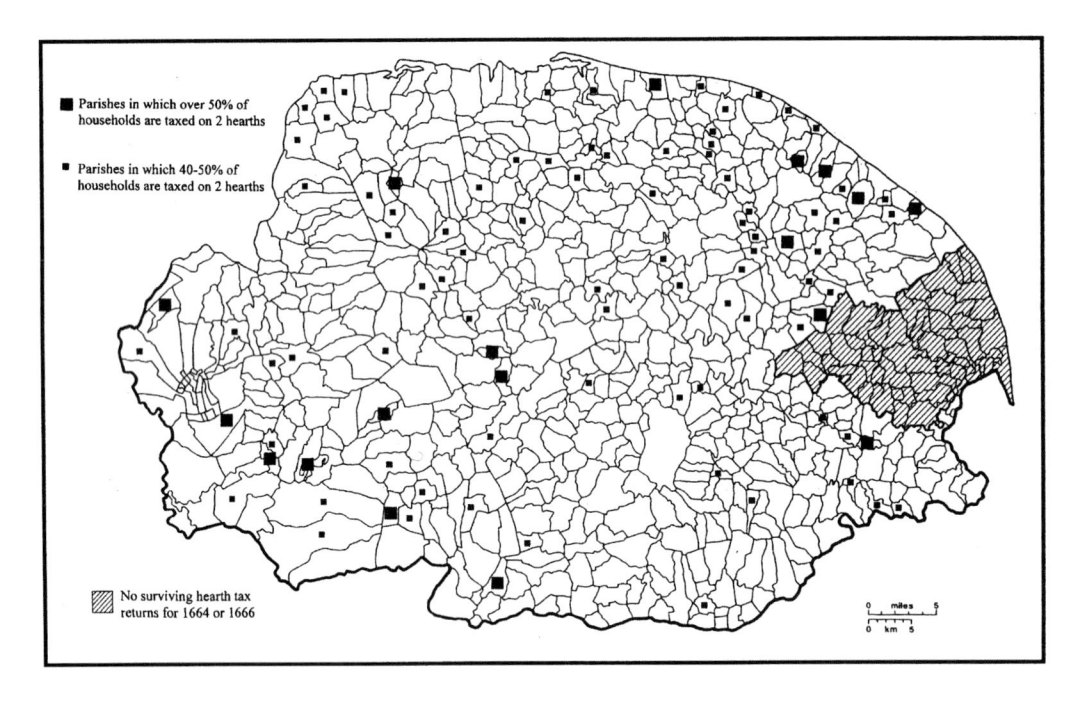

Fig 8.3   Proportion of households in Norfolk taxed on two hearths. © A Longcroft

is the area in which Allison and, more recently, Davison have identified large numbers of shrunken and deserted village sites (Allinson 1957, 116–62; Davison 1993, 84–85; Davison 1996, 72). The Hearth Tax returns strongly suggest that this was also the area where a process of economic polarisation was most advanced by the middle of the 17th century, and where communities predominantly comprised cottagers and lesser farmers with small, unsophisticated dwellings (Yaxley 1984, 88–160). It comes as no surprise that Spufford identified a similar concentration of parishes with a high proportion of cottages on the chalk ridge of Cambridgeshire between Balsham and Woodditton (Spufford 1974, 44).

But what types of houses are under consideration? What would they have looked like? The answer to this question is not entirely dependent on documentary sources, since Norfolk is blessed with a surprisingly large number of small vernac-

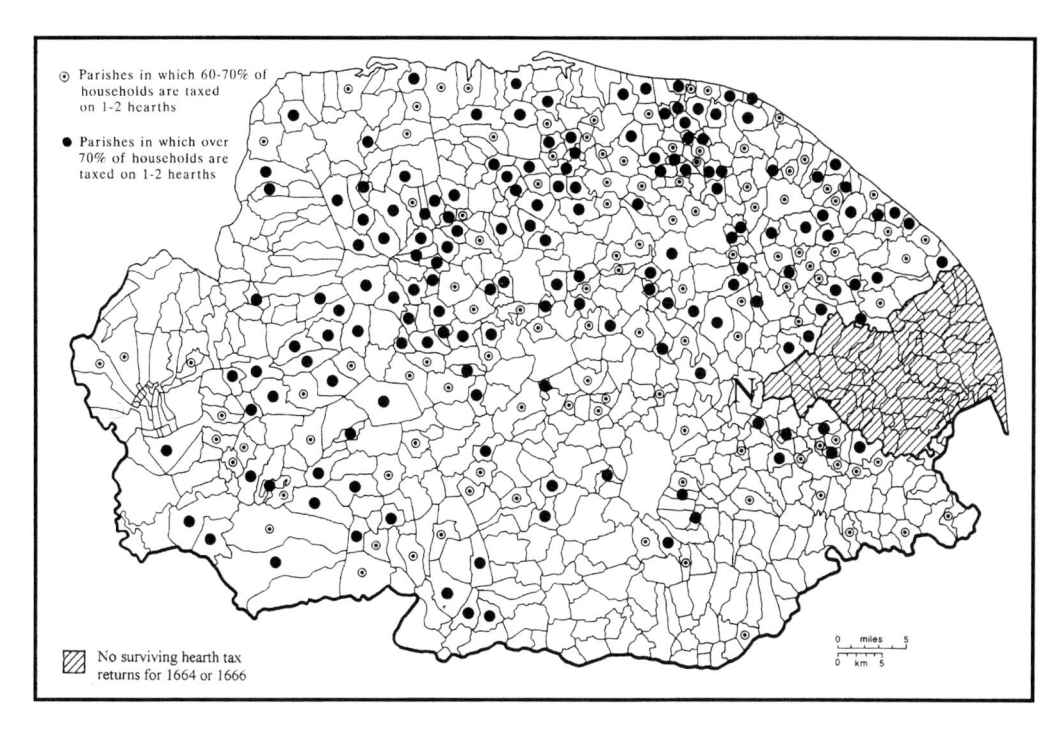

Fig 8.4 Proportion of households in Norfolk taxed on one or two hearths. © A Longcroft

ular houses which survive from the 17th century or even earlier. Tiny cottages with only a single ground-floor room and a solitary fireplace include Apple Cottage and Pip Cottage, both in Stiffkey. Slightly larger houses with two ground-floor rooms and two hearths include 3–5 Bridge Street and 38–40 Wells Road, also both in Stiffkey. The former possessed a cross-passage plan with a gable-end chimney stack, the latter a lobby-entry and a centrally positioned stack (Fig 8.5).

It is fairly safe to conclude, therefore, that the Hearth Tax assessments indicate that small houses with one or two hearths were far more numerous in north Norfolk than anywhere else. But is it possible to be sure who lived in them? As the case of Thomas Amey and Richard London (referred to above) has shown, the answer is usually 'no'. It can be said with some certainty, however, that in East Anglia small houses with only one or two fireplaces were much more likely to be lived in by one social group rather than another. In her study of Cambridgeshire Spufford found that over four-fifths of the occupants of houses with a single hearth had possessions worth less than £50 and their median wealth was £25. Three-quarters of occupants of houses with two hearths, meanwhile, owned goods valued at between £10 and £100 and their median wealth was £60 – double that of the average husbandman in the 1660s. Spufford concluded that 'all persons with three or more hearths are likely to be yeomen' and that 'labourers are very unlikely to occupy a house with more than one hearth' (Spufford 1974, 39–41). A study of over 400 Norfolk probate inventories largely confirms this picture, revealing,

for instance, that in the houses of husbandmen a single hearth is indicated in nearly two-thirds of inventories compared to just over a third amongst yeomen (Table 8.2). Fewer than 6% of husbandman houses contained three hearths or more, whilst for yeomen the figure is much higher at nearly 23%. Labourers' houses containing more than a single hearth were very rare indeed. It would seem, therefore, that there was a marked tendency for members of each of these three social groups to live in houses with different numbers of hearths and rooms (Longcroft 1998, 68–82). Although a number of factors could result in hearths being under-recorded in inventories (Spufford 1990, 144–45), the surprisingly high incidence of yeoman houses with a single hearth indicated in this sample of inventories (38%) should caution against making too many assumptions on the basis of status alone. Moreover, it should be remembered that status could be reflected in different ways. In Wiltshire, for example, Slocombe (1988) has shown that wealth and status were often reflected in the layout of buildings, while in her study of vernacular houses in Avon, Hall discovered that gradations of status could be represented by inner and outer architectural details and the size (rather than the number) of rooms (Hall 1983). Similarly, in his study of gentry houses in East Anglia, Wright found that by the second half of the 17th century, furnishings and the refinement which particular plan arrangements offered were more important in establishing differences within the ranks of the gentry than the size of houses (Wright 1990, 457).

Returning to the Hearth Tax, there are areas

68 Part 2: Regional Studies

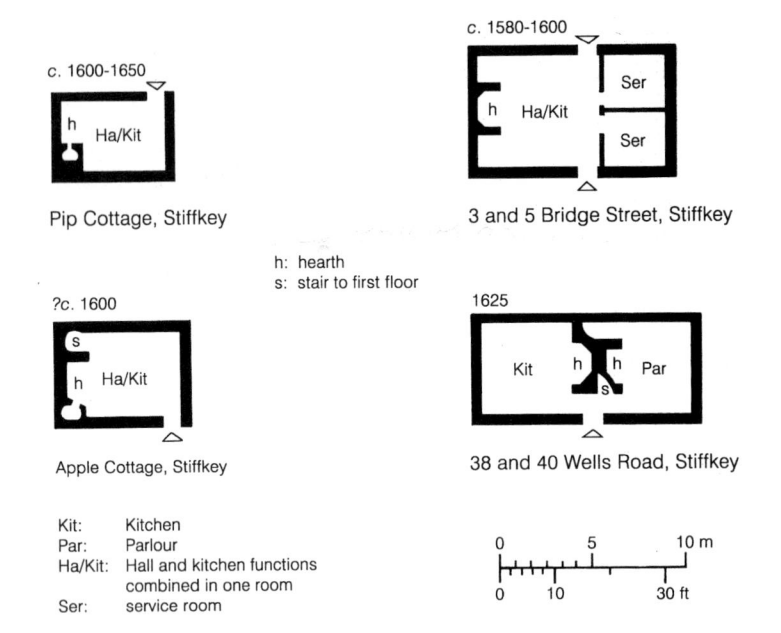

Fig 8.5 One- and two-cell plans in Norfolk: surviving houses of 16th- and 17th-century date in Stiffkey. © A Longcroft

Table 8.2 Numbers of hearths in the houses of husbandmen and yeomen

	Husbandmen	%	Yeomen	%	Total
1520–1629					
1 hearth	53	60.2	45	37.5	98
2 hearths	32	36.4	52	43.3	84
3 hearths	3	3.4	16	13.3	19
4 hearths	0	0	7	5.9	7
Total	88	100.0	120	100.0	208
1690–1729					
1 hearth	25	69.4	72	38.7	97
2 hearths	7	19.4	68	36.6	75
3 hearths	2	5.6	32	17.2	34
4 hearths	2	5.6	14	7.5	16
Total	36	100.0	186	100.0	222
Combined Total					
1 hearth	78	62.9	117	38.2	195
2 hearths	39	31.5	120	39.2	159
3 hearths	5	4.0	48	15.7	53
4 hearths	2	1.6	21	6.9	23
Total	124	100.0	306	100.0	430

within the county notable for not having high proportions of houses with one or two hearths. They include the silt fenlands around Terrington St Clement, the extreme north-west of the county around Sedgeford and Docking, parishes lying on the greensand ridge between Dersingham and Congham, and the claylands of south Norfolk. It is in precisely these areas that the proportion of substantial houses (many presumably inhabited by well-to-do yeomen) with between three and six hearths is correspondingly high (Fig 8.6).

The concentration of larger houses with between three and six hearths is particularly pronounced in south Norfolk, in particular within a triangle between Roydon in the south-west, Norwich in the north and Gillingham in the south-east. Houses

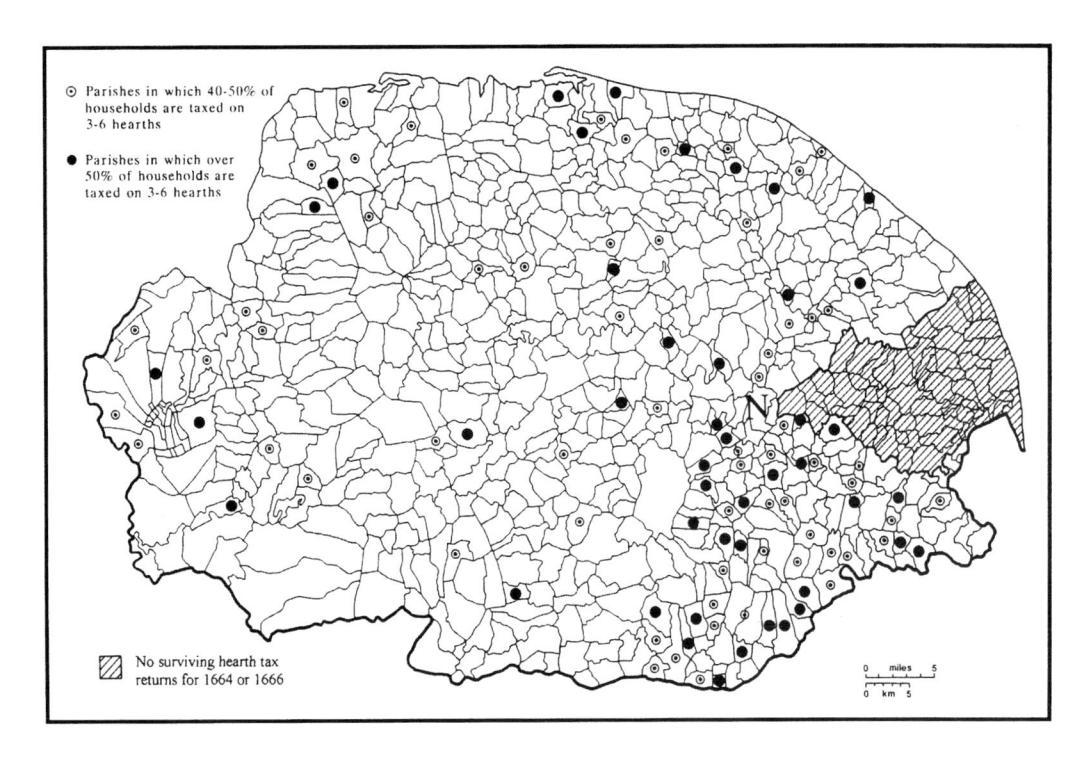

Fig 8.6 Proportion of households in Norfolk taxed on three to six hearths. © A Longcroft

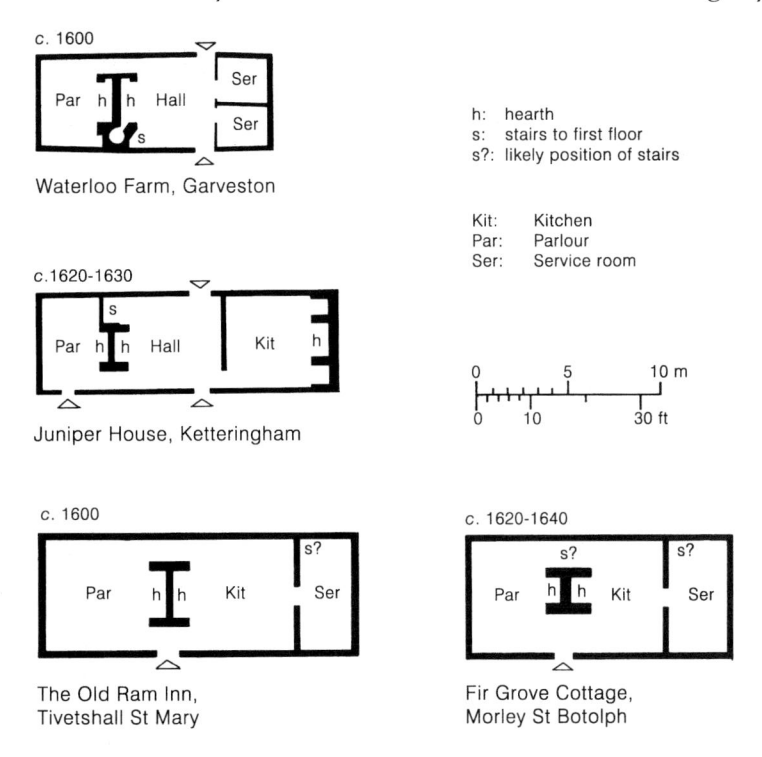

Fig 8.7 Three-cell plans in Norfolk: surviving houses of 16th- and 17th-century date in south Norfolk. © A Longcroft

with between three and six hearths are particularly common along the south-facing slopes of the Waveney valley and along the valley of the River Tas. In both areas such concentrations are likely to be the result of economic prosperity based on fertile soils, plentiful river-bottom meadows, and extensive areas subject to common grazing rights. The heavy clay soils of this area of south Norfolk gave rise to a pastoral economy based on dairying. Weakly manorialised, with a preponderance of free tenures and rural industries such as linen and worsted weaving (Evans 1993, 150–51), wood turning and tanning (Barringer 1993, 152–53), this area became a focus for rural prosperity in the 16th and early 17th centuries. More importantly still, villages were more egalitarian in their socio-

70 *Part 2: Regional Studies*

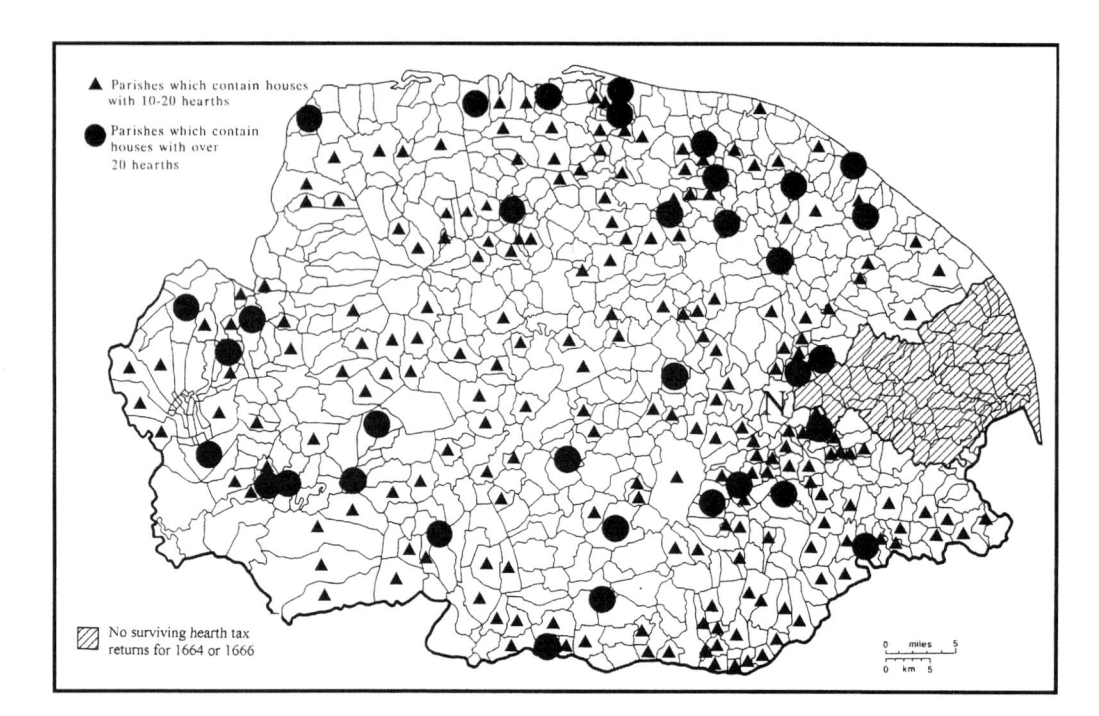

Fig 8.8   Proportion of households in Norfolk taxed on ten hearths or more. © A Longcroft

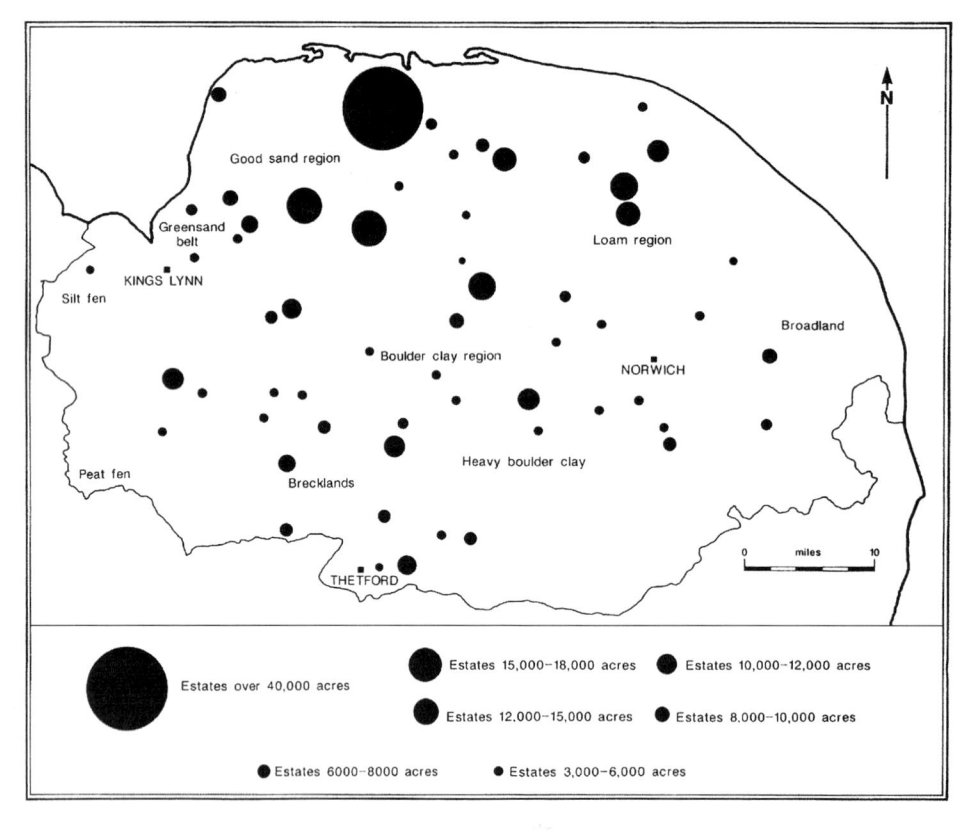

Fig 8.9   The great estates of Norfolk in the 19th century. Source: Wade Martins 1997. Reproduced by kind permission of the author

economic make-up, with large numbers of small to middling-sized farms supporting moderately prosperous yeoman farmers living in substantial farmhouses most of which, by the mid-1600s, boasted elaborate brick chimneys and multiple hearths. Once again, parallels can be found in Cambridgeshire, where a notable concentration of parishes with a high proportion of houses with four hearths or more has been identified on the boulder clays of the western plateau and the clays

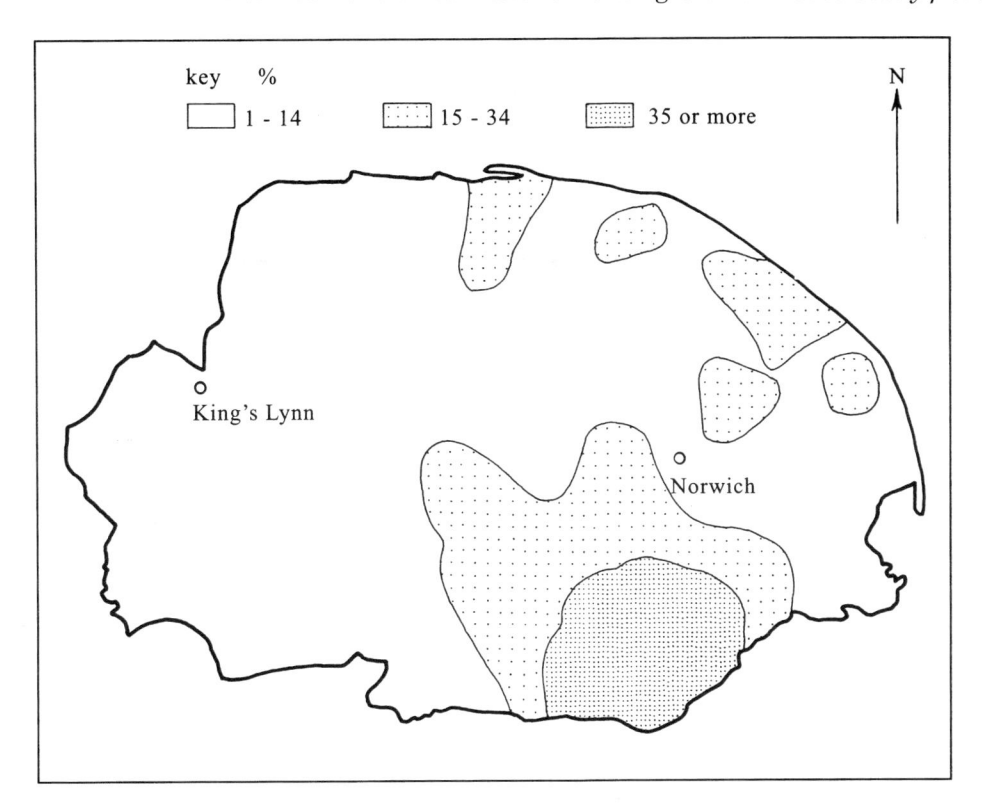

Fig 8.10 Distribution of pre-c 1730 vernacular buildings in Norfolk. Source: Tolhurst 1982. Reproduced by kind permission of the author

in the extreme east of the county (Spufford 1974, 42–43).

In south Norfolk high population densities and an egalitarian social structure provided ideal conditions for the creation of large numbers of multiple-hearth houses in the late 16th and early 17th centuries. High levels of wealth are reflected in significant concentrations of houses with crow-stepped gables, most of which were erected before 1650 (Tolhurst 1993, 112–13). Crucially, brick was also used to construct substantial axial chimney stacks, many of which were endowed with multiple flues. This resulted in a proliferation of multiple-hearth houses from the late 16th century, most of which possessed either a cross-passage plan or a lobby-entry plan. Juniper House, Ketteringham, and Waterloo Farm, Garveston, are good examples of the former, and The Old Ram Inn, Tivetshall, and Fir Grove Cottage, Morley St Botolph, are fine examples of the latter (Fig 8.7).

In contrast, in the north of the county many communities had become socially and economically polarised by the early 1600s, with the gap between the rich and poor becoming wider with each new generation. Surviving 16th- and 17th-century houses in this area were predominantly constructed from a combination of flint and brick. Building traditions here took a different course to those in the south of the county. As a result, chimneys (probably for reasons of economy) were more likely to be incorporated within a gable wall. Larger houses usually had two gable-end chimney stacks, and, after 1650, were often endowed with curvilinear 'Dutch' gables. Large farmhouses with axial stacks were certainly not unknown in this part of the county, but surviving buildings of this type are now thinner on the ground than in south Norfolk. It is possible, however, that the latter have suffered a disproportionate rate of attrition due to changing architectural fashions.

By far the most numerous surviving houses in north Norfolk are small structures like those depicted in Figure 8.5, with either one or two rooms on the ground floor. They rarely possessed more than two fireplaces. The small two-cell house with one or two hearths probably remained the most common type outside south Norfolk throughout the early modern period, the only significant development limited to the repositioning of the front door from the mid-17th century onwards – a process which was linked to a shift from medieval-derived plans to lobby-entry layouts identified in urban as well as rural contexts (O'Neil 1953, 146).

Larger vernacular houses of gentry status (most gentry houses continued to be built from locally sourced materials at this time) also appear in the Hearth Tax and can also be mapped (Fig 8.8). It is interesting to note that, as with medium-sized houses with between three and six hearths, there are significant concentrations of houses with more than ten hearths in the Waveney valley and within a 9.6km (6-mile) radius of the city of Norwich. In addition, large numbers were situated within a 16km (10-mile) wide east–west band across the

72 Part 2: Regional Studies

north of the county and in an area to the west of a line drawn between King's Lynn and Thetford, most especially on the southern fen edge and in the fertile silt fens.

The very largest houses in the county with over twenty hearths were more widely scattered with a concentration, again, in the fens and fen edge of west Norfolk, on the loams of the north-east of the county, and in the rural hinterland of the City of Norwich. This is a very different distribution to that of the 'great estates' that emerged in the 18th and early 19th centuries (Fig 8.9). Most noticeable, perhaps, is the concentration of large estates in the north-west of the county in the latter period, and the almost total absence of the same in the 1660s, as reflected in the existence of large mansions. The Hearth Tax provides a snapshot of the distribution of Tudor and Jacobean mansions such as those at Oxburgh, Holkham, East Barsham, Hunstanton and Blickling, which pre-date the rebuilding of many ancestral seats on a grand scale in the 18th century (as at Holkham, Houghton and Rougham). In the same vein, the Hearth Tax pre-dates the large-scale rebuilding of estate farms and villages by improving landlords, and reveals crucial evidence relating to the characteristics of the housing stock in areas where vernacular thresholds have been recalibrated by programmes of estate improvement and where local building styles have been undermined by a new aesthetic.

Summary

This study has revealed what appear to be significant features within the historic housing stock of Norfolk. Smaller houses with only one or two hearths have a very different distribution to that of larger houses. Moreover, different social groups such as labourers, husbandmen and yeomen tended to live in houses of different size. For example, houses with more than two hearths were far more likely to have been lived in by yeomen than by husbandmen or labourers. Generally speaking, small houses appear to have proliferated in arable areas, in particular, across a broad area of north Norfolk, whilst larger farmhouses with multiple hearths seem to have been thicker on the ground in areas which were dominated by cattle grazing, especially the claylands of south Norfolk. Very large houses with ten hearths or more appear to have been found in large numbers across the county, though there does appear to have been a concentration around the City of Norwich, and along the valleys of the River Tas and Waveney. There also appears to have been a significant dichotomy between the western and eastern halves of the county, the latter having a much greater density of large houses. The distribution of mansions with more than twenty hearths in the mid-17th century seems to have been very different to the pattern of estates which was to emerge in the 18th and 19th centuries.

It seems likely that two key factors affected the distribution of hearths in Norfolk. The first was soil quality. Variations in soil quality resulted in the development of distinctive farming regimes and subsequent geographical variations in rural wealth – both in respect of total wealth and in the way in which this wealth was distributed within communities. In economically polarised communities in which wealth became concentrated into the hands of a few and the gap between rich and poor widened, large, multi-hearth farmhouses were thinner on the ground. In more egalitarian areas, they appear to have proliferated. The second factor was the emergence of divergent vernacular building traditions within the county. Across the north of the county a flint building tradition had emerged by the 16th century. The latter favoured, for reasons of economy, the use of gable-end chimney stacks. In communities where most people could only afford houses with one or two rooms on the ground floor, a single gable stack incorporating one or maybe two hearths at the most usually sufficed. Here the proliferation of hearths occurred within a very limited group of affluent yeoman farmers who were relatively thin on the ground in comparison with pasture-oriented areas like south Norfolk and the silt fens. In the latter area especially, the large number of sophisticated multi-hearth houses reflects not simply the concentration of wealth within a dominant and very large class of moderately prosperous yeoman farmers, but also a well-established tradition of timber-framed construction which favoured the adoption of multiple-flue axial stacks. In south Norfolk, the plan incorporating an axial stack (within the main body of the house) remained the dominant type until changing architectural tastes in the second half of the 17th century dictated the adoption of plans with double gable end chimney stacks which were more aesthetically in tune with the times but less efficient in their use of brick. Early examples of this type of plan, like Dairy Farm, Tacolneston (c 1640), appear at the time of the Civil War, but are more commonly found after the Restoration, as at Crossways Farm, Chedgrave of c 1669 (Carson 1976, 26; Mercer 1975, plate 101).

Finally it is instructive to contrast Figs 8.1, 8.3, 8.4, and 8.6 with the modern distribution of vernacular houses dating from before 1730, as mapped by Tolhurst in the early 1980s (Tolhurst 1982). Tolhurst's map indicates that the largest number of surviving pre-1730 houses is to be found in the southern claylands of Norfolk – precisely where, as we have seen, houses with three to six hearths proliferated in the 17th century (Fig 8.10). Small houses appear, therefore, to have suffered a much higher attrition rate than larger ones. This may be due, at least in part, to the improving activities of large landowners in the north of the county during the 18th and 19th centuries. For every transplanted model village like Houghton and Holkham, there are many other estate villages across north Norfolk where the hand of a great landowner is all too apparent in the almost complete absence of surviving early houses and cottages. The high attrition rate amongst smaller houses may also, however, reflect the fact that they were simply less well suited than larger houses to subsequent adaptation in later periods. Could it be that size really is important after all? In the context of the survival of historic housing stocks it would seem to be a question deserving further research.

Acknowlegements

Thanks are due to Dr Tom Williamson, Mrs Nesta Evans, Dr Robin Lucas and Professor Margaret Spufford, each of whom kindly read early drafts of the text on which this article is based. The author is especially indebted to M S Frankel and P J Seaman whose scholarly published transcriptions of the Norfolk Hearth Tax assessments for 1664 and 1666 form the basis of this study.

9 The Houses of the Dorset Hearth Tax
by Bob Machin

A primary aim of the Hearth Tax Project is to throw new light on the distribution of wealth in late 17th-century England. The news from Dorset is not encouraging.

In 1951 Meekings published a complete transcript of the 1662–64 Hearth Tax returns for Dorset plus a summary of the 1673 returns, listing only the total chargeable hearths, chargeable entries and exempt households for each parish (Meekings 1951). Both returns are defective. That for 1673 has nearly 16,000 entries but most of the names are missing. Meekings therefore decided to publish a composite of the 1662–64 returns but, with just over 11,000 entries, it is clearly incomplete. The discrepancy would seem to be in the exemptions. The 1673 return gives a 31% exemption rate whereas the exempt in 1662–64 is an unbelievable 5%. A distribution map of 1662–64 exempted householders would therefore not be a reliable guide to regional levels of poverty, though one for 1673, using the published summary of exemptions, might be. Since most of the missing exempt in 1662–64 probably lived in one-hearth houses, a distribution map of these would be equally misleading.

There clearly is a relationship between wealth and number of hearths. Most of the Dorset exempt had only one hearth; gentlemen averaged five hearths, esquires twelve, and knights eighteen. But five or more hearths make up only 10% of the total. Was there actually a gradation of wealth from one- to four-hearth householders? Spufford managed to link 101 inventories with Hearth Tax payers in Cambridgeshire (Spufford 2000b, 3). There was a marked correlation between wealth and numbers of hearths, with the two middle quartiles of each group of one-, two-, three-, and four-hearth houses giving a progressively stepped profile. A similar exercise in Dorset produced 109 linkages and quite different results, primarily because there were eight distinctly poorer people living in three-hearth houses. Dorset produced eight more linkages than Cambridgeshire. If these additional linkages had not been found, and if all eight had, by accident, been the poorer inhabitants of three-hearth houses, the Dorset pattern would be similar to that of Cambridgeshire. Unless the data are to be massaged, the verdict on a correlation between wealth and the number of hearths must be 'not proven'. It would seem that the number of linkages in both counties is insufficient to draw firm conclusions. It is most unlikely, however, that further research could add many more examples in either county. It remains to be seen if other counties can produce a much higher rate of linkages.

As a by-product of this exercise, 92 Dorset room-naming inventories, dating from 1640 to 1690, were ranked according to wealth. Here, there was a clear correlation. With few exceptions, more rooms meant greater wealth. But since doubt has just been cast on samples of 100, it would be inadvisable to claim that there is a better correlation between wealth and number of rooms in 92 examples.

An analysis of the 1662–64 Dorset Hearth Tax shows that over 80% of the population lived in houses with one to three hearths. If the substantial but unknown number of missing exempt could be added, these three categories would probably exceed 90% (Table 9.1).

What did these houses look like? This question can be answered with some confidence because so many pre-18th-century Dorset houses survive and have been studied in detail. Dorset was the last complete county survey by the Royal Commission on the Historical Monuments of England (RCHME 1952–75). The vernacular coverage is uneven. The fieldwork for the West Dorset volume was carried out in the late 1930s when minor domestic architecture was not a subject for serious study. The impact of the formation of the Vernacular Architecture Group in 1952 is reflected in the more detailed vernacular coverage of *South-East Dorset* (1970). Subsequent Dorset volumes fall short of that standard. Nevertheless the eight volumes plus the manuscript files behind them provide remarkably full coverage. The author has been adding to and analysing this data since 1970, so that there is now a more comprehensive view of Dorset's vernacular architecture than for most English counties.

Before considering the evidence from the buildings themselves it will be instructive to analyse the information that can be gained from room-naming inventories dating from before the mid-17th century. It will be necessary to restrict the analysis

Table 9.1 Dorset Hearth Tax 1662–64

Hearths	Entries	%	Running Total %
1	4036	37	37
2	3069	28	65
3	1878	17	82
4	882	8	90
5	449	4	
6	252	2	
7	145	1	
8	98		
9	44		
10–19	152		
20+	26		

to ground-floor rooms, since the upper rooms, which were usually a half-storey in the roof space, were merely 'the chamber over *x*'. The basic norm was a hall, and a second ground-floor room known as the chamber or parlour. A quarter of householders had no more. Another 30% of houses, with three ground-floor rooms, merely added a buttery or kitchen. That leaves a substantial 45% with four or more ground-floor rooms. But these more diverse houses usually only had extra service rooms, such as a second buttery, pantry, larder, scullery, or, in the pastoral regions, the ubiquitous dairy.

Two more significant features emerge from the late 17th-century inventories. Increasing numbers of householders moved the best bed to the upper floor, allowing the ground-floor chamber to become a second living room or parlour in the modern usage of the word. This transfer of the best bed may also have encouraged the insertion of fireplaces on upper floors. The second feature is the appearance by 1700 of several houses without a hall. In every case, the former hall furniture was now in a room called a kitchen. Whilst gentry and aristocratic kitchens had always been for cooking, until the late 17th century the farmhouse kitchen was for baking, brewing and laundry.

Published inventories from elsewhere in the country show that Dorset was not exceptional (Machin 1994, 17–18). Everyone below gentry level expected only an all-purpose hall plus a ground-floor chamber or parlour, which doubled as best bedroom and private entertainment room. If more rooms could be afforded, they were usually service spaces rather than domestic ones.

The rarity of fireplaces on upper floors in Dorset before the late 17th century often surprises those more familiar with the Home Counties. This is just one of many ways in which material culture in early modern Dorset lagged behind the south-east. When many medieval houses in Essex or Kent had open halls as high as their fully two-storeyed ends, even substantial Dorset yeomen were building houses that appear externally to be single-storeyed. Open halls here were comparatively low, and any upper end chambers were no more than attics. Inventories show that upper floors were considered to be inferior spaces, suitable for storage of goods or somewhere to put 'second best' beds for children or servants.

Inserting a chimney stack into an existing house was in any case an expensive business. In 1618 Robert Loder of Harwell, Berkshire, spent £6 10s 'about my Chimney ... (and) making my stairs, my window and ceiling and plastering' (Loder 1610–20, 157–58). The Little Ice Age may have made such improvements highly desirable but the expense could be more than the average farmer's annual income. Cob or stone are the predominant building materials in Dorset. Whilst fireplace bressumers (lintels) had to be of timber, several early fireplaces also have timber jambs, and redundant peg holes indicate that many other fireplaces originally had timber jambs that were replaced later in stone or brick. Could it be that most of the early stacks were entirely built in timber? This was an efficient and cheap solution: construct the outline of a tapering flue in timber, in-fill with wattle and daub, then plaster the interior with clay. Surviving examples are rare but have a widespread distribution, indicating an old feature which has been replaced by something better at a later date. Re-used fragments of timber-framed flues suggest as much. At The Laurels, Chetnole, the crucks are joined at the apex by yokes, an early feature. At some later stage, one yoke decayed and someone forced part of a timber-framed flue into the gap to keep the tops of the crucks apart. Presumably this re-used timber was conveniently to hand in the roof space where a timber-framed chimney had recently been replaced by the present stone one. It is easy to add a first-floor flue to an existing stone or cob flue from a ground-floor fireplace but difficult if the original flue is timber-framed. When first-floor fireplaces became desirable, any timber-framed chimneys would have had to be replaced.

Before the 18th century Dorset had a restricted range of farmhouse plans. Most of the surviving houses have either two or three rooms in line; wings and outshots are not part of the local tradition. It would be more accurate to describe these plans as units rather than rooms in line because an outer room was often divided axially to give two smaller rooms, one behind the other. The evidence is clearer in the documentary than the archaeological record. Thus early 17th-century Corfe Castle inventories often list 'the buttery next the street' followed by 'the buttery next the backside', whilst Long Burton inventories list 'the chamber within the hall' followed by 'the chamber within that'. None of the surviving houses in either settlement now has this feature. Smith had a similar experience in Wales. When writing *The Houses of the Welsh Countryside* (Smith 1975) he revisited houses which had axial divisions when he first saw them and found that they had often been removed without leaving any archaeological trace (pers. comm.). Unlike the transverse partitions, outer axial partitions in Dorset, Wales and perhaps other parts of the country were not joined or framed into the rest of the woodwork in the house. This practice means that two-unit houses could have three ground-floor rooms and three-unit houses could have four or even five ground-floor rooms. Thus any inventory with up to five ground-floor rooms can be envisaged within the local planning tradition: six or more ground-floor rooms are exceptional both in inventories and in surviving examples.

Whilst a great deal can be said about surviving two- and three-unit plans, there is almost no information about one-unit plans. After more than a quarter of a century's fieldwork, only five such plans have been found in Dorset. They are too few to sustain any generalisations, and in any case a simple cube with one gable chimney stack offers little scope for analysis. Does the rarity of one-unit plans mean that they were uncommon? Or were they once common and

Fig 9.1 Three-unit central hall hearth passage house, Melbury Osmund, Dorset. One to three hearths originally. © *R Machin*

have been destroyed because they were considered inadequate or poorly built? The latter seems more likely. The majority of Victorian rural labourers lived in badly built cottages measuring 3.6m (12ft) square on average: 13.5 square metres (144 square ft), which is the area of the average modern garage. Very few examples now survive of a house type which was commonplace a century ago.

The pre-industrial poor could not afford to build anything better. But whilst there are detailed accounts of Victorian rural cottages in British Parliamentary Papers, pre-19th-century descriptions are rare. Forty cottages built in Brigstock Little Park, Northamptonshire, between 1600 and 1637, measured 3 × 3.6m (10 × 12ft); 33 cottages built on the waste at Urchfont, Wiltshire, between 1606 and 1639, were a little bigger, with a median average size of 3 × 4.25m (10 × 14ft); but a 1627 roadside cottage at Barford, Wiltshire, measured only 3 × 2.5m (10 × 8ft) (Pettit 1968; Bettey 1982, 28, 30). No one has ever found surviving examples of such small 17th-century cottages. They must have been common, however, and have constituted a significant proportion of the exempted one-hearth houses. Building costs help to reinforce this argument. Early in the 19th century, a one-bedroomed estate cottage cost around £100. Simple late 17th- and 18th-century cottages cost between £3 and £24. By contrast, the smallest surviving pre-1650 farmhouses cost around £37 in cob and £56 in stone (Machin 1994, 29). Any consideration of surviving houses therefore comes with a warning. An unknown but large number of very small, one-hearth houses do not survive and we shall never know what they looked like.

To date 712 surveys of surviving pre-18th-century rural houses in Dorset below the manor house level have been made. Is this a reasonable sample? It has been calculated that there were about 16,000 houses in 1672. If the 1884 urban entries and 812 titled persons in the 1662–64 Hearth Tax returns are deducted, about 13,304 is left as the number of rural houses. The sample of survivors is therefore about one in eighteen houses.

In analysing the plans of existing houses, the main elements are the interrelated location of the entry, the principal fireplace, and the staircase within the two or three units of the ground-floor plan. The traditional entry, since Neolithic times, was by opposed doorways in the long walls. Seventeenth-century Dorset documents called this walkway 'the betwixt doors', but it is usually known now as the cross-passage. In open-hall houses the opposed doorways led straight into the low or service end of the hall.

The replacement of open-hearths by fireplaces in the 16th century led to dramatic changes in planning. One of the most revolutionary changes was the creation of a lobby-entry. A chimney, often with back-to-back fireplaces, incorporating a circular or newel staircase against the back wall, was inserted into the cross-passage. This had the practical advantage of retaining all heat within the house and also gave a new element of privacy: visitors entered a lobby which had doors to left and right into heated rooms. The lobby-entry was devised in Kent in the early 16th century and the idea spread rapidly north and

Fig 9.2 Three-unit unheated central room type, Plush, Dorset. Two hearths originally. © R Machin

west until halted by a 'cultural barrier' where cross-passages were preferred. This barrier is clear in Dorset where the concept of the lobby-entry, learned from Hampshire, is dominant in the east but falters within a few miles so that lobby-entries are rare in central and west Dorset. Back-to-back fireplaces in a lobby-entry plan give a two-hearth house in either the two-unit version (73 examples or 10% of recorded buildings) or the three-unit one (53 examples or 7%). But several one-hearth lobby-entry plans are found in east Dorset.

Dorset is predominantly a cross-passage county (586 examples or 82%). The larger three-unit and smaller two-unit houses each have two variants, giving four common plan types. The older three-unit plan (193 examples or 27%), which often has evidence for a preceding open-hall phase, has a central hall (Fig 9.1). In the open-hall phase the cross-passage was part of the hall, and any staircase to an upper floor was in a chamber beyond the upper end of the hall. The insertion of a chimney stack invariably followed the same plan. A single stack with a hall fireplace was built backing on to the off-centre cross-passage. The stack was always set against the front wall, and entry into the hall involved walking the full length of the back of the stack before turning between its side and a newel staircase set against the rear wall. The rapid standardisation of this improvement is an object lesson in the development of 'new' traditions.

As in the lobby-entry plan, the location of the hall stack made entry to the hall more private, though here the stack also created a barrier against the cross-passage and the room that lay below it. In upper-class medieval open-hall houses this lower end/third unit was usually axially divided to give a buttery and pantry. A few Dorset farmhouses have, or had, this arrangement, though in some cases the third unit is too short and could only have contained a single service room. More examples have a third unit, which seems too long for this traditional usage. Here the lower-end gable usually has a second stack and the room was most probably a kitchen for cooking and perhaps a separate living room for servants in husbandry (104 examples or 15%). It is suspected that this was informed by yet a third older variant, which also has a long third unit, which is often as long as the hall and upper end chamber combined. Here the cross-passage and third unit are straight-jointed against the hall (81 examples or 11%). The simplest explanation would be an addition, though there are no surviving examples of a two-unit plan to which this feature could be added. The most likely alternative explanation is that it represents the rebuilding of a byre end for cattle. Eight surviving Dorset 'long houses' lend support to this interpretation. It would seem that the three-unit long house was formerly widespread in Dorset, but during the 16th and early 17th century the byre ends were rebuilt, most commonly as heated kitchens (see Fig 9.5).

Whilst these improvements were in train, a new three-unit plan appeared in the last two decades of the 16th century and became established as the standard plan for larger farmhouses by the middle of the 17th. Whereas the older three-unit

Fig 9.3 Two-unit Hart's Cottage type, Edmondsham, Dorset. Probably of the 19th century, but it illustrates how small this type often was. One hearth. © *R Machin*

plan had the hall in the middle, this new plan has a central service room flanked by two gable-heated rooms. This 'unheated central room' (Fig 9.2) plan appears to be a complete break with regional traditions (132 examples or 19%). Since this is most unlikely, a derivation from the two-unit one-gable-stack long house can be postulated, but this is not the place to rehearse the arguments. It is sufficient to observe that the unheated central room plan suddenly appears *c* 1590, and within half a century had replaced the old central hall plan.

Initially the unheated central room plan had an off-centre cross-passage with a newel staircase beside the adjacent gable-heated room. The central room was entered through a doorway in an axial partition set at right angles to the cross-passage, requiring a longitudinal passage or corridor, at the other end of which was a door to the second gable-heated room. Since both the preceding and next plans to be considered established the idea that the newel staircase should rise from the hall, it would seem reasonable to assume that the heated room nearer to the entry was the hall. So the second heated room would be the chamber or parlour, privately distant from the entry along a longitudinal corridor. It is always assumed that planning concepts, like stylistic fashions, percolated down the social ladder but here the corridor appears at the vernacular level many decades before it became common in high-style houses. Access to the unheated central service room was equidistant between the two heated rooms, suggesting that it was a buttery equally convenient for both living rooms. This may often have been its use. But many 17th-century inventories confirm what was the case in half a dozen surviving examples where this central room was a dairy.

Enough unheated central room plans survive to establish a 17th-century development typology. First, the cross-passage was suppressed whilst the entry was moved to the centre of the façade, giving a fashionable symmetrical appearance (see Fig 9.6). Then the staircase was moved to the centre, but now in the more convenient straight flights introduced at a higher social level in the late 16th century. Initially the foot of this central staircase was obscured by a doorway, balancing the entry to the unheated central room. For a short period, starting in the last decade of the 17th century, the staircase was set parallel to the front door as a display feature. This was found to be overwhelming, and since the unheated room had already been reduced in area, its functions were moved to a wing or rear lean to, allowing the creation of a more spacious central stair hall. This final development was probably informed by, rather than initiated, the ubiquitous centralised plan of the 18th and 19th centuries.

The two smaller two-unit plans have a parallel development. The older Hart's Cottage type, unlike its three-unit contemporary, continued to be built into the 19th century because it so conveniently combines all the planning elements within a small area (Fig 9.3). Several examples have evidence for an open-hall phase but contribute nothing to our concerns. Hart's Cottage, Corfe Mullen, was the first late 16th-century example identified by the Royal Commission. The gable end of the larger unit is filled by a stack and newel staircase and is entered by an off-centre cross-passage at its other end. This

Fig 9.4 Two-unit Virginia house type dated 1573, Puddletown, Dorset. Two hearths. © R Machin

is obviously the hall. Slightly larger examples have a cross-passage partition towards the hall, giving some degree of privacy, but in most cases the cross-passage was open to the hall. There is always a partition on the lower side with one or two doors into either one small room or two very small rooms separated by an axial partition, giving either a hall/parlour plan or hall plus small parlour and service room alongside. Although the type is smaller than the three-unit plans discussed above, it does not differ in the basic domestic accommodation and several large, well-finished 17th-century examples are as ample in this respect as any three-unit plans (204 examples or 29%).

Prior to the 18th century, vernacular plans are nearly always asymmetrical. An exception is the two-unit house with a central cross-passage and two gable stacks. They usually have newel staircases placed at one or both ends. So far, 57 pre-18th-century examples (8% of the sample) have been found, of which six date from the 1620s and one, Tudor Cottage, Puddletown, has an inscribed date of 1573 (Fig 9.4). Interestingly, the most common early 18th-century plan type in the Chesapeake Bay area of the USA has a similar form. As many of the early colonists in the area embarked at Bristol, it is possible that the origins of this distinctive Virginian house lie in the west country.

In these four common pre-18th-century Dorset plan types, plus the lobby-entry plans in the east, there are exemplars for the one- and two-hearth houses which constitute 65% of the 1662–64 Hearth Tax returns. To get the additional 17% of three-hearth houses, which would bring the total up to 82% of the returns, is not difficult: merely add two gable stacks to the single-stack central hall three-unit plan, or a gable stack to the three-unit lobby-entry plan, and the problem is solved.

However, four basic plan types is an oversimplification. Dorset has several other contemporary plans such a the two-unit lobby-entry with gable stack (17 examples) or the three-unit 'G' plan where the central hall stack is at the upper end of the hall (25 examples). But these and other plan types are rare by comparison with the four plans discussed above.

Envisaging the houses of the Dorset Hearth Tax is confusing enough with only the four basic plans. By definition, the two-unit Hart's Cottage type has only one hearth, just as the two-unit Virginia house and three-unit unheated central room plan have two hearths. But the three-unit central hall plan and the three-unit lobby-entry plan might have one, two or three hearths.

Pearson has argued that overall size rather than plan types would be a better guide to the wealth of householders (see chapter 6). Building always involves expenditure. Economists explain that house building is a diversion of resources into fixed capital formation, which is investment for long-term consumption. A more commonplace formulation might be that people live in the houses that they can afford. Those who built the early 17th-century cottages cited earlier could not afford much; their average ground-floor areas range from 7.5 to 13 square metres (80 to 140 square ft). That is just under the recommended minimum of 3.6×3.6m (12

Fig 9.5   Chetnole Farm, Chetnole, Dorset, where Thomas Downton, yeoman, died in 1668. Two hearths in the returns. © R Machin

× 12ft) for rural labourers in the late 18th and the 19th century. The five surviving one-unit houses in Dorset range from 10 to 23.6 square metres (108 to 254 square ft; the median average is 15.5 square metres or 166 square ft). They feel unbelievably small but are larger than their lost contemporaries, which must be a factor in their survival. This is also true of the oldest surviving Dorset houses. Three-unit open-hall houses cover 81 square metres (873 square ft) on average, while two-unit examples average 63 square metres (675 square ft), approximately 23 square metres (250 square ft) larger than their storeyed successors. But the comparison is flawed. Few medieval houses have been excavated in Dorset, but evidence from elsewhere shows that the majority of three-unit medieval houses averaged 70 square metres (750 square ft) and two-unit ones 37 square metres (400 square ft). Only exceptionally large medieval houses survive, even at the vernacular level.

Of the surviving storeyed 17th-century houses in Dorset, only the two-unit plans correspond in size with excavated medieval predecessors in other parts of the country. Whether they have one or two gable stacks, both average just over 39 square metres (420 square ft). The three-unit plans are smaller than their predecessors. The central hall type averages 61 square metres (640 square ft) and the unheated central room type only 52 square metres (560 square ft). At this point, a modern comparison might be useful: one dwelling in the ubiquitous 1930s semi-detached house covers an area of between 46.5 and 55.5 square metres (500–600 square ft).

The variations arise from the size of the service accommodation. In all four types the basic hall and parlour combination is remarkably consistent at 37.5 to 40.5 square metres (404 to 437 square ft). The parlour is always slightly smaller, except in the two-unit one-gable-stack plan, where the hall is larger than in the other types by about 2.25 square metres (25 square ft). Only three-unit plans have a separate service room. Central service rooms average 11.4 square metres (123 square ft), but the lower-end service accommodation of the central hall plan is nearly twice the size at an average of 22 square metres (236 square ft). That is larger than most halls. If this is not a reflection of their former use as byre ends, an explanation is required as to why the builders of this old-fashioned plan needed such enormous service facilities whilst their contemporaries who adopted the new plan were satisfied with half that area. The most important point to remember in all of this is that the basic hall and parlour combination scarcely varied in area, whatever the overall size of the house.

Costing these dimensions is problematical. Using a range of unpublished building accounts, it is possible to estimate minimal costs *c* 1550–1650 as follows: for a two-unit house in cob, £37, in stone, £56, and in brick, £107; and for a three-unit house in cob, £65, in stone, £98, and in brick, £185. Bowden calculated that the average farmer of *c* 1620 might hope to make a net profit of £5 (Bowden 1967a, 652–57). The cheapest two-unit house therefore cost the total net income of 7.4 years. A modern building society might grant a 50% loan on this basis, but anything more would be too risky. The builders of the surviving houses

Fig 9.6 Iles Farm, Leigh, Dorset, where John Gast, gentleman, died in 1677. Four hearths in the returns. ©
R Machin

considered here were in a similar situation. They needed either a substantial lump sum, from savings or an inheritance, or the income from a farm well above the average size. The latter was probably more often the case. So, as with medieval open-hall houses, the surviving storeyed houses of the 17th century are exceptional rather than typical.

A conclusion that the houses which survive from the time of the Hearth Tax are not typical but only a sample of the largest and best-constructed examples, may suggest some difficulty in presenting arguments based on the tax. But if they are viewed as the 'ideal homes' to which the majority aspired, but could not afford to emulate, it is possible to go some way towards envisaging the houses of the Hearth Tax in the analysis of all this data. There is a danger of losing contact with the expectations and aspirations of the people involved. The poor had little choice; the county gentry and aristocracy had positions to maintain. But is it justified to expect householders with two to four hearths (just over half the entries in the Dorset Hearth Tax) to fill the gap in a sequential economic hierarchy? The linkages between inventory valuations and numbers of hearths in Cambridgeshire support such an expectation; those in Dorset do not.

Amongst the Dorset linkages, two neighbours stand out because relatively more is know about them – and they do not fulfil common expectations. Thomas Downton, yeoman of Chetnole, was valued at £468 when he died in his two-hearth house in 1668, while John Gast, gentleman of Leigh, was valued at £319 when he died in a four-hearth house (with one hearth blocked) in 1677. A yeoman worth £468 with two hearths and a gentleman worth £319 with four hearths is unexpected, and the fact that the gentleman had blocked one of his hearths to reduce his tax payments by two shillings is equally intriguing.

We can identify their houses. Downton lived at Chetnole Farm (Fig 9.5), an old three-unit central hall plan of one and a half storeys. Gast lived at Iles Farm (Fig 9.6), one of the new unheated central room plans of two storeys throughout, built c 1580–1600. Both houses are exceptionally large. Chetnole Farm covers 87 square metres (938 square ft); the type average in the Middle Ages was 60 or 81 square metres (640 or 873 square ft). The 72 square metres (772 square ft) of Iles Farm was enlarged at an early date to 94 square metres (1012 square ft) by the addition of a two-storeyed kitchen against one gable end; the type average in the Middle Ages was 52 square metres (560 square ft).

Iles Farm was built in the last two decades of the 16th century by the younger son of a gentleman, but in 1630 a London merchant foreclosed on his mortgage and sold the property to John Gast, yeoman, of Chetnole. Four years later, Gast married the daughter of one of the wealthiest yeomen in Leigh and with her marriage portion became the fifth wealthiest man in that parish. His adoption of a more expensive gentry lifestyle may explain his low probate valuation: there were chairs and carpeted tables all over the house, and even a long case clock in the hall.

If John Gast illustrates Thomas Fuller's aphorism that 'The Yeoman is a Gentleman in Ore whom the next age may see refined', Thomas Downton held by the proverb that it was 'better to be the head of the yeomanry than the tail of the gentry'. Although he was the richest man in the area and lived in one of the largest houses, his lifestyle was simple comfort in just two domestic rooms, a hall with a bedchamber over it. The rest of this very large house comprised service areas — a kitchen without seating, buttery, milk-house, and cheese loft. The hall had only a single chair, for Downton's own use, and six stools for everyone else. Like Gast, Downton had a livery table in addition to the main table-board, but no carpets on either of them; and if Goodman Downton wanted to know the time, he checked the position of the sun. If Mr Gast offered refreshment, he could bring drink from one of two butteries into either the hall or, if he wished to honour his guest, into an equally well-appointed parlour. If Goodman Downton entertained, he could also bring out a flagon and a silver bowl from his single buttery, but there was nowhere other than his everyday living room in which to entertain guests.

Goodman Downton held fast to the more austere lifestyle of the yeomanry. Neither he nor his successors could see any point in spending lavishly to upgrade Chetnole Farm and he was not going to waste money on foppish things like carpets on the tables. But for all that, he was not totally traditionalist. He ran an arable and livestock farm on a scale which few of his neighbours could afford. But the bulk of his money was invested. He had lent eleven neighbours a total of £310, half of which was specified as two mortgages funding the domestic aspirations of someone else. John Gast spent his way out of the yeomanry; Thomas Downton put his surplus money to work, like the Victorian middle classes, who held similar values to the 17th-century yeomanry.

Two examples prove nothing. But Goodman Downton and Mr Gast exemplify contrary trends amongst the inhabitants of two- to four-hearth houses. Such rulers of the parish described themselves as the 'chief parishioners' or 'better sort of people'. They were 'the middle sort' and 'body of the kingdom' to whom a rebellious Parliament addressed its appeals. They had a position to maintain, and the appearance of their houses was an important element in this.

Those aspiring to gentry status had to spend ostentatiously, and additional hearths represented one badge of superiority. Thrifty yeomen economised to demonstrate their social position. Rather than spend their surpluses, they put them to work either in farming or by way of loans. Half of Downton's neighbours had lent money, and a quarter of them had lent 50% or more of their wealth. Whatever the loans were for (and they might be for extra hearths), the lenders had consciously chosen to forego luxuries (such as an extra hearth).

House size, number of rooms and hearths can reveal something about the inhabitants' wealth at the extremes of the wealth spectrum. But the picture can become fuzzy in the centre. Those who built or improved the middling sort of houses were not just 'economic' men. They were also making statements about their status. John Gast spent to advertise his social aspirations. Thomas Downton economised to demonstrate his social position. Neither conforms to expectation. Both made 'irrational' economic decisions. But they were not socially 'irrational'. It is uncertain how these two elements can be balanced within a research framework, but it is clear from the other chapters in this volume that the 'middling sort' did not always make predictable economic decisions.

10 Bristol: The Hearth Tax as a Decodable Street Directory *by R H Leech*

Introduction

The value of the Hearth Tax as a source for urban architectural history is well established. Counting hearths and exemptions from payment by parish or ward offers the possibility of mapping relative wealth, relating this in turn to the evidence of historic buildings. The extent to which hearths counted in the Hearth Tax returns correspond to the numbers of hearths recorded in surviving buildings in a defined area has often been a concern. Social and economic historians have followed similar approaches. For London and Bristol the Hearth Tax has been an important source for mapping relative wealth across the early modern city (Champion 1993; Sacks 1991).

The purpose of this paper is to offer a new use for the Hearth Tax as a source for the architectural historian. The Hearth Tax, it will be argued, is a decodable street directory for many communities across mid-17th-century England, both urban and rural. The compilation of the Hearth Tax returns was in many instances made by assessors following a clearly defined walking route, in an urban context often up one side of a street and back down the other.

The potential of using the Hearth Tax in this way has already been noted by other writers. In a study of Richmond, Surrey, in the 17th century, Cloake (2001) has identified the Hearth Tax as a decodable street directory; with this realisation it was possible to see the social mix of the town at a level of detail that would not otherwise have been possible. The study of the Hearth Tax for Cambridgeshire has enabled the identification of the walking routes followed by the assessors in two villages (Evans and Rose 2000). In Richmond, and in the Cambridgeshire villages, it was possible through the use of contemporary property records to identify the assessors' routes, enabling properties to be located within the landscape and in relation to one another.

For Bristol the realisation that the Hearth Tax could be used in this way came from research on property holdings in the medieval and early modern town and city (Leech 1997; Leech 2000a), undertaken specifically to inform a study of Bristol town houses now approaching completion (Leech forthcoming). To provide the documentary background as well as archaeological and architectural survey and analysis to the town houses of what was, for much of the medieval period and from the mid-17th to mid-18th centuries, England's second city was a daunting but worthwhile quest.

The potential of medieval and later documentation, especially sources such as title deeds and rentals, has long been realised as a source for systematically reconstructing the historic topography, property ownership, and use. Notable publications reconstructing the topography of a medieval town from such sources have been those for Canterbury and Oxford (Urry 1967; Salter 1960–69). Quite the most detailed study has been that of medieval Winchester by Keene, which now forms an essential starting point for any such work (Keene 1985). These volumes are concerned principally with periods pre-dating the Hearth Tax of the 1660s and 1670s. However, the study of Bristol property holdings is intended to cover the town and city from the earliest recorded times to the later 18th century, the terminal date being effectively the publication of the first street directory for Bristol in 1775 (Sketchley 1775).

To date two volumes have been published by the Bristol Record Society (Leech 1997; Leech 2000a). Initially it was intended to present a selection of tenement histories for the town as a whole, but it rapidly became apparent that so much evidence existed within the documentary records that it would be more useful to cover most streets systematically in something approaching their entirety. This has much facilitated correlation of information on property holdings with the Hearth Tax returns.

The use of the Hearth Tax returns for Bristol has been further assisted by the very complete survival of the records made by the City Corporation. From 1373 until the later 20th century the City of Bristol was a county in its own right. The City's muniments, now held by the Bristol Record Office, are extensive, and include an entirely legible set of five returns for the Hearth Tax contained within what is appropriately named 'the Chimney Book'.[1] Following Parkinson 2001, these will be attributed to Michaelmas 1662 and 1663, Michaelmas 1664–65 (probably updated by annotation in 1668), with the last two returns copied into the book being for 1671 and 1673. The Chimney Book appears to be the locally maintained record of payments. The date 1665 on the cover of the folio volume may be the date at which the transcription of already existing records was commenced. Currently these returns are being transcribed for publication by the Bristol Record Society in anticipation of publication as part of the greater Hearth Tax series. Copies of four returns for the Hearth Tax also survive in The National Archives, for Michaelmas 1662 and Lady Day in 1664, 1671 and 1673. Only those for 1662 and 1671 survive in a legible form.[2]

In the centre of the city sufficient information was available for the ownership and, more importantly, the occupancy of properties to identify that many of the returns for 1662 progressed in house order down one side of a particular street. Once aware of this it was possible to add notes on occupancy derived from the Hearth Tax to entries in the second volume, devoted to the suburb now covered by the St Michael's Hill precinct of the University of Bristol (Leech 2000a). This was a complex process. The pre-1664 returns are made by parish and appear to list housekeepers. The later returns are arranged by ward and list more persons, possibly lodgers as well as housekeepers. Wards may carry the name of a particular parish, yet exclude part of that same parish and include parts of others. Ultimately, by correlating the Hearth Tax returns with the records for property holdings it is possible to identify most of the street sequences and thereby the parishes being traversed within each ward.

Before turning more specifically to the particular insights to be gained from using the Hearth Tax as a decodable street directory, it may be useful to emphasise that the Hearth Tax is but one of a long series of taxation documents, extending from the 13th to the 19th centuries, which can be decoded in this way. The earliest is a list of landgable rents, dated to 1295 (Leech 1997, xiii). It too is arranged by ward. It is apparently the first record of the division of the city into wards, possibly the same system of ward divisions that was still in use in the 17th century. If, for instance, the return for the parish of St John the Baptist is examined together with the record of property holdings, a sequence of properties in Broad Street can be immediately identified. The landgable rents are *de facto* a decodable street directory of 1295 onwards. Only a little later in date is a rental of Arthur's Acre alias Stakepenny, of c 1350. This contains the necessary data to confirm that it too is a rental running in house sequence, providing a decodable street directory of Tucker Street and Redcliff Street to the south of Bristol Bridge (Bickley 1900, **1**, 7–9).

Later than the Hearth Tax is a long series of taxation and rate returns in the Bristol Record Office, first highlighted by Gibson (1985). These cover the years 1679 and 1689, and all years thereafter into the 19th century. They often enable the occupancy of properties to be tracked backwards in time from the first street directory of 1775 to the Hearth Tax returns of 1673 and earlier. Many of these documents, as with some of the returns for the Hearth Tax, are broken down into shorter lists arranged under street headings.

Using the Hearth Tax as a decodable street directory is not an end in itself. The research objective has been to identify through time the occupancy of houses within the city, enabling in turn the identification of precisely or approximately located probate inventories and wills, the reading of which will transform our understanding of household life in the early modern city. Very often a property deed may indicate that a particular person and his or her household occupied a particular property – but 'in the tenure of' or 'in the possession of' do not necessarily confirm occupancy. The Hearth Tax returns, particularly when used in sequence, provide much better data on occupancy.

To date over 200 probate inventories have been correlated with identified properties. Correlations could be made for an even greater number of wills, though they are less useful documents for illuminating household organisation and life. A substantial number of these properties or their immediate and arguably similar neighbours can be seen in plan or in three dimensions. Some 200 houses of the 17th century or earlier in Bristol survive to varying degrees. A much large number are recorded on early photographs, on plans, and in plan books, and on the 2000 and more watercolours commissioned by George Weare Braikenridge in the 1820s (in the Bristol City Museum and Art Gallery), in what we can now see retrospectively as an exercise in preservation by record.

Using the Hearth Tax as a street directory to identify household organisation and daily life is then the purpose of the author's current research and of the transcription of the Hearth Tax returns for Bristol. Its application here has been to link occupants, and also sometimes builders, to particular properties. In the few studies completed of English town houses it is rarely possible to learn to whom a house belonged, who built it, or which households occupied it through time. Studies such as the Survey of London and the Survey of Lincoln Houses have been amongst the few attempting to answer such questions. Using the Hearth Tax returns for Bristol as a street directory has provided a number of new insights into household organisation and life.

Distinctions

In late medieval Bristol a distinction was made between 'shophouses' and 'hallhouses' (Leech 2000b). This, it has been argued, differentiated houses which consisted simply of one or more rooms over a shop from houses characterised by a hall of impressive appearance symbolising the status of the family and household. These houses were seen as distinct from houses which were essentially over the shop. In the shophouse the principal upper room over the shop, usually on the first floor, was frequently referred to as the hall, a term still in use in this context in early 17th-century London but less so in Bristol. In such houses the hall can only have served as the principal living area and social centre of the house, above the shop and below the bedchambers. There were no other rooms for living accommodation, for sitting, eating, and receiving guests. Such a house would have been termed a shophouse, a house over the shop as distinct from one provided with an open hall which might be termed a hallhouse. Shophouse and hallhouse were also shorthand terms used to distinguish houses which reflected polarisations of wealth in the medieval town, between those who could afford only a house of one or more rooms built over the shop, sometimes with no heating, and, at the opposite extreme, those who had the means to live in a larger house with an impressive hall taking up a substantial part of the footprint of the house. In turn, inventories of possessions enable the identification of the hallhouse and the shophouse as *locales* for the enforcement and negotiation of social distinctions.

Hallhouses

Using the Hearth Tax returns and other data, Sacks (1991) identified the parish of St Werburgh as one of the City's wealthiest neighbourhoods in the 17th century. Correlation of the Hearth Tax returns with the documentary records for property holdings enables the reconstruction of the walking route followed by the assessors in Small Street, starting at its north end street and criss-crossing from one side to the other until reaching the north side of Corn Street (Table 10.1).

The house with the greatest number of hearths in Small Street was no. 20, the house of Sir Henry Creswicke. This was a prestigious residence, the home of a family whose relatively recent roots were in south Yorkshire, but whose lineage and status in Bristol were conveyed by the contents and adornments of the medieval open hall rebuilt by an owner 100 years before. On the walls were the arms of Queen Elizabeth, long pre-dating the arrival of the Creswickes in Bristol. A hanging ship symbolised the family's connections with the mercantile city. Arms and weaponry symbolised the family's status in the civic militia (Leech 1999; Leech 2000b). A 19th-century photograph shows the open hall with a first floor inserted and re-used as a printing workshop (Fig 10.1).

The Hearth Tax returns enable the occupancy of two adjacent properties to the south of no. 20 to be identified, those of Sir Robert Cann and Robert Yate, each with ten hearths. The exterior of Cann's property is shown on a watercolour of the 1820s, shortly before it was rebuilt as Albion Court, a medieval entrance from the street still *in situ*. The probate inventory of Cann's possessions made in 1686 provides an interior view. The hall was unheated, furnished with a variety of old tables and cushions, its walls lined with three muskets, ten swords and ten bandoleers. The hall of his city-centre house was a space used symbolically to denote the legitimacy and antiquity of his household, unheated but furnished with arms and armour indicative of

Table 10.1 Small Street, Bristol, in 1662 (street addresses taken from data in Leech 1997)

Names in sequence given in 1662 Hearth Tax return	Number of hearths	House number in Small Street	Notes
John Gunning esq.	9	8 (north part)	Return commences at north boundary of parish, west side of street, then cross over
William Merricke	4	12?	East side of street
William Lysons	6	13?	Ditto
John Speed	6	14	Ditto
Thomas Langton	8	15	Ditto, then cross over
Margaret Cann	11	8 (south part)	West side of street
Richard Streamer	6	7 (north part)	Ditto, then cross over
William Yeomans	9	16 and 17	East side of street, then cross over
George Leamon	7	7 (south part)	West side of street, then cross over
William Hobson	8	18	East side of street, then cross over
John Gwinn	4	6	West side of street, then cross over
William Hazell	8	19	East side of street
Henry Creswicke	15	20	East side of street, then cross over
James Croftes	9	3 and 5	West side of street
Edith Robines	4	?	Ditto?
William Godwin	2	?	Ditto?
Thomas Jefferies	4	?	Ditto? Then cross over?
Sir Robert Cann	10	Between 20 and 25	East side of street, property rebuilt as Albion Court?
Robert Yate	10	25	Ditto, Small Street Court?
Thomas Whitehead	4	26–27	East side of street
Robert Tyler	8	Part of 49	Ditto
Robert Stubbs	4	Part of 49	Ditto
Thomas Haynes	6	51 Corn Street	Turn east into Corn Street

86 *Part 2: Regional Studies*

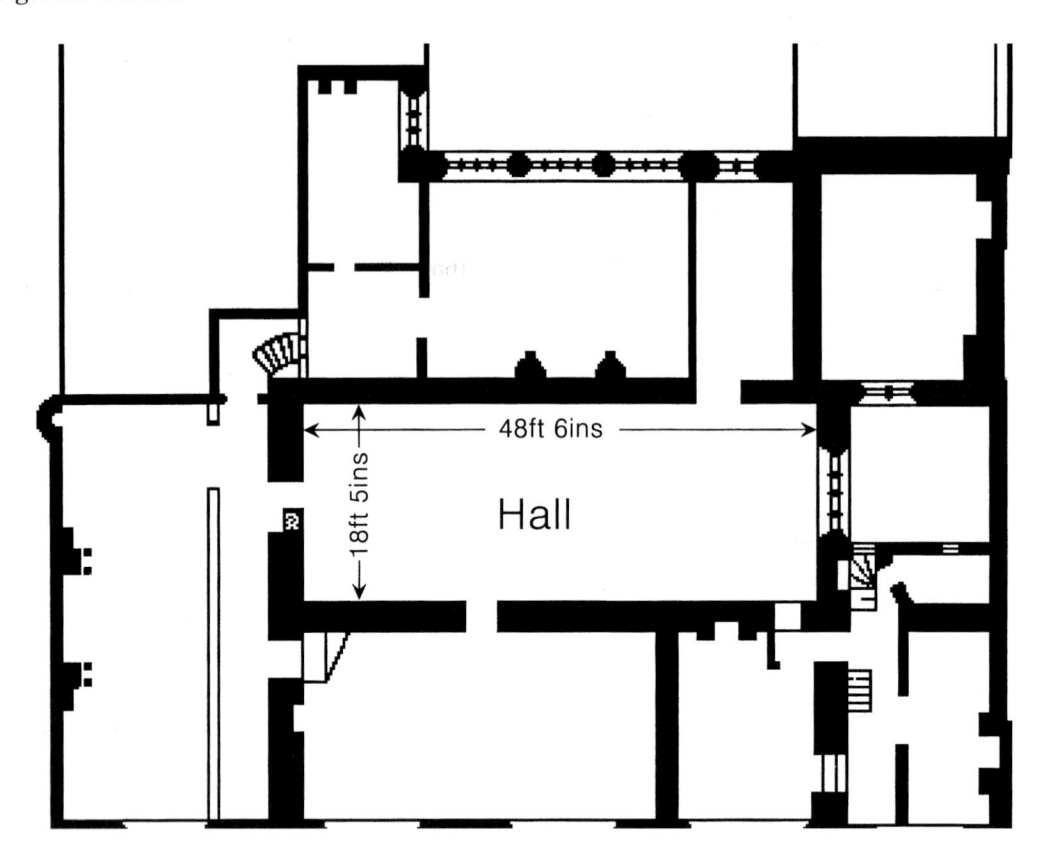

Fig 10.1 20 Small Street, Bristol, the house of John Smythe from c 1540; briefly the residence of Charles I and his sons in 1643, and of Henry Creswicke in 1668. After plan by Dollman and Jobbins, 1863

his status in the city militia (Leech 2003). At Small Street Court an open hall provided a similar entry to the house of Robert Yate, recorded by photography prior to its demolition in 1922 (Winstone 1960, 102). Further north on the same side of the street at nos 16–17, the open hall of the house of William Yeomans survived until its demolition in the 1950s. In 1623 this had been the home of John Butcher, a wealthy draper, alderman and former mayor. His hall was similarly unheated, with the seating confined to panelled benches. Visitors would have noted the hanging candelabra and open roof above, and the walls of the hall adorned with weaponry and armour, all potent symbols of a family's status (Leech 2000b).

Used as a street directory, the Hearth Tax returns for the parish of St Werburgh provide an overview of a neighbourhood of high-status residences in the 1660s. This was a closely knit community linked by intermarriage and by the still open symbolic hall as a potent element of merchant housing culture into the 1680s (McGrath 1968; Leech 2000b).

Shophouses

Bristol Castle had been demolished from 1655 onwards. Its site was rapidly redeveloped for housing by the City Corporation. Castle Street was an existing street within the Castle precinct but was now redeveloped, the new houses being mainly shophouses. Correlation of the Hearth Tax returns with the City's records provides a directory of this street in transition. Part of the south side of the street is examined here (Table 10.2).

The Hearth Tax returns provide confirmation for the location of two shophouses recorded in the probate inventories and wills of Flower Hunt, a tobacco pipe maker at no. 59, and of John Drew, a house carpenter at no. 70.[3] From photographs and plans of nearby contemporary houses it can be argued that the new houses in Castle Street were of three storeys with attics and cellars, and were two rooms deep. One such house, no. 57, with six hearths in 1668, is shown on a late 19th-century photograph (Fig 10.2).

The houses of Hunt and Drew were similarly arranged (Fig 10.3). Below street level were cellars. On the ground floor were a shop and kitchen, the rooms above the 'forestreet' and 'back chamber', those on the second floor similarly named, but prefixed 'upper', with 'garrets' above. In each house the principal reception room was the 'forestreet chamber' over the shop; the term 'hall' was not used. In Hunt's house this room clearly served as the dining room, for six or more guests. To the rear of the house, and distinguishing the Hunts from their neighbours, were the working rooms for the manufacture of clay tobacco pipes. In his bequests to his sons, Flower Hunt viewed his family's status in society as resting on the tools of his craft and on his silverware. The latter included his two inlaid muskets. These were kept in the kitchen along with the close stool, not in a medieval open hall adorned with the royal arms

Table 10.2 The south side of Castle Street, Bristol, in 1664–65

Names in sequence given in 1664–65 Hearth Tax return	Number of hearths	Previous building lease and if acted upon (Y/N)	House number in Castle Street
Margary Andrews	4		
– Chocke	2	1656 – N	55
John Harris	2	1660 – N	56
Katherine Simonds	6	1656 – Y	57
– three with no hearths			
John Hollister	3	?	58?
– [no hearths]			
Flower Hunt	4	1656 – Y	59
Patrick Browne	8	1656 – Y	60?
Francis Ouldstone	7	1656 – Y	61?
Robert Hooke	6	1656 – Y	62?
Thomas Harris	7	1660 – Y	63
Richard Hale	5	1660 – Y	65
Richard Marshall	4	1660 – Y	66?
John Evans		1663 – N	67
Francis Hall	1		
Francis Hobbs	1		
– Hoare widow	1		
John Baker	1		
Edward Bennet	1	1663 – N	Adjacent to 68
one room void			
Richard Hale	3		
– Smart widow	3	1663 – N	68
– Walker widow	1		
– Saunders widow	2	1666 – N	69
John Drew	3	1668 – Y	70

and other symbols of family antiquity and lineage. Hunt's real concerns were for his pipe maker's vices and tools. It was these that were the sole subject of the final codicil to his will. The organisation of Hunt's house and his view of life were fundamentally distinct from those of Creswicke.

Sub-tenants

The Hearth Tax returns for Castle Street and for the houses of Hunt and Drew are also of interest for the information which they provide on the presence of sub-tenants/lodgers and the counts of hearths. Hunt's house was recorded as having four hearths. Questions arise from the schematic reconstruction of Hunt's house: were these hearths in the rooms occupied by Hunt's possessions, and who occupied the rear garret and the second-floor rear chamber? The latter, on analogy with houses of similar plan and date in King Street, would certainly have been heated. The information available for Drew's house provides an answer. Excluding the attic floor, on analogy with the King Street houses unheated, the three remaining rooms containing Drew's possessions correspond precisely to the three hearths recorded for the house in the return. Here it was one of the garrets and the chamber over the kitchen that were not apparently occupied by the deceased's possessions. In his will Drew refers specifically to his 'dwelling house ... now in the several tenures of me the sd John Drew, Richard Bryant and Joan – widow as my tenants'. The rooms unaccounted for in the inventory match exactly the number of tenants recorded in the will. Possibly the tenants were amongst the exempt poor, not yet identified in the 1668 returns.

Redevelopment in progress

Micro-analysis of the Hearth Tax returns for Castle Street also reveals some of the complexities of analysing a street which was in the process of being redeveloped. The returns show that for several plots building leases had been granted but not yet acted upon. Some of these plots were the sites of pre-existing structures, for instance two stables at no. 55 leased in 1656 to Robert Chocke, a 'little house' at no. 67 leased in 1662 to Richard Hale, and a messuage together with a buttress with a room

88   *Part 2: Regional Studies*

Fig 10.2   57 Castle Street, Bristol. Reproduced by permission of Bristol City Reference Library

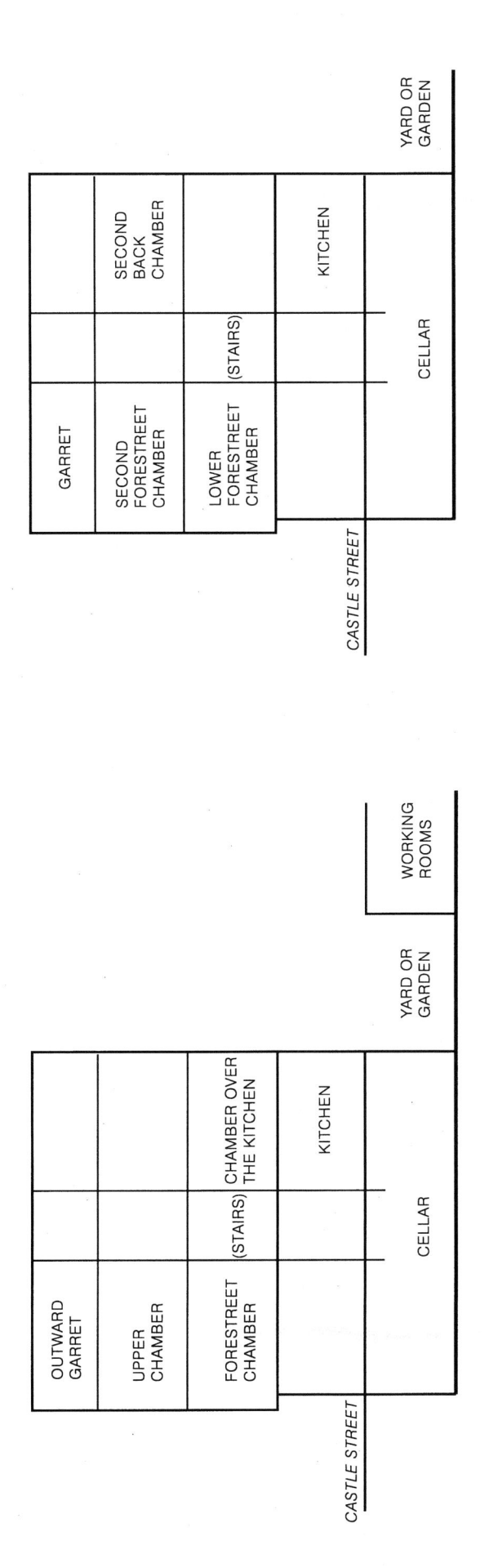

Bristol: The Hearth Tax as a Decodable Street Directory   89

The house of John Drew, 1681

The house of Flower Hunt, 1672

Fig 10.3   57 and 70 Castle Street, Bristol. Schematic section from probate inventories. © R H Leech

Table 10.3 Extract from the Hearth Tax return of 1662 for the parish of St Michael, Bristol, 'Garden houses in St Michael's' (for identifications, see Leech 1997; Leech 2000a)

Names in sequence given in 1662 Hearth Tax return	Number of hearths for garden house	Residence in city centre parish	Street	Number of hearths for city centre house
Thomas Shewell	2	St Leonard	–	9
John Gonning esq.	2	St Werburgh	Small Street	9
John Hillier	3	St John	–	4
Robert Challoner	1	St Nicholas	Welsh Back	5
Edward Tyly	5	St Mary le Port	–	2
Charles Powell	3	–	–	–
Henry Jones	5	St Nicholas	St Nicholas Street	3
Richard Jordan	3	St John	Broad Street	2
Gilbert Moore	2	St Ewen	Broad Street	4
Elizabeth Cugley	1	–	–	–
Leonard Hancocke	1	St Thomas	Redcliff Street	9
George Lane	3	Christchurch	Broad Street	–
Henry Creswicke esq.	1	St Werburgh	Small Street	15
John Haggett esq.	4	Christchurch	Wine Street	8
Anthony Gay	3	–	–	–
Elizabeth Browne widow	2	St Leonard	–	10
Thomas Walter	2	All Saints	–	2
Thomas Bevan	1	–	–	–
Thomas Langton	2	St Werburgh	The Back	8

within first mentioned in 1627 and leased in 1663 to George Hill. Without the Hearth Tax returns one might have concluded that the entire street was rapidly rebuilt in the ten years following the demolition of the Castle c 1655.

Garden houses

The Hearth Tax return of 1662 for the parish of St Michael, on the hillside to the west of the walled city, includes nineteen entries under the intriguing subheading 'Garden houses in St Michael's'. These were mostly the second residences, lodges or garden houses, of prosperous townspeople whose principal residences were located in parishes in the centre of the city. The terms were those used to describe a house which was a place of retreat from the city, a house which was seen as one with its garden. Such houses stood most often within one corner or at one side of a high walled garden. The house was best seen from the garden, or from afar. The view from the house was first of the garden and then into the distance. Such houses were emphatically different in their setting from houses built in continuous rows. As a second residence a garden house could fulfil various needs: a venue for entertainment, a place for more private pleasure, a place for the family on a Sunday, a place for childbirth or an escape from plague (Leech 2000a; Leech 2003).

Using the 1662 return for St Michael's parish, the locations of most of the nineteen garden houses have been identified (Table 10.3). The garden house of Gilbert Moore, a barber surgeon in Broad Street, faced St Michael's churchyard, tower-like and of one room on each floor. In a later extended form Moore's garden house survived until the Second World War (Fig 10.4). The garden house of Richard Jordan was in Park Lane, on the hillside above Moore's house. Its contents were described in the inventory of his possessions made after his death in 1676. The lowest floor was a cellar for storage. Above this was a kitchen, above that a dining room, above that the best chamber, and a garret above in the roof, the inventory account matching exactly the three hearths noted in the 1662 assessment. Jordan was a painter and possessed of considerable wealth. He also had a house in Broad Street in the centre of the city, but it served primarily as his business premises. He kept most of his possessions in what was a sumptuously furnished garden house on the hill. Books, a lute, and Venetian glass would have accompanied music, wine, and carefree summer evenings, looking out over the city, seen and heard by others from a distance. Windows on all sides facing the garden would have provided views over the city to the countryside beyond, and would have underlined the courtly and tower-like qualities of the small garden house or lodge.

In the Hearth Tax returns for other parishes garden houses were sometimes specifically identified, but not always so. Part of the slopes of St Michael's Hill extended westwards into the parish of St Augustine.

Fig 10.4   Gilbert Moore's garden house on St Michael's Hill, Bristol: the further part of the house shown here. Bristol City Museum and Art Gallery Ma.4023. Reproduced by kind permission

Table 10.4   **Extract from the Hearth Tax return of 1664–65 for the ward of St Michael, Bristol (for identifications, see Leech 2000a and Leech 2003)**

Names in sequence given in 1664–65 Hearth Tax return	Hearths	Location
Mrs Woodward's garden house	–	
Mr Jennings	10	S side of Park Row (BRO 04335(5) fol.4)
Mr Bullock: new	–	
Mr Wells	7	Stony Hill below Park Row
- A garden house -	–	
Christopher Cary	4	
Robert Yeamans	9	
John Hellier	3	N side of Park Row, now part of Lunsford House
John Saffin	3	
Mrs Jennings garden	2	
Mr Shewel	2	
- The Red Lodge -	–	The Red Lodge, S side of Park Row, extant
Mary Cox	2	
Capt. Blackwell	9	1–4 Upper Church Lane, N side of Park Row

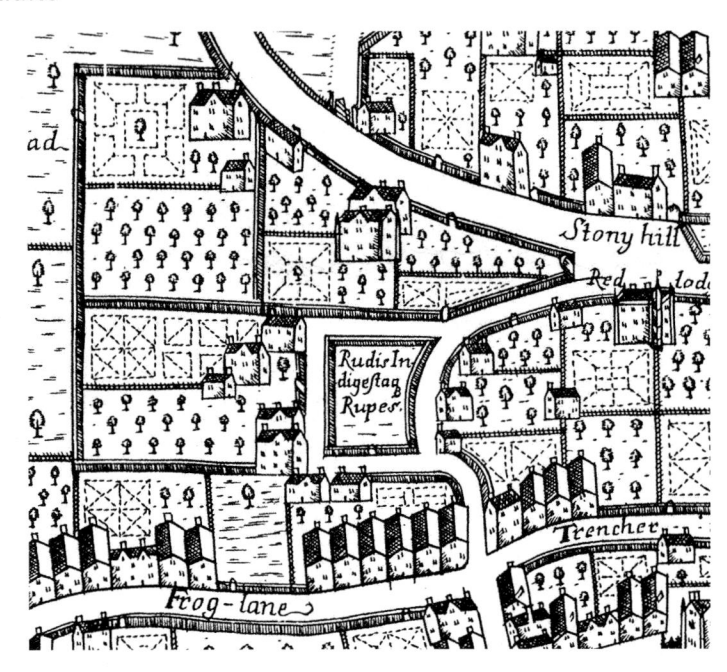

Fig 10.5 Extract from Millerd's map of 1673 of the lower slopes of St Michael's Hill – the garden houses shown include those of Thomas Jennings and Thomas Wells

The Hearth Tax return for St Michael's ward in 1664–65 (not synonymous with the parish) includes a number of named garden houses and other possible garden houses in close succession. Correlation of the return with property records reveals a west to east walking route, crossing Park Row from one side to another and then back again (Table 10.4).

The house of Thomas Jennings, extant by 1662, was on the south side of Park Row, to the west of the Red Lodge. Jennings's business premises were in the sugar house on St Augustine's Back; this was his garden house above the city, typically sited on the uphill side of the walled garden, shown in Millerd's 1673 map of Bristol (Fig 10.5). Below Jennings's house was one newly built by Thomas Wells, a confectioner with business premises in Broad Street. Though built as a second residence, Thomas Wells's lodge, like that of Jennings, provided at least two rooms on each floor.[4] At Wells's death in 1666 this was his house 'new builded', bequeathed together with his Broad Street house to his wife. Wells had been only briefly able to enjoy the pleasures of his new lodge, symbolised in the plasterwork image of the allegorical figure of Abundance in the first-floor chamber (Fig 10.6). Thomas Wells's house was one of a number built in the 1660s, not cited in 1662, but appearing first in a later return for the Hearth Tax.

In brief the Hearth Tax return provides a walking route through a district characterised by the building of garden houses, eastwards to the Red Lodge, now in the care of Bristol City Museum and Art Gallery, beyond to the now demolished garden house at 1–4 Upper Church Lane of Captain Blackwell, the proprietor of the Three Cranes Inn on Broad Quay, and thence to many of the garden houses listed specifically as such in the 1662 return for St Michael's.

Inns

The inclusion of inns in the Hearth Tax returns has posed problems largely unrecognised by historians using the statistical data from the returns as an indicator of relative wealth. The parishes abutting Bristol Bridge, the 'transpontine parishes' of St Nicholas and St Thomas, have been interpreted as amongst the wealthiest districts of Bristol in the 1660s and 1670s (Sacks 1991). But these were the parishes containing many of the inns for travellers, and many of the properties with over ten hearths in these parishes were inns. In the parish of St Nicholas in 1662 four properties had ten or more hearths. Two were inns: the Gillows Inn (William Burroughs) and the Black Boy Inn (John Perdue). On the south side of the Avon in the parish of St Thomas the 1662 return lists nine properties with ten or more hearths. Research to date shows that seven of these were inns or held by individuals who are recorded elsewhere as innholders or in one case as a vintner (Table 10.5). This exercise could be repeated in other parishes with a number of inns, notably those of Christchurch, St John and St Mary le Port. The Hearth Tax cannot be used to assess relative wealth in city centre parishes with large numbers of inns, without first having identified those properties through correlation with other records.

The conclusions of social and economic historians using the Hearth Tax returns for mapping relative wealth in London similarly require reassessment. If these studies had included the Surrey returns, for Southwark south of the Thames, then this would have been obvious enough. Mapping of the returns for the City north of the Thames shows the density of houses with the most hearths to be in the parishes centering on the roads into London from

Fig 10.6 Garden house of Thomas Wells, Bristol, first-floor interior, figure of Abundance on the plaster ceiling. Bristol City Library, Loxton drawings. Reproduced by kind permission

Table 10.5 Extract from the Hearth Tax return for 1664–65 for the ward of St Thomas, Bristol: properties with ten or more hearths (for identifications, see Leech forthcoming)

Names in sequence given in 1664–65 Hearth Tax return	Hearths	Identification
John Pritchard	13	The White Horse, Redcliff Street
Edward Launder	10	Great House at the Bridge?
Ralph Olliffe	10	Bear Inn, Redcliff Street
William Farrier	10	Red Lion Inn, Redcliff Street
John Willoughby	10	House, Redcliff Street
Arthur Stert	24	Recorded as an innholder in 1640, probably the Lamb, St Thomas Street
William Jayne	12	Recorded as an innholder in 1656
Christopher Brimsden	12	Recorded as a vintner in 1672
Joyce Warren widow	11	House, Tucker Street

the north, notable Bishopsgate. Only correlating property records with the Hearth Tax returns for London is likely to reveal the extent to which the properties with the most hearths were not houses but inns.

Expanding cities

It is most apposite for the urban architectural historian that the introduction of the Hearth Tax should have occurred in the 1660s. The Hearth Tax provides a street directory for a period when, for the first time since the 13th century, new housing developments were extending the bounds of England's largest cities, a process which has continued to the present day. In London new streets were being set out in the 1650s between the Strand and the Thames: Essex Street, Surrey Street and others. On the north side of the City, Winchester Street was a new street of the same decade (Leech 1996). In Bristol, too, new streets were being laid out in the 1650s: Castle Green, Tower Street and Castle Street on the site of the demolished castle; King Street beyond the city walls; and new estates of garden houses such as the Little Park on St Michael's Hill, the first new streets in Bristol since the 13th century. Using the Hearth Tax as a decodable street directory should facilitate future research that might explain why urban expansion recommenced in the 1650s – who was building and why – in the 1660s (masked by the Great Fire), and in the 1670s?

There are important questions to be answered here. The renewed expansion of England's two largest cities coincided with the advent of the sugar economy in the West Indies and an unprecedented flow of capital into England. Williams's thesis that slavery and the production of sugar in the Caribbean underpinned the Industrial Revolution in Britain is still much debated by historians (Williams 1944; Morgan 2000, 29–35). The role of the later 17th-century expansion of London and Bristol as a consequence of the advent of the sugar economy has scarcely been discussed (see Leech 2004).

Architectural history can, therefore, focus profitably on questions at the micro level and on the wider scale. Using the Hearth Tax as a street directory for the city of the 1660s and 1670s provides new insights into urban culture and society. New insights may inform our changing understanding of the global economy, the Industrial Revolution and the nature of modernity.

Acknowledgements

Members of staff of the Bristol Record Office are thanked for their help in many ways, John Williams, Richard Burley, Alison Brown and Peter Stone for assistance with general enquiries, and Sheila Lang and Margaret McGregor for checking the transcription of the returns for 1662. Thanks are also owed to Elizabeth Parkinson who has provided much useful advice on the wider context of the returns. For much help in providing indexes and transcriptions of the probate inventories in the Bristol Record Office the author is indebted to the late Edwin George. Finally the author thanks Pamela Leech for many helpful comments on the draft of this paper.

Chapter 10: Notes

1   BRO F/Tax/1A.
2   TNA E179/247.
3   BRO Inventories and Wills.
4   Previously incorrectly deduced to have been of one room on each floor, see Leech 2003.

THE MIDLANDS

11 The Taxable Chimneys of Huntingdonshire in Cambridgeshire *by E M Davis*

Introduction

The administrative unit for the Huntingdonshire Hearth Tax was the hundred. There are four 'double' hundreds recorded in the Domesday Survey. Norman Cross and Hurstingstone hundreds occupy the north-west and north-east of the county, respectively, between the Rivers Nene and Ouse, with a shared boundary along the fen edge. Leightonstone hundred, on the west side of the Great North road and the River Ouse, includes the clay plateau of the 'wolds' of Bromswold. Toseland hundred spans the river terraces of the south and the clay plateau areas on either side of the Ouse (*VCH* 1926–36; Fig 11.1).

Huntingdonshire was a typical East Midlands shire. The hundreds were divided into 104 parishes that had nucleated settlements with some early enclosure. The parishes have a manorial ancestry, and the historic core of the village with its parish church would have been clearly identifiable in the 17th century. Some parishes declined after the 14th century and others expanded; the 'open' villages developed individually and the 'closed', estate villages remained static, many within parkland developments. The Hearth Tax returns, together with other contemporary sources, allow broad comparisons to be made between the nature of village houses and wealth. The population in 1664 was comparatively low on the clay wolds and the fens to the north and west of Huntingdonshire, and was significantly greater along the Ouse valley and in the hinterland of the market towns (Fig 11.2; Carter 1988).

The two important river valleys of the Nene and the Ouse provided the main network for the transportation of goods (see Fig 11.1); they were navigable from the coast up to St Neots on the Ouse, and to Peterborough and the village of Aldwalton on the Nene. By 1674 there were plans to improve the navigation of the Ouse to Great Barford, with the potential of reaching Bedford in 1689 (Bigmore 1979). The improved river navigation, together with the making of the Great North Road into a turnpike road in 1662, gave rise to the great inns at Buckden and Wansford, and in the market towns on the Ouse (Taylor 1979; Frearson 2000). While the Great North Road brought prosperity to the towns and small villages serving the increased number of travellers, it curtailed the movement of cattle. A road, named the Bullock Road in 1662, was used as a droveway avoiding the turnpikes; it linked together existing lanes from Ramsey and the fens to Kimbolton. Joining Ermine Street at Alconbury is the Bullock Track, an ancient ridgeway track that crossed the River Nene at Wansford. Grazing 'guest' cattle before taking them to the London markets was an ancient practice carried out on the fens and wolds of west Huntingdonshire. The drainage of the fens began in the early 17th century and continued after the Restoration. This contributed to the wealth of the fen-edge villages and ultimately to the land available for pasture and agriculture. Milling and malting had always been important on the River Ouse serving an arable hinterland. Wheat and malted barley were exported to London and to the growing brewing industries in the neighbouring counties. The medieval fairs and markets in Huntingdonshire survived throughout the 17th century, though they fluctuated in importance. They were held at Kimbolton and Ramsey, and at Huntingdon, St Ives, St Neots, and Earith on the Ouse (*VCH* 1926–36).

The changes in landscape and geology are reflected in the choice of vernacular building materials. The edge of the limestone belt in the north and west of the county provided stone rubble with ashlar from the quarries for some of the finer building details; boulders and field stones were gleaned from the clay uplands and river valleys as a substitute for stone rubble; and timber from the parish woodlands was used for timber-framing. Scattered in post-Dissolution buildings throughout the county are the medieval masonry remains of the former monastic houses. Timber and bricks were imported from Wisbech or King's Lynn on the Wash, and there are records of ready-framed buildings being transported up the Ouse in the late 17th century.[1] The local manufacture of brick was first recorded in the 13th century in the Ramsey Abbey Cartulary, and brick was in use as a building material by the 16th century. It was used in the 16th-century rebuilding of the Bishop's Palace at Buckden and in the new house at Hinchingbrooke (Pevsner 1968, 215–16; RCHME 1926). Brick became commonplace in chimney building by the mid- to late 17th century though there is a clear social division between the use of brick and stone, or timber-frame as building materials in the 17th century, and this applied to the building of chimneys. Bricks vary from parish to parish and can be roughly dated (Davis 2000).

The Hearth Tax returns

The Hearth Tax returns for Michaelmas 1662 and 1664 generally combine two years, and marginal notes explain the discrepancies between them where there are details of the demolition and addition of chimneys. The returns for Lady Day 1674 are about

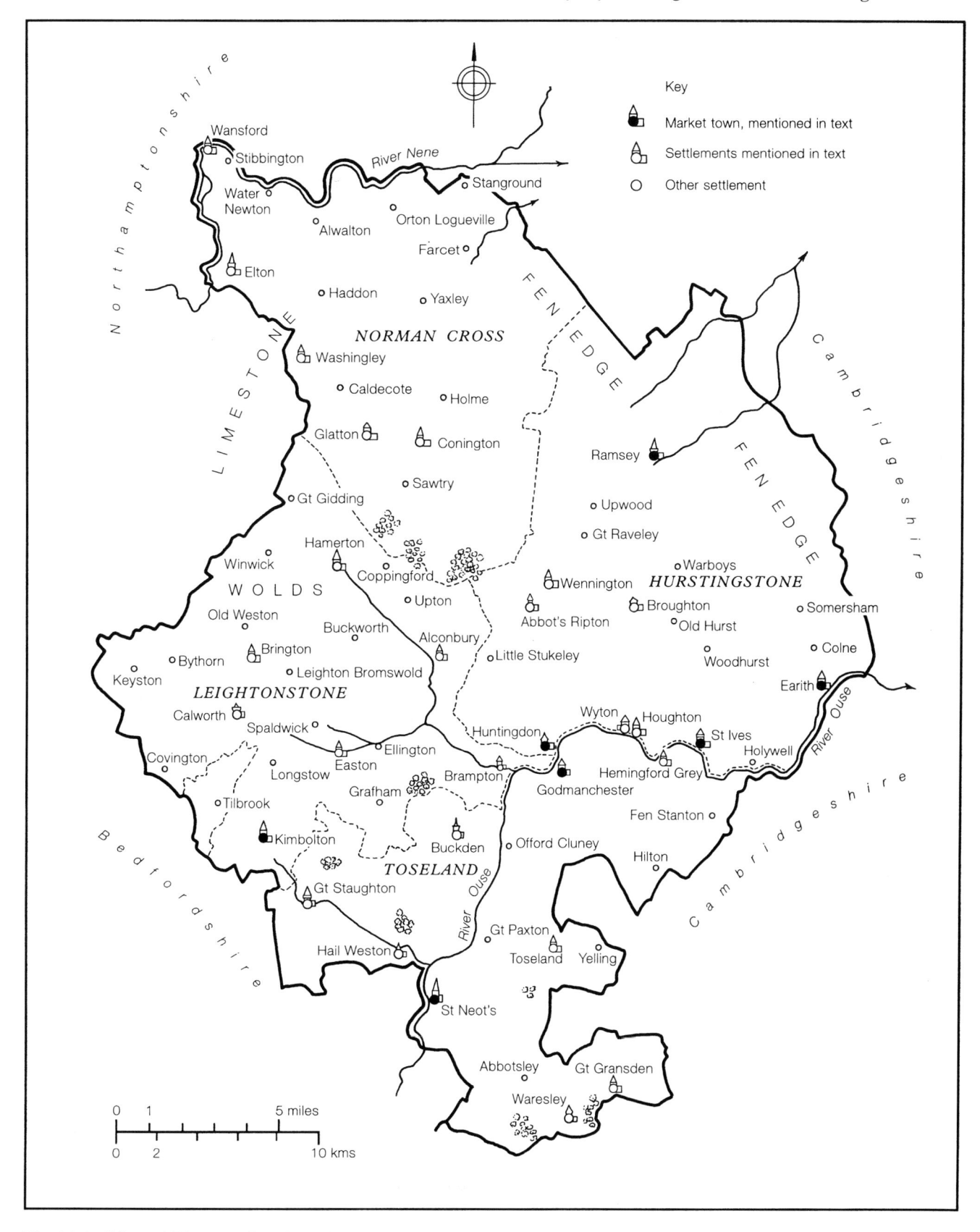

Fig 11.1 Map of Huntingdonshire. © English Heritage. NMR

20% longer, possibly due to under-registration in the 1660s. Exempt households in 1662 may have been 'improved' by 1674 and rendered taxable. The increased returns for 1674 compares with Cambridgeshire and Kent (Evans 2000; Evans and Rose 2000; Harrington et al 2000). The names of properties on the list may not identify a single building but one with several occupants or households, and may include a number of separate buildings, especially for the large estates. Connington Hall, for example,

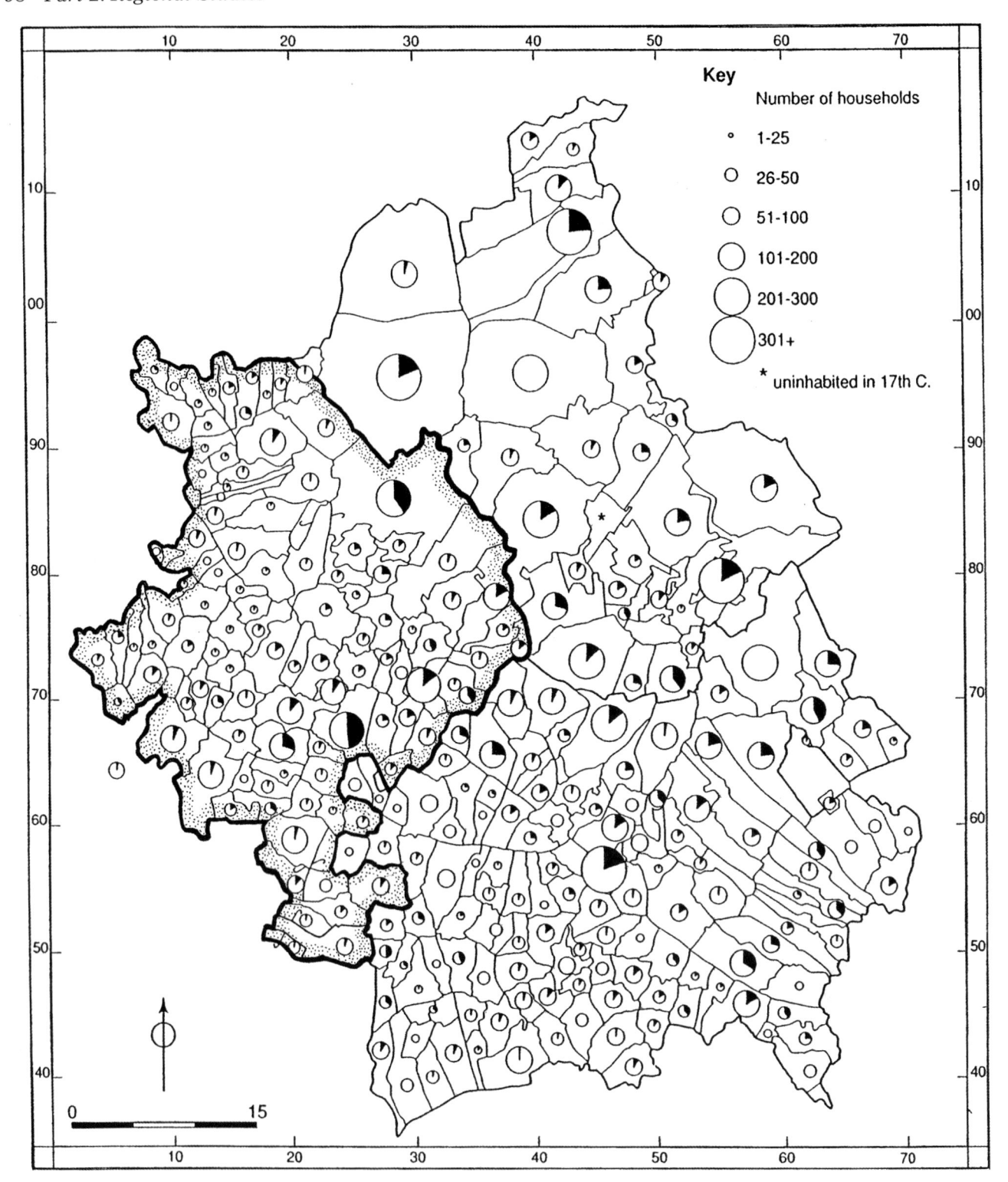

Fig 11.2 Hearth Tax return 1664 for Huntingdonshire (shaded) and Cambridgeshire: number of hearths and exemptions showing population density. Kirby and Oosthuizen 2000. Reproduced with permission

may have included an accommodation range, while at Hinchingbrooke House the gatehouse and accommodation range may have contributed to the total.[2]

The improvement and rebuilding of the large houses of the new estates is shown by the increasing numbers of chimneys in the three Hearth Tax returns. In 1674 there are eighteen houses with more than twenty hearths, and there are 60 with ten or more hearths, representing 1% of all households (Carter 2003). The households with more than nine hearths are concentrated in the towns of the Ouse valley and in Kimbolton near to the Castle. The number of hearths in the 1674 returns relates to the size of each estate and large house: Kimbolton Castle (54), Hinchingbrooke House, Huntingdon (44), Ramsey Abbey (40), Buckden Palace (36), Connington Hall (23), Hamerton (26), Waresley (21), Brampton (21), Washingley (21), and Elton

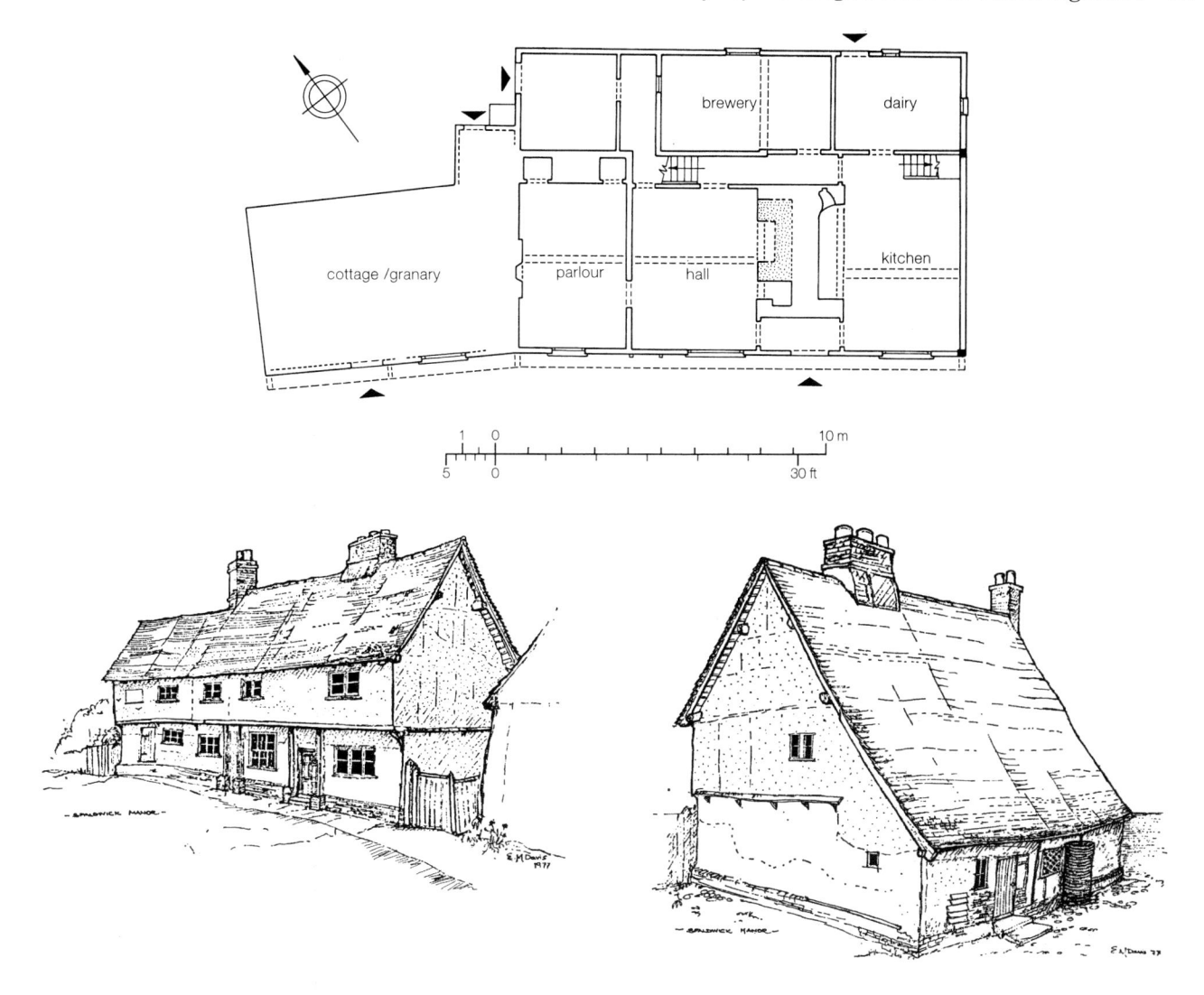

Fig 11.3 Spaldwick Manor, Huntingdonshire, built by the First Earl of Manchester c 1630. © E M Davis

Hall (16) (*VCH* 1926–36; RCHME 1926). Hinchingbrooke House and Ramsey Abbey were built from the remains of monastic buildings and were the original houses of the Cromwell family. The Sandwiches and Montagues, Cottons and Probys were the rising families of the 17th century. The Bishops of Lincoln at Buckden fared less well during the Civil War because of their Royalist sympathies, and the sequestration of some other estates at the time of the Restoration brought about similar changes. The rebuilding of Elton Hall at the time of the Hearth Tax by Sir John Proby and his young wife, the daughter of Sir John Cotton, was registered in the Hearth Tax returns. They rented the old manor of Elton, the Berrystead, which was the home of the Selby family. Sir John accounted for a sum for the Hearth Tax that was due to John Selby, whose name appeared in the 1662 and 1664 Hearth Tax returns with five hearths; Elton Hall was completed by 1674, and Sir John Proby was then found in the Elton list with sixteen taxable hearths (Clark 1992). The notable country seats of Huntingdonshire were being established in the 17th century, and the newly acquired 'estate' villages were being improved. The Earl of Manchester's Kimbolton estate included the Soke of Spaldwick, which he purchased in 1627. Improvements were made in c 1630 at Easton (dated church roof). Spaldwick Manor house was newly built with a long jetty and rear outshut. It had a main chimney stack for three hearths and another chimney heating the parlour (Fig 11.3).

The most obvious buildings in the lists of names are those with more than five hearths. These households act as benchmarks in the Hearth Tax returns for 1664/67 where they represent 6% of the households. Matches have been made with existing buildings by comparing the lists with other sources. Two good examples are at Elton and Brampton. In Elton the rectory had nine hearths and, in the probate inventory dated 1675 for the rector's widow Elizabeth Cooper, it can be seen that the old house had been improved with an extension, and that there was a coal fireplace in one chamber.[3] In Brampton, Samuel Pepys extended his family home by underbuilding the long jetty and adding a new red-brick

First-floor plan

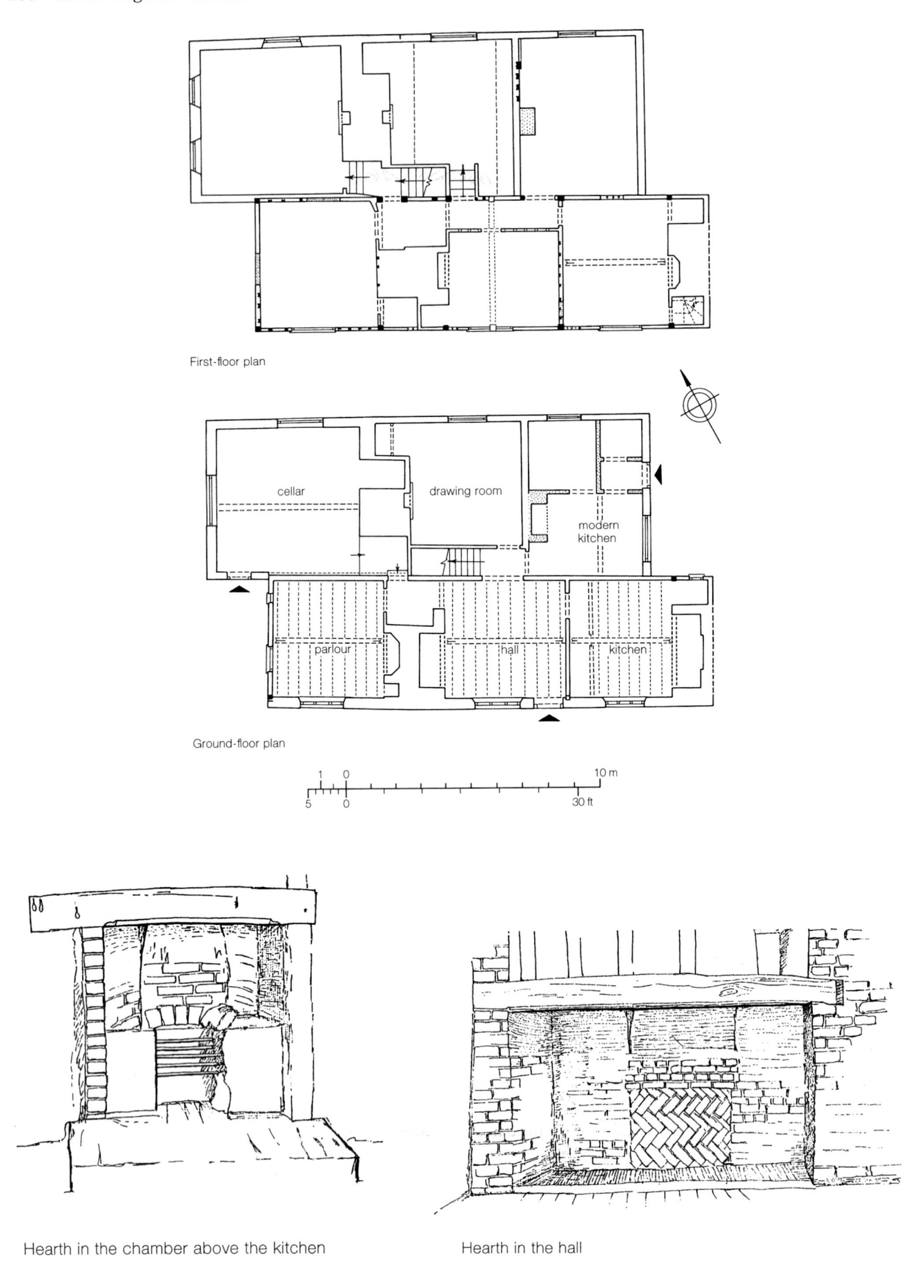

Ground-floor plan

cellar | drawing room | modern kitchen
parlour | hall | kitchen

1 0 10 m
5 0 30 ft

Hearth in the chamber above the kitchen

Hearth in the hall

Fig 11.4   Plans of Pepys House, Brampton, Huntingdonshire, and two hearths. The green painted stripes of the hall hearth imitate timber framing. © E M Davis

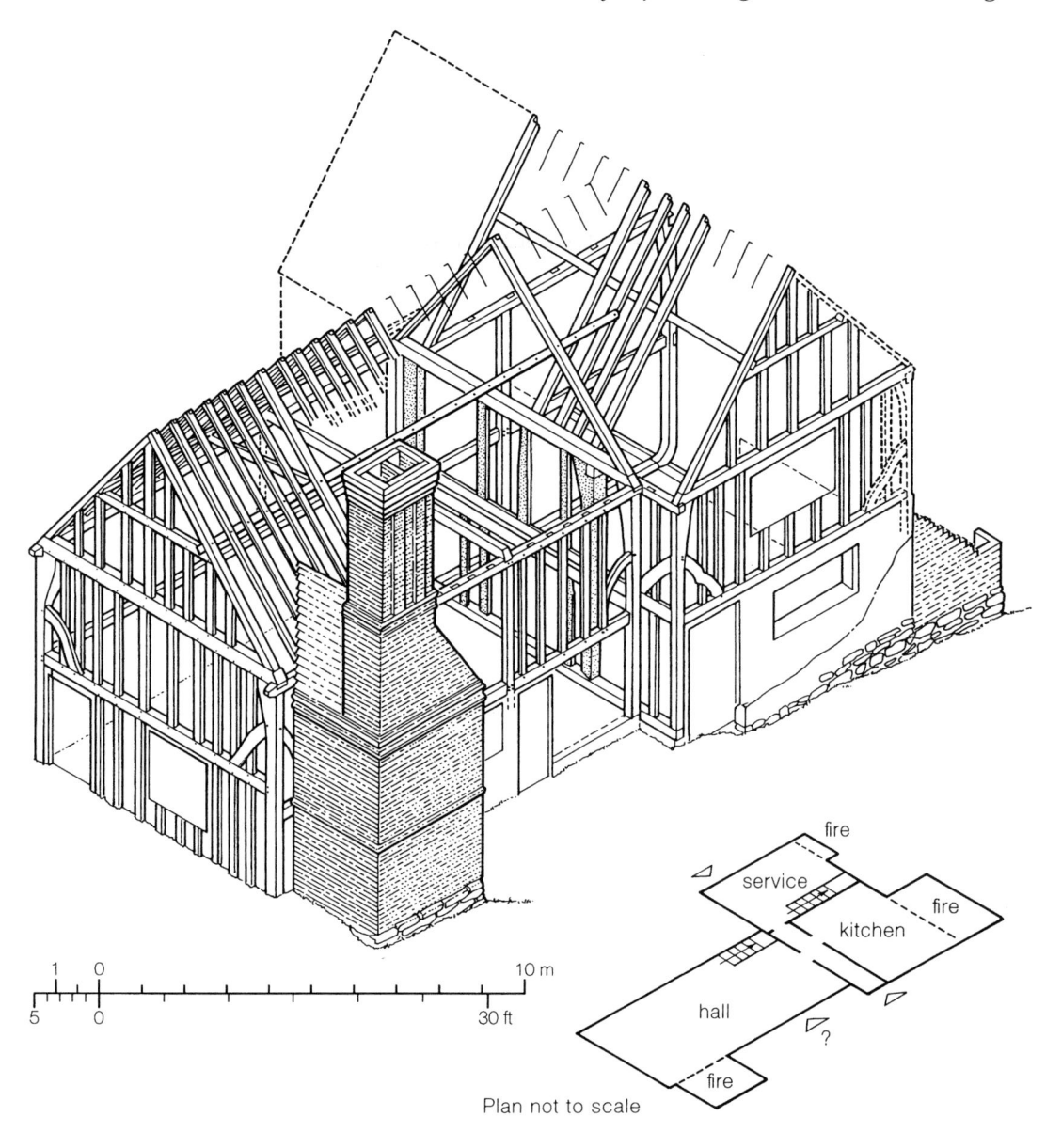

Fig 11.5 Brook End Farmhouse, Great Catworth, Huntingdonshire. Remains of an earlier building, possibly built 1647 by Henry Thompson (demolished 1980). © E M Davis

parallel wing to the rear of the existing house: it had a cellar and a parlour at mezzanine level, perhaps similar to his London house, with a coal cellar. The original west gable had been replaced in brick, with a chimney stack for three hearths, one each in the kitchen, a chamber above and an attic room (Fig 11.4). In the 1667 tax returns Samuel Pepys was taxed for nine hearths. Later in the 1680s Pepys was still improving the house (Tomalin 2002). There are many examples of the parapet gabled chimney stack similar to that in Pepys House, especially in the Ouse valley; this feature was clearly influenced by Dutch immigrants. There are some fine mid-17th-century brick farmhouses with shaped parapet gables and stout square internal stacks in the north-west wold villages at Hamerton and Broughton (Cudworth 1932; RCHME 1926).

The riverside parishes, where trade and farming were combined, demonstrate wealth in improved and new buildings (RCHME 1926). In Ermine Street, Godmanchester, there are three surviving farmhouses built from 1601 to *c* 1630. They are on sites of former hall houses and are built intriguingly around earlier chimney stacks, one with an earlier cross-wing. These buildings have five or more hearths and are innovative in their plans and framing methods (Davis 1996). At the same time, and earlier, conventional long-jettied houses were being built in the town, fourteen of which still exist, with lobby entries and with three to five hearths; these are buildings possibly representing the 'freemen' class of the borough of Godmanchester. The kitchen and dairy were important in these buildings. New markets may have encouraged a dairy industry and cheese rooms are often mentioned in probate inventories. Individual properties in other Huntingdonshire villages, especially along the Ouse valley, have dated chimneys. Other homeowners expressed wealth in different ways. At Catworth, for example, Henry Thompson built a fine house in 1647 with two external brick stacks heating a hall and parlour and their chambers, and with a rear kitchen chimney bringing the total to five hearths. In 1688 the farm was sold and tenanted to Thomas Croxton. He was a butcher who owned 100 cattle, and, when he died in 1708, he was worth £301 in his 'inventory of the goods and cattle'. Although he is just out of the study period he was perhaps typical of his local community (Davis 1979; Fig 11.5). The most common of the surviving buildings today, representing 15% of all households, are those with three or four hearths, which may represent the homes of the yeoman farmer or husbandman, shopkeeper or labourer. It is difficult to make a distinction between wealth and title. Comparisons and contrasts can be made between the areas of low population on the clay plateau and the thriving Ouse valley (see Fig 11.2). In the more sparsely populated areas there seem to be more converted hall houses and very few new vernacular buildings. The hall of a house in Brington had a chimney stack but was not chambered over (Mercer 1975, 172). This may have been a common practice where the household preserved older traditions of sleeping in the hall or parlour, and using the attic floor for storage. Improvements often came in phases with rising prosperity.

In the 1674 Hearth Tax returns, 25% of all taxable households had two hearths and 55% had only one. The highest proportion of these households is in parishes away from the market towns and the riverside, as Carter demonstrates by comparing parishes in the hinterland of St Ives, a part of Hurstingstone hundred (Carter 1988). The surviving buildings show clearly that many one- to four-hearth houses of the 17th century were reasonably well built. Some 15th- and 16th-century cottages and farmhouses in Abbots Ripton that were improved by the estate in the 17th century had substantial timber frames, and they may not all have had inserted floors in the hall. There are smaller 17th-century vernacular buildings, clustered particularly in Glatton, and villages on the fen edge, and one of note in Wennington (Davis 1982; VCH 1926–36).

Shops and workshops are represented in the Hearth Tax lists but need to be identified from other sources. The baker Thomas Goode had acquired two adjacent properties in the High Street of Kimbolton at the time of his death in 1668. His household and shop, described in his probate inventory, had twelve rooms. In the Hearth Tax return he was assessed for two hearths; the shop, mentioned in his probate inventory, was unheated, and the bakehouse, possibly in the yard, was excluded from the tax.[4]

Wood was the main or only fuel, collected from woodland or hedgerows, or gleaned from the underwood and burnt as bundles of faggots mixed in the fen-edge villages with peat or cow pats. Coal was used in the homes of the gentry, where additional flues were added to existing chimneys; in the villages away from river transport, householders tended to retain the large hall hearth for cooking and warmth, and had fewer heated rooms.

House plans

By the end of the 17th century the house plan in Huntingdonshire had developed from the medieval hall and cross-wing into the lobby-entry house of one storey and attic or two storeys and attics. It would be two or three rooms long in plan and may have had a rear kitchen wing or an outshut. These houses could have one to five hearths. The chimney stack inserted into the cross passage of the open hall had created the lobby entry. Added to this main range would be a kitchen wing, making a T or L plan. The rear kitchen wing with a gable-end stack and large cooking hearth may have had outshuts as service rooms or dairies. Medieval houses continued to be added to in piecemeal fashion and in accordance with whatever could be afforded. Medieval stone frequently found its way into chimney building: a good example of this can be seen in Wornditch, Kimbolton, where a new kitchen chimney stack was built against the frame of an older building. Against this kitchen wing is a newly built range with a back-to-back two-flue chimney stack (Fig 11.6).

Chimney stacks

There was clearly a desire for comfort in the 17th century, which may have been deterred by the 'chimney tax'. Samuel Pepys refers to resentment felt against the 'chimney men' who had right of entry to inspect hearths during daylight hours. There is no evidence for hearths being blocked in the 1664 tax return. The survey of chimneys in the Huntingdonshire Hearth Tax returns broadly indicates that most householders were living in traditional buildings derived from the medieval hall plan. They had one or two hearths, with a smaller number having three to five hearths, depending on the house size and type of chimney. The one- and two-hearth households most probably had timber-framed chimneys or smoke bays, and were without chamber hearths. More than three hearths in a house possibly indicated that there was a brick chimney stack with a hall chamber hearth, and there could be multiples of this form in larger houses.

The general desire for display, innovation, and some conformity in 17th-century building can be seen in the different forms of chimney stacks. In large houses chimney stacks had a hierarchical significance: those built for display clearly identified the most important rooms of the house, the hall or a parlour cross-wing. The functional kitchen hearth frequently terminated the kitchen end or wing

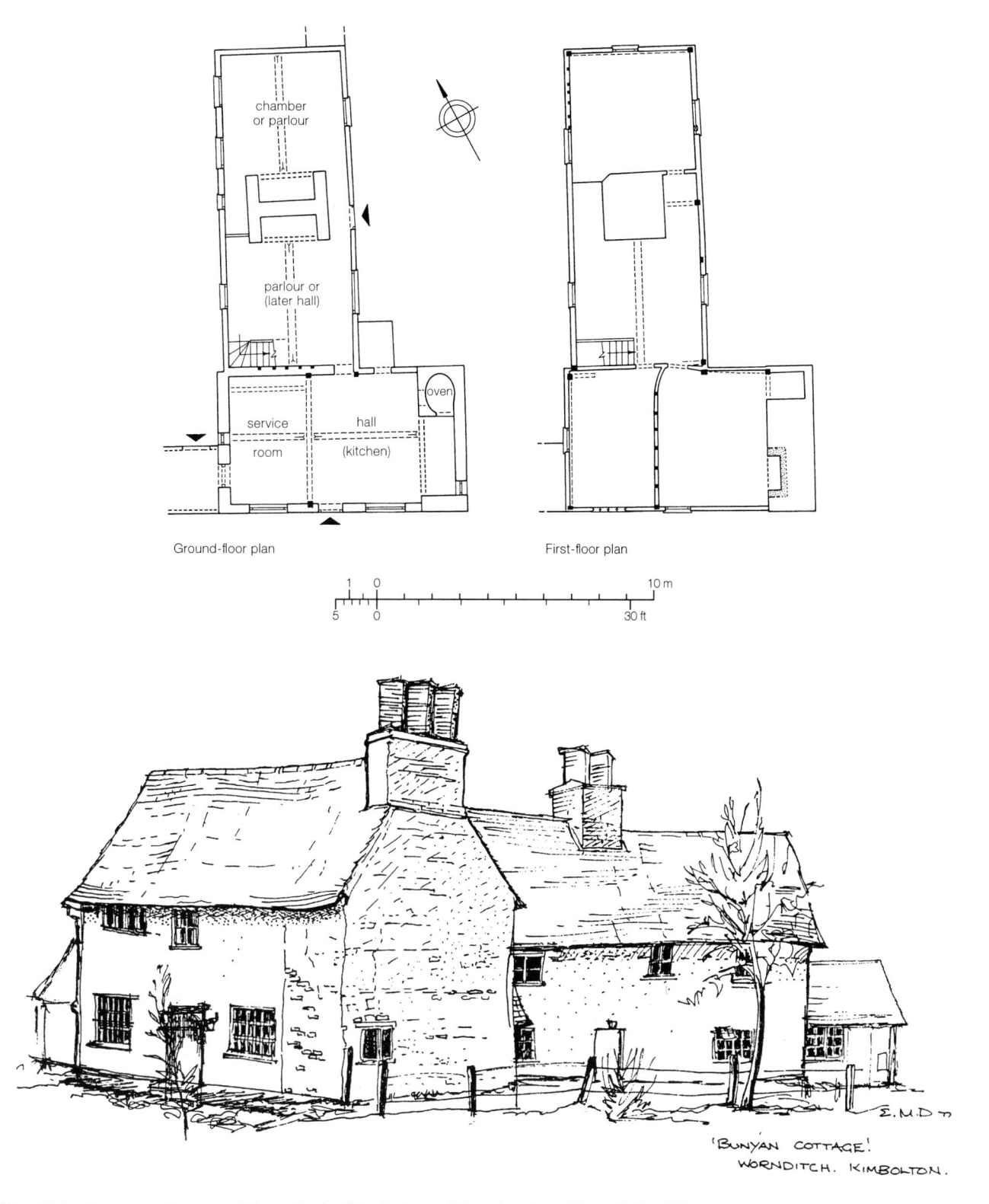

Fig 11.6 Bunyan Cottage, Wornditch, Kimbolton, Huntingdonshire. © E M Davis

and was generally a large, single stack, possibly combined with a loft for smoking bacon. Manor Farm at Alconbury has three types of brick stack: the parlour wing with a huge side stack terminated by co-joined diagonal shafts, a large multiple hall stack, and a tall simple rear kitchen stack (RCHME 1926).

Daniel Defoe's account of the hurricane in 1703, when numerous chimney stacks were blown down over the country, provides us with the terms that were used for the hearth and the chimney: a chimney has a flue from one hearth, a number of chimneys co-joined form a stack, and the shafts on the stacks are funnels (Defoe 1704). The most elaborate of

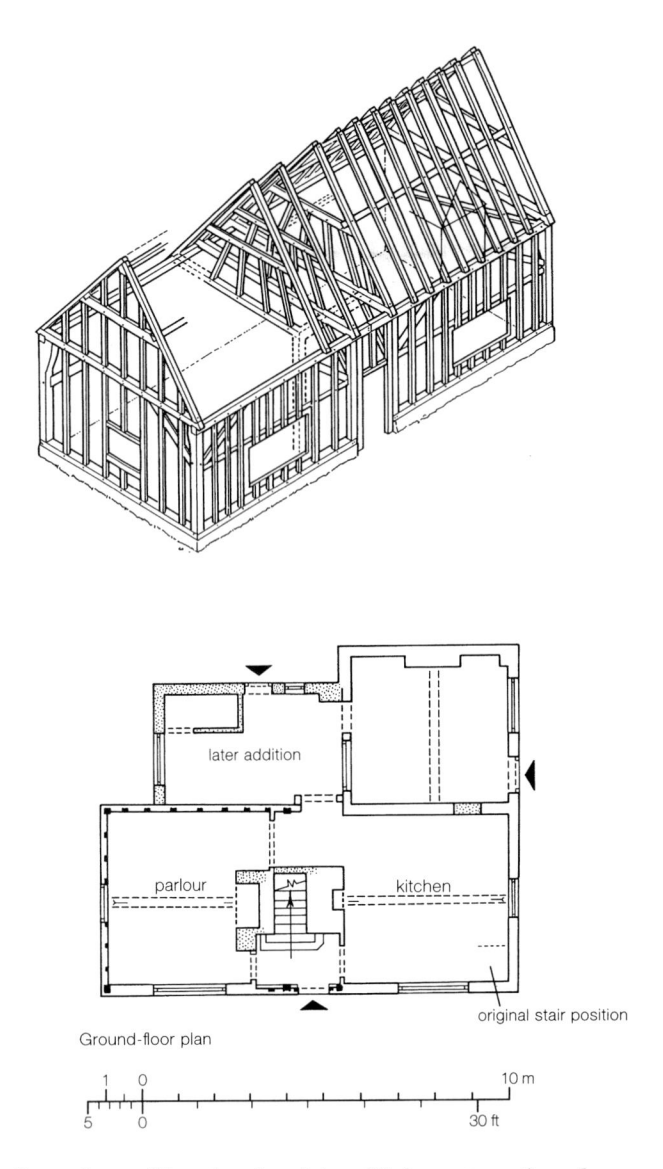

Fig 11.7 Highbury, Great Staughton, Huntingdonshire, 17th-century farmhouse with integral framed chimney. © E M Davis

houses in Huntingdonshire is Toseland Hall, a symmetrically planned lodge built for the merchant Sir Nicholas Luke who died in 1613, which displays a forest of 'funnels' (*VCH* 1926–36).

The earliest chimneys that survive in Huntingdonshire, apart from the 12th-century wall chimney of Hemmingford Grey Manor, date from the early 16th century. They are octagonal in plan, and the shaft has a cap that is sometimes crenellated. This form of shaft can be grouped on the chimney stack and easily counted by the tax assessor, but sometimes shafts were there for display only. Very few of these early chimneys survive today. The most common chimney of the 17th century has brick shafts set individually and diagonally on the stack. A later version of this has shafts that are grouped together or conjoined, creating an illusion of multiple flues, and certainly more than the actual number of hearths. Some of the 17th-century chimney stacks have panels for monograms and dates, while others have arches with classical details. In the northern parishes the chimneys have separate shafts of ashlar limestone with a common entablature similar to those in Stamford. The rectangular planned brick chimneys, in their plain version, have a string course at the height of the original stack with a continuation of the stack above this divided into panels of brickwork, usually terminated by a bold cornice (RCHME 1926). These rectangular-planned stacks have a definite Puritan influence, and seem to make their appearance in the mid-to late 17th century. The map of the Ramsey Estate dated 1706 for Susan and Katharine Titus shows a variety of chimneys: the side stack of Cromwell's Ramsey Abbey with a tall octagonal shaft and cap, the rebuilt stacks of Bodsey Grange in the early 17th century with diagonal shafts, and the new small farmhouses on the estate beside the windmill pumps that have a standard Puritan version of chimney stack. These last were possibly built on the new reclaimed land of the fen.

Fig 11.8 Photograph, demolition in 1936 of Hail Weston, Huntingdonshire, farmhouse with a double-framed chimney stack. CROH PH39/4. Reproduced by permission of the County Record Office Huntingdon

Occasionally, the chimney stack is sited outside the building as a side stack. There are examples in Great Gransden, Houghton and Easton where they were clearly added to existing small buildings, and there was a fine example of a building now demolished at Catworth belonging to a yeoman farmer, already described (see Fig 11.5).

There are several examples of timber-framed chimneys with cobble or stone hearth backs. They were inserted into existing buildings with a single and occasionally a double back-to-back hearth. Some were framed independently within a purpose-built chimney bay, open to the rafters. Some chimney bays served as the chimney. None of these timber-framed chimneys had chamber hearths. The framed chimney generally terminated at the roof collars and a brick stack was built above the collar and purlin. There must have been examples where the frame of the chimney projected beyond the roof. A fine house with beautifully moulded ceiling beams in Kimbolton has a timber-framed hearth, possibly added to a former unheated room. In the neighbouring parish of Great Staughton a timber frame has been constructed as part of three internal trusses providing a back-to-back chimney with a brick stack above the collars (Fig 11.7), and at Hail Weston there is an example of an independently framed double chimney, exposed while the building was being demolished (Fig 11.8).

Chimneys in the 17th-century house demonstrate the changing styles, functions and economic circumstances of the householders or owners. Few 16th-century chimneys survive in Huntingdonshire. Many late 17th- and early 18th-century chimneys have stacks that were rebuilt from soft red bricks in a simple rectangular plan, often leaving smoke-blackened rafters in the roof as evidence of their earlier form. Some of these red brick stacks may be replacements for decaying older chimneys while some could have replaced chimneys demolished by the great storm of 1703.

Acknowledgements

I would like to thank Mary Carter and Ken Sneath, co-authors of the forthcoming publication of the Huntingdonshire Hearth Tax, for sharing unpublished information with me that has helped with the interpretations I have made in this paper, and Nesta Evans for permission to use her map of the distribution of exempt households and those paying the Hearth Tax for Huntingdonshire in Cambridgeshire.

Chapter 11: Notes

1. Beford Record Office, Bedford navigation correspondence 1671–89.
2. CROH Hearth Tax returns.
3. Ibid.
4. CROH Probate inventories for Kimbolton.

12 The Hearth Tax in Warwickshire *by N W Alcock*

Introduction

Warwickshire has been picked out as the most fortunate county for Hearth Tax studies (Arkell 1986–87). It has more surviving assessments than any other county: complete returns for six years and a large part of two more – all in virtually perfect condition – and it has extensive supporting evidence, such as exemption certificates.[1] However, even the Warwickshire returns have their weak points and close examination cautions against taking every name and figure in them as the whole truth (Arkell 2003).

The following analysis aims to provide an overview of 17th-century Warwickshire society as revealed by the Hearth Tax, and also to move from the general to the particular, identifying individual houses (either as standing buildings or as drawings) that can be matched with their Hearth Tax entries, and so give actuality to the raw data of the assessments. The underlying implication that the number of hearths is a surrogate for wealth has been carefully examined by Husbands (1992), who concludes that the assumption is valid, though it needs to be applied with caution. In particular, he does not indicate the extent to which regional variations in living standards may affect the correlation on a national scale. The proportion of houses with specific numbers of hearths varies greatly in different parts of England. For example, in Cumberland, 90% of houses have one hearth, whereas in Sussex the corresponding figure is 33% (Arkell 2003, 156). This must indicate either that the distribution of wealth was very variable, or that the housing aspirations of individuals with particular amounts of disposable assets might vary greatly from region to region. Although both factors may influence the quality of housing, the latter seems likely to dominate regional variation in numbers of hearths.

Statistical analysis for Warwickshire

Warwickshire was divided into the four hundreds of Hemlingford, Knightlow, Kineton and Barlichway,

Fig 12.1 Administrative divisions of 17th-century Warwickshire; the two detached portions of Kineton hundred are marked K. B = Bedworth; C = Chilvers Coton; Cd = Curdworth; Cl = Claverdon; Cov = City and County of Coventry; S = Stoneleigh. © N W Alcock

broadly located in the north-west, north-east, south-east and south-west of the county (Fig 12.1), each with four internal divisions; in addition, the borough of Warwickshire was treated as a separate division of Kineton hundred in the assessments. The large City and County of Coventry formed an enclave in the centre of Knightlow hundred and has surviving returns for 1664, of relatively poor quality, and much better ones for 1666.[2] In its agrarian economy, the county was divided between two clearly distinguished regions (eg Thirsk 1967b, 89–99; Skipp 1979, 26, 132, 152). To the south and east (broadly Kineton and Knightlow hundreds) lay the Felden, an almost treeless area dominated by open-field arable farming. The western half of the county (broadly Barlichway and Hemlingford hundreds) comprised the Forest of Arden or Arden region, well-wooded with an emphasis on pastoral farming, characterised by dispersed and hamlet settlement, assarting and medieval enclosure.

In conjunction with the Roehampton Hearth Tax Project, Arkell and the author have worked with two Warwickshire assessments, that for 1669–70 which has the highest overall number of entries, and that for 1673–74 which is nearly as full for most of the county, though it lists those paying the tax separately from those exempt, and so is less useful for topographical analysis. The maps and statistics in this chapter relate to the 1673–74 return, which has 98% of the highest total of households for the county as a whole for any year and so can be accepted as virtually equivalent to the 1669–70 master year, with very limited evasions and omissions (Arkell 1986–87).[3] It includes comments such as that for Bedworth (B on Fig 12.1) – 'In this parish there are 204 poor persons that receive collection and that live on the common'[4] – suggesting that the listing is close to comprehensive. The 1673–74 data have been combined throughout with the 1666 Coventry return, which gives the impression of being a well-taken assessment in regard both to those paying the tax and to the exempt.

Arkell (2003) has identified the percentage of houses with three or more hearths as being the statistical measure least sensitive to inadequate recording of exempt households, and the variation in this figure is examined below. However, the lower levels of society, we need to look principally at those with fewer hearths. For them, the best comparative measure appears to be the proportion of one-hearth houses, coupled, for the poorest in the county, with the proportion of exempt households.

What can be seen for Warwickshire in this information depends critically on the extent to which it is aggregated. The county as a whole included 18,303 households in 1673–74, of which 11,626 (63.5%) had one hearth. This percentage hardly varies over the four hundreds, ranging only from 62.2% in Knightlow to 65.5% in Hemlingford. The divisions within the hundreds are almost as uniform, but with two exceptions. The borough of Warwick and the whole City and County of Coventry have no more than 50% one-hearth households, compared to 62–70% in the other divisions. As might be expected, areas within the towns also show marked fluctuations. Thus, in Coventry, one of the rich inner-city wards has only 27% of households with one hearth, compared to 53% in an outer suburb.

Within the superficial uniformity of rural Warwickshire, individual parishes have to be examined to see the dramatic variations in housing standards, as in the proportion of one-hearth houses (Fig 12.2a). This is closely related to the proportion of exempt households (Fig 12.2b). Both show high proportions of relatively poor people concentrated in three areas: along the western side of the county, identifiable as those working for and supplying Birmingham's growing industries, in north central Warwickshire (discussed below) and in an area to the east and south-east of Warwick. This last area is something of an enigma. Its poverty is only relative, more marked in the proportion of those with only one hearth than in those excused payment at all, and may identify a group of villages still fully involved in open-field arable farming and with a relatively large number of smaller half- or quarter-yardland holdings.[5] Both maps show some parishes with particularly high proportions of one-hearth or exempt households, notably the cluster in the north-centre of the county made up of Bedworth (with the highest exempt percentage in the county) and the adjoining Chilvers Coton to its north, Exhall, Foleshill and Walsgrave to its south. As discussed in more detail below, they formed a proto-industrial community using the resources of the North Warwickshire coalfield.

The third map shows the percentages of houses with three or more hearths (Fig 12.2c). Much of the county is relatively uniform at around 20%, but the high and low areas are essentially the inverse of the map of one-hearth houses, low in the north-west and east-centre, and high in the south and, surprisingly, in an area north and west of Coventry. The patchwork of areas of relative prosperity and higher living standards reveals the fine texture of Warwickshire lifestyles.

Turning to the opposite end of society, the statistics for substantial houses have been examined at two levels. The first map (Fig 12.3a) identifies the elite at parish level. In other studies, ten hearths has been used to indicate this section of society (eg Harrington *et al* 2000, map 6), but a consideration of the evidence for Warwickshire has pointed to houses with between eight and nineteen hearths as making up the most informative grouping. They are not plotted as percentages, but rather as the number of such houses in each parish, so that the distribution is not influenced by the proportion of exempt households. Of the 235 parishes in Warwickshire, only 109 have houses with ten hearths or more, but 145 are included if eight hearths is taken as the determining level. Furthermore, many gentry and a few esquires occupied houses with eight or nine hearths, including such local notables as Francis Gramer of Mancetter Manor, with nine hearths. Thus, this

108 Part 2: Regional Studies

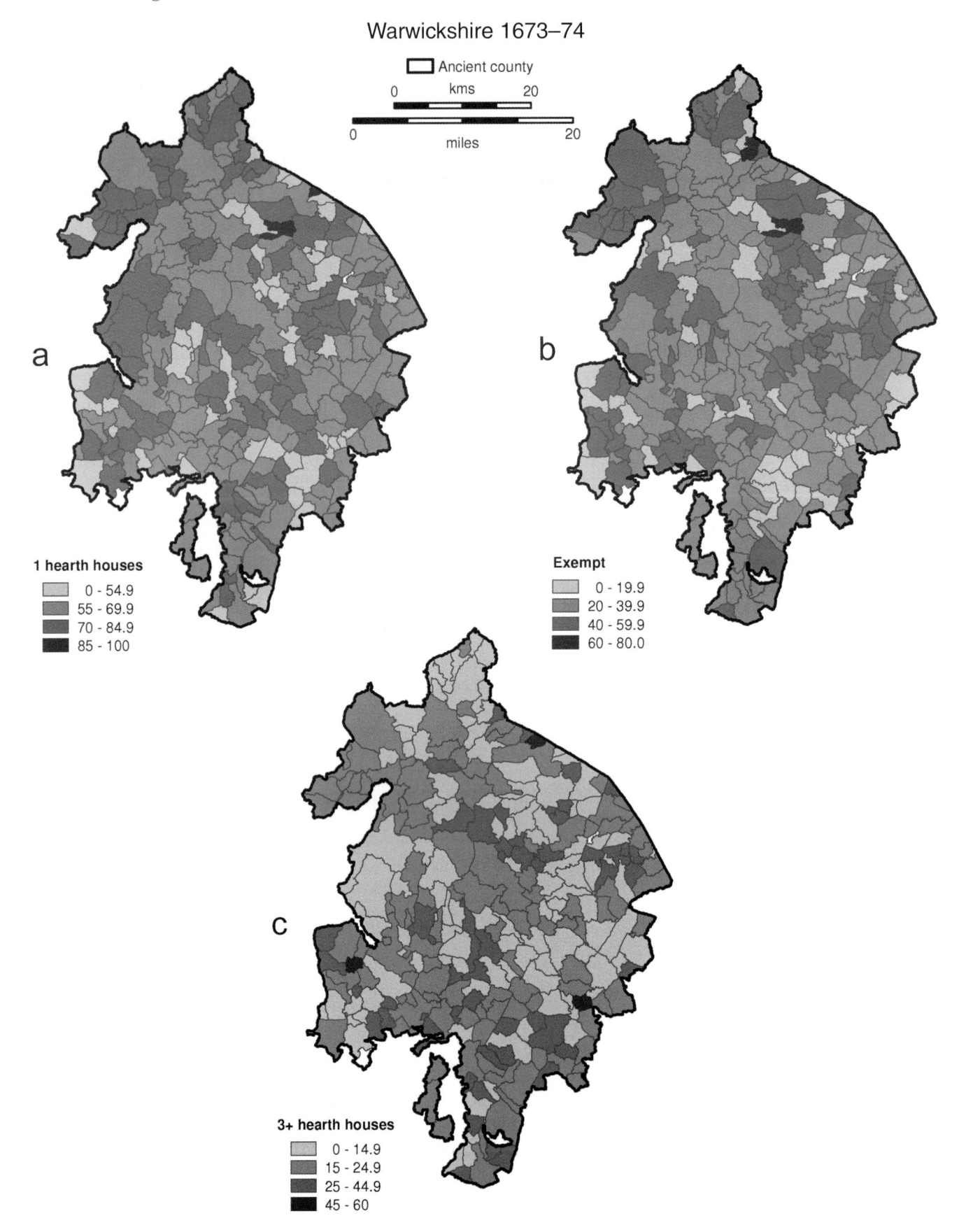

Fig 12.2 Mapping of Hearth Tax statistics for Warwickshire: percentages of total hearths in 1673–74 (from Slater forthcoming)

a Percentages of one-hearth households (including both exempt and paying), b Percentages of exempt households, c Percentages of households with three or more hearths. For the positions of Birmingham, Coventry, Stratford-upon-Avon and Warwick, see Fig 12.3. Reproduced with permission

map should point out the elite of each parish. An unexpected corollary of this mapping is the 40% of parishes whose leaders were no more than yeomen and do not feature on the map. In this respect, Warwickshire contrasts greatly to, for example, Kent (Harrington *et al* 2000) or Cambridgeshire (Evans and Rose 2000, map A9), where almost every parish had one or more house with ten or more hearths.[6]

The distribution of these substantial houses within Warwickshire is surprisingly non-uniform, with concentrations in the north and the extreme south of the county. The differences are real, even if difficult to explain. In Hemlingford hundred (north-west), 66% of parishes have one or more such houses, but in Barlichway (south-west) the corresponding figure is 38%. As specific examples, in the moderate-sized north-western parish of Curdworth (Cd on Fig 12.1), John Ridgley, esquire, and Doctor Wagstaff had houses with nine and eight hearths respectively; in the similar-sized Claverdon (Cl on Fig 12.1), the three largest houses had five hearths each, and only Mr Thomas Higgins was dignified with a specific status.

The concentration in the south corresponds approximately to the Jurassic belt, in which stone was the dominant building material (Fig 12.4; Wood-Jones 1963). It may be that the use of stone encouraged the provision of additional fireplaces, so that a house in this region might have eight or nine hearths, when a similar building in the timber-framing area would only have had four or five. If confirmed, this suggestion would associate the houses with relatively large numbers of hearths with a difference in the character of the buildings, rather than in the social structure of the area, as seems possibly to underlie the concentration in the north-west of the county.

This map shows one other notable feature, an urban emphasis. Coventry, Warwick, Birmingham and Stratford-upon-Avon have respectively 50, 32, 14 and 11 substantial houses. The names of their owners reveal a social mixture. Taking examples from the largest group, those in Coventry, it can be seen that they were partly urban gentry like Sir Richard Hopkins living in Palace Yard, Earl Street (sixteen hearths) – and one more 'in his hall which he refuseth to pay for', surely a surviving open hearth;[7] partly the urban professionals and merchants like Alderman Billers in Broadgate, a mercer whose estate was valued at £3300 in 1676 (9 hearths: Alcock 1996, 11, 17); partly also the tenants of a particularly urban phenomenon, the grand inn, such as the Star in Earl Street, where John Lax, described as 'innholder' in his 1688 probate inventory, was charged for fifteen hearths.[8]

Beyond this swathe of gentry houses, Warwickshire society included another layer – the great houses. These have been defined (as elsewhere: Evans and Rose 2000; Harrington *et al* 2000) as those with twenty or more hearths, running up to the 70 hearths of Lord Leigh at Stoneleigh Abbey (the largest in the county) and the 51 of the Earl of Craven at Combe Abbey (Fig 12.3b). This select group of 35 houses included essentially all of the nobility and the knights and some of the esquires, such as Henry Ferrers at Baddesley Clinton and his cousin John at Tamworth Castle, both with twenty hearths. But the map has one or two surprises. In Warwick is Lord Brooke at the Castle and Sir Henry Puckering at the Priory,[9] but also Mr Moses Holloway in High Street. He was the keeper of the Swan Inn, clearly the finest in the county, with twenty hearths and 34 bays of building when it was burnt to the ground in 1694 (Farr 1992, 137). This example substantiates the tendency noted above for substantial houses to be concentrated in the towns, and for inns in particular to have large numbers of hearths.

The distribution of the great houses seen in Figure 12.3b is no less enigmatic than that on some of the other maps, with concentrations in the south-west and north-west of the county, and a virtual blank to the east. Although the presence of one great house and its estate is likely to inhibit the existence of another very close to it, this cannot explain the large blank area east of Warwick and Coventry, measuring some 16km (10 miles) broad by 48km (30 miles) long. Although this does correspond quite closely to the Felden area of the county, it is difficult to see why this agricultural micro-economy should have prevented the development of great estates.

Individuals and their houses

The second part of this paper examines the reality behind these statistics. What did one-, two- or three-hearth houses look like, who lived in them and how did they live? It is possible to use architectural evidence to determine the number of hearths that an individual house seems to have had, but this can easily lead to error, with hearths having been added, or sometimes removed, at uncertain times. Thus, it is much more satisfactory to match actual houses with their Hearth Tax assessment. This is easy at the level of the great houses, and some of the gentry houses. The owners are well known and their residences feature in guidebooks. Below that level, some special cases can be identified, particularly parsonages (though they have often been rebuilt), also perhaps mills or inns, and of course houses whose history has been investigated in detail (see, for example, the case studies in Alcock 2003). Houses in towns also tend to be more readily identified than those in the country; tax assessments and rate lists may well be taken topographically, and title deeds often describe property in terms of its abuttals.

Study of the standing 17th-century buildings of the county as a whole suggests a reasonable uniformity, with the great majority built in timber framing, apart from the south-eastern fringe (Fig 12.4). Thus the identification of some houses provides pointers to the context of similar examples. A number of Warwickshire parishes have late 17th-century maps, but they mostly lack further documentary evidence. However, in a couple of places in Warwickshire con-

110 *Part 2: Regional Studies*

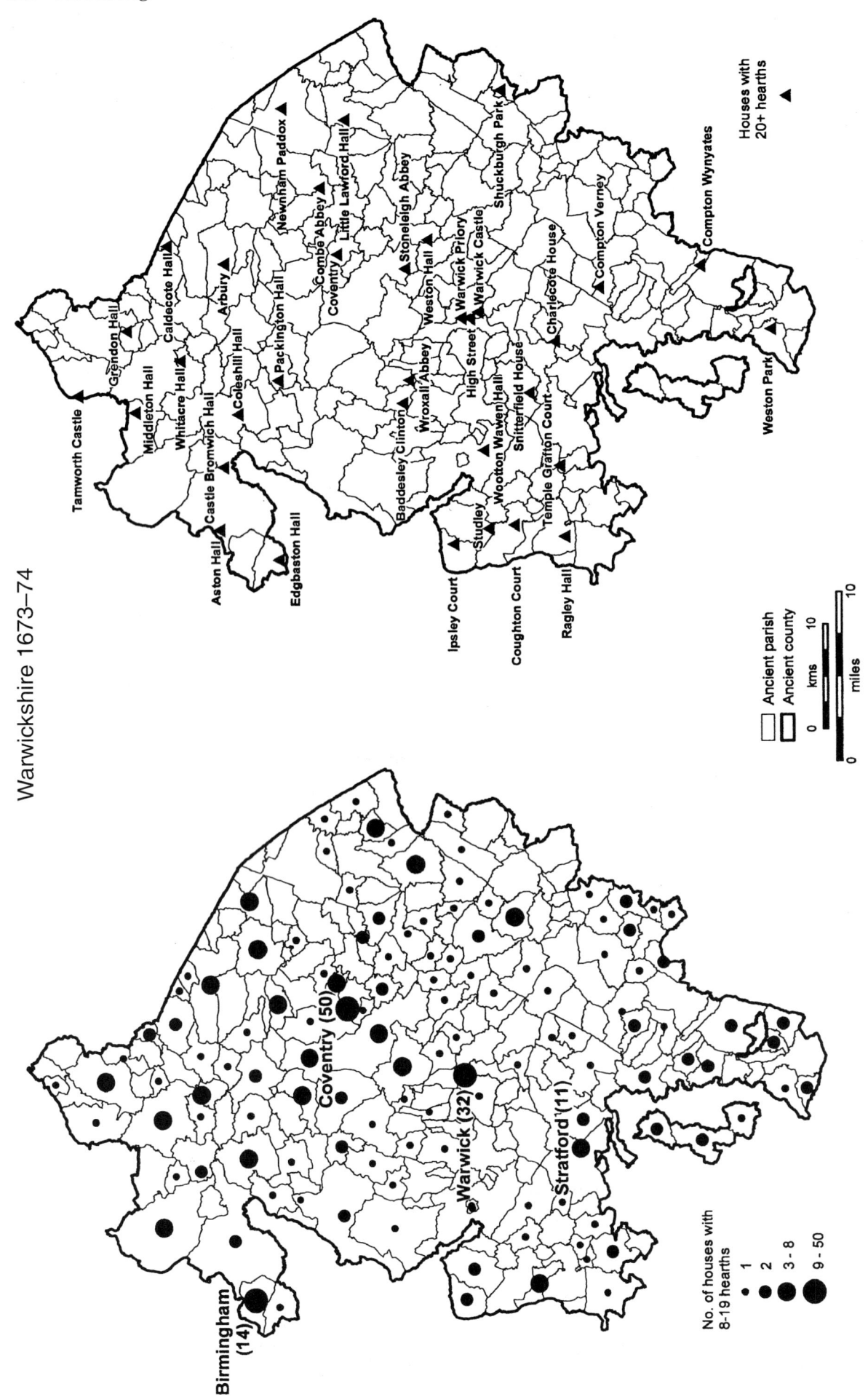

Fig 12.3 Mapping of Hearth Tax data for gentry and great houses in Warwickshire (from Slater forthcoming)

a Numbers of houses in each parish with eight to nineteen hearths. For Birmingham, Coventry, Stratford-upon-Avon and Warwick, all wards are combined.
b Individual houses with twenty or more hearths. Reproduced with permission

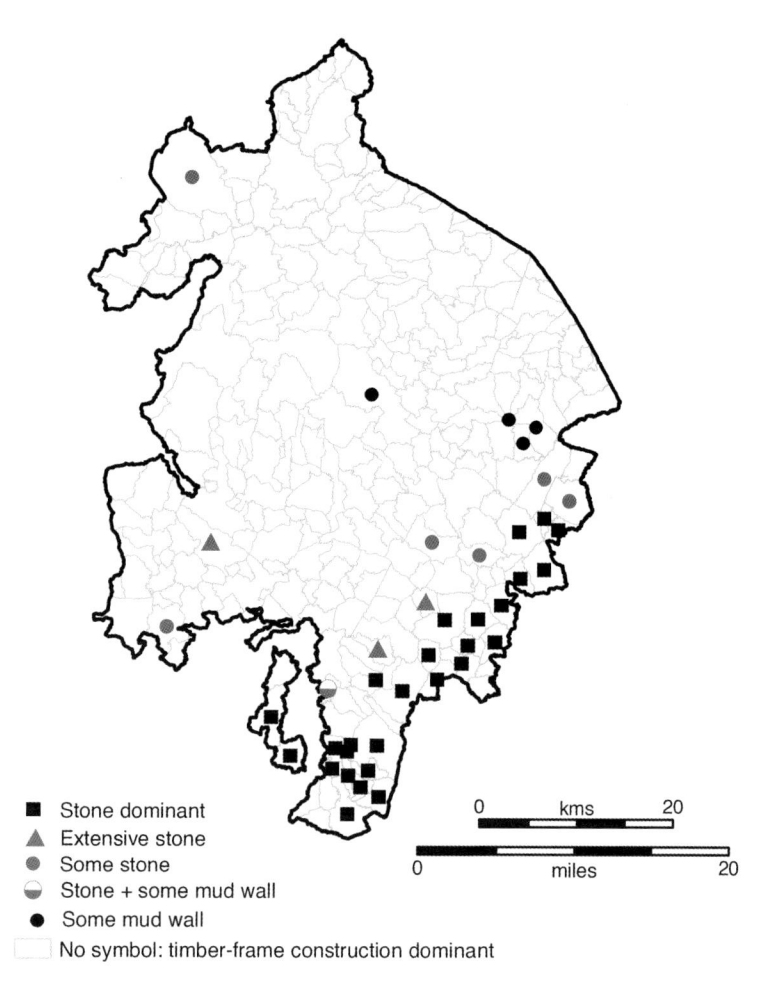

Fig 12.4 Building materials in Warwickshire (from Slater forthcoming). Those areas dominated by timber framing are left blank. Reproduced with permission

temporary sources can be used to go further, both to locate the houses listed in the assessments and to identify the social position of their occupiers. A magnificent map was made of the village of Chilvers Coton in north Warwickshire (C on Fig 12.1) in 1684, and this is accompanied by a series of surveys identifying both the landholdings and the household structure.[10] Material evidence from the 17th century is, however, almost non-existent, as the village is situated on the outskirts of Nuneaton and has been swallowed up in the growth of the town; there is only one blurred photograph to represent all its timber-framed houses (Veasey 1984, 20). The second is Stoneleigh in the centre of the county (S on Fig 12.1), which retains many early standing buildings. It is recorded fully in maps of 1597 and 1766, and is covered by extensive longitudinal data series, allowing the Hearth Tax entries to be identified with mapped holdings. The parish, its buildings and documents have been very extensively studied and it has been possible to correlate most of the buildings with their Hearth Tax entries, and in many cases with room-by-room probate inventories as well (Alcock 1993).

These two parishes also have the advantage of exemplifying the differences in social structure found in the county as mapped in Figures 12.2a and b. The inhabitants of Stoneleigh were modestly prosperous, with only 22% exempt households and 65% living in one-hearth houses. Those in Chilvers Coton were among the poorest in the county, with 81% of one-hearth houses and 55% exempt. They also show the variations that can arise on a micro-scale. Chilvers Coton was made up of four parts: Coton village itself, which was extensively industrialised, Griff and Woodland, which were mainly farming communities (though Griff later became another industrial village), and Arbury, with one house only, the Hall itself. Both Griff and Woodland have lower levels of exemption, 55% and 29% respectively, compared to 62% in Coton itself. Surprisingly, though, Woodland had no less than 87% of its households with only one hearth, as against 73% in Coton.

Chilvers Coton

The major documentary evidence for Chilvers Coton is of three types: the map of 1684, which gives convincing thumbnail sketches of the houses,[11] surveys of tenants and their holdings, and the most remarkable item, a full listing of

112 *Part 2: Regional Studies*

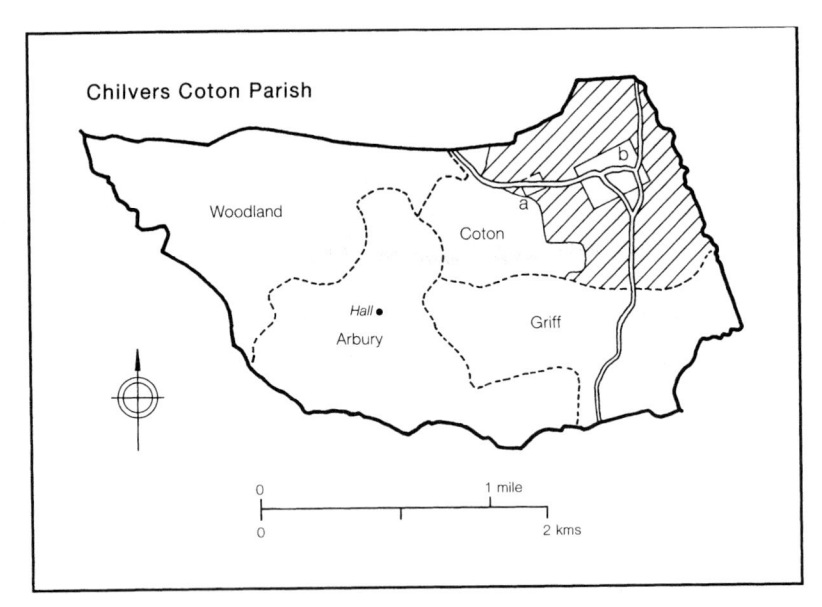

Fig 12.5   The parish of Chilvers Coton, Warwickshire, in the 17th century, showing its administrative divisions and the location of the main settlements of Coton and Griff. Boxes indicate the approximate positions of Figs 12.7 and 12.8. © N W Alcock

each of the 175 households with the names, ages and occupations of all the family members.[12] Thus, a better picture of these families can be obtained than for anywhere else in the county – indeed it is one of only a handful of such listings for the country as a whole.[13] About half of the 175 householders can be matched directly with the names in the 1674 Hearth Tax, so it is possible to correlate occupation and life cycle position with standing in the assessment. The listing also illuminates the underlying cause of the poverty of the parish. It was an incipient industrial community, containing fifteen colliers working the local coal outcrop, a locksmith, three masons, eight nailers, seven rake makers, three sawyers, seven silk weavers, two tailors and two other weavers. Virtually all of these are to be found among the exempt one-hearth households.

Of course, the parish also included all the normal range of occupations to be found in an agricultural community. Starting at the top was the landowner, Sir Richard Newdigate at Arbury Hall (Fig 12.6). He had 32 hearths (Fig 12.3) and a 'family' of 36 people at the Hall (Table 12.1). Serving him, his wife and their seven daughters,[14] were sixteen men including two bailiffs, the butler, cook, brewer, postillion, shepherd and wainman, and eleven women including ladies' maids, nursemaids and two dairymaids. Moving into the village, standing near the cross (Fig 12.7) were two relatively substantial houses. Henry Baker, a young husbandman farming half a yardland (about 6 ha or 15 acres), had a hall and cross-wing house, but apparently only one hearth;[15] his household comprised only himself, his wife and two young children (Table 12.2). Across the street, John Parker, gentleman, lived in one of the largest buildings shown on the map, an L-shaped house, with three hearths; he owned both the adjoining cottage and his own farm of 1¼ yardlands (12–16 ha or 30–40 acres) and had a large household by village standards, with both a man and a woman as live-in servants, as well as his wife, son and daughter (Table 12.2). The other houses on the north of the street all had one hearth, owned respectively by a gardener, shoe maker,[16] blacksmith and rake maker, locksmith and carpenter (William Hough, Samuel Brown, George Wagster junior, Samuel Suffolk and Richard Sutton). The map shows one fewer house than the number of households listed, and from the names on the map it seems that Brown and Wagster (the blacksmith and the rake maker) were sharing.

In the poorest part of the village, along the lane leading to Heath End (Fig 12.8), was a group of labourers' cottages. The corner house (top left) was shared by Thomas Abbotts, nailer, and Ann White. She was an elderly widow living on her own, perhaps in the cross-bay that the map sketch suggests; he had his wife and two boys (stepsons?) in the house (Table 12.2). Two more widows and two labourers lived down the lane opposite in the typical small houses shown on the map, so this was a very homogeneous area. It is notable that only three of those living nearby can be identified in 1674, Francis Sergeant, a silkweaver, and two labourers, William Mortemer and William Randle (with only himself and his wife making up the household, see Table 12.2); each of them had a single hearth and was certified as exempt. Such a rapid turnover is perhaps to be expected at this end of the social scale and the possible bias introduced needs to be taken into account in comparing sources like these separated by a number of years.

Fig 12.6 Arbury Hall, Warwickshire, in the early 18th century (from a drawing in the Aylesford Collection, Birmingham City Archives). Reproduced with permission

Table 12.1   Household of Sir Richard Newdigate (from WCRO CR136/v.12)

Name	Position	Age	Name	Position	Age
Sir Richard Newdigate	Baronet	40	Men		
The Lady Mary N	(wife)	38	Robert Johnson	[unstated]	42
Mrs Amphillis	(daughter)	15	Ja: Dowell	bailiff	31
Mrs Mary	(daughter)	09	Sam: Moore	bailiff	22
Mrs Frances	(daughter)	07	Geo: Nott	butler	28
Mrs Ann	(daughter)	05	James Lines	cook	27
Mrs Jane	(daughter)	03	Gervas Whithead	gardener	35
Mrs Eliz	(daughter)	02	Tho: Tomson	brewer	22
Mrs Julian	(daughter)	01	Richard Drakford	coachman	37
Mr Scott Mr A & F: L: l: p:*	[unstated]	26	Jo: Clark	postillian	19
Women			Jos: Dagle	under gardner	18
Mrs Sarah Searle	[unstated]	28	Tho: Bolt	foot boy	17
Jane Sanders	ladys maid	19	Wm Clark	sheepherd	60
Grissell Armstrong	Mrs Am: maid	28	Jo: Stones	husb'	38
Margaret Pace	nurse maid	37	Edw: Brian	wainman	38
Kath: Thissell	under nurse maid	31	Robt Serg^t	[unstated]	17
Jane Whistons	chambermaid	31	Edw: White	[unstated]	14
Isabell Bates	chambermaid	20			
Mary Clements	under cooke	22			
Margaret Johnson	dairy maid	40			
Lidia Beamish	under dairy maid	22			
Sarah Johnson	middle maid	22			

* The name of Mr Scott is followed by a series of undeciphered abbreviations.

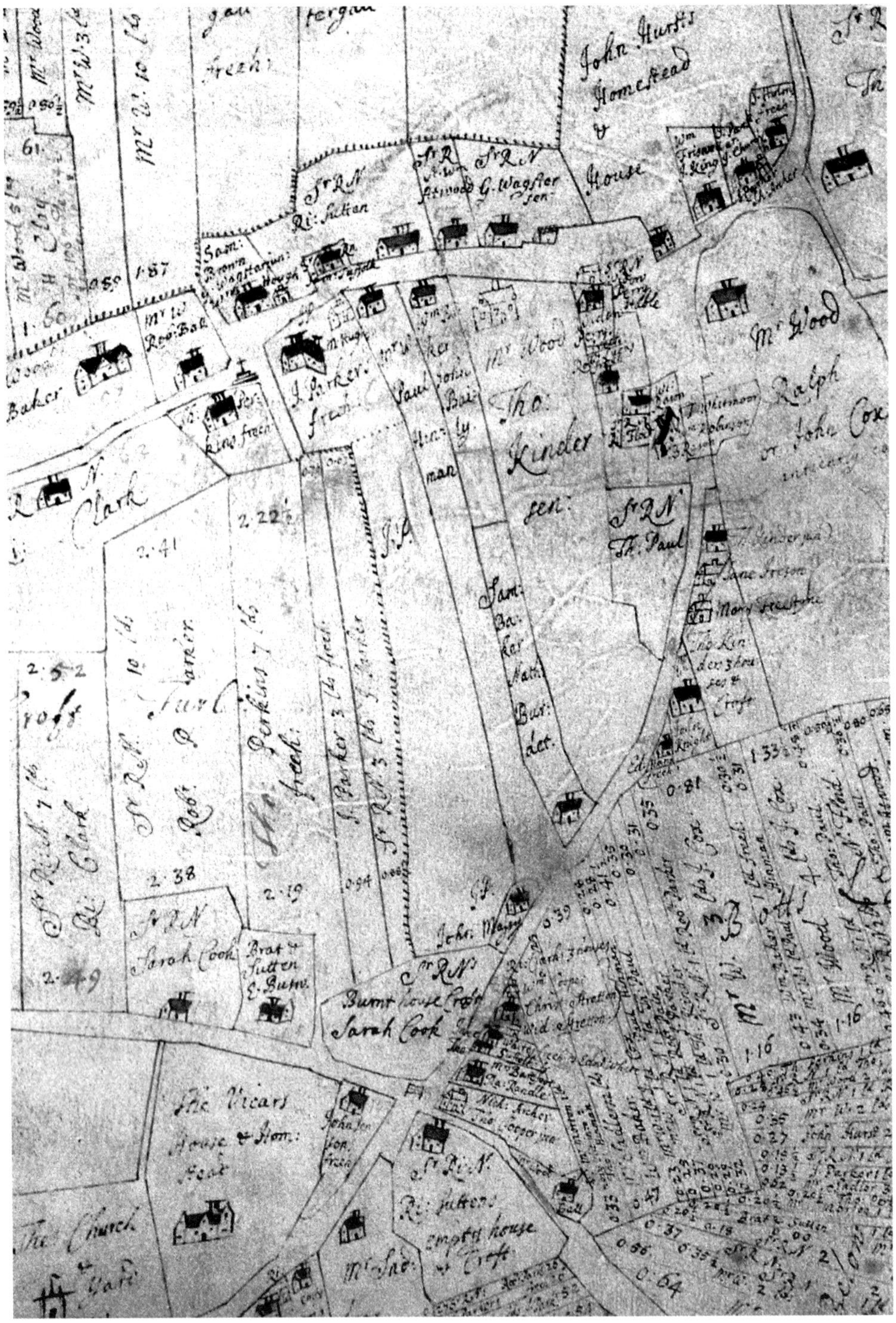

Fig 12.7 Chilvers Coton village (Warwickshire) in 1684, area A (extract from WCRO CR136/M14). Reproduced with permission

Stoneleigh

Although the Chilvers Coton map gives an indication of the character of these poor houses, it is only when a whole group of buildings can be matched with their Hearth Tax assessments that we can confidently identify what sort of house had a particular number of hearths. This has been possible for the parish of Stoneleigh, just south of Coventry, because of the survival of both extensive estate documentation and of some 60 houses dating from the 17th century or earlier (Alcock 1993); the assessments for some 50 of them are known.[17] Unlike Chilvers Coton, its economy was essentially agricultural, with about half the land still in open fields in 1674. The proportion of one-hearth houses (64%) is about average for the county, but it had relatively few exempt households (22%). The houses that can be identified range from those of the nobility – Stoneleigh Abbey with its 70 hearths – through minor, or not so minor, gentry houses, to the poorest single-hearth homes. Strikingly, a higher proportion of the smaller houses survive than the larger ones in the assessments, the result

The Hearth Tax in Warwickshire 115

Table 12.2 Households of Henry Baker, John Parker, Thomas Abbotts, Ann White and William Randle
(from WCRO CR136/v.12, ff 64f with sequence numbers)

Name	Position	Age	Name	Position	Age
Henry Baker (42)			Tho: Abbots (68)		
Henry Baker	husbandman	28	Thomas Abbotts	nailor	35
Mary [Baker]	his wife		Ann	his wife	38
Mary [Baker]	([presumably	6	Peeter Smyth	(stepson?)	14
Ann [Baker]	(daughters]	2	Edward	(stepson?)	12
Mr Jo: Parker (35)			Ann Whites (67)		
John Parker	g[ent]	56	Ann White	widow	62
Ann [Parker]	his wife	46	Wm Randles (88)		
Ann [Parker]	his daughter	15	William Randle	labourer	60
John Parker	[presumably son]	5	Katherine	his wife	50
Margaret Attwood		34			
Henry King		18			

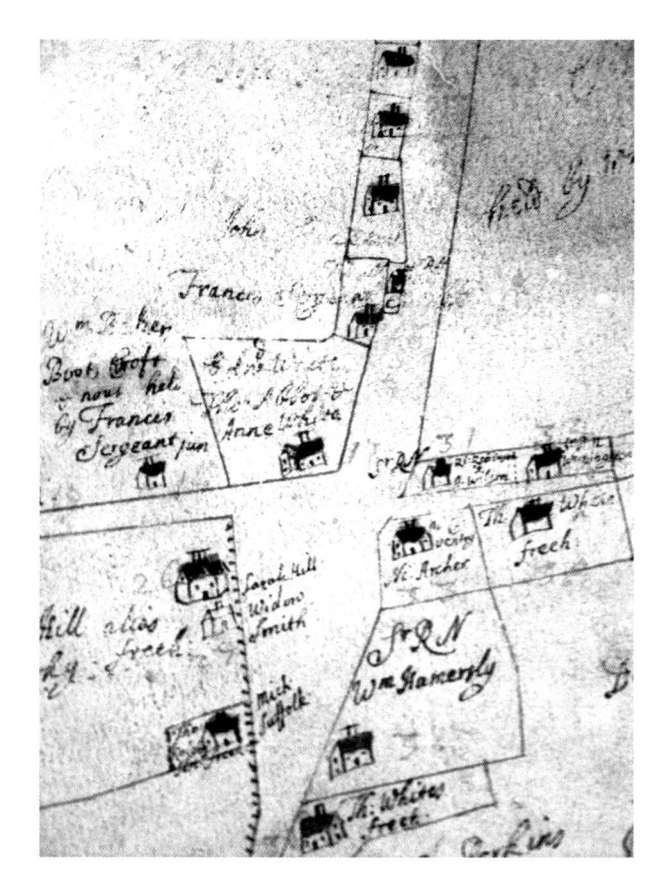

Fig 12.8 Chilvers Coton village (Warwickshire) in 1684, area B (extract from WCRO CR136/M14). Reproduced with permission

probably of the later policy of the Stoneleigh estate towards its housing stock.

At the top of local society (apart from Lord Leigh) stood Christopher Leigh, esquire, great-uncle to Baron Leigh; he leased a moderate-sized farm in the village (30 ha or 73 acres) from the estate, though he had considerable other financial resources. He lived in Manor Farm (Fig 12.9), which had nine hearths and twenty rooms (according to his 1673 probate inventory). He had enlarged the house by the addition of a parlour wing (on the right-hand side in Fig 12.9) in 1664, when the Hearth Tax records four hearths 'in building'. Thus, the house corresponds precisely to the group of gentry houses with eight to nineteen hearths discussed above. Interestingly, later in the century the house proved too large and was divided between two tenants of more modest status.

None of the three other 'gentry' houses (eight hearths or more) in the parish survives, and the next largest houses now standing had three hearths. Typical of these is 11–12 Coventry Road, Stoneleigh (Fig 12.10), a 24 ha (60 acre) farm with two hearths in the house, and one in a detached kitchen (since demolished).[18] The village inn was a substantial building with some fourteen rooms, but it also had only three hearths – clearly not comparable to the great urban inns. Houses with two hearths can be illustrated by that of a slightly smaller farm (10 ha or 25 acres), new-built earlier in the 17th century (Fig 12.11); presumably the first hearth served the hall/kitchen in the main range and the second the parlour in the wing.

Below this level, everyone obviously had only one hearth, and the distinction between those exempt and those paying the tax is not obvious in their houses – and often varied from assessment to assessment. Among the numerous examples are found smaller farms, for example, one of 20 ha (50 acres: two bays – Fig 12.12a), craftsmen's houses, including those of a shoe maker (three bays – Fig 12.12b) and a carpenter: all these paid the tax. A medieval two-bay cruck house (Fig 12.12c) without any significant landholding was occupied by Francis Whitmore, probably a labourer, exempt from payment. The final example (Fig 12.12d), a medieval box-frame house reconstructed in the 17th century, was occupied by a fuller in 1612, when it was associated with a landholding of about 10 ha (25 acres), but in 1664 when Katherine Dyto succeeded her husband Francis, the landholding was apparently reassigned to another

Fig 12.9   Manor Farm, Stoneleigh, Warwickshire, with nine hearths in 1674. © N W Alcock

Fig 12.10   11–12 Coventry Road, Stoneleigh, Warwickshire, with three hearths in 1674. © N W Alcock

tenant, and she was always recorded as exempt from the tax on her one hearth.[19]

The smallest of these standing buildings sometimes come close to the minimum quality for which longevity can be expected, but their character is clear. The single-hearth houses generally had two rooms in plan, sometimes three, though it should be remembered that the ten almshouses were built with one-up, one-down plans (Alcock 1993, 141).

As well as identifying standing buildings in the Hearth Tax listing, the Stoneleigh evidence allows it to be related to 62 room-by-room probate inventories from the period 1660–1700 (Alcock 1993; here collected in Table 12.3).[20] The overall impression given by the table is of a close and believable correlation between the number of hearths and the number of rooms, though with too few examples of houses with upwards of six hearths for meaningful statistics. The evidence is clearly biased in one direction – proportionately fewer of the smaller than the larger houses are recorded; this undoubtedly reflects the general bias of probate inventories towards the better-off.[21] However, the Stoneleigh evidence extends remarkably far down the social scale, as is demonstrated by the presence of six inventories for those exempt from the Hearth Tax. There is no reason to believe that those who entered the probate process because they had rather more worldly goods than their neighbours would automatically have larger houses.

The correlation visible in the table confirms the *a priori* expectation: the more rooms in the house,

Fig 12.11 Ivy Farm, Canley, Warwickshire, with two hearths in 1674. © N W Alcock

Fig 12.12 Warwickshire Houses with one hearth.
a Bridge Cottage, Stoneleigh
b 1–2 Coventry Road, Stoneleigh
c 3 Birmingham Road, Stoneleigh
d Fir Tree Cottage, Ashow

118 Part 2: Regional Studies

Table 12.3 Correlation of 1674 hearths and rooms in Stoneleigh probate inventories (data from Alcock 1993)

Hths	Tot	Id	2	3	4	5	6	7	8	9	10	>10	Room Mean	Mean (£)
1E	36	6	1	1	3	1							3.8	49
1	68	20		3	5	10		2	(1)*				4.7	69
2	25	15				5	4	2	4	2	2		7.5	146
3	16	8				1	2	2	1			13, 17	8.6	148
4	3	4+					1		1	2			8.0	281
6	3	1										11	11	273
7	3	1							1				8	551
8	2	0												
9	1	2+									1	20	15	1,432
10	1	2+										12, 14, 16	14	255
70	1											102	102	16,471

Tot = Number of houses with the stated number of hearths. Id = number with identified inventories. Mean (£) relates to the gross inventory value without allowance for debts.

* Known to have been rebuilt before the date of the inventory. Excluded from calculations.

+ Two separate inventories refer to the same four-, nine- and ten-hearth houses; the third ten-hearth house had this number at the date of the probate inventory in 1665 but eight hearths in 1674.

E exempt

the more hearths are provided for them. For the smaller houses, the pattern corresponds closely to that seen in the standing buildings. Houses of two or three bays with one or two bays floored (three to five rooms) had one hearth; houses with two hearths (or indeed three to four hearths) would have about eight rooms, typically representing three fully floored bays with a couple of single-storey service rooms. It is worth commenting particularly on the smallest house inventoried at this period, that of John Morice (1697). He lived in a cottage on the heath and had just a dwelling house (living room) and a 'leanto to the house', in which he slept. His inventory totaled £33, and he owed £5 in debts, but of the total, £22 was represented by debts owed to him; it was probably because of the wish to collect these debts that his estate was probated. He has to stand for the whole under-stratum of poor Warwickshire householders.

Within the county as a whole, apart perhaps from the stone-building region (see Fig 12.4), the pattern of the houses is consistent within their groups, with a clear differentiation between those with one, two, three, or more hearths; however, the one-hearth houses of the exempt appear to have differed from those paying the tax, as would be expected from the inconsistency with which people appear in either category. What varies most dramatically from area to area is the mix of larger and smaller houses, which depended on the prosperity and social structure of each parish.

Chapter 12: Notes

1 Perhaps because of the quality of the main assessments, the exemption certificates have hitherto been little used, but in the context of the impending publication of the 1669–70 return (Arkell and Alcock forthcoming), they are now being examined by Tom Arkell

2 TNA E179/259/9 (1666); E179/259/10 (1664). A much later return also survives but has not been studied: E179/259/11 part 1 (c 1680).

3 At the time of the preparation of the paper, a checked text and reliable statistics were only available for the 1672–74 return. The maps here have been prepared as part of Slater forthcoming.

4 WCRO QS11/55.

5 The emphasis on arable farming is characteristic of the Felden part of Warwickshire. The suggested economic structure of these villages is more difficult to establish.

6 The information for Kent is not precisely equivalent as, for technical reasons, it is plotted for rather larger areas.

7 TNA E179/259/9 membrane 6. This remarkable comment by the assessor or the constable seems to be unparalleled elsewhere.

8 Lichfield Joint Record Office, probate records. Coventry City Council Legal Department deed bundle 4214 (relating to 31 Earl Street and examined with kind permission of the Department) includes a lease and release of 7–8 October 1840 that describes the property as part of the former Star Inn, formerly in the tenure of John Lax, innholder; also TNA CP43/542 membrane 2, enrolled deed of 1718. The Herbert Museum, Coventry, holds four trade farthings (SH.A.953/25/1–4) that are inscribed: obverse – 'JOHN.LAX.AT.THE' with a six-pointed star

in the centre; reverse – 'I.M.L.' in the centre, circled by 'IN.COVENTRY.1659' (Huw Jones, pers. comm.). Edward Childes had the largest number of hearths in Coventry (21). He cannot be identified in other Coventry records, but on the evidence of a marginal note in a later Hearth Tax assessment (TNA E179/259/11) was probably also an innkeeper, at the Bull Inn in Smithford Street.

9   Though not Nathaniel Stoughton, esquire, at St John's House, the third large gentry house in the town, who only had seven hearths.

10 I thank Tom Arkell for drawing this notable source to my attention. He has discussed it in general terms in Arkell 1987.

11 WCRO CR/136/M14. As shown on Fig 12.5, this covers Coton but not Griff or Woodland, though all three settlements are included in the surveys.

12 The whole survey is divided into five parts, WCRO CR126, volumes **12** (census of inhabitants on 64ff), **13**, **101** (list of tenants on 23ff), **109**, **122**.

13 Gibson and Medlycot 1992. It has been convincingly suggested by Spufford (Spufford and Watt 1995, 13) that the Chilvers Coton census was inspired by Gregory King's interest in establishing the national population structure.

14 The four sons living at this date, Richard (16), Walter (13), John (12), and Gilbert (10) were perhaps away at school. For the family, see Larminie 1995, 210.

15 The apparent second cross-wing seems to be the end gable of the house, drawn facing the viewer. Henry Baker cannot be directly identified in the Hearth Tax sequence, and is probably too young to have been a tenant in 1674, but in the relevant part of the list, those houses with more than one hearth can be identified with other tenants.

16 According to the census, but called 'fidler' on the listing of tenants in WCRO CR136 volume 101.

17 The small parish of Ashow is included with Stoneleigh, as it shared the same ownership and documentation. Stoneleigh village was the largest nucleated settlement in the parish of the same name.

18 As reconstructed from the probate inventories for the house (Alcock 1993, 64–70).

19 The holding was stripped of its land at some time between 1650 and 1697, though the precise date is unknown because of the absence of estate rentals for this period (Alcock 1993, 14, 16). It is an inference that it took place when Katherine Dyto succeeded her husband.

20 Of the matched inventories, seventeen relate either to predecessors or successors of those listed in the Hearth Tax. Seven further inventories (five to eleven rooms) could not be linked to Hearth Tax entries, while one inventory has been discarded as its list of rooms appears to be incomplete. A further 33 inventories from this period do not give room names.

21 In Stoneleigh, virtually everyone was a tenant (Alcock 1993, 182), so no bias arises from the exclusion of real property from inventories.

THE NORTH

13 The East Riding of Yorkshire
by Susan and David Neave

Introduction

The historic East Riding of Yorkshire, bounded on the east by the North Sea, and on the north, west and south by the Rivers Derwent, Ouse and Humber respectively, has a physical and cultural identity that distinguishes it from the rest of Yorkshire (Neave 1998, 187–96). It consists of four main natural regions: the plain of Holderness to the east, the chalk Wolds in the centre, the Vale of Pickering to the north and the low-lying Vale of York to the west. The economy of the area in the late 17th century was based almost entirely on agriculture, as it has been throughout history. In the early 19th century H E Strickland noted: 'The surface of this Riding is little calculated for manufactures of any kind, having neither coal, nor wood for charcoal within itself, nor any rapid streams for working machinery' (Strickland 1812, 284).

Industry and commerce were confined to the towns, of which the port of Hull was the most populous in the late 17th century. Around 1370 households are recorded there in the Hearth Tax assessments which, using a multiplier of 4–5 people per household, suggests a population of between 5500 and 7000. Beverley, the tenth largest provincial town in England in the late 14th century, had 620 households, and Bridlington with its port at Bridlington Quay had a total of 350. There was a handful of smaller market towns, including Hedon, Howden and Pocklington, but the bulk of the riding's population lived in nucleated settlements with fewer than 60 households. The mostly thinly populated areas were the Vale of Pickering and the high Wolds. In the early 18th century Daniel Defoe recorded that the central part of the East Riding was 'very thin of towns, and consequently of people, being overspread with Woulds' (quoted in Woodward 1985, 54). The most populous townships were north and west of Hull, in north and south Holderness, and in the west of the riding along the River Ouse (Neave and Neave 1996, 44–45).

The East Riding has a paucity of surviving smaller domestic buildings from before the mid-18th century. There are a number of fine Elizabethan and Jacobean country houses and manor houses, but only a handful of farmhouses and cottages that can with any certainty be dated before the late 17th century. Sources of information on the houses that have gone are limited, and the Hearth Tax assessments of the 1670s therefore provide an invaluable record. Few homes will have been unrecorded by the assessors, since even the poorest cottager would have had a fire.

Hearth Tax assessments

For the East Riding as a whole surviving Hearth Tax assessments are confined to the years 1670–73.[1] For the purposes of analysis the assessment for Michaelmas 1672 is the best preserved, although it does not include Hull and Hullshire. The document comprises 117 parchment membranes, arranged by wapentake, with single columns of names written on both sides of each membrane. There are generally two lists for each township, the first giving the names of those liable to pay tax followed by the names of those discharged from payment. Against each name is the number of hearths for which that householder would normally be liable. As might be expected, the majority of those discharged had only one hearth, although there are exceptions. The gaps in the 1672 return can be filled by reference to other years, or by reference to the paper books used for enrolling the 1673 assessment. These survive for several wapentakes, and show almost no variation from the 1672 assessment.

For many places there are also exemption certificates of a similar date.[2] These often distinguish between those exempt because they were not liable to pay poor or church rates, or because they paid no more than £1 annual rent for the house they occupied, or because they had personal estate worth £10 or less, and those who were paupers, that is, in receipt of parish relief. This is especially useful as there is sometimes no record of the latter in the Hearth Tax returns. The exemption certificates also contain references to almshouses, demolished houses or chimneys, and newly built houses. For one township, Scampston, the destruction of thirteen houses by fire is recorded.

Population decline

A comparison between the 1672 Hearth Tax figures (households) and the 1743 and 1764 archiepiscopal visitation returns (families) indicates that the population of the majority of East Riding villages declined to a marked extent between these dates (Neave 1990, 52). The township of Watton, in the Hull Valley to the north of Beverley, provides a well-documented example. A former monastic estate, it belonged to the Earl of Winchilsea in the late 17th century. A map dated 1707 (Fig 13.1a), but described as having been drawn from an old survey, shows the nucleus of the village comprising two streets forming an L-shape, with houses lining both sides of each street. In total the map shows about 70 houses in Watton (including outlying farms), of which 48 were

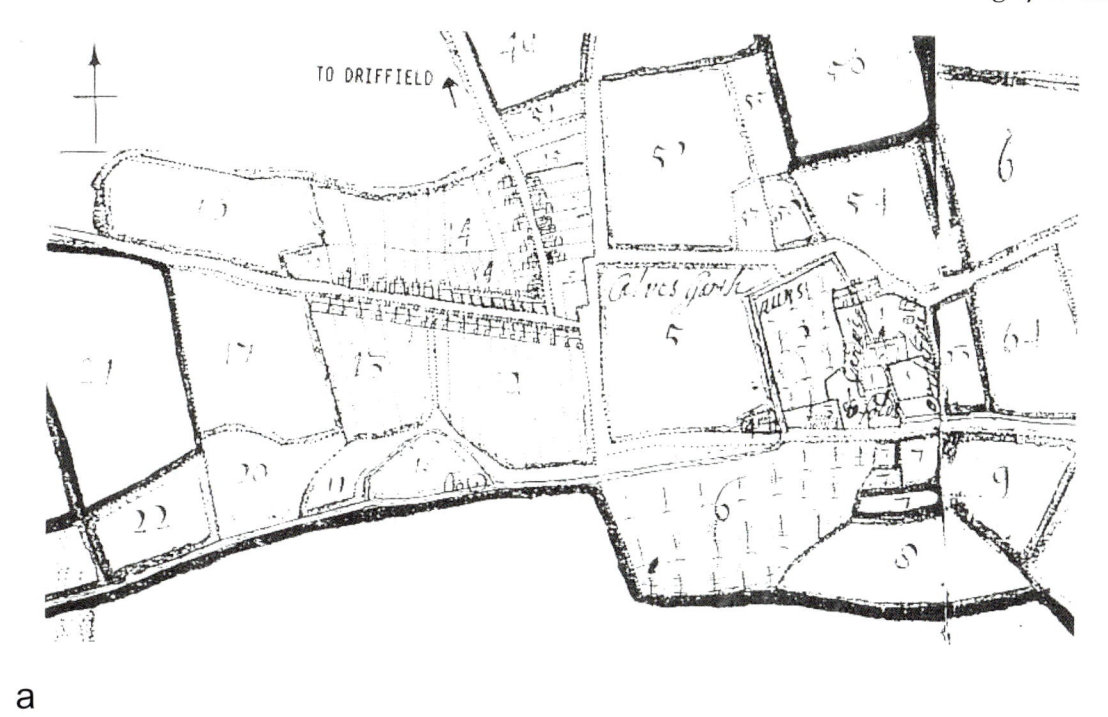

Fig 13.1 Maps of Watton, East Riding of Yorkshire, showing decrease in housing

a 1707, but drawn from an earlier survey
b 1761
(East Riding Archive Office DDRI Acc 2980)

in the village nucleus. This corresponds well with the Hearth Tax figure of 71 households in 1673. A second map, dated 1761 (Fig 13.1b), shows dramatic changes to the shape and size of the village nucleus. The street running east–west contains far fewer houses than on the earlier map, and that running north–south has only empty garths. In 1764 it was reported that only 36 families lived at Watton, half the number recorded in the 1673 Hearth Tax return.

The Hearth Tax assessments are equally useful for examining the timing of village desertion. Of the East Riding settlements classed as 'deserted medieval villages' by Beresford and Hurst (1971),

Fig 13.2 Oak Cottage, South Dalton, East Riding of Yorkshire. This early 17th-century cottage was thatched until the early 20th century. © D Neave

30 were taxed separately in 1672. Of these, seven fell into the category of 'very shrunken' (four to six households), but nineteen townships still had seven or more households, and of these two-thirds had twelve or more households. This suggests that in the East Riding, an area of nucleated rather than dispersed settlements, many 'deserted medieval villages' were still viable communities at the end of the 17th century.

Vernacular buildings and the Hearth Tax

With a lack of vernacular buildings from before the 18th century surviving in the East Riding there is a reliance on archaeology, illustrative material and documentary sources, in particular probate inventories, glebe terriers and estate surveys, for information about their construction and appearance.

The East Riding is not rich in natural building materials. Good-quality stone is confined to a narrow belt of Jurassic limestone and sandstone to the west of the Wolds. Chalk was used extensively for cottage building on the Wolds, but much of it was of poor quality and weathered badly. The exception is the chalkstone once quarried in the north-east corner of the riding, near the coast, which is much more durable. In Holderness cobblestones from the beach were also used for house building. There was a paucity of timber, although there are recorded examples of both box- and cruck-framed cottages, and many buildings were constructed simply of mud, with thatch as the universal roofing material. It was not until the late 18th century that brick and pantile farmhouses and cottages began to dominate the East Riding landscape (Pevsner and Neave 1995, 23–29).

Archaeological evidence and the few extant vernacular buildings suggest that East Riding farmhouses built in or before the 17th century followed three main plan types. Long houses, which provided accommodation for the family, stock and crops under one roof, with a common through-passage entrance for humans and animals, were found both on the Wolds and in the Vale of York, but none is known to survive. There are a handful of houses with the hearth-passage plan, seemingly derived from the long house plan, such as Oak Cottage (Fig 13.2) at South Dalton, a three-bay timber-framed house perhaps dating from the early 17th century. More numerous are examples of the lobby-entry plan type where the entrance opened onto the stack, with a room either side, allowing for a hearth in each room. This plan type was still common in the early 18th century, and most of the surviving examples in the riding are probably of this date.

Even in counties where 17th-century vernacular buildings can be found in much greater numbers, what survive are the homes of farmers or craftsmen, rather than of the labouring poor. A drawing of a cottage at Wheldrake (Fig 13.3), a large settlement in the Vale of York, gives some clue to the type of building in which an East Riding agricultural labourer might have lived. The ramshackle single-storey cottage, almost devoid of windows, has a roughly thatched roof. It probably consisted of only one room. The most prominent feature is the wooden chimney. Of 115 households recorded at Wheldrake in 1672, 83% had only one hearth, as this cottage would have done.

Fig 13.3 Cottage at Wheldrake, in the Vale of York, drawn by Henry Cave c 1800. Private collection

Figure 13.4 shows those East Riding townships where 75% or more of the houses had only one hearth; in a third of these settlements the figure was at least 90%. The wapentake with the largest percentage of one-hearthed houses was Buckrose, at the north-west corner of the riding, an area dominated by high Wolds parishes, closely followed by the adjoining Bainton and Wilton divisions of Harthill wapentake which lay immediately south, and Dickering wapentake to the east (Table 13.1). The better-hearthed communities were concentrated in the southern half of the riding, in the fertile low-lying areas or close to Hull or York. The poorest village in the whole riding seems to have been Filey, a fishing community at the north-eastern tip of the riding. Of the 77 houses recorded in the 1672 assessment, 69 (90%) had only one hearth and 60 householders (78%) were exempt from paying tax. In contrast, only eleven (22%) of the 49 householders at Scampston, in Buckrose wapentake, were exempt although 47 (96%) of the houses had only one hearth.

In 1697 Celia Fiennes described Brandesburton in Holderness as a 'poor sad thatch'd place' (quoted in Woodward 1985, 50); of 85 households recorded in 1672 only ten had more than one hearth. Many of the inhabitants were tenants of Emanuel Hospital, Westminster. A survey made in 1700 describes several houses as 'mean' or in a bad state of repair; two had fallen down within recent years, and a third was on the point of collapse.[3] If Brandesburton is typical of other townships, this suggests that the housing stock of the East Riding in the late 17th century left much to be desired, and that its rebuilding in the 18th and 19th century was a necessity. There is no evidence to suggest that the high percentage of one-hearthed houses indicates that the East Riding was less prosperous than better-hearthed rural areas in the south. The pattern of landholding, with large estates and few small freeholders, lack of good building materials and cultural influences probably dictated that the houses in the riding were generally small and poorly heated.

Probate inventories

More information on the size of late 17th-century houses is provided by probate inventories, where the goods of the deceased are often itemised room by room. In the East Riding, wills and probate inventories made before 1688 survive only in those townships which came under the 'peculiar' jurisdiction of an ecclesiastical court other than that of the Archbishop of York.[4] Inventories chiefly give an insight into the homes of the more prosperous members of a community, but in the East Riding such people often lived in comparatively modest houses. In 1672 Robert Johnson of North Newbald, a roper, was living in a house with one hearth. An inventory made six years later, soon after his death, mentions only three rooms. The heated room, in which the family lived and where the cooking was done, was simply called the 'house' although elsewhere the terms hall, hall house, fore house or fire house

126 *Part 2: Regional Studies*

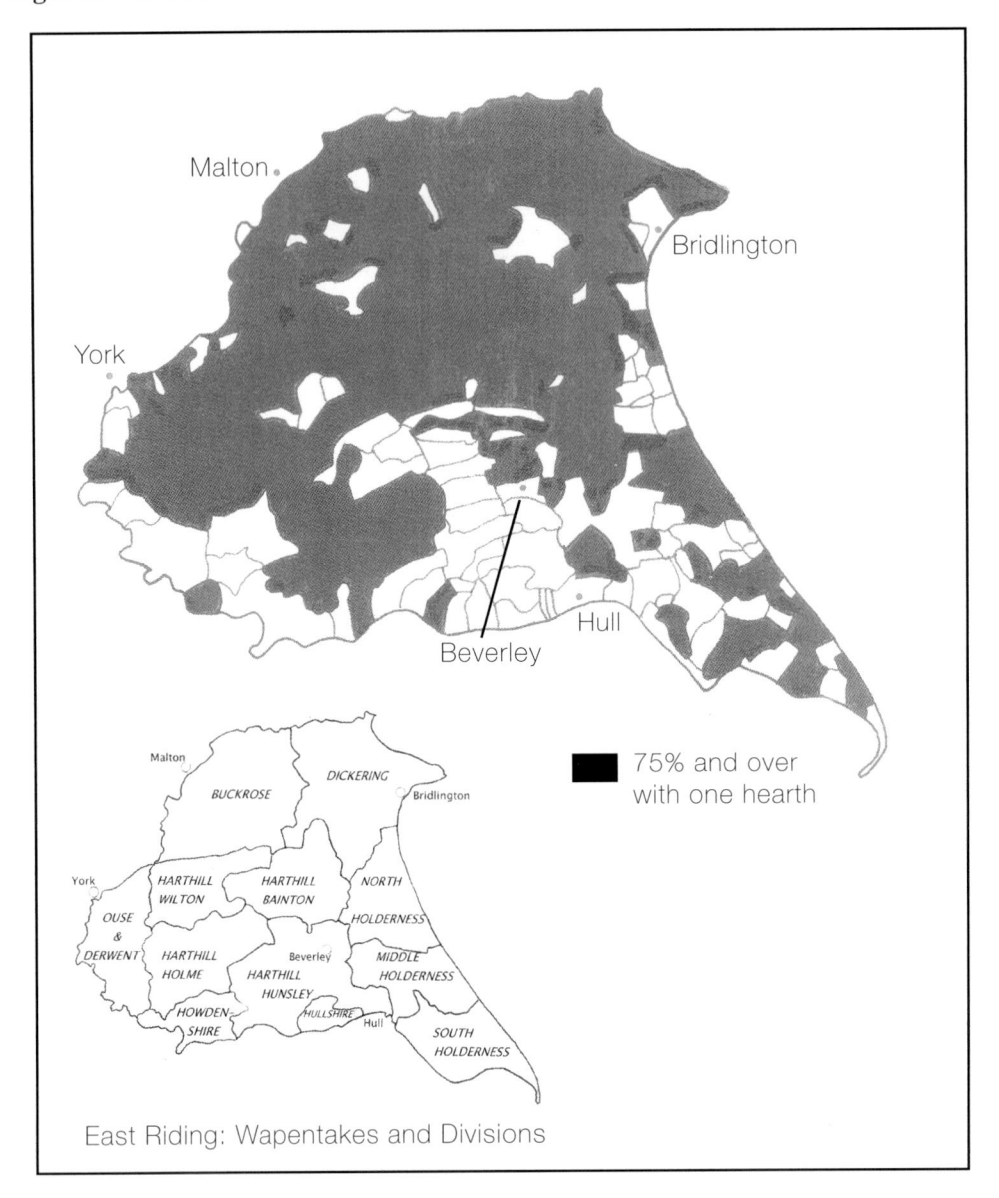

Fig 13.4 East Riding townships where 75% or more of the houses had only one hearth in 1672

are used. This room had a 'gallow balk', a regional term for the bar that hung over the fire on which the cooking pots were suspended. There was also a table, chairs and stool, a cupboard, and some brass and pewter. The parlour (presumably unheated) was where the family slept. In it there were two beds with bedding, chests containing linen, and other items. Over the parlour there was a chamber where corn was stored. Evidence from other parts of the East Riding suggests this layout was typical of the homes of many small farmers and craftsmen.

Inventories for those discharged from payment of the Hearth Tax are rare, and offer a particularly valuable insight into the lives of the less affluent. William Cropton of Langtoft, who was discharged from payment of tax on his one-hearthed property in 1672, died the following year leaving goods valued at £9 8s 6d. An inventory of his possessions mentions only one room, the 'house', in which he also slept.

One of the best-hearthed settlements was Preston, the most populous township in Holderness with around 127 households in 1672–73.[5] Of these, 13% had three or more hearths. The largest house, occupied by Mr Sanders, had eleven hearths; six houses had four to six hearths, and a further nine had three hearths. Houses with two hearths accounted for 24% of the total, and the remaining 63% had only one. Preston came under the jurisdiction of the Sub-Dean of York, and inventories with room names have survived for thirteen residents who are named in the Hearth Tax assessments and died within the following decade. Of these, three were assessed on three hearths, six on two hearths, and four on one hearth. The wealthiest of the deceased was Adam Acie, a yeoman with goods valued at £207. His modest house, on which he paid tax on two hearths, apparently had only a parlour, house with chamber over, and a milk house. Marmaduke Smith, described as a husbandman, had goods valued at £62. He also paid tax on two hearths, but his inventory refers to a hall house, great and little parlours, a kitchen, milk house, buttery and chamber. Robert Wallas, a

Table 13.1 East Riding of Yorkshire: households and hearths by wapentake 1672

Wapentakes and Divisions	1 hearth households inc. exempt	2 hearth households inc. exempt	3–4 hearths	5–9 hearths	10+ hearths	Total households	Total exempt households
Buckrose	1,231 87%	108 7.5%	47 3.5%	24 1.5%	9 0.5%	1,419	445 31.5%
Dickering	1,811 81%	217 9.5%	146 6.5%	53 2.5%	9 0.5%	2,236	786 35%
Harthill Bainton Beacon	849 84%	82 8%	48 5%	22 2%	8 1%	1,009	295 29%
Harthill Holme Beacon	869 80%	132 12%	57 5%	20 2%	7 1%	1,085	153 14%
Harthill Hunsley Beacon	939 69.5%	239 18%	118 9%	45 3%	7 0.5%	1,348	194 14.5%
Harthill Wilton Beacon	808 84.5%	77 8%	47 5%	18 2%	3 0.5%	953	221 23%
Holderness North Division	904 79%	146 13%	67 6%	18 1.5%	6 0.5%	1,141	222 19.5%
Holderness Middle Division	773 65%	235 20%	122 10%	44 4%	9 1%	1,183	174 15%
Holderness South Division	736 74%	160 16%	73 7%	23 2.5%	5 0.5%	997	244 24.5%
Howdenshire	703 65.5%	221 21%	110 10%	34 3%	3 0.5%	1,071	195 18%
Ouse and Derwent	888 71%	210 17%	97 8%	38 3%	10 1%	1,243	231 18.5%
Hull and Hullshire	653 40%	385 24%	333 20%	229 14%	36 2%	1,636	301 18.5%
Beverley and Liberties	377 50%	139 18.5%	141 19%	85 11.5%	6 1%	748	208 28%
EAST RIDING	11,541 72%	2,351 14.5%	1,406 8.5%	653 4%	118 1%	16,069	3,669 23%

husbandman, left goods valued at £157 in 1680, yet had been paying tax on only one hearth in 1673. His house consisted of a parlour, hall house, milk house, two chambers and kitchen. Perhaps he had moved between 1673 and 1680, or had extended his house, but it is more likely that the 'hall house' was the only heated room. At the lower end of the scale, it would seem that the Hearth Tax figures tell us little about the prosperity of an individual, nor are they a reliable guide to house size.

Rarely is it clear from probate inventories what rooms, other than the principal one, were heated, but the Hearth Tax provides some evidence. The houses of Robert Williamson (died 1679) and Robert Carlill (died 1680), both of Elloughton, a village west of Hull, each had a 'house' with a range, a parlour, and a chamber. In 1672 Williamson paid tax on only one hearth, whereas Carlill was assessed for two, suggesting he had a heated parlour, although there is no indication of this from the probate inventory. There is often a surprising lack of reference to fireplace goods, even in houses known to have had several heated rooms.

Some inventories do offer clues as to the types of fuel used. The lack of wood in the East Riding may well have contributed to the modest number of hearths in rural dwellings. References have been found in inventories to whins, turves and 'elding' (fuel), and more rarely to coal. In some townships such as Weaverthorpe on the Wolds, where in 1673 only three of the 38 houses had two hearths, and the rest one, there are references to 'cassons'. The archaeologist John Robert Mortimer, who was born at nearby Fimber on the Yorkshire Wolds in 1825, wrote in his reminiscences:

> The cottagers of Fimber and the adjoining wold villages were often in great straits for fuel, and at times were constrained to burn the dried excrements of the cows. This kind of fuel was called 'cassons', and was burned in a somewhat similar manner to peat (quoted in Hicks 1978, 6).

At that date several substantial cruck-framed long houses still stood at Fimber. Of the twenty houses recorded in the 1672 Hearth Tax assessment four had two hearths and the rest one.

The larger houses of the East Riding

A rare example of a probate inventory that can be linked to an East Riding house that survives, albeit

128 Part 2: Regional Studies

Fig 13.5   Elmswell Old Hall, East Riding of Yorkshire, built c 1635 for Henry Best. University of Hull Photographic Service

in a derelict state, is that for John Best of Elmswell, who died in 1669. Although the house near Driffield in which he lived, now known as Elmswell Old Hall (Fig 13.5), is much grander in scale than the houses previously described, it provides an opportunity to test how accurate a picture an inventory can give of a house at the time of the Hearth Tax. The brick manor house was built around 1635 for Henry Best, who wrote the well-known *Farming* and *Memorandum* books, which were published in a new edition by the British Academy in 1984 (Woodward 1984). The house is of two storeys with attics, and has three massive stacks. The layout as recorded in the inventory of Henry's son John is still apparent, with three principal rooms on each floor, and garrets above. On the ground floor there was the parlour, the hall (in which there was an iron range and gallow balk) and the kitchen (also with a range). Above were three chambers where the family slept: the parlour chamber, middle chamber and kitchen chamber. At the top of the house were the three garrets, which contained bedsteads and various other items. There is no indication as to which rooms, apart from the hall and kitchen, were heated, but John's widow Sarah was assessed on nine hearths in 1672. This suggests all the rooms mentioned were heated, yet there is no evidence of the attic rooms ever having had fireplaces.

Several other manor houses survive that were built before or around the time of the Hearth Tax. In the case of Portington Hall, in Howdenshire, the assessments give a useful clue to when the house was built. In 1672 Henry Portington esquire paid tax on his nine-hearthed house, but he was also liable for tax on 'his old house' which had seven hearths. Another newly built house was Marton Hall near Bridlington, an attractive brick house with a fine late 17th-century staircase. Gregory Creyke married in 1672, and his arms and those of his wife are incorporated in the stucco decoration inside the house. In 1674 he was required to pay tax on one hearth and six more 'new built'.

The largest house in the East Riding in 1672, with 40 hearths, was Burton Constable Hall, seat of the Constable family, a medieval building greatly enlarged in the late 16th and early 17th centuries. Next in size was Burton Agnes, seat of the Boynton family, with 32 hearths. Another six houses had more than twenty hearths, and 36 (excluding those in Hull) had between twelve and twenty. The last group included four houses in Beverley, the largest of which was that of Michael Warton, adjoining the North Bar, with twenty hearths.

A detailed inventory of Warton's house, drawn up in 1688, lists, but does not value, the contents of every room (Hall 1986, 15–40). There are numerous references to items connected with fireplaces such as fenders, fire prods, fire shovels, coal rakes, bellows and iron backs, as well as a stock of coal. It is possible to identify eighteen rooms that were heated (including service rooms such as the laundry), accounting for the majority of hearths. All the principal rooms had fireplaces, and it was

Fig 13.6   Wilberforce House, Hull, built c 1660. © D Neave

chiefly the garrets, where the servants slept, that apparently had no heating. A few years after his death Michael Warton was described in the diary of Abraham de la Pryme as having been the richest commoner in England with an estate worth £15,000 a year (Hall 1986, 4).

The ports of Hull and Bridlington

In the late 17th century Hull was an expanding inland port, trading with the Baltic and the Low Countries. Hollar's plan of 1640 shows it was still a compact town at this date, confined within its medieval walls. The merchant community was centred on High Street, which ran parallel to the River Hull. Many of the merchants' houses backed on to the river and had private wharves. In 1672 there were fourteen houses in Hull with between twelve and twenty hearths, of which the largest had seventeen. Several Hull residents paid additional tax for garden houses. In about 1644 there was a report of a bricklayer from Amsterdam persuading people in Hull to have their chimneys altered.[6] At this time the wealthier merchants were replacing their timber-framed buildings with fashionable brick houses. Although both Hull and Beverley had brick works in the Middle Ages, it was not until the 17th century that brick was used extensively for domestic buidings. Several of these new houses were in the 'artisan-mannerist' style, where the architectural details echo those commonly found on buildings in the Low Countries with which the port traded. The best example is Wilberforce House on High Street, now a museum (Fig 13.6). It was built around 1660 for the merchant Hugh Lister, whose widow was assessed on twelve hearths in 1672. The nine-bay rusticated brick front has pilasters to the first floor, stone Corinthian capitals and a three-storey porch with pilasters decorated with diamond- and lozenge-shaped stone 'jewels'. Similar details are found at the remnant of Crowle House, also on High Street, which is dated 1664. Both houses were undoubtedly the work of William Catlyn, a remarkable Hull builder-architect to whom can be attributed a series of buildings in this distinctive style on both sides of the Humber estuary (Neave 1996). Illustrations suggest other contemporary buildings in Hull had curved or crow-stepped gables, features also commonly found in the Netherlands. A fine East Riding example of a mid-17th-century brick house with shaped gables is Knedlington Old Hall, near Howden, which was built for the Arlush family, who paid tax on eight hearths in 1672 (Fig 13.7).

The small port of Bridlington, on the coast, was flourishing in the mid-17th century. A description of the town by Richard Blome in 1673 mentions the 'very good and commodious quay for ships to load and unload at, which hath occasioned it (of late) to be a place of good trade' (quoted in Woodward 1985, 29). The merchants traded overseas, carrying corn, malt and West Riding cloth to the Low Countries and the Baltic, and importing timber, although the greater part of the trade was coastal, chiefly carrying coal and salt from Sunderland and Newcastle. In the 1670s the trade exceeded that of Scarborough, yet according to the Hearth Tax assessments Bridlington was, at this very time, the poorest town in the East Riding, with more than a third of the inhabitants discharged from payment. It may be that trade

Fig 13.7   Knedlington Old Hall, East Riding of Yorkshire. © *D Neave*

was temporarily affected by the Anglo-Dutch Wars. In the summer of 1672 the 70 ships of the English fleet sought refuge off Bridlington, and 400–500 sick men were taken on shore. The fleet was under the command of the Duke of York, the future James II (Neave 2000, 91).

Although the percentage of people discharged from paying the tax was especially high, the Bridlington Hearth Tax figures still reflect the pattern typically found in towns. Many residents were experiencing some degree of poverty in the late 17th century, but 20% of the town's population lived in houses with three or more hearths, a very different situation from that found in the surrounding rural settlements. This reflects the more diverse urban economy and the presence of professionals, merchants and substantial tradesmen who were rebuilding their houses. The availability of imported coal as a source of fuel in coastal towns may also have influenced the number of hearths.

Bridlington was divided into two distinct areas of settlement, the port or 'Quay' and, a mile inland, the 'Old Town', centred on the former priory church. Several merchants lived at the Quay, such as John Bower, who was assessed on eleven hearths in 1672, but many chose to live in the Old Town. A number of houses along High Street and its continuation, Westgate, were rebuilt in the latter part of the 17th century by merchants or professionals for whom a new house was an overt display of wealth. These include 7–9 Westgate, a fine brick house built in the 'artisan-mannerist' style in 1682 by the merchant Thomas Wilson.

Within a short distance of Wilson's house is the grandest 17th-century house to survive in Bridlington, 43 High Street (The Toft), which Hearth Tax assessments revealed was built by his father-in-law, William Hudson, woollen merchant. Behind the early 19th-century façade is hidden a sumptuous late 17th-century interior. The artisan-mannerist woodwork includes door surrounds of numerous different designs and elaborate chimney pieces. A fine staircase once led up to a lookout from where Hudson would have been able to watch his ships entering and leaving the harbour. There can be little doubt that the fine interior was known to William Kent, architect, landscape and furniture designer, who was born in Bridlington and grew up in the house next door.

Hearth tax assessments proved especially useful in verifying the date of building the house, said formerly to have had 1673 on a rainwater head, and in identifying the owner. In the 1673 assessment, where the houses along High Street seem to be listed more or less in order, there is the revealing entry 'Mr Hudson new house building', and Hudson's ownership has been confirmed from deeds.

Conclusion

In the late 17th century large numbers of people in the East Riding, especially those in rural areas, lived in houses with only one hearth. To some extent this must reflect the poor quality of the housing stock in this region, where there was a lack of good natural building materials. A shortage of fuel may also have been a factor. For the wealthy a house with several prominent chimneys would have been a status symbol, but for the majority it was acceptable to have only one heated room, irrespective of income or social standing. The introduction of a

Hearth Tax may have actively discouraged small owner-occupiers from building extra chimneys and thus incurring additional expense, though for the many who were tenants the choice was not theirs to make. There is no doubt that hearths were occasionally blocked. The 1674 certificate for the township of Leppington tells us that Tobias Ashbourne had 'two chimneys hearths clearly down and hath no more but four hearth in his house'.[7] In 1672 he had been assessed on six hearths.

In the East Riding, if there was a 'great rebuilding', it occurred in the 18th century, considerably later than in many other parts of England. Economic prosperity, the availability of locally made bricks and pantiles, and the relocation of farmhouses outside the village centres after enclosure were important factors. The extent of this rebuilding was such that few vernacular houses that were standing when the Hearth Tax was collected now survive. These taxation documents provide useful information on the quantity and, to some extent, scale of buildings for which there is virtually no other record.

Chapter 13: Notes

1 This chapter is based on work in progress. An edition of the East Riding Hearth Tax is currently being prepared by the Roehampton Centre for Hearth Tax Research. We are indebted to David Purdy for his early work on the Yorkshire records, in which the East Riding assessments are described more fully (Purdy 1991, 30–33).

2 Many of these certificates have recently been transcribed by Duncan Harrington as part of the Roehampton Project.

3 City of London Record Office Emanuel Hospital papers, Box 3.8.

4 The probate inventories referred to are all at the BIA.

5 Part of the 1672 assessment for Preston is illegible; the gaps have been filled by reference to other years.

6 Hull City Record Office M 189.

7 TNA E179/350 (Duncan Harrington, pers. comm.).

14 The West Riding Hearth Tax returns of 1672 and the Great Rebuilding *by Colum Giles*

Introduction: themes and sources

When William Harrison wanted to convey to his Elizabethan audience something of the spirit of improvement and confidence which marked his time, he chose to remark not on commerce, industry or science, but on material evidence, plain to see to his contemporaries. He noted how plate and drinking glasses had lately replaced wooden tableware, and how tapestries, silk hangings and carpets adorned the houses not only of the great but also of 'inferior artificers and many farmers'. He remarked on the common use of timber for house building, but demonstrated that the gentry and nobility had recently turned to the use of brick and stone in their dwellings. Those dwellings, and the homes of poorer people, were commonly lit by windows filled not with lattice but with window glass, for the first time both plentiful and cheap. Two changes in material culture were identified by Harrison as particularly significant and remarkable. First, there had been a 'great (although not general) amendment of lodging', for where earlier generations had suffered with straw pallets and 'a good round log under their heads instead of a bolster or pillow', now mattresses, beds of down or feathers, and pillows were *de rigueur*. And, second, in frustratingly scanty detail, he noticed 'the multitude of chimneys lately erected' in new houses (Harrison 1587, 195–201). For Harrison, national progress could be measured in material prosperity, and changes in the standard of living for what he implies was a significant proportion of English society were evident in the houses of the people.

Harrison's few words have been taken by modern writers on vernacular architecture as evidence for what W G Hoskins memorably labelled 'the great rebuilding' (Hoskins 1953). The complexity of this process is now better understood, and it might now be argued that this rebuilding represents only one of the more visible and obvious stages in a much longer history of changing living standards, ultimately affecting all levels of society. Nevertheless, it is a useful concept, one which serves to focus attention on how the quantity and quality of building varied in

Fig 14.1 Wood Lane Hall, Sowerby, West Yorkshire, built in 1649 by John Dearden, was assessed at eight hearths in 1672. The inventory of Joshua Dearden, drawn up in 1696, names the hall (open through two storeys), five parlours, a kitchen, and a number of heated chambers (RCHME 1986, 216). © Crown Copyright

time and place across the country. If Harrison identified a particular stage in the process, other sources provide further evidence for other places and other periods. The Hearth Tax returns, compiled almost a century later and very different in nature from Harrison's limited and anecdotal account, offer a unique opportunity to test the development of living standards across much of the country. This chapter uses the returns, supplemented by other sources, to ask a question of fundamental importance in the study of regional housing: how far had the great rebuilding progressed by the 1670s in West Yorkshire?[1]

Three principal sources may be brought to bear on this question. The Hearth Tax returns of 1672, of course, form one; the second comprises contemporary or near-contemporary probate inventories; and the third is the evidence of surviving houses. Few properly contemporary probate inventories survive for West Yorkshire, but inventories from the 1680s and 1690s probably represent something close to the way of life common at the time of the Hearth Tax in the early 1670s. The principal question concerning the use of surviving houses as evidence relates to the degree to which these buildings represent a reasonable sample of housing conditions in the last third of the 17th century. The answer must be that the relationship is unlikely to be precise, but that surviving houses nevertheless provide one of the best sources for the development of material culture in this period. The value of their evidence is not disputed; how that evidence may be used and interpreted is the issue. The important thing about these sources is that they complement each other: the Hearth Tax returns provide a global quantitative overview at a single point in time; inventories and houses are less systematic, concentrated and comprehensive, but they provide invaluable qualitative material, one showing how houses were furnished, the other giving three-dimensional and visual evidence. Together, they do much to illuminate the question of how far the process of improvement in living standards, celebrated by Harrison in the 1570s, had progressed a century later.

The focus of analysis will be on the lower levels of society, that is, on the ranks below the gentry. Gentry and nobility provide an important context for the discussion of the living standards of the lower ranks, but this will be described briefly, since it can be argued that these social groups had, long before the late 17th century, adopted the improved living standards noted by Harrison: their state of grace is not in question. Having learned how they lived, attention can be turned to the yeomanry, Harrison's 'inferior artificers', and the labouring poor to ask how far these had progressed from a notional standard characteristic of medieval life.

Housing in late 17th-century West Yorkshire: the gentry and nobility

Harrison makes it clear that already by the mid-16th century the great families of the land enjoyed houses with many heated rooms, and the benefits of greater comfort and privacy came to be shared by more modest titled families in the course of the late 16th century and throughout the 17th century. The most significant trend in the way in which gentry houses were used has been identified as 'an increase in their numbers as rooms changed from spaces that were shared to spaces that are private, and from rooms with more general functions to more specialised ones' (Cooper 1999, chapter 8). The influences which brought about this multiplication and specialisation were the desire for more privacy, the changing social relations within the gentry household, and changing expectations of how life at this level should be conducted. New standards are apparent in contemporary documents, and it has been remarked that the probate inventories of the gentry give 'a sense of rapidly growing sophistication in taste, manners and comfort' (Cooper 1999, 275).

Changes in the way of life of noble and gentry families are evident in their houses. In West Yorkshire as elsewhere, the most obvious change was the frequent abandonment of the open hall, supplanted in many new houses by a floored hall with a chamber over, the hall's earlier principal functions having been removed to other parts of the house. The desire for comfort and privacy is expressed most conspicuously in the proliferation of parlours and chambers and in their architectural treatment. The imposing, but compact, house built by Robert Smythson at Heath near Wakefield in the 1590s had five heated parlours on the main floor and a number of heated chambers on the upper floor (RCHME 1986, 50–54). Nearly a century later, in 1675, Sir Thomas Wentworth's house at Bretton had eight parlours (four heated) and eight chambers, including a great chamber (Brears 1972, 145–52). Many of these heated rooms were identified by the users' names, and in many (but not all) cases this indicates use as a personal, private space. Wentworth's Bretton house had chambers for Mr Mathew, Mr Wentworth and the Lady (the last with a bed worth £30), and when Sir Richard Hawksworth died in 1657, his house contained a heated hall and a dining room, six heated chambers (his own and the 'Yong Mr's' identified by the user's name, others by status or decoration – the 'great chamber', the 'red chamber'), two heated nurseries, and a kitchen and bakehouse (Brears 1972, 145–52; RCHME 1986, 64, 72–73, 198–99).

This sophisticated division of space and high degree of comfort had percolated through to the new gentry by the early and mid-17th century. When the Murgatroyd family rebuilt the lower end of their house at East Riddlesden in 1648 they provided a heated dining parlour and kitchen on the ground floor and a number of heated chambers, including a diminutive room over the porch; and at Wood Lane Hall, Sowerby, built in 1649, the hall, at least two parlours, the kitchen and at least two chambers were heated (Fig 14.1; RCHME 1986, 60–72, 206–07; 57, 59, 216). Parlours and chambers could be elaborately decorated, both with carved stone fireplaces and with ornamental plasterwork.

The Hearth Tax returns show that by the late 17th century the West Yorkshire nobility and gentry had erected their own multitude of chimneys to match that of Harrison's Essex families a century earlier: a modest gentry house like Wood Lane Hall was assessed at eight hearths; the more substantial East Riddlesden Hall at sixteen hearths; and the houses of the nobility at considerably more – Sir John Lewis paid tax on 25 hearths for Ledston Hall (with six additional hearths being noted as unfinished); Sir John Savile had 43 hearths at Methley Hall; and the highest taxpayer in the modern county was Lord Irwin of Temple Newsam, assessed at 45 hearths. Even these large mansions were overshadowed by Skipton Castle, for which Lady Clifford, the most heavily taxed person in the old West Riding, was assessed at 60 hearths.

Housing in late 17th-century West Yorkshire: the yeomanry and lower ranks

In an examination of improved living standards, it is helpful to establish a point of departure, from which different levels of society, at different rates, moved as they became able to afford something which matched changing expectations of what a house should provide. Harrison implies that the single-hearth house was the norm in the medieval period for almost all levels of society below that of the great families, claiming that 'religious houses and manor places of their lords always excepted, and peradventure some great personages', each man 'made his fire against a reredos in the hall, where he dined and dressed his meat' (Harrison 1587, 201). Even if he does not state as much, the implication is that the fire in the hall was the only hearth in the house, and the reader is invited to accept this as a reference point describing the medieval norm. But it is instructive to examine the extent to which the evidence of houses supports the conclusion that the existence of a single hearth in a house connoted a minimum standard of living, one which showed no advance on that of the poorer levels of medieval society.

The idea that a single hearth must inevitably be associated with the lowest levels of society is contradicted by what we know of medieval houses in West Yorkshire. It is likely that some gentry houses had more than a single hearth in the Middle Ages, and there is documentary evidence that gentry and yeoman houses might have used braziers to heat rooms other than the hall (Moorhouse 1981, 812–14). But surviving medieval yeoman houses have only a single identifiable hearth: in the Pennine aisled house of the late 15th or early 16th century the main room, the housebody, was heated by a fire beneath a firehood, and other rooms lack structural evidence for heating. This lack of multiple hearths does not mean, however, that houses of this type were of inferior quality. They were substantially constructed, and in some cases they had sophisticated plans and features, with a dais canopy at the upper end of the housebody and a cross-wing containing parlours and chambers (RCHME 1986, 27–36). These houses, the homes of wealthy yeoman-clothiers, sheltered families living in some style, certainly far above what might today be taken as a minimum standard.[2]

Similar caution is needed when we turn to the 17th century. Surviving 17th-century houses are, almost invariably, of modestly substantial form, and it may be inferred that they sheltered modestly prosperous families. Most families, of course, were not modestly prosperous, and the vast majority of their houses are lost, at least as standing buildings. It is probable that large numbers of people still, in the late 17th century, lived in houses which were little different from those of their medieval forebears. Indeed, many of the households listed in the Hearth Tax returns may well have lived in houses which were already old: some at least were doubtless medieval in origin. A few were recorded by curious antiquaries in the 19th century: probably conscious of their antiquity and vulnerability – even perhaps of their historical significance – these men recorded them as evidence of a vanishing way of life. A small cottage in Baildon, for example, was observed in some detail in 1884. The cottage was

> of singularly primitive construction. The rock ... had been bared and levelled, and in it were sunk four holes ... Four massive oak timbers, shaped something like a boomerang ... were inserted into the holes, two and two, so that each pair met at the top ... A wall has been built round, and a fireplace and chimney in the middle completed the cottage. I saw this picturesque and interesting building in 1884; it was pulled down shortly afterwards' (Baildon 1913, 48–49; RCHME 1986, 42, 191).

It is likely that similar cottages sheltered large numbers of families in 17th-century West Yorkshire. In the Hearth Tax returns, the house would register as one assessed on a single hearth, and the general notion might be accepted that this simplest form of house represented a way of life that differed little from that endured by the majority of families in the Middle Ages. Perhaps only the use of a firehood rather than an open hearth distinguished this cottage from its medieval precursor.

These tiny cottages are not, however, entirely representative of the single-hearth houses recorded by the Hearth Tax assessors. Many new and much more commodious houses were built in the 17th century with just a single hearth. Flailcroft, near Todmorden, was probably constructed in the middle of the century with a relatively simple form: a heated housebody, a divided inner cell giving an unheated parlour and small service room, and chambers over (RCHME 1986, 108, 218). Despite the simplicity, Flailcroft offers far superior accommodation to the miserable

Fig 14.2 The open housebody at Birks, Slaithwaite, West Yorkshire. A small linear house of three cells, probably entirely single-storeyed originally. © Crown Copyright

hovel in Baildon, but nevertheless the Hearth Tax assessors, while doubtless appreciating that very different ways of life were conducted in them, would have made no distinction between them, for that was not their business. It is important, therefore, to be aware of the wide range of lifestyles which might be hidden within a single taxation category.

The Hearth Tax returns for West Yorkshire demonstrate that, as in most other parts of the country, overwhelmingly the most common type of house was the single-hearth dwelling. Leaving aside townships with just a single great house, all townships had some single-hearth houses. There were some wealthy townships (9% of those in the county) where such houses made up less than a third of the dwellings: in the populous township of Southowram,

Fig 14.3 Green Top, Marsden, of 1671, West Yorkshire. It is a substantially built house, originally heated only by the fireplace in the housebody; the fireplace heating the parlour is a later addition. © Crown Copyright

near Halifax, for example, only 22% of houses were assessed on a single hearth. At the other extreme, single-hearth houses made up more than two-thirds of the dwellings in 13% of the townships: in upland Haworth and in the agricultural township of Bramhope, respectively 76% and 82% of houses were rated at just a single hearth. Between these extremes lay the majority of townships, 78% in all, with between one- and two-thirds of its houses assessed on a single hearth. In 56% of West Yorkshire townships, half or more of the chargeable houses had just one hearth, in both upland areas such as Heptonstall and Thornton, and in lowland areas such as Thorpe Audlin and Clifford.

Probate inventories help to give a picture of the workings of these simple dwellings. Some may have had a single room, but probably more common were houses with two ground-floor rooms and one or more chambers. Judeth Almen, of Sandal, near Wakefield, occupied a dwelling consisting of a house or housebody, the main living room used for cooking and containing spits, pans, pewter, tables and chairs; a parlour, used for sleeping and storage; and a chamber, again a room for sleeping and storage of crops. Only the housebody was heated.[3] Instead of a parlour, Daniel Smith of Sowerby had a shop, with a bed and a loom, alongside the housebody,[4] and Henry Johnson of Mirfield had a housebody for cooking and sitting, an unheated parlour for sleeping, and a shop for sleeping and storage.[5] Some inventories identify only a single hearth, in the form of a range or cooking utensils, in houses of some size: Richard Denton of Stainland had a range in his housebody, but neither his sun parlour nor two further parlours appear to have been heated, his kitchen was used for storage and salting meat rather than for cooking, and none of his three chambers, used variously for sleeping and storage, had a hearth.[6] This austerity is, of course, possible, especially where houses may have been already old in the late 17th century, but confidence in the source, or at least in our ability to interpret it, weakens when it describes such large and elaborate houses with minimal provision of heating.

Something of the range of housing encompassed within the category of single-hearth dwellings can be illustrated by surviving houses. The simplest dwellings, perhaps little different from the type of house occupied by most families in the Middle Ages, were similar to the small single-storey cottages recorded by antiquaries in the 19th century. Birks, in Slaithwaite, was probably built in stages in the 17th century and later and formed a linear house of three cells, the central one providing the one heated room, open to the roof (Fig 14.2). While it might provide just a single-storey range of rooms and one hearth, it was constructed in durable and well-worked building materials. More substantial are houses like Green Top, Marsden, built in 1671 and therefore brand new when assessed for the Hearth Tax, with a heated housebody, unheated parlour and service rooms to the rear, and with full chambers over both cells (Fig 14.3). Seventeenth-century houses like these were unpretentious, lacking expensive woodwork, stonework or decorative features, but they were well enough built to survive into the modern period. Many, furthermore, had a full range of chambers, and this probably distinguished them from earlier small houses. On more than one count, therefore, they were a significant advance on the dwellings of most of the rural population in the Middle Ages. Quite what proportion of the single-hearth houses recorded in the Hearth Tax returns were, like Green Top, new-built improved dwellings of the 17th century cannot be known, but the relative rarity of surviving examples when set against the numbers recorded in the Hearth Tax returns suggests that the proportion may have been low. The majority of single-hearth houses listed in the Hearth Tax were, therefore, probably small, poorly built, perhaps in many cases already old, and sheltered families who lived very much as their medieval forebears had done.

If single-hearth houses were the most common house type in late 17th-century West Yorkshire, larger and more elaborate dwellings were nevertheless present in large numbers. These houses are significant in many ways, but especially so for the purpose of this analysis, for they provide evidence for the degree to which better living standards had percolated through to social levels below the gentry. The graph of hearth size is predictable: in most townships, the numbers of houses diminishes as the number of hearths rises, so that, after the single-hearth house, the most common number of hearths is two per household, then three, and so on.

In two-hearth houses, inventories demonstrate that the housebody continued to be the hub of the dwelling, the site of the cooking hearth and the centre of family life. What was different in many of these houses was that the parlour was also heated and in some cases appears to have acquired a higher degree of comfort. Inevitably in houses of modest size, room uses tended to remain general and mixed, so that parlours doubled as bedrooms and sitting rooms, perhaps even as dining rooms in some cases. In some houses, there was a single parlour: when Anthony Milner of Skircoat died in 1693, his heated parlour was used for sleeping and for sitting and dining. The rest of the house was made up of housebody, buttery and milkhouse, a shop and shop chamber, and a further chamber over the housebody.[7] Many houses had more than a single parlour, but only the best parlour had a fireplace. In 1668 Edmund Bothomley of Slaithwaite had a heated great parlour, used for sitting and sleeping, but his unheated little parlour was a plain bedroom (Brears 1972, 134–38). There were four parlours in Robert Reade's house in Huddersfield, but only the lower parlour appears to have been heated and was used as a sitting room: upper, little and little lower parlours were unheated bedrooms.[8]

In houses where the housebody was still the main room for cooking, heated almost invariably by a firehood, the parlour was heated by a fireplace in a stone or brick chimney stack. Fireplaces and chimney stacks, in stone or brick, had been used in the houses of the gentry since the late Middle Ages, but the parlour fireplace and stack were innovations for the West Yorkshire yeomanry in the 17th century, found first in larger houses and then increasingly in smaller houses such as Ivy House, Bingley, of 1676. Houses of this type, size and date are quite common in parts of West Yorkshire, and show the effect on house design of rising living standards.

Greater sophistication and more specialisation in room use are evident at the level of the three-hearth house. These houses demonstrate a significant development, that is, the removal of all or most of the cooking to a kitchen. This allowed a more 'polite' use for both the housebody and the principal heated parlour, although the opportunity was apparently not always taken. In 1693 Daniel Thorpe of Sharlston died with a house where both housebody and kitchen were used for cooking, but the 'new parlour' was a well-furnished heated sitting and dining room, not used also as a bedroom.[9] John Hanson, of Warley, had a housebody (not specifically listed in his inventory as containing fire tools, but we may assume that it was heated), a heated kitchen with spits and cooking pans, and a heated dining parlour, again not used as a bedroom.[10] Beds had been banished to the first floor, an important step on the road to modern ways of living.

Three-hearth houses in West Yorkshire show some variety of plan and design. In the larger yeoman houses of the first half of the 17th century, the kitchen was housed in a gabled rear wing. These large houses usually had a workshop below the passage at the lower end of the main range. Similar in the size of their living accommodation, but lacking the shop end, are two-cell variants of the plan form, where the kitchen wing lay behind a main range made up of housebody and parlour (RCHME 1986, chapter 5).

In some houses, the three heated rooms are arranged in a linear form on the main front. Ryecroft, in Tong, near Bradford, is a splendid example of the type, built in 1669 by Christopher Nettleton, and therefore very new when the Hearth Tax assessors arrived three years later. The house has a central open housebody, heated by a firehood; a heated parlour, with a fireplace in a stone chimney stack, at one end; and a kitchen, with a firehood against the end gable, at the other (Fig 14.4). The use of an open housebody at this late date suggests that Nettleton, a wealthy tanner, wanted the best of both old and new: the open housebody may have been a status

Fig 14.4 Christopher Nettleton, a farmer and tanner, built Ryecroft, Tong, West Yorkshire, in 1669. The central room was a housebody open through two storeys, at the far end lay a parlour, and at the near end was the kitchen, heated by a firehood against the gable wall, lit by the two-light fire window. © Crown Copyright

feature used to suggest the family's ancient lineage, but the additional heated rooms demonstrate that the medieval way of life had been left far behind (RCHME 1986, 136, 219). The mystery at Ryecroft is the discrepancy between the modern interpretation of the 1669 house as having had three heated rooms and the Hearth Tax assessors' identification of only two hearths, undoubtedly those beneath the firehoods in the housebody and kitchen. It is possible that the parlour was originally unheated, and that a fireplace was added before Nettleton's death in 1693, when his inventory shows that the great parlour was a heated sitting room.

In houses of three or fewer hearths, the advances made in heating before the late 17th century were confined to the ground floor. Houses with two or three fireplaces on the ground floor might have had a full range of chambers, but they were very rarely heated. The low status of first-floor rooms is indicated by probate inventories, which show that they were used for sleeping for lesser members of the household and for storage. In Samuel Swaine's house in Horsforth in 1688, there were three chambers: all contained a bed, the sun chamber had an ark of meal, the middle chamber had an ark with flitches of bacon, and the north chamber was used to store oats. The best bedrooms, both heated, were ground-floor parlours.[11]

It is not entirely clear when the three-hearth house, with housebody, parlour and kitchen, but with unheated chambers, became common in West Yorkshire. Inventories and Hearth Tax demonstrate its presence in some numbers by the late 17th century, but there are few reliably dated and certain three-hearth houses remaining today to allow us to establish when the form was introduced. It is likely that it was established by the mid-17th century in some areas, but more consistent work is needed to verify this claim. This is important, since it would be significant to know whether styles of living percolate from high to low in sequence, or whether some improvements were adopted at the same time by people of different ranks and wealth.

If most yeomen, even those of some standing, failed to match gentry ways of living, the wealthiest amidst their ranks, made rich by agriculture or industry, were able, from the first decades of the West Yorkshire rebuilding, to build large dwellings. Substantial numbers of untitled men, mainly yeomen, were assessed at four or more hearths in the Hearth

Fig 14.5 Peel House, Warley, West Yorkshire. To the right of the porch (dated 1598) is a workshop, originally unheated; in the centre are the housebody and, at the rear, the kitchen (the stone caps to the firehoods heating these rooms are both visible); and to the left is the parlour wing, originally heated not by the present central stack but by one on the side wall, combined with a garderobe. © Crown Copyright

Tax returns. In Skircoat, near Halifax, for example, there were nineteen untitled heads of households with more than three hearths out of a total of 58 households. Inventories show that yeoman houses of this size, as well as having the expected heated housebody, parlour and kitchen, enjoyed a significant supplement to this accommodation in the form of a heated chamber, hitherto one of the badges of the gentry way of life. George Boyle, of Jackroyd in Shelf, was assessed on four hearths in 1672, and his inventory, of 1693, corresponds with this rating, listing hearths in the housebody, the sun parlour, the kitchen, and the sun chamber. Also listed were an unheated parlour and three unheated chambers, all poorly furnished compared to the heated sun chamber, with its bed, livery cupboard, books, chest and chairs.[12] Yeoman houses with more than four hearths could have two or more heated chambers: Thomas Priestley of Ovenden had a heated best chamber and chamber over the house in 1693,[13] and Edward Perkin, clothier, of Slaithwaite, had fireplaces in the Master's chamber and in the chamber over the housebody.[14]

Jackroyd was probably a hall and cross-wing house like Peel House, Warley, dated 1598, where firehoods originally heated the housebody and rear kitchen wing, and a stone chimney stack provided fireplaces for a ground-floor parlour and a first-floor chamber (Fig 14.5). The use of a firehood for cooking was not, however, invariable, and by the end of the century the housebody, and sometimes also the kitchen, might be heated by a large stone fireplace. The size of the fireplace indicates its likely use: smaller fireplaces, particularly when in the housebody, were not well equipped to serve as the principal cooking hearth, but large fireplaces could do this.[15] Changes in heating arrangements at Peel House show how room uses could alter over time. The late 16th-century house had firehoods in both housebody and kitchen, suggesting that cooking was shared between them. But in 1691 the housebody was upgraded with the replacement of the firehood by a stone chimney stack: the new fireplace, dated on the lintel, was adequate only to heat the room rather than to cook in.

By the mid-17th century the West Riding clothiers included in their ranks men of great wealth, able to build substantial houses with the same sort of specialised rooms, the same degree of comfort, and something of the same magnificence as were found in the houses of the contemporary lesser gentry. Lower Old Hall, in Norland, was built in 1634 by George Taylor, a dyer. It is not a very large house, but it is imposing, with a fine gritstone triple-gabled ashlar façade, a kitchen wing at the rear, and a number of fine heated rooms. These included a housebody heated by a carved fireplace and decorated with a plaster frieze (Fig 14.6), a heated parlour, again with plasterwork over the fireplace, and a heated chamber. The source of Taylor's wealth is evident in the house design, for the lower end of the main range is a simple single cell, probably an unheated workshop or warehouse for his dyed goods (RCHME 1986, 208).

A second yeoman-clothier's house, High Bentley, in Shelf, demonstrates a process of slow improvement, generation by generation. The house began as a timber-framed aisled hall, probably of late 15th-century date, but underwent significant extension and alteration over the following two centuries. The workings of the house in the late 17th century are revealed by the 1693 inventory of Samuel Wade and by the records made of the house before dereliction destroyed its features (Fig 14.7). The centre of the house was the housebody, open through two storeys, and thereby betraying its medieval origin, but updated by the insertion of a stone chimney stack with a plaster overmantel. The original cross-wing contained a sun parlour and a sun chamber as well as rooms to the north, and the added rear wing contained a kitchen. The inventory lists eight ranges, indicating the existence of a corresponding number of heated rooms. The room contents demonstrate the sophisticated division of functions within the house. The housebody, with its gallery, decorative fireplace and plasterwork, was a sitting and dining room, with ten chairs, a long table, a form, a round table and clocks. The sun parlour doubled as the best bedroom and as a sitting room or dining room, with a long table, a form and six chairs, and there were two further parlours. The kitchen was clearly the site of the cooking hearth: probably still heated by a firehood, it had spits, pots, pans, and the household stock of pewter. The chambers were simple bedrooms, although some of the better ones must have been heated. The inventory ends with a list of goods at the lower end of the house, the site of the shop and shop chamber. Here were the tools of Wade's trade, including shears, scales and a loom, and a considerable stock of cloth.[16]

Conclusion: housing standards in late 17th-century West Yorkshire

Students of vernacular architecture have argued for many decades over the concept of the great rebuilding. The present examination of housing in West Yorkshire has addressed the heart of this question and has used a range of sources to test the evidence for an improvement in living standards in the 17th century. Some conclusions, relating both to the principal issue itself and to the degree to which the Hearth Tax returns may be used as evidence, have emerged from the study.

First, virtually all households of gentry rank and above occupied complex, sophisticated houses with a high degree of comfort and specialisation in the use of rooms. The sources reveal, in fact, that they had enjoyed these conditions for a considerable time before the Hearth Tax assessors visited them in 1672. Second, it has been seen that a small number of non-gentry families lived in houses of similar sophistication. These houses may have been generally smaller and less sumptuous than those of the gentry and nobility, but they were nevertheless distinguished by clear differentiation in room use and by high standards of comfort. The prosperity generated by the textile industry was clearly responsible for the strength of the yeomanry in some parts of the county, and the difference between the simple accommodation offered by a timber-framed aisled house of the 15th century and the larger and more comfortable stone houses of the 17th century provides unambiguous evidence for raised expectations of material life on the part of the richest yeoman-clothiers. Third, something like a half of the households in the county had more than one hearth in their house. Even the two-hearth house repre-

Fig 14.6 The elaborate fireplace and plaster overmantel in the housebody of Lower Old Hall, Norland, West Yorkshire, of 1634: the wealthiest yeomen could afford to live in style. © Crown Copyright

Fig 14.7 The remains of High Bentley, Shelf, West Yorkshire. The transomed window lit the open housebody, the cross-wing contained sun parlour and sun chamber, there was a kitchen wing at the rear, and a shop wing has been removed from the right-hand end. © Crown Copyright

sented a significant advance on the living standards which, Harrison would have readers believe, all but a very few endured in the Middle Ages.

The Hearth Tax returns, it may be concluded, can be used with some confidence to indicate living standards where houses had more than a single hearth. This is especially true for the larger houses: there can be little doubt that a house with five hearths could accommodate a better and more expansive way of life than one with only two hearths. But the returns cannot be used with the same confidence where they relate to single-hearth households. Half the households in the county overall, and a much larger proportion in some small areas, lived, as far as heating was concerned, in conditions identical to those of their medieval forebears, with domestic life centred on the single household hearth. If only the provision of heating is taken as a measure of how far the great rebuilding had progressed by the late 17th century, then it must be concluded that the Hearth Tax returns record only the half-way point, in terms of population if not of chronology, in movement away from the minimum living standard.

The situation is, however, far more complex than this single measurement allows: many new houses of the 17th century were built with a single hearth, but in other respects – quality of construction, the incorporation of chambers – they show considerable advances on medieval ways of life and should certainly be counted as part of the great rebuilding rather than as a perpetuation of medieval forms. To this extent, therefore, the Hearth Tax cannot, on its own, be used to demonstrate with great accuracy the extent of change from medieval standards of living, for by far the most common house type – the single-hearth house – could describe a wide range of material comfort. The returns make no distinction between the tiny cottage, perhaps built 200 years before and crumbling around its poor occupiers, and the new stone houses of modestly prosperous families. Quite what proportion of the single-hearth houses recorded in 1672 were indeed unimproved hovels will never be known. What is known is that many of these hovels, or later versions of the same, survived into the late 19th century, when antiquaries were noting their existence as curiosities. It was only in this later period that housing standards improved widely at the lower social levels, as the new urban working class moved in to solid terraced housing. It is an interesting piece of historical perspective to recognise that the mechanic or craftsman of *c* 1900, living in a speculator-built terraced house with three, four or even five hearths, had at last attained something of the degree of differentiation in room use and of comfort, represented by the number of fireplaces, that Harrison's 'inferior artificers' had enjoyed 300 years earlier.

Chapter 14: Notes

1. Much of the material discussed in this chapter is taken from RCHME 1986, which gives additional detail about many of the houses mentioned in this account.
2. For documentary evidence for medieval housing in West Yorkshire, see Moorhouse 1981.
3. BIA Inventory of Judeth Almen, June 1689.
4. BIA Inventory of Daniel Smith, October 1689.
5. BIA Inventory of Henry Johnson, May 1689.
6. BIA Inventory of Richard Denton, September 1689.
7. BIA Inventory of Anthony Milner, November 1693.
8. BIA Inventory of Robert Reade, June 1697.
9. BIA Inventory of Daniel Thorpe, December 1693.
10. BIA Inventory of John Hanson, August 1693.
11. BIA Inventory of Samuel Swaine, May 1689.
12. BIA Inventory of George Boyle, September 1693.
13. BIA Inventory of Thomas Priestley, April 1693.
14. BIA Inventory of Edward Perkin, November 1693.
15. For a discussion of the changing technology in the kitchen of Yorkshire gentry houses, see Brears 1984, chapter 2. It is likely that kitchens in yeoman houses operated with the same sort of equipment, albeit on a reduced scale and perhaps with some time lag.
16. BIA Inventory of Samuel Wade, May 1693.

15 The Durham Hearth Tax: Community Politics and Social Relations *by Adrian Green*

Introduction

The Hearth Tax records are notoriously tricky and demanding sources. Wilson, in an effort to encourage social historians to engage with scientific and intellectual history, has commented that 'if we can master (say) Restoration Hearth Tax records, then surely we can come to grips with (say) the writings of Boyle and Newton' (Wilson 1993, 30). The reasons why the Hearth Tax records are so difficult to use relate to the complexities of administration in a society that was structured according to local patterns of authority, yet was experiencing an unprecedented degree of state centralisation in the late 17th century (Braddick 1996; Braddick 2000; cf chapter 2). Collecting taxes is a key function of the state, and at the Restoration in 1660 the Exchequer took control of all revenues. The Hearth Tax, introduced in 1662, was granted in perpetuity and levied on an indicator of wealth, and as such represented a permanent tax on income. Yet, the agents of the state on the ground – village constables, parish churchwardens and county justices – were involved with local social relations which conflicted with the effective gathering of revenue. Only in the context of community relations can their tolerance of under-assessment and sometimes generous interpretation of the exemption criteria be understood. This chapter will explore the issues related to the community politics of taxation in County Durham, and will consider what the micro-politics of taxation meant for issues of recording. This presents a means to glean yet more information about 17th-century society from the records by attending to the reasons for omissions in the data. These should not be assumed to be the result of administrative error; rather explanations should be sought for why those responsible for assessing and collecting the tax, and allowing exemption, acted as they did in the context of their communities.

Before turning to the micro-politics of taxation, this chapter summarises what the Hearth Tax returns for Lady Day 1666 and 1674 reveal about housing and social relations in the contrasting communities of urban, industrial and agricultural County Durham (Fig 15.1). The issues highlighted here are explored in much greater detail in Green 2006, which includes the full transcript of the tax for Lady Day 1666, tabulated data for Lady Day 1674, exemption certificates for the 1670s, and transcripts of surviving local records, along with maps and tables for hearth-ranges by township. These data are also analysed, and there is a discussion of the Hearth Tax and surviving houses.

Housing and social relations

The general character of Durham society in the late 17th century can be summarised on the basis of the Hearth Tax returns. County Durham had an exceptionally high level of relative poverty, with around four in ten recorded households exempted from the tax in 1666 and 1674. Rural settlements were characterised by a majority of single-hearth households, inhabited by cottagers and wage labourers, most of whom were exempt from the tax. Over half of charged households had single hearths, with more than a third in the middling bracket of two to four hearths. Lesser craftsmen and husbandmen, along with better paid specialist workers in industrial employment, had one or two hearths, and a smaller number of more wealthy farmers and middling tradesmen in towns occupied houses with three or four hearths. A generally sparsely spread gentry (with clusters in certain towns and villages), as well as wealthy tradesmen and professionals in towns, usually lived in houses with over five hearths. This broad élite represented less than 10% cent of charged households, and just 5% of the recorded population. There were only a few great houses with over twenty hearths (twelve are recorded in 1666), and houses with over ten hearths made up less than 1% of all recorded households. Even in the towns, fewer than 2% of householders had establishments with over ten hearths and there were no large households in a majority of rural communities.

The relative absence of families of consequence reflected the extensive estates of the Church, and few communities were dominated by the gentry or nobility. The social distance between the élite and the rest of society was exacerbated by the tendency for the wealthy to be clustered together. This was especially pronounced in the north of the county, where communities either had several households with over ten hearths or none at all. These larger households were often funded from commercial wealth, and indicate the social polarisation between coal owners and coal workers. The location of wealthier houses was also related to patterns of sociability, and ease of access to the county town. The greatest concentration of households with ten or more hearths, and a considerable number of five- to nine-hearth houses, lay within a 16km (10 mile) radius of Durham City. The strong preference for dwelling near others of similar social standing is also evident in the marked clustering of householders with status designations in 1666, such as Mr, Mrs, Esq, or Gent.

Across England, the five-hearth house has been taken to represent an important threshold in relation

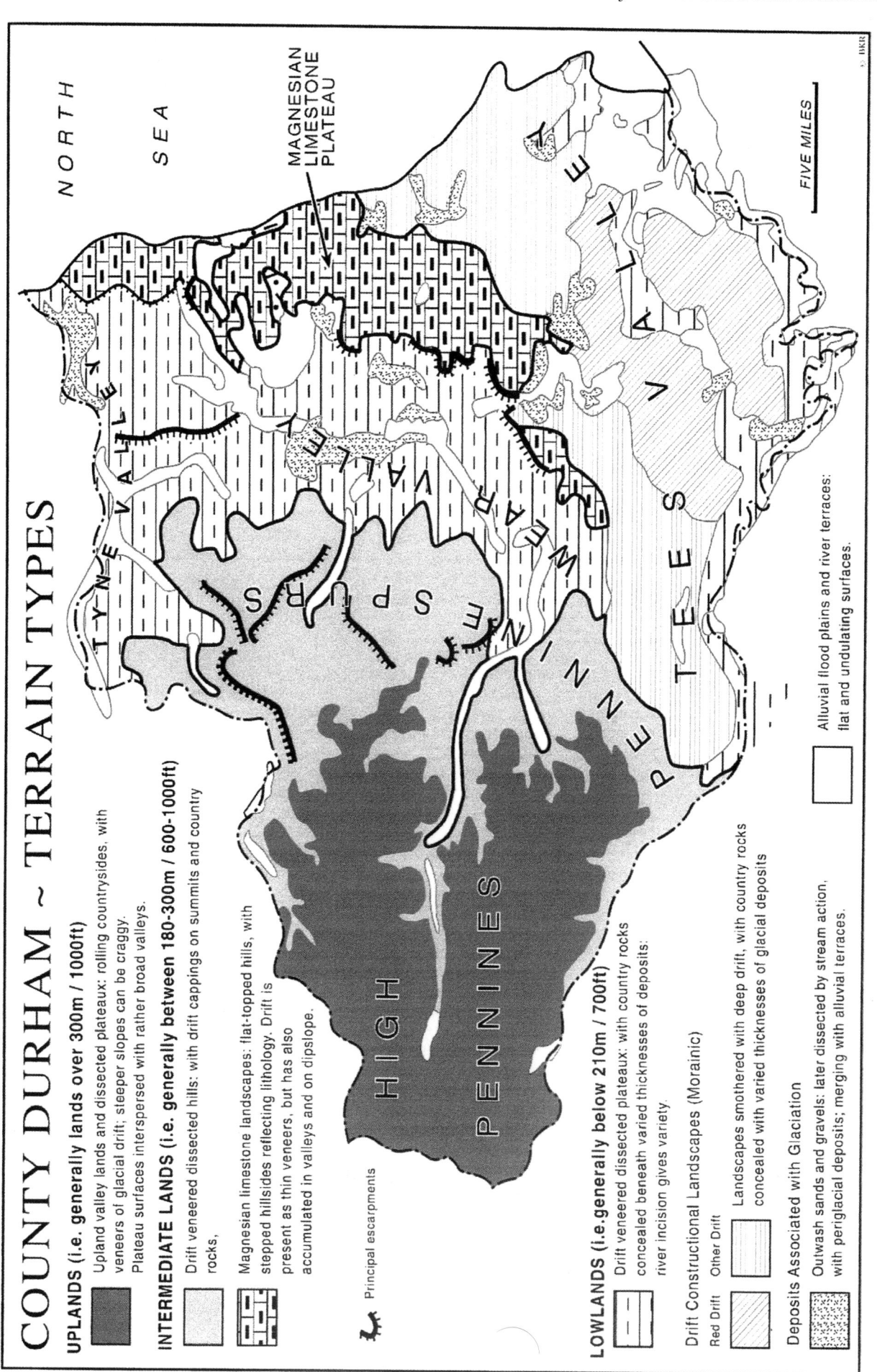

Fig 15.1 Terrain map of County Durham by B K Roberts. Source: Green 2006

to social status, and Gregory King believed that the gentry usually occupied houses of five hearths or more (Spufford and Watt 1995, 9). In Durham City, the gentry, merchants and professionals mostly lived in houses with between five and nine hearths. In the coal mining parish of Whickham, households with five to nine hearths were those of the lesser gentry – 'the wealthiest and most prominent members of parish society' (Levine and Wrightson 1991, 158) – and this was generally true in the more rural parts of the county. Yet five hearths was not an absolute threshold for status or wealth, and across County Durham the lesser élite had a somewhat broader range of hearth numbers, with many persons of status in 1666 paying on houses with four or even three hearths.

Around 1000 households were listed with three of four hearths in 1666. There were some gentry and professionals with houses of four hearths, more rarely three, and a number of prosperous widows and unmarried women. Generally, however, the three- and four-hearth category relates to the wealthier middling sort, particularly the more prosperous farmers, craftsmen and tradesmen. Yet the opportunities for accumulating sufficient wealth to fund a three or four-hearth house were limited, and they represent just 15% of paying households, and less than 10% of all households. This is half the proportion in Kent, where 22% of households had three or four hearths (Harrington et al 2000, xlv). The relatively small size of the prosperous middling element in Durham, with few houses having more than two hearths in most communities, highlights the distinctive nature of Durham society. Middling affluence was ultimately limited, and it might be presumed that members of this class had less of a stranglehold on social mores than in much of southern England.

Whereas wealthier middling households might have three or four hearths, two hearths generally related to the lower middling sections of society. This distinction between middling sorts of people is not absolute, and represents differences in degrees of wealth. Houses with three, two or one hearths, for those in craft and agricultural occupations, were often not dissimilar – except for the number of heated rooms. Better-off husbandmen and some yeomen lived in two-hearth houses with several unheated rooms. The second hearth usually heated the parlour or a kitchen where cooking took place separately from in the hall. But both hearths were not always in domestic use: John Adamson had a shop with one hearth and a separate house with one hearth at West Auckland in March 1672.[1] Households with two hearths rarely amounted to more than a quarter of the population in Durham communities in 1666, and many places had fewer than 20%. In Kent, by contrast, few areas had less than 25% (Harrington et al 2000, xlvii–xlviii). Yet Durham did contain higher proportions of two-hearth houses where prosperity allowed, and lowland farming villages with over 25% of houses with two hearths existed along the Rivers Tees and Wear, and a few places in the south and west of the county had over 40%. The east coast was less prosperous with fewer lower-middling houses of two hearths, except for the port towns of Hartlepool, Sunderland and South Shields. The social profile of Tyneside was more in keeping with the agrarian parts of the county than is commonly assumed, as the proportion of lower middling households with two hearths was generally under 20%, and pockets of middling prosperity were often surrounded by large numbers of single-hearth households.

Single-hearth households predominate in County Durham to a degree unparalleled in many southern counties. Whereas the map of one-hearth households for Kent (Harrington et al 2000, xlvi) does not even have a category for places with over 70%, the equivalent map for Durham (Fig 15.2) shows communities with over 70% of households with a single hearth throughout the county (the main exception being the more prosperous settlements along the River Wear). This map shows that the industrial districts were less distinct from the rest of the county – in terms of the proportion of households with one hearth – than might be expected. Rural communities in County Durham were characterised by a majority of single-hearth houses, some of which were occupied by those dependent on wage-labour and most were exempt from the tax. Over 50% of paying households also only had a single hearth, and husbandmen and craftsmen occupied houses with several rooms but only one hearth. Households paying on one or two hearths represent the more prosperous of the lower orders, with a secure income. This group may be distinguished from those single-hearth households exempt from the tax, as although exemption does not represent a poverty line it is possible that the form of housing had some bearing on whether assessors regarded a household as up to paying.

The Hearth Tax and housing

The Hearth Tax falls midway through a period of protracted change in the provision and heating of space in houses. The relatively high social status of most surviving domestic buildings constructed before 1700 has tended to obscure the degree to which people continued to occupy houses which did not comply with the requirements of their wealthier and increasingly socially distant neighbours. Only for the most successful middling households, usually based on married couples with secure incomes, is it possible to posit the replacement of an open-hall house (with an inner room to the high end and service rooms at the low end, both of which might be floored) by a hall and parlour house with a full upper storey and a greater number of service rooms, including a kitchen for cooking. The desire to heat some of these rooms, primarily the hall and kitchen, but also the parlour, and sometimes upstairs chambers, determined the number of hearths a house might

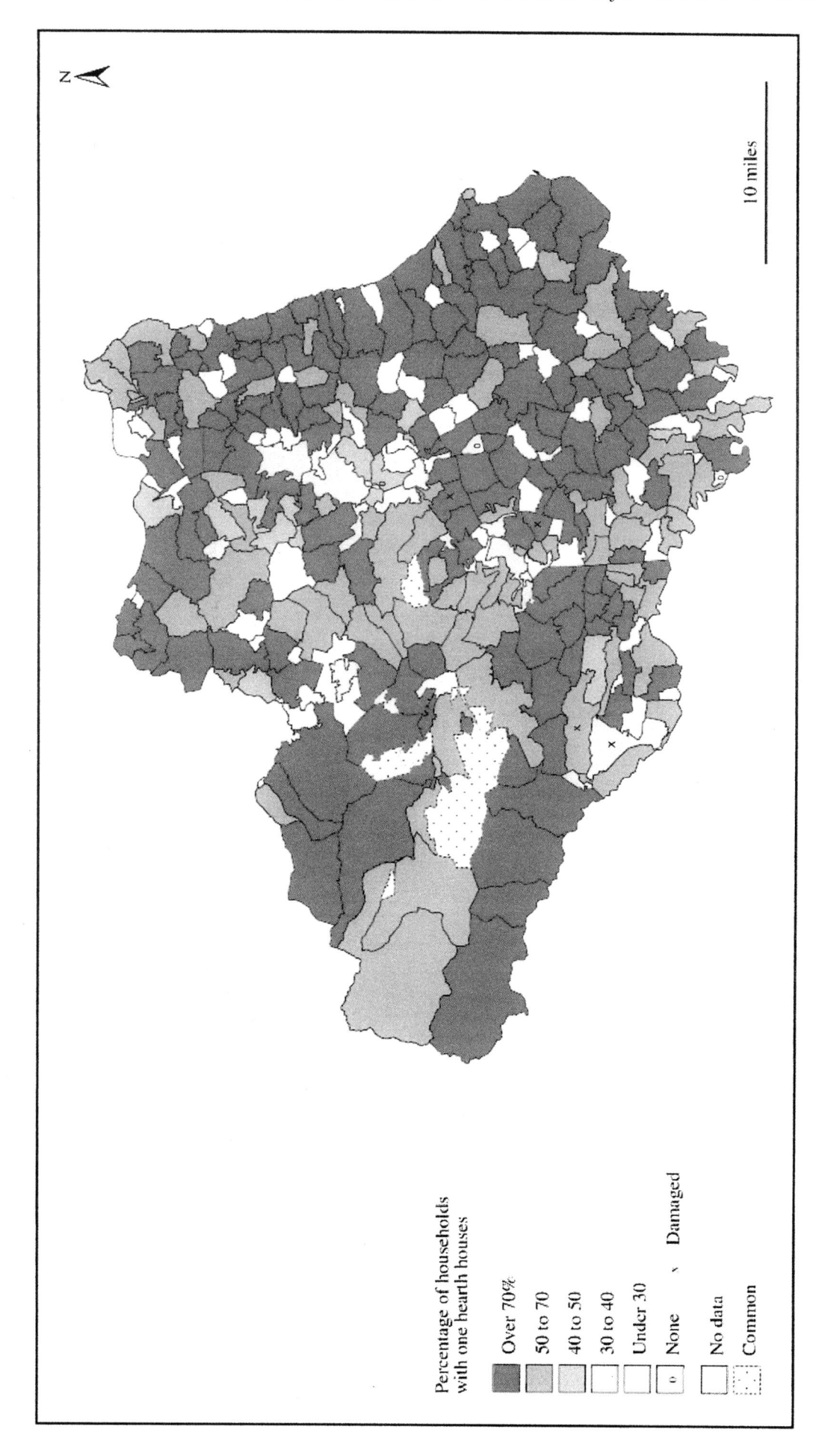

The Durham Hearth Tax: Community Politics and Social Relations 147

Fig 15.2 Map of one-hearth households in 1666 in County Durham. Source: Green 2006. © British Record Society

Fig 15.3 Old Queen's Head, Wolsingham, Weardale: 17th-century stepped chimney stack. © A Green

have. While much attention has been given to the changing social relations involved with enclosing the open hall (Johnson 1993), the increased use of upper floors was equally important and helps explain the introduction of chimneys. Chimney stacks provided a means of heating rooms on upper floors, and while this usually refers to houses with three hearths or more, many houses with one or two hearths on the ground floor had unheated rooms above which required the smoke from their hearths to be evacuated by a flue. The increasing use of coal, especially prevalent in County Durham, provided a further motivation for the cultural preference of containing smoke within a flue. From outside the house, chimney stacks signified wealth, and the large projecting stepped stacks on 17th-century houses made this an overt social statement (Fig 15.3).

Although middling rural and urban houses were being rebuilt in the early 17th century (Green 1998; and Fig 15.4), a greater proportion of houses were probably rebuilt in the later 17th century. For County Durham, 1666 may be slightly too early to record many of these. By 1674 a significant number of those assessed for two or more hearths had been enlarged, and there were considerably more houses with between five and nine hearths in 1674 than in 1666. This indicates increasing prosperity for those of more than moderate wealth in the 1660s and 1670s, while the bulk of the population remained in smaller dwellings with only one hearth. Yet, the pattern of housing change was more complex in detail, and the 1670 altered assessment records both demolished and newly built houses as well as reductions and additions to houses both large and small. At West Cassop, a five- and a three- hearth house were both 'pulled down', but in neighbouring Pittington a two-hearth house increased to nine hearths and a nine-hearth house had 'decayed' to eight hearths. Nearly half of the 224 legible entries refer to changes of occupier without any alteration in hearth numbers, and eight empty properties, reflecting something of the housing market. Of the remainder, over two-thirds relate to houses which had been newly built or had hearths added, while the other third had either been demolished or experienced a reduction in the number of hearths in use.[2] The demolition of single-hearth houses followed in some instances from enclosure, especially in the agrarian south-east of the county where settlements were contracting, whereas the greater number of new builds and increases in hearth numbers indicate a preference for investing surplus income in improvements to housing.

Limitations of survival make it difficult to gauge the degree of changes in the use of hearths in County Durham. Over 95% of the dwellings documented in the Hearth Tax no longer survive. Many of these would have been comparable to the moderately sized single-hearth houses known from excavation (Pallister and Wrathmell 1990), while timber-framed houses would have been similar to those still standing south of the Tees (Harrison 1991). Others, especially the two- and three-hearth houses, would have been comparable to surviving stone-built houses. Figure 15.5 illustrates a late 17th-century yeoman farmhouse – a two-and-a-

Fig 15.4 Westernhopeburn Farmhouse, Eastgate, Weardale: an early 17th-century upland farmhouse. © A Green

Fig 15.5 Slashpool Farm, Hett village, County Durham: a late 17th-century yeoman farmhouse in the Wear lowlands. © A Green

half-storey hall and parlour house (with two or three hearths) and a byre at the low end rebuilt as a kitchen in 1708. For workers' housing in the north of the county, documentary sources compensate for the lack of archaeological investigation. Pitmen were often provided with accommodation – and coal to fuel their hearths – by their employers (Levine and Wrightson 1991, 189–90). These workers often lived away from the established areas of settlement, frequently in temporary shelters near the coal pits and spoil heaps. It is likely that the inhabitants of these 'hovels' were the kind of people who were not always counted as householders among the exempt and did not appear in the Hearth Tax returns at all. More securely employed workers in the coal trade had commensurately more permanent housing, and the later 17th century witnessed the beginnings of pitmen 'rows', with each household centred on a single room with one hearth. Managerial and better-paid skilled workers occupied houses with several rooms and often had more than one hearth. In Whickham, two- and three-hearth households were occupied by the 'superior employees and semi-independent middlemen of the coal trade', as well as yeomen and better-off craftsmen (Levine and Wrightson 1991, 159–60). Workers employed in glass and metal manufacture, and salt panning, occupied a similar range of accommodation. The concentration of these industries, along with ship building and rope making, encouraged the development of terraced housing, often referred to as 'rows' or 'onsets' of cottages in the late 17th century (Green forthcoming).

The more securely employed on Tyneside and Wearside were thus in better accommodation than is normally imagined, and may have been better housed than agricultural labouring families, who were usually on lower incomes. The widespread enclosure of fields in 17th-century Durham – motivated by the market for produce presented by the waged population in industrial employment – required an increasing proportion of the rural population to become dependent on wage-labour, which in turn resulted in the greater need for relief from poverty through under-employment, especially in old age. Many migrated to find industrial employment, and settlements in the south and east of the county were contracting or deserted in the later 17th century. The remaining labouring families occupied smaller cottages, often subdivisions of older houses or newly built in rows. These cottages were not necessarily an improvement on earlier housing, as the families occupying them in the later 17th century would often have had great grandparents in long houses, who raised their own food, a hundred years before. Indeed, housing conditions probably worsened for a majority of the poor and wage-labourers in 17th-century Durham. Meanwhile, the prosperous craftsmen, skilled labourers and farmers experienced an improvement in housing conditions. Those benefiting from economic change (especially enclosure) experienced a 'great rebuilding' from c 1600, with further rebuilding from c 1670, more in line with housing change in southern England. While a large proportion of the population were in smaller houses, with only one hearth, those with a degree of prosperity and higher social status occupied houses comparable to those in southern England (Green 1998). It is the proportions between the various forms of housing, rather than uniform relative poverty, which differentiates County Durham from more affluent areas.

Politics of taxation

Taxation was a political issue and from its inception this novel form of tax aroused considerable opposition, as reflected in anti-Hearth Tax ballads such as *The Chimney's Scuffle* (1662). Most historians have emphasised opposition to chimney men entering the home, which occurred from 1664 (*Statutes of the Realm* 1810–28, 16 Charles II c 3) when professional tax collectors were employed in place of the local constables (see chapter 2). Contemporaries were certainly annoyed by tax assessors having access to their houses, and the 1689 'Act for taking away the revenue arising by hearth money' asserted that the tax was 'a badge of slavery upon the whole people exposing every man's house to be entered into and searched at pleasure by persons unknown to him' (*Statutes of the Realm* 1810–28, 1 William and Mary c 10). Whig historians subsequently asserted that the Hearth Tax offended English liberty by intruding upon property. But opposition to the tax pre-dated 1664 and people were conscious of a more Tory concern in their hostility towards what was effectively an income tax. Sir William Petty in his 1662 'Treatise of Taxes and Contributions' identified the number of hearths as a measure of an individual's purchasing power (Evans and Rose 2000, xiii; Hull 1899). Such permanent taxation on wealth was widely regarded as unjust and this partly explains resistance to the Hearth Tax.

Restoration taxation had a particular political context in the Bishopric (or County Palatine) of Durham, where the bishops held considerable secular power. The Civil War and Commonwealth removed these prerogatives, but at the Restoration Bishop Cosin was equipped with the powers of his predecessors and the Church estates were restored. The reported enthusiasm which greeted Cosin's entry into the Bishopric and City of Durham in 1661 has been taken to indicate that the Restoration was welcomed. A portion of the population was undoubtedly sympathetic to a return to the order and authority of the 1630s – when several communities had been keen on the 'thorough' administration of Church and secular affairs (James 1974, 108–37). Such communities, invariably those with a gentry presence, were more deferential to authority and more amenable to taxation. Unsurprisingly, the two Durham communities with surviving local Hearth Tax lists both relate to villages with active gentry families, the Catholic Salvins at Tudhoe, and the Edens at West Auckland.[3] In many other communities, the attitude to authority was very different, especially where Protestant dissenters were numerous (and the county contained a notable number of Quakers, among other groups). Their demands for religious freedom in the 1660s were

Fig 15.6 East Oakley House, West Auckland, County Durham: home of John Kay, hearth tax collector, assessed for three hearths in 1666 and the 1670s. © A Green

accompanied by appeals for lower taxation (Hutton 1986, 205).

The Restoration circumscribed the political and economic, as well as religious, freedoms enjoyed by Durham's populace during the 1650s. Individuals had been able to purchase the freeholds of sequestrated lands and houses, but in July 1660 Charles II ordered the seizure of both Crown and Church lands in Durham, and the interregnum purchasers forfeited their freeholds (Hutton 1986, 140). To add insult to injury, the restoration of the Church estates entailed the payment of arrears on the restored leaseholds – in some cases these were not cleared until the end of the century (Mussett with Woodward 1988). The propertied inhabitants of Durham also lost their representation in parliament, briefly gained in the 1650s but reverting in 1660 to virtual representation via the bishop in the House of Lords (Heesom 1988). Traditionally, lack of representation in parliament went with lack of central taxation in the Palatinate of Durham (Lapsley 1900, 294–300). The imposition of the Hearth Tax in 1662 might therefore have been expected to have fuelled resentment towards the Restoration regime. Radical opposition was certainly present in the north-east of England, which spawned one of the greatest threats to the Restoration nationally in the Derwentdale Plot of 1663–64, which included the abolition of the Hearth Tax and freedom of religion in its programme.[4]

In some Durham communities, local officials refused to co-operate in the first years of the Hearth Tax. In parts of Easington ward, the high constables made no returns whatsoever for Michaelmas 1662, and constables in every ward made no or limited returns in 1662 and 1663. Further lassitude was present in Gateshead, where parish officials allowed a very large number of households to be returned as exempt on between three and seven hearths.[5] For the county as a whole there were considerable arrears by Lady Day 1664, when only 65% of the assessment was collected. A further indication of non-cooperation is that the assessment itself had been limited. William Christian, appointed receiver for the county in July 1664, managed to increase the assessment, and Michaelmas 1665 witnessed a 14% increase on the number of chargeable hearths, though Christian was only able to collect 51% of the amount assessed (Parkinson 2001; Green 2005). Christian signed off his list of those in arrears for 1662–64, with the declaration 'that the severrall persons not mentioned in this schedule are either so poor that no distress can be had against them' or 'are run away so that the said duty could not be collected from them'.[6]

The collection of taxes in the first phase of the Hearth Tax from 1662 to 1664 was devolved upon the lowest office-holders – the constables in individual towns and villages – overseen by the county magistrates and sheriff. The constables were men of ordinary status, usually serving in rotation as the established householders of their communities (Kent 1986), and the authority of the justices and even the sheriff relied on their local standing (Braddick 2000). In some places, community sentiment failed to comply with the expectation that householders should pay the rates and serve their turn as constable. The inhabitants of Ketton were refusing to contribute 'according to their proportion to the Book of Rates' and 'to the several charges' of the petty constable in 1664, while in Stanhope there were problems with finding petty constables to serve in the outlying parts of this large upland parish.[7] Disputes over filling the office of constable also occurred in communities where we might expect a more compliant attitude to authority. At West Auckland, the gentry Eden family occupied the largest house in the village (assessed for eight hearths in 1666), at the western end of the village green, while the three-hearth house of the grieve, John Kay (whose initials remain on the parlour fireplace), stood at its eastern end (Fig 15.6). Kay served as constable in the 1670s and entered Hearth Tax lists meticulously in his notebook. His notebook also records a protracted dispute over who should serve as constable, eventually resolved in about 1700. On the basis of good neighbourliness, and in the presence of John Eden Esq, it was agreed that all householders should serve in rotation on the basis of the location of their house, 'whereas heretofore there hath very often and for the most part every year strifes and dissents been raised ... concerning the serving of the office of Constables'.[8]

Even where the obligation to serve as local officers was upheld without difficulty, both constables and justices were necessarily alive to local circumstances and how far they could go in extracting revenue. 'In exercising political power early modern office-holders and officers were embroiled in negotiation, and built into the functioning of the state was a sensitivity to expectations outside the ranks of the formally empowered' (Braddick 2000, 79). The collection of taxes involved interactions between neighbours, and administration of the Hearth Tax by local office-holders 'prompted suspicions that widespread evasion and underassessment were being encouraged by office-holders sensitive to the views of their neighbours' (Braddick 2000, 256). It was the failure of the constables to collect anything approaching the full potential revenue from the Hearth Tax in its first two years (and the returns from Durham were exceptionally low) that led to the experiments in tax farming which privatised tax collection. It was this innovation that led to vociferous opposition to the 'chimney men' who were entitled to enter homes to collect the tax, if necessary by the seizure of goods when accompanied by a constable. The constables and justices proved widely reluctant to prosecute those who failed to comply (Braddick 1994, 262), and there appears to be no evidence for prosecutions relating to the Hearth Tax in the Durham Quarter Sessions. The population of County Durham, moreover, were aware that the authorities could be lenient. They had perhaps heard that the Mayor of Newcastle in 1666, facing riots in Sandgate ward, proclaimed in public that only those willing to pay need do so. 'The mayor, recorder and aldermen all went in the afternoon to appease the tumult, and to explain the intentions of the collectors of the duty, and only to be taken from those who were able' and 'the collectors were only ordered to take from those who were willing, but the ruder people stoned them away'.[9]

In other parts of the country in the winter and spring of 1666, householders turned to disorder when the evasion allowed by constables and justices was made more difficult under the tax farmers. Such disorder sometimes involved whole communities, with the tacit support of gentry and justices, and the 'constables were notoriously disinclined to intervene, and there is a significant absence of prosecutions resulting in most surviving Quarter Session records' (Hutton 1986, 257–58). In north-eastern England there were Hearth Tax riots in Hexham as well as in Newcastle, and in the North Riding of Yorkshire (Braddick 1996, 234–35; Purdy 1991, 19–29). County Durham might have been expected to participate in this disorder, especially since in May 1666 the coal pits were closed and the miners left unemployed (Hutton 1986, 237). Yet no disorder against the Hearth Tax is recorded in the Bishopric. This absence of disorder reflects the success of the county government in ensuring good order. In the autumn of 1666, Bishop Cosin, as lord lieutenant of the county, was warning his deputy-lieutenants to guard against disorder resulting from rumours connected with the Great Fire of London, and they responded by issuing instructions to their officers 'to double their guard, and to keep patrols constant in the night, that we might not be surprised or taken unprovided' (Osmond 1913, 274). With order a priority, the collection of the Hearth Tax was presumably conducted in such a way that local grievances were catered for. This clearly has implications for the reliability of the data compiled in the Exchequer returns. Under-recording of hearths and households may well relate to lenient practices at a local level that the tax collectors – and tax payers – regarded as legitimate, with or without the sanction of higher authority. As Arkell and Braddick have emphasised, there was considerable variation in the ways in which local officers interpreted the central legislation (see chapter 3; Braddick 1994, 231–70). It was part of the logic of late 17th-century authority that neighbourly relations had a greater immediacy than central government. Office-holders might represent the authority of the Crown, as the royal coat of arms heading the imposing document requiring the Mayor of Durham and others to take the oath of Hearth Tax officers in 1685 attests,[10] but it was within communities that established residents agreed upon who counted as householders, who received favourable treatment, and who might reasonably be excluded from tax assessment altogether.

Inter-personal relations could result in leniency for individual Hearth Tax assessments, but could equally allow for stricter interpretation of the rules where constables were not well disposed to householders attempting evasion. The constable at Tudhoe noted in 1670 that one of the Byerleys' five hearths was 'not paid by W.B. senior pretending it a Butcher Shop'.[11] The constable was perhaps not prepared to allow this evasion because the Byerleys had paid on five hearths in previous years. While the local assessments for 1666 and 1668 record the Byerleys as having five hearths, the Exchequer return for 1666 lists William Byerley senior and junior separately for two and three hearths respectively. This is not the only discrepancy between the constable's lists and the Exchequer records for Tudhoe. These reveal significant under-recording in the Exchequer returns. The constable's 1670 assessment, being a full survey of the township for a new administration of the tax, provides the most complete index of Tudhoe households and their hearths. It lists households in topographical order, with the non-liable intermingled with the chargeable. Sixty-five households are recorded, and the parish officers certificated an additional thirteen as exempt. In all other years the Tudhoe constables recorded a lower number of households and hearths, indicating that the local records themselves usually include a degree of under-recording. Compared to the constable's survey of 1670, the under-recording in the 1674 Exchequer return is 40%. The Tudhoe lists also reveal significant under-recording among the chargeable population, of between 10% and 20% of both householders and hearths. Comparison with under-recording rates for other areas (Evans and Rose 2000, xxiv–xxv; Webster 1988, xxii), suggests that 20% under-recording may be general in the Exchequer returns. This under-recording mainly omitted the poor. The assessment of exemption in local lists is generally more comprehensive than the final returns enrolled for the Exchequer, and similar discrepancies can be found for West Auckland and St Helen Auckland on the basis of John Kay's notebook. Even local lists, however, rarely give an entirely accurate record of all households and hearths, being most likely to have excluded those who did not count as householders within settled parish society.

Poor relief was the most divisive issue affecting parish society in the 17th century, and the shifting pattern of employment and high degree of enclosure in County Durham created acute difficulties. At Long Newton in the 1660s, local officers identified three sorts of poor: those already in receipt of poor relief; those who kept livestock 'and so maintained themselves and their families, but that employment being taken away by the inclosure . . . are likely to be wholly burdensome to the town', and those 'with divers children and nothing to maintain them but the poor man's hand labour'.[12] For those who were regarded as part of the community, poor relief was an obligation of neighbourliness, but for those who were not deemed to be part of settled parish society it was a financial burden to be minimised (Hindle 2004; Rushton 1989). The lack of fit between the administrative structure and settlement pattern of County Durham – with large parishes containing several settlements administered as separate townships – created additional difficulties, especially after the Settlement Act of 1662 confirmed the administration of poor relief by township. Individual townships that felt over-burdened by their poor might petition the magistrates to oblige the entire parish to pay towards their relief. This occurred at Tudhoe, where the Quarter Sessions ordered that the poor of Tudhoe township shall 'be maintained at the charge of the whole parish' of Brancepeth.[13] The parish of Darnton was similarly required to contribute to the maintenance of the poor in Darnton township, and disputes over payment of the poor rate were brought to Quarter Sessions for Byers Green in 1675 and Greatham in 1677.[14] Underlying these disputes was an equitable sense that more prosperous neighbourhoods should support the poor. In 1675, the inhabitants of Crossgate in Durham City petitioned the magistrates that their wealthier neighbours in Framwellgate, 'who are part of the Chappelry of Saint Margarets' and 'who have great estates' yet paid less in poor rates, should contribute to 'the great number of poor' in Crossgate constabulary.[15]

The conflicts over poor relief between the smaller civic units and their larger parish directly affected the Hearth Tax because assessment and collection at township level did not always correlate with exemption by certificate at parish level. In the Exchequer returns, the areas for payers and non-payers are thus not always the same. Exemption from the Hearth Tax was granted on the basis that householders were not required to pay the poor rate, or that they occupied houses whose rentable value was less than £1 a year, and did not use or own land or tenements worth more than £10 a year. The property qualification that disabled new householders from being forced out under the 1662 Settlement Act was anyone who rented a house worth £10 a year or more (Slack 1988, 194). Those beneath this threshold were at the mercy of the local officers. For those establishing a household in a new community (without settlement rights from service, apprenticeship or marriage for women), the best way to become a part of parish society was to pay the rates and even offer to serve as a local office-holder (Snell 1991, 382). Anyone unable to do so, and regarded as likely to become chargeable to the parish, might be excluded from lists of the exempt in the Hearth Tax in case this in itself conferred any recognition of entitlement to poor relief. Since entitlement to poor relief generally included the elderly but excluded the able-bodied, we should expect those listed as exempt in the Hearth Tax to reflect life cycle poverty, but not always under-employment. As Arkell has emphasised (chapter 3), exemption from the Hearth Tax was not in itself a measure of poverty and those officers responsible for both poor relief and the Hearth Tax had some disincentive for recording those likely to become chargeable to the parish.

Those dwelling outside the established areas of settlement were especially likely not to be recorded in the Hearth Tax, and cottages on commons were frequently the resort of those excluded from parish society. The specific requirement to list cottages on commons in the printed instructions issued to Hearth Tax collectors in 1684 implies that they had not been regularly recorded previously (Arkell 1992, 47–50). Settlement on commons occurred across north and central County Durham, where immigration exceeded the existing housing stock and where the established villagers were reluctant to allow newcomers within the main settlement. In other places, especially villages and market centres where there was an increased need for employment, there was a greater tolerance of population increase and permanent housing was allowed to develop on the open village greens. It is unclear whether the initial semi-permanent cottages, or 'huts' as they were called, were included in the Hearth Tax. They may plausibly have been excluded if they lacked chimney stacks.

The Hearth Tax records certainly reveal a lack of rigour in the accurate recording of the exempt. The 1670s exemption certificates surviving among the Exchequer records indicate a considerable degree of copying between Hearth Tax lists, and the consistency in the numbers of recorded exempt for individual places suggests that they do not accurately record the flows of population on the ground.[16] The ultimate purpose of exemption lists was to ensure that those eligible under the assessment criteria did pay, and the tax aimed to maximise revenue for the Exchequer not to record the entire population. That the exemption lists do not enumerate the entire population, and omit the poorest, reflects an ultimate lack of ability on the part of the state to record those who were never going to be able to contribute to the revenue, or who stood outside of parish relief. Some, I suggest, were deliberately excluded at a local level. Receiving poor relief or contributing to taxation implied reciprocal obligations with the community, which they may not have been welcome in, or wanted to join. This is especially likely for areas of County Durham where irregular industrial and maritime employment encouraged high levels of population mobility: people who appeared shiftless and faceless to the established households. Similar strategies for deliberate social distancing occurred in agricultural villages as well, although there was some sympathy for those immediately disadvantaged by enclosure. Non-payers in the Hearth Tax returns are best taken as recording the more stable sections of the population. Given the high degree of population mobility, the under-recording of the poorest and most transitory groups must have been considerable.

Conclusion

In Durham, evidence of resistance to the Hearth Tax is muted. There was significant initial refusal by constables and parochial officials to cooperate in 1662, 1663 and 1664, and the levels of assessment were far below the national average. Yet no disorderly resistance is known to have occurred, and 1666 was remarkably quiet in comparison with other counties. This suggests some accommodation between ordinary householders and those in authority, and the context of tax collection certainly warrants considerable caution over under-recording, both in omitting households and in under-assessing numbers of hearths. Some people, especially those at the margins of parish society, were entirely excluded from assessment, even among the exempt. Local office-holders seem to have found it desirable not to list some people at all. It may also be the case that those who lacked a chimney stack were not regarded as eligible to pay chimney money. Under-recording in the Hearth Tax has usually been regarded as the result of administrative complexity and error. Yet the underlying reasons for omissions in the data also relate to community politics. It was in this community context that the micro-politics of taxation encouraged tolerance of under-assessment, high levels of exemption, as well as the desire to exclude the poorest and marginal from recording. By contrast, those communities where full recording can be demonstrated may represent places where social relations were stable and authority was exercised with due deference for the law. Yet even where we can detect full recording on the basis of linking the Hearth Tax with house plots or other lists of householders, we should remember that outlying areas of waste might contain the marginal who were excluded from all these forms of record. Surviving evidence from Tudhoe township indicates that perhaps 40% of householders were omitted from the Lady Day 1674 Exchequer return for County Durham, excluding the poorest of the population. Under-recording also reveals a larger truth: that a significant proportion of the population was beyond the reach of state authority.

Chapter 15: Notes

1. DUA Halmote Court Doc M 95.
2. TNA E179/375/5.
3. DRO D/Sa/E 882–90; DUA Halmote Court Doc M 95.
4. DUA Mickleton MS 31, f 58 cited in Hutton 1986, 204–05.
5. TNA E179/106/20 and 2.
6. TNA E179/106/23.
7. DRO Q/S/OB 5, 215 and 225.
8. DUA Halmote Court Doc M 95.
9. *Calendar of State Papers Domestic*, 1666–67, 330–31 cited in Braddick 1994, 256.
10. DRO D/Lo/F 382.
11. DRO D/Sa/E 882–90.
12. DRO D/Lo/F 196(2) quoted in Rushton 1989, 145.
13. DRO D/Sa/E 899.
14. DRO Q/S/OB 6.
15. DRO Q/S/OB .
16. TNA E179/327 parts 2 and 3.

16 Northumberland, Newcastle upon Tyne, Berwick upon Tweed, and North Durham: One County *by Grace McCombie*

The context

With regard to the country I found that England at a distance of from 50 to 60 miles from the frontier, and especially the county of Northumberland, was very poor, uncultivated and exceedingly wretched, while for many miles on the other side of the frontier I seemed to be travelling through uninhabited deserts. This proceeds from the sterility of the ground and also from the perpetual wars with which these nations have savagely destroyed each other.

These were the words in 1617 of Giovanni Battista Lionello, the Venetian Secretary in England, writing to the Doge and the Senate after he had reached Edinburgh (*Calendar of State Papers Venice* 1908, 550). He considered Northumberland's character to be 'exceedingly wretched' then, and the buildings of Northumberland reflect that past, that of a troubled border county.

While such disorder affected all buildings, it is vernacular houses which are the particular focus of this book. What the Hearth Tax returns can reveal about these buildings in this, the most northerly English county, has to be considered in the light of the unusual political and social situation of the Anglo-Scottish borders. The view presented here is provisional, and may need to be reconsidered when the Roehampton Institute has finished preparing the maps and tables for Northumberland, and analysis has been completed. When the conference took place in November 2004 that stage had not been reached.

Topography and character

The county has three principal elements: the coastal plain, the hills with river valleys cutting through them, and the once industrial south-east. In the north and west are the grass-covered Cheviot Hills, with hill forts and sheep pasture, and cut by the valleys of the Rivers Coquet and Rede; in the south-west are the Pennines, cut by tributaries of the River Tyne. To the south-east is the heavily populated area which developed around the Tyne with the growth of the industries of coal mining, ship building, and engineering.

Northumberland's boundaries partly follow the courses of rivers: the Tyne in the south-east, and the Tweed in the north-east. Berwick grew at the mouth of the Tweed as a garrison town, sometimes belonging to England and sometimes to Scotland. Its great Elizabethan defences have long been the subject of research, and knowledge of the houses of the town is increasing, partly through archaeological work. Further upstream, Scotland encompasses both banks of the Tweed, and the country and county boundary runs along the watershed of the Cheviots, the land of the reivers, of border raids, of political and private struggles. The combatants were not always armies — the men of one valley often raided a neighbouring valley, one 'name' or 'clan' against another (Newton 1972, 102; Meikle 2004, 227).

The raids were many and frequent; systems of keeping watch, and of providing safe refuge on the approach of raiders along the valleys, were essential. The houses which the Hearth Tax collectors would have found in those border lands were not like those in most other rural areas of England. If they were not strong, they would not survive: even small houses had thick stone walls. Raiding continued after the Union of the Crowns in 1603, when James VI of Scotland became James I of England, right up to the 1640s and the Civil War (Newton 1972, 105; Watts and Watts 1975, 134; Charlton 1987, 50). The centre of trade in stolen horses was in North Tynedale, reaching from Hexham almost to the Scottish Border. The first use of the word 'moss trooper', a border raider and horse thief, is recorded by the *Oxford English Dictionary* as occurring in the middle of the 17th century.

Figure 16.1 is the map of Northumberland, published in 1622, from the second volume of Michael Drayton's long poem *Poly-Olbion, a Chorographicall Description of all the Tracts, Rivers, Mountains, Forests, and other Parts of this Renowned Isle of Great Britain*. It shows hills, rivers and towns, all personified. North of the River Tyne Hadrian's Wall is shown as the Picts' Wall (in present-day England, the media often wrongly use 'north of Hadrian's Wall' to mean 'Scotland'). The Emperor Hadrian's great linear barrier became in later years a source of stone for the vernacular buildings of the area, but it had no significance as a border in the medieval period, and was certainly not the border which caused the wretchedness reported by the Venetian Ambassador in 1617. That was rather the present Scottish border, the north-western boundary of Northumberland, and it is that which is relevant to a study of the development of the settlements and the buildings of the county.

That national border was finally established in 1237 by the Treaty of York, when England took

Fig 16.1 Map of Northumberland and the Bishoprick of Durham from Michael Drayton's Poly-Olbion, *1622. Reproduced by permission of Newcastle City Library*

control of the lands which became Cumbria and Northumberland (Lomas 1996, 32). There was some uncertainty even in those apparently defined terms: large areas between the two countries were known right through Tudor times as 'the debateable lands', and special measures were in place for the government of the border marches by wardens who were directly responsible to the monarch (Grey 1649, 41; McCord and Thompson 2004, 70, 78). The buildings of the region reflect that troubled history of invasions and raids, the river valleys forming easy routes to and from potential targets. In addition, the fortunes of some families were brutally affected by the Pilgrimage of Grace (1536–37) and the Rising of the Northern Earls (1569–70).

These political, economic and social uncertainties have caused the buildings of the county to have particular characteristics: houses might not have survived at all unless they were of stone, for timber framing was too vulnerable to attack. However, in Newcastle and Berwick, towns that were protected by encircling walls, there are still timber-framed houses. In Newcastle there were many until a hundred years ago, of which a few survive; in Berwick one timber-framed structure is visible. It is not likely that the number of hearths in a house would vary according to whether it was built of timber or of stone, but the Hearth Tax, in giving information about numbers of hearths and densities of multi-hearth houses within an area, may eventually yield some understanding of the development of house plans in the years leading up to the 1660s. That stage has not yet been reached in the Northumberland research, but it is possible to consider some of the houses that have survived from that decade.

Large rural houses

In the 1660s the only houses in the deep valleys of the Cheviot Hills were probably shielings. They would have had only one hearth, and the Hearth Tax collectors might not have reached such remote summer dwellings. But in the lower valleys there would be medieval castles, late medieval towers, and stronghouses at critical points such as at Edlingham (for discussion of the forms of such houses see Pevsner and Richmond 2001, 58–67).

Edlingham Castle (Fig 16.2) was thought to be a tower house until excavations by Fairclough revealed that it was a moated house to which the tower had been added (Fairclough 1984). While it can be seen that in the tower interior there were fireplaces on two floors, the lower with a fine joggled lintel (lintel of interlocking stones), the total number of hearths must have been greater than two. The book of rates for Edlingham in 1663 records that Sir John Swinburne, the owner of the estate, was assessed on £160, but in the Edlingham Hearth Tax assessments for that year the highest assessment is that of Mr Ralph Carr, with three hearths, and there is no householder called Swinburne (Constance Fraser, pers. comm.; Hodgson 1820–58, **1**, 264; Vernacular Architecture Group 1998, 26).

Many of the Northumberland buildings which survive from the 1660s have regional rather than national characteristics despite belonging to the nobility and gentry. Whether castles and houses high in the social scale can be considered to be 'vernacular' is a difficult question — they are of local materials, and were probably built by local craftsmen, but they are national in their design principles and

Fig 16.2 Edlingham Castle, Northumberland: a mid-14th-century solar tower added to a mid-13th-century manor house. © G McCombie

Fig 16.3 Chipchase Castle, Northumberland: a house of 1621 added to a mid-14th-century tower, the house with Georgian and Victorian alterations. © G McCombie

Fig 16.4 Belsay Castle, Northumberland: a tower of c 1370 to which a manor house was added in 1614. The porch of this survives in front of the 1870 house in the Jacobean style. © G McCombie

their aspirations. However, many of the buildings known as 'castles' were not great systems of fortifications such as those at Newcastle, Alnwick and Warkworth, but sizeable houses that had been built in such a way as to ward off attackers.

Chipchase Castle is a house of high status, originally consisting of a tower house looking out over the wide valley of the North Tyne (Fig 16.3). To the medieval stone tower a more comfortable house was added in 1621, and the building was further enlarged and altered in the 18th and 19th centuries. Sir Cuthbert Heron was assessed on 23 hearths in Chipchase in March 1666, though the Hearth Tax will be difficult to interpret in more detail for such a complex. Like Chipchase, Belsay is a tower house (Fig 16.4). The property of the Middleton family from the 13th century, it was probably originally a hall to which the tower was added, with the hall then replaced with an early 17th-century house of which the porch survives in front of a late 19th-century house (Pevsner and Richmond 2001, 167). The Hearth Tax return for 25 March 1666 shows that Sir William Middleton paid on fifteen hearths: were they all in the 17th-century house? There might have been a west wing as part of that build and the Hearth Tax might be thought to support that theory; even though Buck's view of 1728 shows an apparently 18th-century wing, the sash windows may be an alteration in older fabric. Of that wing, only one fragment of the south wall survives above ground. There is also the question of whether an owner paid for hearths in his tenants' houses as well as his own. When it is possible to find inventories more will perhaps be found, but in the case of Belsay the plan of the building seen by the Hearth Tax assessors may have been irretrievably lost in the 19th-century reconstruction.

Mitford, a true castle, with mound, keep and bailey, is now a ruin. It was abandoned in the Middle Ages in favour of a modest but long-vanished manor house east of the church. West of the church, the present Mitford Manor is probably slightly earlier than its sophisticated entrance porch dated 1637. By 1816 that house too was a ruin and now only its rear wall survives with a single wall of the left rear wing, while the right wing was remodelled in the 1990s. Humphrey Mitford was rated at £300 for fifteen hearths, but, as at Belsay, there are scant remains of the 17th-century house on which tax was paid.

Aydon Castle is more fortified manor house than castle. It consists of a strong walled enclosure of about 1300 with a late 13th-century first-floor hall, a 14th-century kitchen range, and 16th- and 17th-century roofs (Vernacular Architecture Group 1998, 27). The Hearth Tax assessments for Lady Day March 1666 show no household in Aydon paying on

Fig 16.5 Elsdon Tower, Northumberland: long known as a 'vicar's pele'. The 14th-century tower on this site has been altered and added to, and has some 16th-century features. © G McCombie

more than one hearth, and it will therefore be particularly interesting to see whether the documentation relating to the tax adds anything to knowledge of the house.

A slightly less grand category of house comprises the so-called 'peles', a term now much discussed and disputed. Distinct within them is the group of 'vicars' peles'. Most famous among these is that at Elsdon, the medieval tower given greater comfort by 18th-century alterations and a Victorian addition (Fig 16.5; Pevsner and Richmond 2001, 268), but others survive at places including Corbridge, Embleton and Ford.

Smaller rural houses

The smaller houses of Northumberland are not as pretty as a chocolate-box picture in the way many in the south of England are, but bold, stern and strong. The only small homes known to have survived in rural areas from the decades leading up to the Hearth Tax are the bastles. The type is exemplified by Hole Bastle, near Bellingham in the valley of the North Tyne (Fig 16.6; Vernacular Architecture Group 1998, 34). Such buildings have long been recognised as characteristic of the Anglo-Scottish Borders, found wherever farmers needed to protect their families, their horses and their cattle when thieves came over from the next valley or across the county or national border. They needed to be defensible even though they are small, and to have no direct access from the outside to the family room on the first floor. There was always a strong door to the ground floor with deep slots in the jambs where a long draw-bar could be housed ready to secure the door against attack. That floor, the temporary shelter for livestock when raiders were approaching, can either be vaulted or have strong beams to support a stone floor above. Access to the upper floor was generally by a ladder through a hatch, but occasionally by an intra-mural stair or by an external ladder to the door. Many bastles have had external stairs added in more peaceful times. Windows were on the first floor only, and were very small. Only the upper room had a fireplace. Sometimes there is a whole village of bastles, as at Wall, near Hadrian's Wall, and north of Hexham, where (now with ground-floor windows) they enclose a large green, like a ring of covered wagons in Hollywood's Wild West. It will be very interesting to see how many of the existing bastles in Northumberland can be identified in the Hearth Tax analysis. Ryder says that between 200 and 300 bastles still survive in Northumberland (pers. comm.), and over 250 bastles and towers are listed on the Northumberland County Council website (www.keystothepast.info). In addition, there are some in Scotland, in Cumbria, and in the north-western parts of County Durham.

Fig 16.6 Hole Bastle, Northumberland, a typical bastle of the late 16th to early 17th century, its living floor quite separate from the strongly built ground floor. © G McCombie

The research process

The process of research on the Northumberland Hearth Tax requires, first, that the boundaries the tax collectors worked to are established, so that the areas covered by each entry in the documents can be identified in the present-day landscape and townscape. Then any buildings within those boundaries that survive from the 1660s are identified, and, finally, those buildings must be related to the 1660s statistics. After research into other sources including rentals, wills and probate inventories, it should be possible to identify the owners or occupiers of at least some of them, and so to locate the buildings in the Hearth Tax assessments, and to use further information about houses, such as the presence of chimneys, scuttles, tongs, fire irons and other fireside equipment, for comparison with the tax returns.

The evolution of Northumberland's boundaries

In respect of boundaries as in other things, Northumberland is not as most other counties: it had no hundreds. Before the County Council was formed in 1889, the county was divided into wards which were subdivided into townships; there were also boroughs, the old towns. Newcastle alone had the special status, granted in 1400, of town and county (only becoming a city in 1882). Before 1880, the parishes of Bedlington, Norham, and Holy Island formed part of the liberty of the Bishop of Durham and were called North Durham (Lomas 1996, 151–52). In the 19th century they were taken into Northumberland, and it was the later 19th-century boundary which was used by the County History Committee, by many earlier County Histories, and by *The Buildings of England* (Pevsner and Richmond 2001). Comparing the medieval with the modern boundaries is further complicated by the fact that in 1974 the county of Tyne and Wear was created out of the south-eastern part of Northumberland and the north-eastern part of County Durham, with Newcastle, on the north bank of the Tyne, as its largest and most populous settlement.

Urban houses

In 1649 William Grey, the first historian of Newcastle and author of one of the earliest town histories, wrote of the region,

> Since the union of both kingdoms, the gentry of this country hath given themselves to idleness, luxury and covetousness ... and hath consumed of late their ancient houses (Grey 1649, 39–40).

He nevertheless used the present tense to describe the border thieves:

> there is many dales ... the chief are Tynedale and Reedsdale ... these Highlanders are famous for thieving, they are all bred up and live by theft.

Fig 16.7   Denton Hall, Northumberland, dated 1622 for the Errington family; some windows enlarged in the late 19th century. © G McCombie

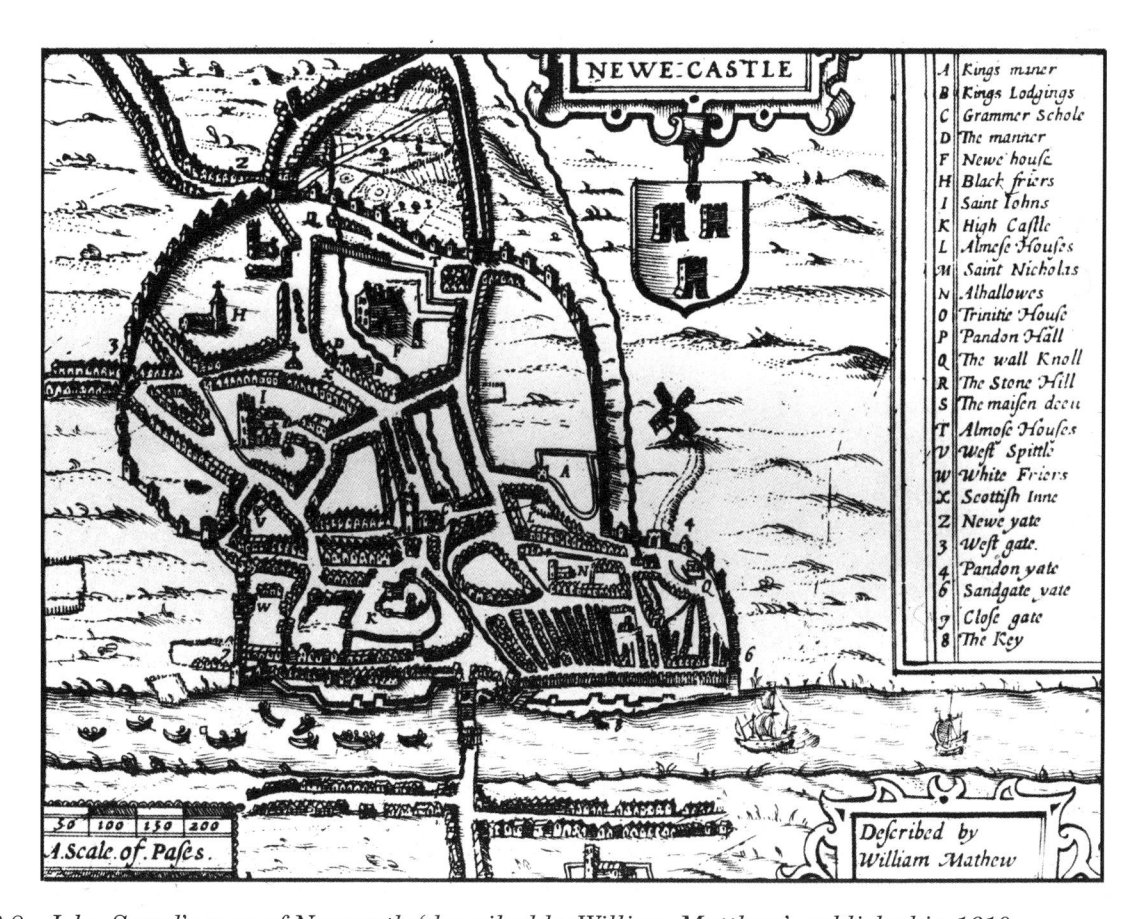

Fig 16.8   John Speed's map of Newcastle 'described by William Matthew', published in 1610

Fig 16.9 41–46 Sandhill, Newcastle upon Tyne: timber-framed houses, mostly of the mid-17th century, some with 18th-century brick fronts. © G McCombie

They come down from these dales into the low countries, and carry away horses and cattle... There is many every year brought... into the gaol of Newcastle and at the assizes are condemned and hanged... (Grey 1649, 41).

Standing at the lowest bridging point on the Tyne, the New Castle founded in 1080 by William Rufus became the focus of growth which made Newcastle upon Tyne the most important town in the county – so important that in 1400 it became a county in its own right. It had its own Hearth Tax return, distinct from that for Northumberland, and among its inhabitants were many wealthy merchants, and owners of coal mines or of land over which coal had to be transported. It grew rich on the export of coal and the import of luxury goods, all made possible by its position on the coalfield and on the tidal river.

In the countryside outside the town, and within easy travelling distance from it, there were a few large houses belonging to coal owners and farmers, such as the Errington family's Denton Hall on the line of Hadrian's Wall, dated 1622 (Fig 16.7). Its windows were enlarged in the late 19th century, but even so it is a remarkably undefended house for its date, and its proximity to Newcastle must have been felt to be security enough. Slightly further west is Welton Hall, a 15th-century tower and an adjoining house of several dates.

In the middle of the 16th century Newcastle upon Tyne was shown by an unnamed cartographer/artist in a birds'-eye view which Harvey suggests might have been drawn in 1545 by Gian Tomasso Scala when new fortifications were being constructed at Tynemouth (Harvey 1993, 70). It seems designed to display the town's strength and high status: not only are castle and town wall given prominence, but large chimneys are shown on all houses. These are invariably on the back wall, where surviving historic houses still have fireplaces.

In 1610 John Speed published the first plan of the town in the corner of his map of Northumberland (Fig 16.8). It shows the medieval street pattern, which was to remain undisturbed up to the 1780s: two streets alongside the river from the bridgehead, and a crow's foot of roads stretching north and west to the countryside from the high ground above. By the time the Hearth Tax was being levied, Newcastle was finally emerging from a very difficult period after Scottish siege and occupation in the 1640s. There had been great damage and much loss of property. Many wealthy merchants lived near their place of business: the river, the Quayside, and Sandhill (where the Exchange, the Merchants' Court and the Town Chamber were all in what is now known as the Guildhall, next to the bridge). West from Sandhill ran the Close, with burgage plots on both sides, those on the south running down to private quays on the river; eastwards ran

Fig 16.10 Alderman Fenwick's House, Newcastle upon Tyne: a late 17th-century house in Pilgrim Street, shown in the margins of the c 1723 survey of Newcastle by James Corbridge. © G McCombie

the street called Quayside, the town wall separating it from the public Quay, and with houses on only the north side. Between the two streets was the bridgehead on Sandhill. For some sites, the names of the owners in the 1660s are already known, and for others they may yet be discovered. A particularly well-known group is the row of timber-framed houses, some of them with later brick front walls, on the north side of Sandhill (Fig 16.9). Like the Town Hall or Guildhall opposite, they were extensively remodelled in the 1650s. Another survivor from the 17th century is the building now known as Alderman Fenwick's House, in Pilgrim Street in the higher part of the town but only a few minutes' walk from the river (Fig 16.10). It has 18th-century windows, but an earlier stair and first-floor great room. Wills and inventories exist for the Sandhill group, but research has so far revealed no information before the end of the 17th century for the Pilgrim Street house. The owner in 1693 was a tanner, Thomas Winship, whose daughter inherited it then; but in 1666 he appeared in another ward in the tax (Heslop and McCombie 1996, 132). If ever the owner before Winship is identified it will be fascinating to see how many hearths there were and perhaps to reconstruct the first phase of the house.

Conclusion

The county of Northumberland has a tremendous range of townscapes and landscapes. Between bustling, prosperous Newcastle and the bleak Border hills, there are many 'castles' and small stone bastles which provided refuge from raiders. In the plains and valleys of the countryside, the houses of farmers, clergy and gentry were built for protection first and comfort second, while the Borders were still outside the normal rule of law. It is hoped that the Hearth Tax will assist in creating a better understanding of both great and small Northumbrian houses and of their owners and occupiers.

17 The Hearth Tax and Housing in Westmorland
by Colin Phillips

The publication of texts of the Hearth Tax documents for England and Wales by the Roehampton Hearth Tax Project and the British Record Society offers historians an opportunity, at least, to go beyond the archival sources and look at surviving buildings which might both retain something of their later 17th-century form, and contain some of the chimneys, if not the hearths, that figured in the tax between 1662 and 1689. The present chapter comes sufficiently early in the development of the project for Cumberland and Westmorland for broad brush strokes to be required: for example, detailed maps are not yet available, and some of the complexities of the surviving Hearth Tax records for Cumberland in The National Archives are still being explored.

The documentary evidence

Two Hearth Tax documents for Westmorland have been examined: the account from 1669,[1] and a survey made over the winter of 1674/75.[2] The 1669 document is an assessment, township by township, of the tax liability of each household listed by giving the number of hearths in the household, and, for most townships, it differentiates between those households liable to pay the tax and those excused. The 1674/75 documents were the first stage in a new levy of the tax, when the tax collectors recorded, that is, surveyed, the number of hearths in each household. The survey of the county did not distinguish between those who would pay tax and those who would be excused, for that judgement would be the result of a subsequent administrative process involving the justices of the peace. Indeed, the document survives as a copy made for the Westmorland justice Sir Daniel Fleming. The survey for Kendal and Kirkland, archivally separate from Fleming's manuscript, exists alongside records of the exemption process. In fact, the poorest households in borough and county had probably been omitted during the survey (Phillips 1981, 128, n30). Compared to the 1669 document, the larger numbers of multi-hearth households, if not the larger number of households in all, must be attributed to the zeal of the surveyors working for private tax farmers rather than the state.

The distribution of single hearths in Westmorland

Anyone scrolling through the microfilm of the 1669 Hearth Tax account for the county, or turning the pages of the 1674/75 Hearth Tax survey, will immediately be impressed by the preponderance of one-hearth households. This is shown in Table 17.1, which includes comparative Cumbrian material where useable tax accounts survive. The map (Fig 17.1) outlines the areas referred to in the table, and divides Westmorland into the Barony of Kendale (the south of the county, Diocese of Chester) and the Bottom of Westmorland (the north of the county, Diocese of Carlisle).

According to the 1669 Westmorland Hearth Tax return 80% of households had one hearth. Indeed, 24 collection areas, all in the north of the county, contained only single-hearth households. Any natural scepticism of the historian that the preponderance of one-hearth tax payers might be the product of tax evasion is weakened by the survival of the 1674/75 survey, which contains many one-hearth households, though, at 73%, proportionately fewer than the 80% in the 1669 document. One-hearth households were therefore commonplace, unless widespread fraud on the part of the tax assessors is alleged.

To start with, one-hearth households may be examined through the perspective of a sample of probate inventories for the county close in time to the two tax documents.[3] For the rural inventories, the relationship between overall gross value of probate estates and numbers of hearths shows some consistency: only one person with three hearths ranks below the top quartile of gross inventory values, but the most wealthy has one hearth (Table 17.2). Of course, measured by average or median, those with more than one hearth were valued more highly than those with one hearth, but the ranges are so wide as to be meaningless. It seems strange that some rural people of significant personal estate lived in one-hearth houses (even if the wealthiest of these did record building materials in his probate inventory). Exemption from the tax offers another insight into one-hearth households. In Westmorland in the 1669 document 28% of one-hearth households were exempt: that is 32% exempt in the north, and 21% exempt in the south of the county. In the other areas on the map, the proportions of one-hearth households exempt in accounts varied between 65% in Leath ward, and 42% in Furness. It is clear from the varying proportions of the exempt, and from the data in Table 17.2, that the one-hearth category was not a monotonous homogeneity, but, instead, was characterised by some diversity, perhaps even prosperity.

The number of single-hearth households may be so large because of some way in which the constables, tax assessors and tax gatherers defined the members of a household. Alternatively, the number of single-hearth households may result from a substantial proportion of families choosing to match

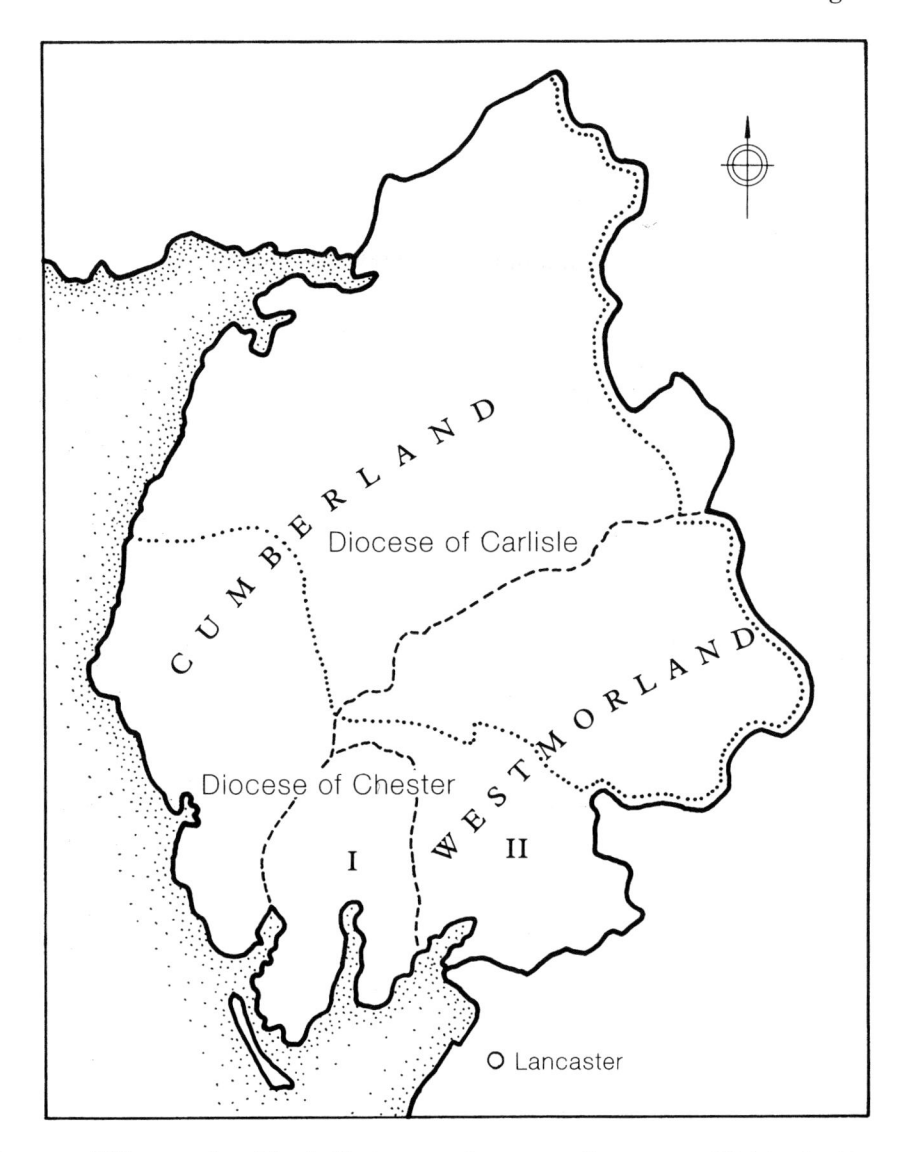

Fig 17.1 Sketch map of Westmorland jurisdictions and surrounding areas. Within the Diocese of Chester: I = Furness Deanery, II = Parts of Kendal and Lonsdale Deaneries. Adapted from Phillips 1973, 45

their resources with one hearth, either in a building inherited with, or constructed with, one hearth. They might further be occupiers of properties divided into a number of one-hearth tenements. But what if a family lived in a multi-hearth house, and transient circumstances arose in the normal life cycle of that family which caused it to divide the house to accommodate more than one household? A parent or sibling might settle by a deed, or bequeath residential rights in the property to children or to siblings. It is not clear how, for example, after 1679, Henry Jopson's brother was to maintain his sister for her life in his house at Regill,[4] but in Kendal in 1660 William Fenton dealt with the problem by letting an out of repair room towards the backside of the house to his sister for her life. She was to repair it and build it a stone chimney.[5] In the large burgage properties of Kendal, subdivision could still leave multi-hearth houses: thus the Revd William Brownsword had five hearths in his part of his burgage in Stricklandgate in 1669; the other portion of the property, containing four hearths, was occupied by a different family.[6] Other Kendal families, however, struggled: the Stramongate cordwainer John Hinde, with two hearths, divided his house between his two sons so that one had the forehouse and shop, and the other the kitchen and two lofts, and so apparently one hearth each, with a share each of the stable and garden.[7] Another example is Brian Brathwaite. In 1658 he divided his burgage at Far Crossbank between his son and daughter, a division which held for at least twenty years and into their adult lives, though the property was conveyed as an entity in 1698.[8]

Where a wife survived her husband, she enjoyed widow's rights in a varying proportion of her husband's real property according to the custom of the manor. Many widows enjoyed the whole customary real estate for their chaste widowhood, others received a half or a third, according to the different customs.[9] There are plenty of references to testator husbands following such customary provision. In these circumstances, an eldest son and

Table 17.1 Westmorland: households (entries) by numbers of hearths, 1669 and 1674/75.
Sources: Westmorland: text notes 1 and 2; Furness: TNA E179/250/11; Cumberland Leath ward: TNA E179/90/76

Westmorland	one	one as % of total	two	three	four	five	six	seven	eight	nine	ten & more	TOTAL	three & more	% of total	1675 as % of 1669
All Westmorland															
1675	4986	73	1111	324	170	68	66	27	21	17	21	6811	714	10.5	208
1669	4124	80	659	144	89	39	24	12	15	5	16	5127	344	6.7	
South															
1675	2077	65	608	239	136	50	46	10	15	11	9	3201	516	16	212
1669	1477	68	467	107	64	29	15	11	11	1	5	2187	243	11	
North															
1675	2909	81	503	85	34	18	20	17	6	6	12	3610	198	5.5	196
1669	2647	90	192	37	25	10	9	1	4	4	11	2940	101	3.4	
Comparisons															
Furness 1664	1898	91	122	22	16	5	4	1	0	0	7	2075	55	2.7	
Cumberland Leath ward 1674*	2526	90	182	55	24	11	11	5	4	0	1	2819	111	3.9	

*Some areas missing, and 170 damaged entries excluded.

Table 17.2 Westmorland: rural gross probate values and numbers of hearths (excludes Appleby and Kendal). Source: text notes 1–3

	range		average	median	number
	£	£	£	£	
1 hearth	3	771	63	41	101
2 hearths	4	228	91	71	16
3 and 3+ hearths	63	404	193	187	10

eventual inheritor of the property who was married presumably shared the customary tenement with his mother (unless he had a tenement or cottage of his own). In 1673 Thomas Fleming of Rydal's will provided meat and lodging for his mother according to the agreement he made at his father's decease in 1670; his father had paid tax on one hearth in 1669. Mabel Hallhead of Natland, widow, was owed rent by her son Nicholas, and what was due to him for her table was to be paid out of this rent, yet the widow owned the usual fire irons and pans.[10] Nicholas paid tax for one hearth in 1669 after his mother's death, and, presumably as 'Nicho: Hollett', was surveyed for two hearths in 1674/75. The practice of the Flemings and the Hallheads may explain why both Westmorland documents list a low proportion of women occupiers, 10% in 1669 and 14% in 1674/75. There is a presumption that the customary rights of widows were in some way given up.

Prima facie instances of a house divided by life cycle circumstances as an explanation for the preponderance of one-hearth households can be detected in the Hearth Tax documents using surnames: in both 1669 and 1674/75 about 15% of entries had the same surname as the next or previous entry. Unmarried siblings would share the same surname, as would widows and their sons, and sequential entries with the same surname would be expected. Even in the unlikely event that all these sequential surname entries in 1674/75 were to involve the division of properties, one-hearth households would still comprise almost two-thirds of the total.

The manor of Rydal provides an insight into something of the diversity of the single-hearth house and household. Nearly a century ago a detailed study by Armitt (1916, 331–88) used a rental of 1655 to identify some fourteen tenements in the village of Rydal. For the 1660s and 1670s there is little to say about five of these farmholds, only one of which can be identified, once, on the two Hearth Tax documents. Armitt followed the descents of most of the farmholds and their inhabitants well into the 19th century, if the property had not decayed or been engrossed into the manor earlier. The names of the tenants of ten of these holdings appear under Rydal in the 1674/75 Hearth Tax survey, all save one (perhaps two) as single-hearth households. Four names in the survey do not fit the descents, but were probably those of sub-tenants.[11] Armitt concluded that some of the Rydal tenants struggled to keep their holdings going in the 1660s and 1670s. William Walker, she noted, fled in debt in 1679. The heirs of another, John Thompson who died in 1670 in debt, sold his holding to the estate steward John Bankes who built a four-hearth house on it by the 1674/75 survey. The inventories of three Rydal one-hearth tenants (not in my probate sample) fall below the median values of the sample, supporting Armitt's argument. However, before too readily equating one-hearth households with economic decline, we should note that the probate sample includes two of Armitt's heads of households who left personal estates with values substantially in excess of the median value of the sample, as did another one-hearth tenant not in the sample.[12] Perhaps significantly, these men, as Armitt demonstrated, enjoyed income generated from non-agricultural activities, but they were styled yeomen or husbandmen.

Armitt concluded that the tenement called Hart Head, with one exempt hearth in 1669 and one hearth in the 1674/75 survey, was not substantially rebuilt until 1840. If this is correct, then Green's etching of 'Hartshead' 1822 (Fig 17.2), showing a single chimney stack, may offer some impression of the house at the time of the Hearth Tax. That said, the open porch, first-floor windows, and slated roof may not resemble the 1670s, though in 1692 Thomas Machell was conscious (Machell 1692, 133, 149) of the use of common slate quarries in the area, and also commented that '... the houses in Rydal are all of stone...' (as on Fig 17.2). The occupant of Hart Head survived the 1670s, but his probate records do not survive.

Multi-hearth houses and their occupiers

If yeomen occupied single-hearth houses one might expect the occupants of those houses with multiple hearths to be of a higher social status. Three hearths may be taken as the lowest level of multiple-hearth households in order to obtain a measure of modest prosperity above the household with one cooking room and one other directly heated room. The social status of those with more than two hearths was very varied. It is important to classify occupiers by social status for the gentry would be expected to live in very different properties from, say, husbandmen, and some historians of vernacular architecture therefore exclude the great gentry houses from their studies. The 1674/75 survey is the more vague of the two documents in its use of status indicators. Both documents use the terms Mr, Mrs, esquire and Sir, but not the terms yeoman or husbandman. The proposition that those with most hearths were of the higher social status proves to be only partially correct. In the 1669 document just under half of those households with three or more hearths were not assigned any indicators of social status, of which more than 30 had five to nine hearths. The reverse test, that those with a title indicative of status would have the most hearths, similarly fails. Some

Fig 17.2 A one-hearth house of shortly before 1670 in Rydal. 'Hartshead' in Rydal, from an etching by W Green, 1822, reproduced from Armitt 1916, facing 331

253 people were given a title, of whom rather more than a quarter had fewer than three hearths. There is a further complication, in that about a third of those given titles were townsmen. Many of those called 'Mr' in a town would not be ranked as gentry in the countryside.

These tests show that a social classification of those named in the Hearth Tax documents is difficult to carry out. However, it is possible to recognise in the 1669 account the houses of two peers who were non-resident, three Westmorland gentry who were non-resident, and two non-Westmorland gentry, with, allowing for the vagaries of social mobility, some 80 resident gentry (Phillips 1973, 7–17). In fact, in the countryside, 29 of those called 'Mr' were not gentry at all, but clerics and lawyers. The claim of a further 73 called 'Mr' or 'Mrs' to gentry or professional status is unclear.

In 1669 the proportion of households with three or more hearths in towns or market towns was just over half, but in 1674/75 this dropped to about a third. The frequency of houses with three or more hearths in the borough towns of Kendal and Appleby is supported by the near contemporary sketches by Gregory King, which suggest buildings with chimneys at either end. In Kendal, rather than Appleby, King indicated two, and sometimes three, storeys.[13] For houses with three or more hearths in the countryside, the naming of multiple rooms in probate records *a priori* makes multiple hearths not unlikely. A clear divide between north and south Westmorland so far as the occurrence of three or more hearth houses is concerned was apparent (Table 17.3).

Table 17.3 **Westmorland: households with three and three-plus hearths. Source: text notes 1 and 2**

	North		South	
	No.	%	No.	%
>2 hearths				
1669	101	3.4	243	11
>2 hearths				
1675	198	5.5	516	16
areas without hshlds >2				
1675	21	24.0	3	5

Multi-hearth, vernacular, rural houses

The current interpretation of Westmorland vernacular housing at the time of the Hearth Tax is predominantly the work of Brunskill, the distinguished historian of vernacular architecture. He worked from surviving buildings and descriptions c 1800 of old buildings, but also using probate records and the 1669 Hearth Tax account, to set the earliest date for surviving vernacular buildings below the level of the great gentry houses at about 1650, though Denyer (1991, 18, 66–67) has suggested some pre-1600 survivals. Brunskill explains the 1650 date by arguing that from 1625 tenurial conditions for the lower levels of society became legally certain, and this created the confidence to build in more lasting materials. He has established a number of plan types of Westmorland and Cumbrian houses of the mid-17th century: commonly they have one hearth, but each type originally ranged from more to less grand forms. These plan types also became more elaborate over time. The simple two-unit house developed ' . . . later, a full gabled wing at the rear [which] might contain a separate kitchen with a chamber above it in a T- or L-shaped plan' (Brunskill 2002, 67). It was further developed by outshuts from about 1730 (Brunskill 2002, 77). Cross-passage houses with a 'downhouse' were present in the 1660s, and the downhouse was open to the roof, ' . . . but later it was lofted . . . Eventually the downhouse was provided with a fire place and made into a kitchen . . . ' (Brunskill 2002, 70). Denyer, concentrating on a smaller sample of houses drawn only from the Lakeland core of Cumbria, has elaborated some of Brunskill's plans (Denyer 1991, 54–72). The county has not, however, figured prominently in the 'great rebuilding' debate (cf Garnett 1988).

The historian trained on documents but not in architecture enters this arena with some trepidation. Brunskill's historiography suggests that the rebuilding posited for the mid-17th century began with a range of vernacular forms, from the simple towards the grand, and that later, in the 18th century, the forms in that range were elaborated. It follows therefore that the mid-17th century was backward. However, a less backward view of Westmorland buildings emerges if two types of precisely dated document are used alone: the 1674/75 Hearth Tax survey, and probate records of the 1670s. The 1674/75 Hearth Tax survey (Table 17.1) shows that for the whole of Westmorland the number of households with three or four hearths was twice that in the 1669 account. In fact the number was up nearly threefold in the countryside, but only increased by some 60% in the towns. There was also a significant 69% upward movement in the recorded number of two-hearth households (there is no space to consider them in this paper). The 1674/75 survey better states the variety of small house types in the mid-17th century than does the 1669 document. The survey shows that the third quarter of the 17th century contained a more elaborate housing stock than the initial, simple, plans of the Brunskill model suggest.

Furthermore, some probate records from the time of the Hearth Tax documents list more rooms than Brunskill's type plans suggest. Where probate inventories can be linked to names in the Hearth Tax returns, they suggest that internal subdivision and the construction of extra rooms, which Brunskill understands as elaborations of simple plan forms, had been underway for some time. While it is possible that probate appraisers did not need to list every room in a building, there is no suggestion that appraisers invented rooms, even if their listings may make visualising the buildings involved difficult. Many properties of course had lofts used for sleeping and/or store rooms or work rooms. But more developed buildings were inventoried, that of William Shepperd of Field End in Patton, for example, listed an entry, great chamber, house (fire), study, larder, buttery, buttery loft, kitchen (fire), kitchen loft, and lower kitchen.[14] The 1669 account charged him with three hearths, and he had five in the 1674/75 survey, even though his inventory locates only two. William Fell of Dryslack in Whinfell seems to have lived in a simple two-unit plan house.[15] But an extra wing appears to have been added, with a kitchen with a chamber above it, and perhaps a milkhouse. The inventory locates hearths in the kitchen and house, but the whereabouts of the third hearth in the 1674/75 survey is unclear at probate. None of the rooms of Shepherd or Fell was referred to as new, though in other inventories some rooms, even whole houses, are described as 'new'. At Whitwell and Selside, George Mawson's inventory referred to a kitchen, as opposed to the hearth in the house, for cooking, but went on to list an old kitchen, with its loft.[16] The present kitchen had a hearth with all the usual iron fittings, but also, and unusually, an iron oven, valued at 5s. According to the 1669 tax account Mawson had two hearths, with a third listed as 'unerected'.

Multi-hearth houses: the houses of the gentry

The 1669 Hearth Tax is imprecise in its infrequent use of social status terms, and, where it does give status, not infrequently duplicates individuals. Some 80 gentry heads of household occupied houses with from one to 22 hearths. The 1674/75 survey gives a similar picture, though many names differ between the two documents. Pevsner (1967, 27, 31, 33, 36–37) noted some new gentry building in Westmorland in Elizabeth's reign, and again in the 18th century, but only two Hearth Tax period houses, and they of the 1680s. The 1692 tour of south Westmorland by the antiquary Thomas Machell found many old-fashioned gentry properties. The later 17th century was, then, largely a time of alteration rather than major construction for the gentry, who seem already to have installed numbers of hearths. In north Westmorland Sir John Lowther's mid-century additions to his house at Lowther included rooms with chimney pieces intended to be of marble, perhaps as elaborate as the doorway in Figure 17.3. In 1664 he had the smoky chimney of his own chamber in the old tower

Fig 17.3 Lowther Hall, Westmorland in the 1680s, reproduced from the sketch by Thomas Machell, CROC Machell Mss, III, f 45, by kind permission of the Chapter of Carlisle Cathedral

repaired (Phillips 1979, 242, 250) and this was presumably one of the fifteen hearths he was taxed on in 1669. At Newbiggin one of Mrs Crackenthorp's ten hearths was a 14th-century fireplace (Sawrey-Cookson 1979, 127, 129). Sir Daniel Fleming (1671, 21) noted extensive recent building at Acornbank in Temple Sowerby, presumably that which the Royal Commission (RCHME 1936, 226) dates to 1656. In the south of the county, at Levens Hall, the hall was replastered if not re-orientated late in Elizabeth's reign, and Pevsner (1967, 27, 269) was impressed by that work and by the chimneys of rooms of this date, as well as those at nearby Sizergh Castle. Here were the most taxable hearths in the south of the county, and Goodall (2002, 237–38) reported that c 1618 even rooms fitted out for servants were given chimneys. Elsewhere, the 'good old house', in Fleming's parlance (1671, 13), at Grayrigg Hall had, in 1662, a number of unheated rooms.[17] Three of the eight store and service rooms had fires, which left seven taxed hearths in 1669 distributed between twelve sitting rooms and bedrooms, plus the hall. Grayrigg was not entirely immune from modern influences: by 1662 the parlour and great chamber had evolved to become sitting rooms, there was a modern-sounding colour-named room, the green chamber, and a 'new chamber'.

Multi-hearth houses: Kendal

As for multi-hearths in the towns, it is the borough towns of Appleby and Kendal, rather than the rural market towns, which display a range of hearths in buildings. Brunskill has suggested that in Kendal the houses might be older than in the rural surrounds (Brunskill 1974, 92). The number of multi-hearth houses for the town in both tax documents raises expectations for sophisticated house types, which provided work space as well as domestic accommodation. Kendal's social structure depended on manufacture, trade, and the professions, and the use of such status terms as Mr, or even esquire, by its prominent residents differed from the rural areas. One-third of Kendal households in the 1669 account with three or more hearths had a title, so the housing patterns are those of the pseudo-gentry. However the buildings were laid out on them, Kendal's burgage plots were typical of most towns: narrow fronts onto the street with long backs.

A review of the building stock about the time of the Hearth Tax through the inventoried rooms in the Kendal sample suggests development of house plans. On the ground floor the mode of entrance to the residences on the burgage plots is unclear, but some mention an 'entry' or 'entry passage' usually by reference to a loft over it. However, porches had made an appearance in the town, and there were two two-storey porches. 'Entry' and porch were evidently different, as one rural inventory of 1678 (not in the sample) had both an 'entry' loft and a porch loft.[18] Lofts were as ubiquitous as they were in the countryside. Kitchens were well established in the sample, and though the habit of inventory appraisers of listing fire irons out of location makes it uncertain whether all kitchens had a fire, rather more than half certainly did. A kitchen fire could indicate that cooking had been shifted out of the house or hall, leaving that as a heated sitting room. None of the kitchens was described as new, though one was referred to as old, so that kitchens do not appear as a novel feature of the third quarter of the 17th century. There were kitchens in some Kendal properties in the 1630s,[19] but a generation later their absence in a third of sampled properties suggests that there was still time for this development to occur, either as a conversion of existing space or as a new build. Half of those inventories which did not mention a kitchen did have an existing space which could have been converted to a kitchen. The only other heated room mentioned on the ground floor was, in two inventories, the parlour.

Stairs, another progressive feature in Brunskill's model plans, are mentioned in two of the sample inventories, but not in the evidently three-storied properties. Incidentally, the houses of Henry Atkinson and Roger Fenton had contained stair heads a generation earlier in 1630s Kendal.[20] There is nothing to suggest where these staircases were located. Fires were located on an upper floor in three houses in the sample. Up-to-date housing ideas were certainly known in Kendal c 1670, as references to dining rooms and to the use of window curtains in the inventory sample indicate. Building work recent enough to be described as 'new' was mentioned in five probates in the sample, involving the building of one new house on the edge of the town, one new house and one partial rebuild in the centre of town, and the fitting out of new lofts in two houses. In combination with title deeds and probate documents the Hearth Tax does help to build up a picture of the bigger houses fronting the town's main streets. Behind these main streets, on the backsides of the burgages, in some short side streets, and up the hill

The Hearth Tax and Housing in Westmorland

Table 17.4 Kendal: occupiers of part of the east side of the north end of Stricklandgate, 1669–95. Source: text notes 1, 2 and 21

1669		Hearths	1674/75		Hearths	1695		
north			*north*			*north*		
			Roger	Britch	1			
Anthony	Warriner	1	Robert	Brough	1			
John	Tyson	1	James	Nicholson	3	Nicholas	Dawson	
Edmund	Adlinton	5	Richard	Duckett	6	John	Singleton	
James	Moore	3	James	Moore	5	James	Moore	
Henry	Holme	2	Henry	Holme	3	Margaret	Holme	widow
Mrs	Towers	4	Ann	Towers	4	Mrs	Towers	
William	Akerigg	1	Wm	Ashridg	1	Wm	Gurnell	
Christopher	Barrow	3	Cristo	Barrow	4	Alice	Barrow	widow
			Wm	Atkinson	1	Wm	Noble	
Mr	Simpson	4	James	Simpson	4	Thomas	Midleton	
Mr George	Wilson	8	Geo	Wilson	5	George	Wilson	
			Geo	Wilson	6			
Blackhall			Blackhall			Blackhall		
south			*south*			*south*		

on the western edge of the town, called Fellside, lay the 42% of households with one hearth.

Houses in Stricklandgate, Kendal

One of the advantages of the Hearth Tax is that it lists the names of the head of the occupying household. In Kendal we have two Hearth Tax lists, and a list of occupiers compiled under the so-called Marriage Duties Act dated to 1695.[21] Wills and title deeds allow some of these households to be located on the ground. It is thus possible to watch the physical nature of one area of the community and its buildings change over time at the northern end of Stricklandgate, on the east side (Table 17.4 and Fig 17.4). According to the Hearth Tax records, although Stricklandgate was the most wealthy part of the town, this wealth was not omnipresent: Stricklandgate had 44% of houses with three or more hearths, compared with 36% and 37% in the other two gates. By about 1670, three of the buildings were divided. 'Under one roof' as one deed put it, the northernmost building may in fact have been divided into three at the time of the 1674/75 survey.[22] At one end of the social spectrum, in 1674/75 the occupiers of the lesser subdivisions had one hearth, and one of the three was exempt from the Hearth Tax. But at the other end of that spectrum, the building called the Blackhall at the southern extremity of the study area was divided into one occupied house with six hearths, and another, empty, house with five hearths (Table 17.4). By 1695 the buildings at the two extremities were united, but the subdivided property in the centre of the study area, now occupied by William Noble, was still present. The property occupied in 1695 by William and Ann Gurnell is obscure, and may have been a backside dwelling. By 1695, then, a wealthy area of the town was still socially mixed. The buildings surviving in c 1900 (Fig 17.4) reflect only the wealthy, as do those which are extant today. Two of those survivors, however refronted, date from at least the 16th century, and the inside of a third also can be dated to the 16th or 17th century, while one survivor seems to be an early 18th-century replacement of two 17th-century buildings. The rest have to be imagined, for their burgage plots are largely filled by modern service and retail premises.

Conclusion

The view that the rural Cumbrian built environment emerged as a mass of simply formed houses in the mid-17th century, now reflected in one-hearth houses in the Hearth Tax documents, carries with it connotations of social, even economic, backwardness. The nature of the built environment before 1650, it has been argued, is unknown. Those forms of buildings which emerged c 1650 were elaborated subsequently to allow more comfort and sophistication. But probate and Hearth Tax evidence suggests a higher degree of comfort and sophistication than has hitherto been allowed. First, the higher number of occupiers in 1674/75 than in 1669 with three or more hearths indicates more heated rooms. Second, the nomenclature of rooms, and evidence towards their use, indicated in probate inventories shows that some of the development in building forms that supposedly came after 1700 was already present at the time of the Hearth Tax. Denyer has pushed back the date of the surviving built environment into the

172 Part 2: Regional Studies

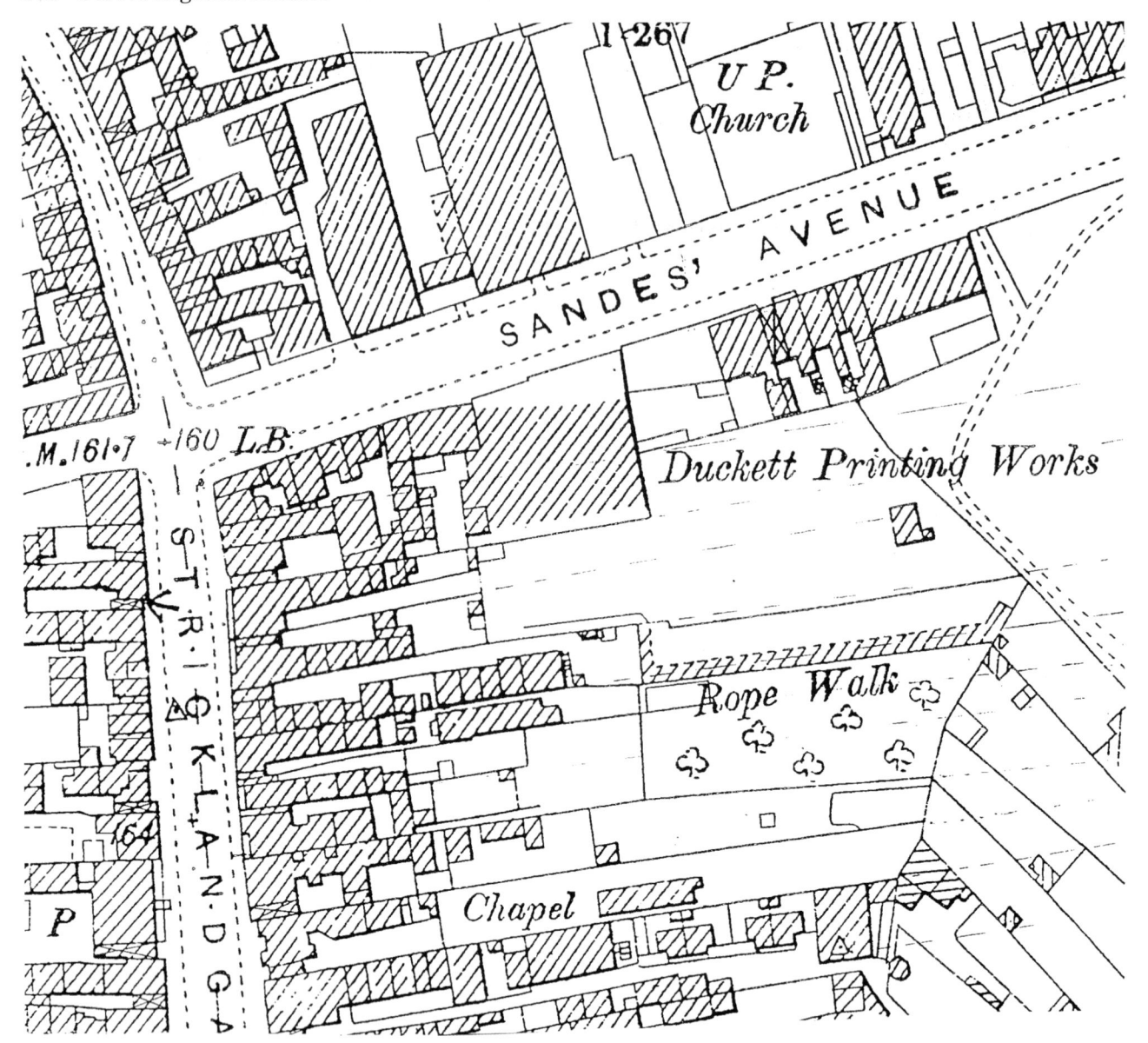

Fig 17.4 Part of north-east side of Stricklandgate, Kendal, 1898. Ordnance Survey 6-inch map. The property of Nicholas Dawson, Table 17.4 under 1695, was cut into by the southern edge of Sandes' Avenue, constructed 1887 (Ordnance Survey).

16th century. It may be that the rooming recorded in my sources lay in buildings which date from earlier than 1650, in which case the backwardness of the mid-17th century needs a re-assessment. Or, it may be that the records of rooming discussed here refer to a building stock which was replaced in the middle of the century with durable materials, but in less elaborate and therefore less comfortable forms? If so, why?

Chapter 17: Notes

1. TNA Exchequer, lay subsidy rolls, E179/195/73, including Kendal borough. I have used a transcript prepared for the project. The document was printed as extracts in Farrer 1923–24; and, without the exempt, in Curwen 1932.
2. CROK Fleming of Rydal papers, WD/Ry, Ms R, for Westmorland excluding Kendal borough and Kirkland (heavily edited in Ramsden 1998); and CROK Kendal Corporation Manuscripts, WD/MBK, HMC/A9, for Kendal and Kirkland.
3. The whole sample comprised: 152 from CROC Diocese of Carlisle probate records, microfilm, 1669–80 for north Westmorland; plus 234 from CROK microfilm of Diocese of Chester, Archdeaconry of Richmond, probate records, Kendal Deanery (LRO WRW/K), excluding Kendal borough; plus 79 for Kendal borough (LRO WRW/K). In what follows, microfilm documents from Kendal deanery are noted as WRW/K, but documents at the LRO as LRO WRW/K, both followed by the year of probate. There is nothing in this sample for Lonsdale in the Archdeaconry of Richmond.
4. WRW/K, 1673.

5 CROK Kendal Corporation Deeds (KCD), bdle 657, Fenton to Fenton, 7 April 1660.
6 LRO WRW/K, 1673.
7 LRO WRW/K, 1674. Widow Hyne had two hearths in 1675; in 1669 one John Hinde had two hearths, the other had one.
8 CROK miscellaneous deposits, WDX/967/2–5.
9 Eg Nicolson and Burn 1777, 113 (Grayrigg, also TNA Chancery bills and answers, C5/41/49), and 616–18 (Bleatarn); manor of Rydal, CROK WD/Ry, original Ms T, p 12; for the Richmond fee, south Westmorland, Bagot 1962, 238; for Crosby Ravensworth,TNA Chancery enrolled decrees, C78/446, no.16, C78/1205, no. 7; for the barony of Barton, TNA Exchequer, depositions by special commission, E134/ 12 Chas I, Mich 30.
10 Thomas Fleming of Rydal, LRO WRW/K, 1671, and WRW/K, 1673; Mabel Hallhead, WRW/K, 1669.
11 By note 10, an eleventh name, 'Marg[aret] Fleming', is the daughter-in-law of Thomas (pr 1671) living in his 'ould house'.
12 LRO WRW/K, Edwin Grigg, 1670; Thomas Fleming, 1671; and Charles Wilson, 1664; plus Edwin Green, 1667.
13 Professor Margaret Spufford kindly loaned me her copies of King's sketches from The College of Arms, London, C39, Westmorland church notes, between pages 14 and 15.
14 WRW/K, 1676.
15 WRW/K, 1679.
16 WRW/K, 1672.
17 LRO WRW/K, Anthony Ducket, 1662.
18 LRO WRW/K, Thomas Warriner of Bowthwaite in Selside, 1678.
19 LRO WRW/K, Robert Atkinson, 1637; Miles Burkitt, 1632; Stephen Newby, 1634; and John Nicholson, 1636. Of a small, unscientific sample of twelve probates for that decade, eight did not mention a kitchen.
20 LRO WRW/K, 1630 and 1638, respectively.
21 CROK WD/Ry, box 32.
22 CROK KCD, bdle 43.

PART 3: CONCLUSION

18 Houses, Hearths and Historical Inquiry
by P S Barnwell

One of the most significant questions bearing on the uses to which historians can put the evidence of the Hearth Tax is that concerning the relationship between the numbers of hearths on which a household was assessed and the wealth of that household. Contemporaries believed that such a relationship existed, some justifying the tax on the grounds that it was related to the economic means of its payers, and others, such as Gregory King, using its evidence to draw conclusions concerning the geographical distribution of wealth (Husbands 1992, 66). At a simple level the contention may appear to be vindicated by surviving buildings of the later 17th century, at least in some parts of the country and in relation to the higher social classes, members of the upper sub-gentry class of Hertfordshire, for example, consciously displaying their affluence by adopting an architectural style with prominent decorative brick chimney stacks (Smith 1992, 111; Hunneyball 2004, 26, 162–63).

The contributors to the second part of this volume have each been concerned with an individual county or equivalent major urban area. Using, in varying measure, the evidence of the Hearth Tax returns, probate inventories, and the houses which survive from the period, most of them agree that the extremes of the distribution of hearth numbers within a county or city are related to wealth: a householder assessed on five or more hearths was almost certainly more wealthy than his counterpart who was assessed on only one or two. At more refined levels of analysis, however, the question is more open. Individuals might choose, for social or economic reasons, to invest their money in things other than buildings or expensive moveable goods, so that neither the number of hearths on which they were assessed, the value of their goods, their houses, nor even a combination of the three, necessarily bears a direct relationship to their wealth (Machin; Phillips; cf Husbands 1992, 68). In a county such as Kent, where a large stock of substantial older houses was occupied by the relatively affluent, it is also possible that the number of hearths in newer dwellings built by members of slightly less prosperous social groups might for a time exceed those in the older dwellings of the wealthier (Pearson; cf Harrington *et al* 2000, especially lxvii–lxviii). Furthermore, even within one county the speed of the increase in the number, and of the evolution of the character, of hearths and chimneys could be affected by the availability and cost of different kinds of fuel, the history of which has yet to be systematically studied (Spufford).

Teasing out the relative significance of factors such as these is a challenge even in regions where there is a high degree of differentiation in the numbers of hearths, but it is considerably more difficult in those dominated by houses assessed on only one hearth. While some of those areas, such as County Durham (Green), undoubtedly contained a high proportion of poor or very poor people, in others the occupiers of one-hearth houses ranged from the poor to the modestly prosperous (Giles; Neave and Neave; Phillips). Even in counties, such as West Yorkshire, where the Hearth Tax returns indicate greater differentiation, similar proportions of houses with different numbers of hearths could mask significant variations in social structure (RCHME 1986, 125–26). These differences are compounded when comparisons between counties are attempted. The Neaves succinctly make the point when they comment that no evidence suggests that many of the occupiers of single-hearth houses in the East Riding of Yorkshire were less prosperous than those assessed on a greater number of hearths in more southern counties. That observation, made by authors who are as familiar with the buildings as with the Hearth Tax, strengthens the case Arkell has recently made, on the basis of the documentary sources alone, for investigation of the possibility that there were significant differences in the social and economic circumstances of the occupiers of houses with the same number of hearths in different parts of the country, particularly at the lower end of the scale (Arkell 2003, 165).

The essays in this volume, most of which represent work in progress, show some ways in which a combination of different forms of evidence can be used, and begin to refine the questions. While they constitute the largest corpus of county-based case studies of vernacular houses and the Hearth Tax so far assembled, they do not attempt a national overview, nor are their approaches sufficiently uniform readily to permit the kind of direct comparison which would furnish a set of concrete findings. Instead, they suggest that there remain fundamental questions concerning the characteristics of the evidence (both written and physical) and the ways in which it can be interpreted that must be resolved before the true value of the Hearth Tax for understanding the distribution of wealth can be assessed. It is on some of those issues that this concluding chapter will concentrate, in the hope of suggesting ways in which the subject might be developed in future.

The evidence of probate inventories

If the relationship between numbers of hearths and wealth is to be tested, the Hearth Tax assessments must be compared with another source (or sources)

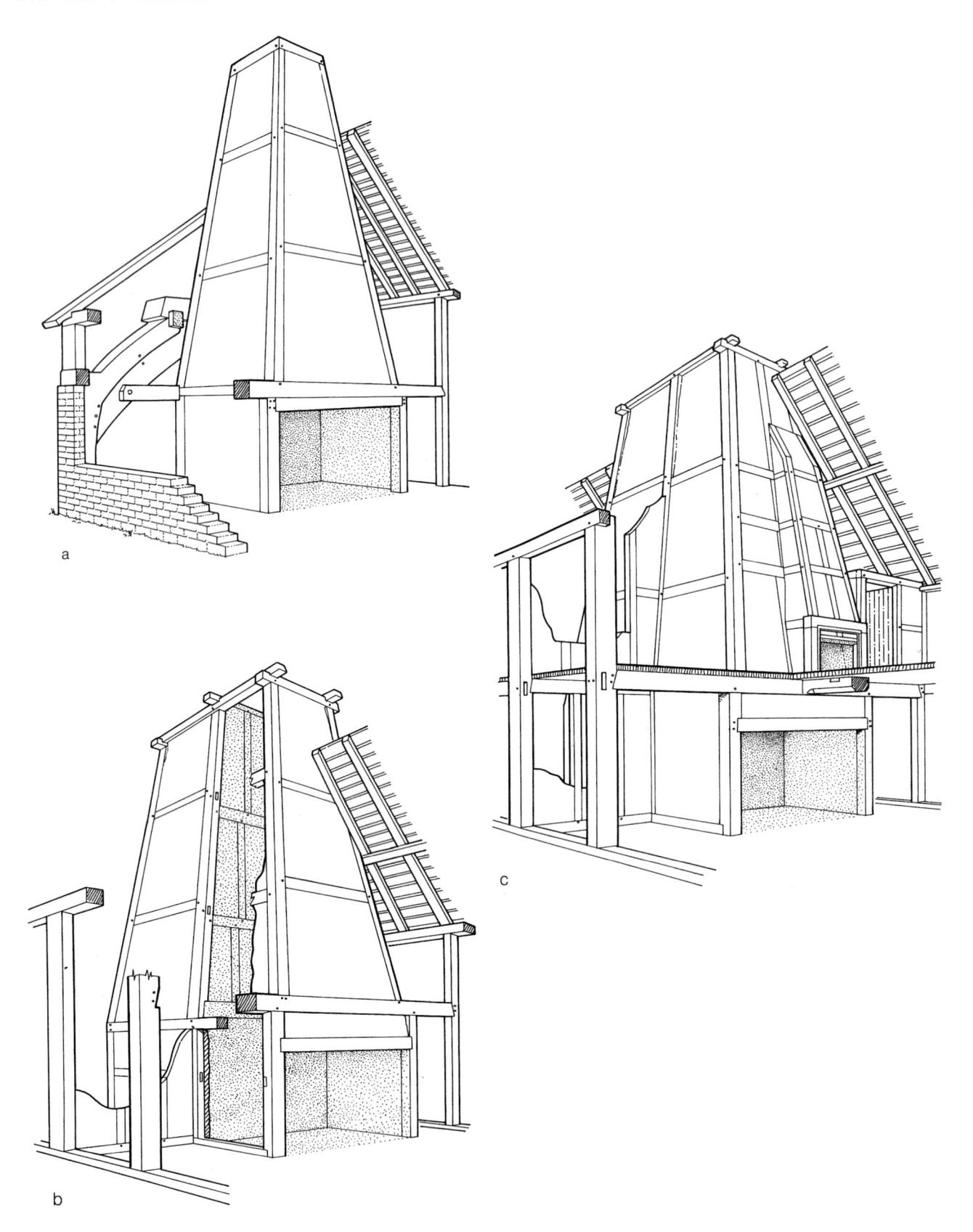

Fig 18.1 Timber Chimneys.
a: single ground floor fireplace: Nightingale Farm, Yalding, Kent.
b: two ground-floor fireplaces: conjectural reconstruction based on Hail Weston Farmhouse, Huntingdonshire (see Fig 11.8).
c: fireplaces on the ground and first floors: conjectural reconstruction informed by drawings of The Medicine House, Blackden, Holmes Chapel, Cheshire (moved there from Wrinehill, Staffordshire), contained in Vernacular Architecture Group 2000, 12–13.

> **Timber chimneys**
>
> In the late-16th and the 17th century, timber chimneys were a common feature in many parts of the country, though most were later replaced in brick or stone and only survive, if at all, in fragmentary form. By far the most common form contained a single ground-floor fireplace (a). Paired ground-floor fireplaces such as that at Hail Weston, Huntingdonshire (b), and examples in Hertfordshire (J T Smith 1992, 185), and Montgomeryshire (L J Hall 2005, 177), are much rarer. Possibly the only timber chimney with a first-floor fireplace so far known is that at The Medicine House (c), though the fact that the house was dismantled and moved from another site means that not all of the present structure may be original. (The evidence for timber chimneys in particular counties is discussed elsewhere in this volume by Spufford, Pearson, Ryan, Machin, Davis, and Green, who advance varying interpretations of their significance.)
>
> It is unlikely that multiple-flue timber chimneys were ever more than an extreme rarity. The lists of rooms and fire implements in probate inventories do not suggest that the timber chimneys in houses with which they can be matched served first-floor fireplaces. The nature of the physical evidence, however, is such that it would be very difficult to tell whether the timber predecessor of a brick or stone chimney had contained a first-floor flue. The ground-floor fireplace opening often retained its original proportions when the chimney was rebuilt, and the timber jambs and bressumer (or the pegholes for its tenons) may survive. A first-floor fireplace, however, would have been structurally dependent on the main flue, the removal of which would have necessitated the complete destruction of the upper one. While in the vast majority of cases the provision of multiple fireplaces was associated with a change in building material, there may have been exceptional instances where it was not. Further evidence for understanding the dates and phases of brick chimney stacks, and particularly whether the first-floor flues were original or added may be provided by the developing technique of luminescence dating (Antrobus 2004).

of evidence for wealth. The most commonly used form of evidence is that provided by probate inventories. Writing more than 40 years ago, Spufford demonstrated that in Cambridgeshire the levels of wealth represented by the goods recorded in inventories were reflected in numbers of hearths, though only within very broad and overlapping bands (Spufford 1962). While that conclusion finds an echo in several of the contributions to this volume, Machin's discussion of the evidence from Dorset urges caution in applying the model in different regions without testing it. Furthermore, the nature of probate inventories, which Spufford herself has more recently explored (Spufford 1990), suggests that even where a direct correlation between their evidence and hearth numbers is found, it must not be taken at face value.

Inventories only record moveable goods, and not all of them. In particular, they only record goods owned by the deceased householder himself rather than all those owned by the household, for they omit those owned by a spouse or by resident children, the existence of whom may well not be noted as they were not relevant to the purpose of the valuation; they also omit goods left to the executors, and some of the specific bequests, the latter often amongst the most valuable goods (Spufford 1990, 142, 144–45). Recent work by Overton and Weatherill has explored more sophisticated ways of handling the evidence of inventories, concentrating on particular kinds of goods which may be indicative of social status, and which may have been fairly consistently recorded (Overton *et al* 2004; Weatherill 1996). However, the evidence of inventories in relation to wealth remains problematic, at least when it is considered in isolation from that of other sources. For example, because inventories were made at the time of death, they may often reflect the value of only such moveables as were retained in old age, rather than that of those possessed by the deceased at the time of building, modernising, or acquiring the house in which he or she lived (cf Havinden 1965, 10, where specific emphasis is placed on under-representation of farm stock). In addition, inventories do not record the often substantial debts of the deceased: when such debts are revealed, usually by a surviving probate or administrators' account, they can substantially alter the picture of the net worth of the individual both in absolute terms and in relation to his neighbours, with the result that tabulations of comparative wealth within a community may be severely disrupted (Machin; Spufford 1990, 150–73). Finally, inventories take no account of real estate: as with debts, there is a likelihood that both individuals and social groups will have invested varying proportions of their total assets in land and buildings. The survival of the will as well as the inventory may furnish a partial remedy, but it does not always do so (Spufford 1990, 142; Havinden 1965, 10). The sum and nature of the exclusions from inventories therefore render tenuous the link between their evidence and both the actual net assets of an individual and comparative levels of wealth within a community or area, especially when related to houses built or acquired some time before death.

The evidence of houses

Given the limitations of probate inventories, the physical evidence of buildings acquires particular significance, since the size and quality of a house and its fixtures may reflect the economic circumstances of its builder. That argument, however, only relates to the moment at which the householder built or acquired it. Many people, particularly the elderly, will, as today, have had substantial means but have chosen not to keep their dwellings up to date, whether with chimneys or in other respects; others, by contrast, may, also as today, have continued to occupy large and well-furnished houses even though having relatively little disposable income or capital. The problems are compounded when seeking comparisons between regions, for very little is known about the cost of the materials and labour for building at the vernacular level: the Neaves identify the problem when they suggest that the shortage of good building materials in large parts of the East Riding may have meant that a modestly proportioned one-hearth house in fact represented the same or a greater level of investment than a larger two- or three-hearth house in another part of the country (chapter 13). Understanding the pattern across England is a considerable task, not least because the relative cost of different materials (timber, stone, brick) varied with time as well as place (Machin 1978, 139–41). Documentary and building historians need to work closely together to identify both the unit costs of materials at different times and places and the number of 'units' represented by the surviving houses from the same times and in the same places. The task is considerable, but the outcome may have the potential to fill one of the gaps in the evidence of probate inventories which cannot be made good by wills or administrators' accounts even where the latter survive.

Similar factors are relevant to understanding the numbers and character of hearths in individual houses. While there is a typological progression from the open hall to the smoke bay, the timber chimney and the multi-flue stone or brick chimney, each providing a greater level of sophistication or 'comfort', the rate of adoption of each new type of smoke management and fireplace was very variable. Old houses might have been built with an early form of smoke containment, or have had one inserted into them, long before the 1660s, but not have been upgraded again (Harrington et al 2000, ci). This may have had a significant effect on the number of hearths, for, while it was structurally feasible for timber chimneys to be built with back-to-back ground-floor fireplaces, and it was structurally possible for there to be a first-floor flue, the vast majority contained only one hearth (Fig 18.1). In parts of the country where wood, peat or dung continued to be burnt, large fireplaces with no grates may have remained desirable, the heat from such slow-burning fuel burnt on the hearth stone spreading throughout even quite large buildings. In places where coal was burnt, by contrast, a larger number of fireplaces may have been required to spread warmth through the same size of house, while the need to provide a grate to create an underdraught (Fenton 1981, 34; Smith 1992, 186) may have meant both that fireplaces could be smaller and that flues might be as well, to avoid all the heat disappearing up the chimney.

The adoption of multiple chimneys built in new materials may, therefore, sometimes have had less to do with the financial means of the householder than with the availability and cost of different kinds of fuel (Davis; Neave and Neave; Harrington et al 2000, xcviii n 211). In Lancashire, for example, 23% of houses in the county as a whole were assessed on more than one hearth in 1664, but in the vicinity of the Douglas Valley, where coal was readily accessible and the pits were owned by the local gentry, the proportion rose by 16% (Miller 2002, 67–70 cf 30–31), though how much of that should be attributed to the cheapness of coal and how much to the wealth coal created for the pit owners is unclear. On the North York Moors, where coal was only exploited from the mid-18th century, and almost 200 years later people still burnt the moorland peat to which their tenancies gave them free access, the timber firehoods of single-hearth houses were sometimes elaborately decorated, even panelled, creating an impression of some prosperity (RCHME 1987, 11; Hartley and Ingilby 1990, 73–81; Harrison and Hutton 1984, 236).

The evidence so far available suggests that there is the potential for systematic study of chimneys and the houses in which they stand to supply unique primary evidence to provide differentiation within the vast number of single-hearth houses. Part of the equation concerns the ages of houses and chimneys, but alongside that the relationship between variations in the availability of fuel in different places and the dates at which chimney design changed needs investigation.

Economic circumstances and investment cycles

One of the patterns which emerges from analysis of the Hearth Tax returns is that, in some of the well-hearthed counties of the south-east, parishes with fundamentally arable economies seem to have contained a larger proportion of single-hearth houses than those where there was a greater emphasis on pastoral farming (especially Longcroft; cf Spufford 1962). Part of the reason may be that arable farming supported a small class of relatively wealthy landlords and a large number of relatively poor tenants who often had little opportunity to engage in secondary activities to increase their income (see Harrington et al 2000, xcii, for discussion in relation to Kent), whereas a more pastoral economy allowed greater access to common resources and greater freedom for tenants to engage in additional activities (Thirsk 1984b). That the availability of secondary sources of income was an important, if not determining, factor in at least some areas is clear in West Yorkshire (Giles; RCHME 1986), but it was not always the case. In discussing Yetminster in Dorset, a parish with a predominantly pastoral economy, which contains a greater number of 17th-century houses than its arable neighbours, Machin found that it was a less significant factor in relation to investment in building than the greater flexibility and potential profit margins of livestock-based economies than grain-based ones (Machin 1978, 125–35; cf Machin 1977, 46–47). When Machin wrote, some of the detailed data upon which his argument is based was only available up to 1640 (Bowden 1967a; Bowden 1967b), and it has yet to be seen whether it holds for the later 17th century, though comparable information has now been published (Bowden 1984a; Bowden 1984b).

The position is, however, likely to be more complicated than simply a matter of pastoral economies creating greater surpluses which could be invested in houses, for if that were the case less of the predominantly pastoral west (and perhaps even north) of England should have been dominated by single-hearth houses. An avenue for further exploration might be the relationship between the location of pastoral wealth, as reflected in houses and hearths, and access to markets. One strand of investigation might concern the power of the London market, which drove much of the economy of the south-east and may have encouraged an increase in specialisation in agricultural and proto-industrial production in the region. That may have created a need for local markets for exchange within a region such as East Anglia (Holderness 1984, 199), enabling pastoral farmers there to take advantage of the flexibilities of their position in terms of both secondary occupation and/or of profit margins, in a way not open to pastoral farmers in areas with a less well-developed market economy.

Areas with comparable access to markets but with different agricultural economies, might, in addition, give rise to different cycles of investment. Between 1500 and 1650 grain prices rose steeply, so that arable farmers, particularly in places with developed market systems, may have had sufficient surplus to have been able to invest in new houses or to improve older ones in what will often have been the period when timber chimneys were the best available form in the locality, so looking 'poor' in the Hearth Tax returns. Thereafter, the price of grain fell, and the position of arable farmers was considerably weakened, while the prices of pastoral products remained stable (Bowden 1984a; for a less technical synthesis see Thirsk 1997). Up to the middle of the 17th century, some pastoral farmers with good access to markets may have been better placed to invest in larger houses or in ones with more sophisticated heating arrangements at the same time as their arable counterparts, or to modernise older houses by, for example, adding fireplaces. Other such farmers, however, may only have chosen to invest as the general trend of prices moved in their favour after about 1650, so that the Hearth Tax could reveal their improvements or new houses, created when brick and stone multi-flue chimney stacks were more common, as more 'wealthy' than those in comparable arable areas. In pastoral regions with poorer market access the decision to invest might often have been delayed until the stability of the livestock economy was more firmly established, thereby pushing it into the 1660s or 1670s: if that were the case, the Hearth Tax, which provides a snapshot of a period of little more than a decade, might catch them in transition (as in the Yorkshire Dales: Harrison and Hutton 1984, 185–86), or even shortly before significant modernisation or rebuilding began.

A further layer of variation may arise from the destructive and unsettling effects of the Civil War (discussed in general terms by Porter 1994), which may have had some similarity to that of the instability and uncertainty caused more locally in Northumberland by the border raiders (McCombie). Physical destruction of property was relatively little felt to the east of a line drawn from King's Lynn to Cambridge, London and Arundel, a line which bears a crude similarity to that around areas with the highest proportions of houses with three or more hearths (see Arkell 2003, 157 fig 1 and 158 fig 2); the exception is that places further west along the south coast have a high number of hearths, perhaps on account of their access to ports and, therefore, to both internal and foreign markets. While destruction of property in the more severely affected areas was relatively modest, directly affecting only about 1% of the population, and was concentrated in towns, the effects of the War may have been felt much more widely: disruption of markets in the affected towns may have restricted economic development in their hinterlands; even if the movement of armies did not destroy crops, a climate of insecurity in the countryside may have discouraged investment in new building; after the War there may have been a shortage of skilled builders in rural areas as they were sucked into the towns to repair the damage, in the same way as Guillery notes that parts of London outside the area affected by the Great Fire suffered a pause in building activity in its aftermath. The Civil War lasted long enough for the uncertainty it caused to have continued for some time afterwards, and the repair of many towns was not completed until the 1660s or even later — in the case of York and Gloucester, some suburbs were not reconstructed until after 1700. In lower social strata, the effects of uncertainty, even when a direct economic setback was not encountered, may therefore have lasted into the period when the Hearth Tax was imposed, so that low numbers of hearths may not always reflect actual levels of wealth. For members of higher social levels, even if their own country houses were not destroyed, the economic stability and psychological condition of the gentry and aristocracy was damaged by the fining or dispossession of Royalist supporters during the Interregnum, and again by Charles II's dispossession of the purchasers of former Crown and Church lands (Green), so that building work may not have been immediately undertaken in the areas affected.

Cultural factors

Differing agrarian systems may not only have affected the economics of rebuilding and heating houses, but may also be related to different requirements in terms of space, or the provision of heat: the storage of grain, for example, may have led to a preference for heating arrangements different from those where large quantities of cheese and meat were kept in the house, smoking of the latter requiring a large flue, preferably over a wood or peat fire. The number of hearths may also have been affected by other cultural factors: in areas where there were few gentry, or few gentry buiding houses with elaborate chimneys in the aftermath of the Civil War, there may simply have been fewer examples for social emulators in lower classes to copy, and less pressure on them to do so, as there may also have been in areas of sparse population. That cultural factors might have significance is suggested by the well-known fact that parts of northern England saw a proliferation of parlours, usually used as bedrooms (Barley 1984, 656); their presence indicates both a way of using houses which was different from that in the south-east, and that northern houses might have as many, or more, ground-floor rooms as their southern counterparts, even if they had fewer hearths.

It is perhaps in relation to these issues, rather than to wealth, that the evidence of inventories comes into its own. Used with a caution which seeks to identify occasions when goods were moved into a small number of rooms for valuation, inventories can provide evidence for the numbers of rooms in houses, which can sometimes be set against the evidence of buildings themselves. In addition, the contents of rooms may give an indication of the way in which they were used. Even when the number and designation of rooms is suspect, the types of goods listed within the house as a whole are one of the vital clues both to regional economies and to the purposes to which space in houses was put. What is required is a refinement, development, and marrying of the approaches adopted 40 years ago by Barley in relation to houses (Barley 1961) and Thirsk in relation to the identification of agrarian regions (Thirsk 1967b; cf Spufford 2000c, especially 18–19), both of which were based on inventories.

Conclusion

The papers in this volume represent work in progress, not only towards the medium-term aims of the British Academy Hearth Tax Project to publish returns for each county for which there is no adequate existing publication, but also towards the much larger task of understanding what the Hearth Tax returns actually mean. They illustrate a variety of ways in which the buildings and documentary sources can be used together, ranging from addressing questions of rebuilding (especially Giles and Phillips), to using the Hearth Tax returns to begin to reach a layer of humble dwellings with have disappeared (as suggested by Guillery and Longcroft in particular), to using the topographical structure of the returns as a key to assist in linking other documentary sources and the people recorded in documents to individual houses (Leech).

One of the most telling comments in the book, however, is made by Alcock, when he refers to the way in which study of the buildings standing at the time of the Hearth Tax brings 'actuality' to the tax returns. That does not mean that they merely 'illustrate' them. It is already quite clear that there was tremendous variation in the kinds and ages of house represented by the different number of hearths recorded by the tax assessors, both within and between regions and counties (Spufford 2000c, 9–10), and the buildings are a unique and vital source of primary evidence. Such variations do not simply reflect different levels of wealth, but a much more complicated mix of economic and social factors including sources of income, access to markets, the level of confidence to invest, and the different investment cycles they engendered; the implications of those cycles for the nature of the 1660s' and 1670s' housing stock; and more nebulous cultural factors still to be identified. In terms of assessing wealth, probate inventories need to be handled with increased sophistication, and more routinely only in conjunction with the much smaller number of related wills and administrators' accounts, so that a picture of net assets can be established, taking into account both the ownership of real estate and the value of debts. Even then, the value of the houses themselves will remain to be considered, and that can only be achieved by studying the buildings themselves in conjunction with documentary evidence for the prices of materials and labour. Only when all these factors are understood will it be realistic to approach with conviction the question of the extent to which the mapping of hearth numbers truly reflects that of wealth, and will it be possible to assess the extent to which the tax on hearths really did act as a tax on assets as intended.

No one source, or even pair of sources, will provide the answers. It is only by using all available types of material, combined with an appreciation of the limitations of each, that the full potential of any one kind of evidence will be realised. All kinds of source can be fallible, may on occasion only survive incompletely, or may contain evidence which appears baffling, but combining them, particularly in fairly large samples, can enhance the reliability of the overall pattern.

Until very recently, inquiry of this kind has been hampered by the inability of interpreters of the physical evidence to produce dates both reliable and precise enough to fit the short periods covered by many kinds of documentary source including the Hearth Tax returns. When he wrote about the rebuilding debate in the 1970s, Machin's firm evidence for buildings was restricted to a handful of houses with date stones which seemed trustworthy (Machin 1977). Now both tree-ring dates and the luminescence dating of brick are beginning to provide the more precise dates required, though both are expensive, capacity to undertake the work is limited, and the latter technique is still in its infancy. While the two techniques are developing and a corpus of dated houses and chimneys is built up, there is much which can be achieved by the traditional disciplines working more closely together than they often have. Thirty years ago, Machin concluded his re-assessment of the 'great rebuilding' debate with the statement that progress would only be made if students of buildings thought in more historical terms and if historians recognised the value of buildings as primary evidence (Machin 1977, 55–56): that conclusion can equally trenchantly be drawn today in relation to the study of the Hearth Tax.

Acknowledgements

I am grateful to Malcolm Airs, Colum Giles, Sarah Pearson and Margaret Spufford for debate during the writing of this chapter, and for comments and reactions to the draft text. Thanks are also due to Allan Adams for drawing the illustration.

Bibliography

Alcock, N W, 1993 *People at Home: Living in a Warwickshire Village, 1500–1800*. Chichester: Phillimore

Alcock, N W, 1996 Documentary Records, in M Rylatt and M A Stokes, *The Excavations at Broadgate East, Coventry 1974–5*. Coventry: Coventry Museums

Alcock, N W, 2003 *Documenting the History of Houses*. London: British Records Association

Allison, K J, 1957 The Lost Villages of Norfolk, *Norfolk Archaeology*, **31**(1), 116–62

Andrews, D D, Ryan, P, Stenning, D F & Tyers, I, 1997 New House Farm and Hungry Hall, Cressing: The Disintegration of the Cressing Temple Estate or the Great Rebuilding?, *Essex Archaeol and Hist*, **28**, 156–64

Antrobus, A, 2004 Luminescence Dating of Brick Chimneys, *Vernacular Archit*, **35**, 21–31

Arkell, T, 1986–87 Assessing the Reliability of the Warwickshire Hearth Tax Returns of 1662–74, *Warwickshire History*, **VI**(6), 183–97

Arkell, T, 1987 The Incidence of Poverty in England in the Later 17th Century, *Social History*, **12**, 23–47

Arkell, T, 1992 Printed Instructions for Administering the Hearth Tax, in Schürer and Arkell 1992, 38–64

Arkell, T, 2003 Identifying Regional Variations from the Hearth Tax, *Local Historian*, **33**(3), 148–74

Arkell, T, & Alcock, N W, forthcoming *The 1669–70 Warwickshire Hearth Tax return*. Stratford upon Avon: Dugdale Soc

Armitt, M L, 1916 *Rydal*. W F Rawnsley (ed). Kendal: Titus Wilson

Baer, W C, 2000 Housing the Poor and Mechanick Class in 17th-Century London, *The London Journal*, **25**(2), 13–39

Bagot, A, 1962 Mr Gilpin and Manorial Custom, *Trans Cumberland & Westmorland Antiq & Archaeol Soc*, new ser **62**, 224–45

Baildon, W P, 1913 *Baildon and the Baildons*. Privately printed

Barley, M W, 1961 *The English Farmhouse and Cottage*. London: Routledge & Kegan Paul

Barley, M W, 1984 Rural Building in England, in Thirsk 1984a, **2**, 590–685

Barley, M W, 1986 *Houses and History*. London: Faber & Faber

Barley, M W, 1988 Nottinghamshire Houses, in Webster 1988

Barnwell, P S, & Adams, A T, 1994 *The House Within: Interpreting Medieval Houses in Kent*. RCHME. London: HMSO

Barringer, J C, 1993 Tanners and Tanning, in Wade Martins 1993, 152–53

Beier, A L, & Finlay, R (eds), 1986 *London, 1500–1700: The Making of the Metropolis*. Harlow: Longman

Beresford, M W, & Hurst, J G (eds), 1971 *Deserted Medieval Villages: Studies*. Woking: Lutterworth Press

Bettey, J H B, 1982 Seventeenth-Century Squatters Dwellings: Some Documentary Evidence, *Vernacular Archit*, **13**, 28–30

Bickley, F B (ed), 1900 *The Little Red Book of Bristol, volumes 1 and 2*. Bristol and London: Hemmons and Sotheran & Co

Bigmore, P, 1979 *The Bedfordshire and Huntingdonshire Landscape*. London: Hodder & Stoughton

Bowden, P J, 1967a Agricultural Prices, Farm Profits, and Rents, in Thirsk 1967a, 593–685

Bowden, P J, 1967b Statistical Appendix, in Thirsk 1967a, 814–70

Bowden, P J, 1984a Agricultural Prices, Farm Profits, and Rents, in Thirsk 1984a, **2**, 1–117

Bowden, P J, 1984b, Statistics, in Thirsk 1984a, **2**, 827–902

Braddick, M J, 1994 *Parliamentary Taxation in 17th-Century England: Local Administration and Response*. Studies in History, **70**. Woodbridge: Royal Historical Soc

Braddick, M J, 1996 *The Nerves of State: Taxation and the Financing of the English State, 1558–1714*. Manchester: Manchester University Press.

Braddick, M J, 2000 *State Formation in Early Modern England, c 1550–1700*. Cambridge: Cambridge University Press

Brears, P C D (ed), 1972 *Yorkshire Probate Inventories 1542–1689*. Yorks Archaeol Soc Record Series, **134**. Leeds: Yorks Archaeol Soc

Brears, P C D, 1984 *The Gentlewoman's Kitchen: Great Food in Yorkshire 1650–1750*. Wakefield: Wakefield Historical Publications

Brinkworth, E C R, Gibson, J S W, and Dannatt, G H (eds), 1985 *Banbury Wills and Inventories. Part 1: 1521–1620*. Banbury: Banbury Hist Soc

Brooks, H, 2004 Beeleigh Abbey, near Maldon, Essex: Report on the Fourth Phase of Excavations, 2003. Unpubl report for Maldon Archaeol and Hist Group

Brunskill, R W, 1974 *Vernacular Architecture of the Lake Counties: A Field Handbook*. Reprinted 1987. London: Faber & Faber

Brunskill, R W, 2002 *Traditional Buildings of Cumbria, the County of the Lakes*. London: Cassell

Calendar of State Papers, Venice 1615–17, 1908. A B Hinds (ed). London: HMSO

Calendar of Treasury Books Preserved in the PRO,

1904–57. W A Shaw (ed). 7 vols in 10. London: HMSO

Carson, C, 1976 Segregation in Vernacular Buildings, *Vernacular Architect*, **7**, 24–29

Carter, M P, 1988 Urban Society and Its Hinterland: St Ives in the 17th and early 18th Centuries. Unpubl PhD thesis, University of Leicester

Carter, M P, 2003 Huntingdonshire Hearth Tax Records: Context and Analysis. Unpubl typescript

Chalklin, C W, 1965 *Seventeenth-Century Kent*. London: Longmans

Chalklin, C W, 1995 The Towns, in A Armstrong (ed), 1995, *The Economy of Kent, 1640–1914*. Woodbridge: Kent County Council, 205–34

Champion, J A I (ed), 1993 *Epidemic Disease in London*. Centre for Metropolitan Hist Working Paper, **1**. London: University of London, Institute of Hist Research, Centre for Metropolitan Hist, 35–52

Champion, J A I, 1995 *London's Dreaded Visitation: The Social Geography of the Great Plague in 1665*. Hist Geography Research Ser **31**. London: University of London, Institute of Hist Research, Centre for Metropolitan Hist

Chandaman, C D, 1975 *The English Public Revenue 1660–1688*. Oxford: Clarendon Press

Charlton, B, 1987 *Upper North Tynedale: A Northumbrian Valley and its People*. Newcastle: Northumbrian Water

Clark, A G, 1992 *Elton, A History of its Lost and Ancient Buildings*. Stamford: Spiegle Press

Cloake, J, 2001 *Cottages and Common Fields of Richmond and Kew*. Chichester: Phillimore

Colman, S, 1971 The Hearth Tax Returns for the Hundred of Blackbourne, 1662, *Procs of the Suffolk Institute of Archaeol*, **32**(2), 168–92

Cooper, N, 1999 *The Houses of the Gentry 1400–1680*. New Haven and London: Yale University Press

Crossley, D, 1999 Iron and Glass Industries, in K Leslie and B Short (eds), *An Historical Atlas of Sussex*. Chichester: Phillimore, 62–63

Cudworth, C L, 1932 Dutch Influence in East Anglian Architecture, *Procs of the Cambs Antiq Soc*, **37**, 24–42

Currie, C R J, 1988 Time and Chance: Modelling the Attrition of Old Houses, *Vernacular Archit*, **19**, 1–9

Curwen, J F, 1932 *The Later Records Relating to North Westmorland or the Barony of Appleby*. Cumberland & Westmorland Antiq & Archaeol Soc Record Series, **8**. Kendal: Titus Wilson & Son

Davis, E M, 1979 Brookend Farm, Catworth. *Records of Huntingdonshire*, **9**, 5–9

Davis, E M, 1982 Weepers: A Small Late Medieval Aisled Hall in Cambridgeshire, *Medieval Archaeol*, **26**, 158–62

Davis, E M, 1996 Tudor Farm, Godmanchester. Unpubl report

Davis, E M, 2000 Vernacular Building Down to 1700, in Kirby & Oosthuizen 2000, 39–40

Davis, R, 1962 *The Rise of the English Shipping Industry in the 17th and 18th Centuries*. London: Macmillan

Davison, A, 1993 Deserted Villages and Rural Depopulation, in Wade Martins 1993, 84–85

Davison, A, 1996 *Deserted Villages in Norfolk*. North Walsham: Poppyland Press

Defoe, D, 1704 *The Storm*. R Hamblyn (ed), 2003. London: Allen Lane

Denyer, S, 1991 *Traditional Buildings and Life in the Lake District*. London: Victor Gollanz

Edwards, A C, & Newton, K C, 1984 *The Walkers of Hanningfield: Surveyors and Mapmakers Extraordinary*. London: Buckland Publications

Emmison, F G, 1978 *Elizabethan Life, 4: Wills of Essex Gentry and Merchants Proved in the Prerogative Court of Canterbury*. Chelmsford: Essex County Council

Emmison, F G, 1982–2000 *Essex Wills*. 12 vols. Chelmsford: Essex County Council

Evans, N, 1993 Worsted and Linen Weavers, in Wade Martins 1993, 150–51

Evans, N, 2000 *The Cambridgeshire and Huntingdonshire Hearth Tax Returns, Michaelmas 1664*, in Kirby & Oosthuizen 2000, 48–49

Evans, N, & Rose, S, 2000 *Cambridgeshire Hearth Tax Returns Michaelmas 1664*. British Record Soc Hearth Tax Ser **1**. Cambs Records Soc **15**. London: British Record Soc

Evelyn, J, 1661 *Fumifugium or the Inconveniencie of the Aer and Smoak of London Dissipated*. London: G Bedel & T Collins

Everitt, A, 1966 *The Community of Kent and the Great Rebellion*. Leicester: Leicester University Press

Fairclough, G, 1984 Edlingham Castle, Northumberland, *Trans of the Ancient Monuments Soc*, new ser **28**, 40–59

Farr, M W (ed), 1992 *The Great Fire of Warwick. The Records of the Commissioners Appointed under an Act of Parliament for Rebuilding the Town of Warwick*. Publications of the Dugdale Soc, **26**. Stratford upon Avon: Dugdale Soc

Farrer, W, 1923–24 *Records of Kendale*. J F Curwen (ed). Cumberland & Westmorland Antiq & Archaeol Soc Record Ser, **4, 5**. 2 vols. Repr 1998–99. Kendal: Titus Wilson & Son

Fenton, A, 1981 *The Hearth in Scotland*. Edinburgh: National Museum of Antiquities of Scotland

Finlay, R, & Shearer, B, 1986 Population Growth and Suburban Expansion, in Beier and Finlay 1986, 37–59

Fleming, D, 1671 *Fleming-Senhouse Papers*. E Hughes (ed), 1961. Cumberland Record Series, **2**. Carlisle: [Cumberland County Council]

Frankel, M S, & Seaman, P J, (eds), 1983 Norfolk Hearth Tax Assessment. Michaelmas 1664, *Norfolk Genealogy*, **15**

Frearson, M, 2000 Transportation in Early Modern Cambridgeshire and Huntingdonshire, in Kirby & Oosthuizen 2000, 46–47

Frenzel, B (ed), 1994 *Climatic Trends and Anomalies*

in Europe, 1675–1715. Stuttgart: European Science Foundation

Garnett, M E, 1988 The Great Rebuilding in South Lonsdale, 1600–1730, *Trans Hist Soc of Lancs and Chesh*, **137**, 55–75

George, M D, 1925 *London Life in the 18th Century*. Repr 1964. New York: Harper & Row

Gibson, J S, 1985 *The Hearth Tax, Other Later Stuart Tax Lists and the Association Oath Rolls*. Plymouth: Federation of Family Hist Socs

Gibson, J S, & Medlycot, M, 1992 *Local Census Listings, 1522–1930*. Birmingham: Federation of Family Hist Socs

Goodall, I H, 2002 Privacy, Display and Over Extension: Walter Strickland's Rebuilding of Sizergh. *Antiq J*, **82**, 197–245

Green, A, 1998 Tudhoe Hall and Byers Green Hall, County Durham: 17th and Early 18th-Century Social Change in Houses, *Vernacular Archit*, **29**, 33–42

Green, A, 2006 *The County Durham Hearth Tax Returns for Lady Day 1666*. British Record Soc Hearth Tax Ser, **4**. London: British Record Soc

Green, A, forthcoming Houses and Landscape in Early Industrial County Durham, in T Faulkner and H Berry (eds), *Northern Landscapes: Representations and Realities*. Woodbridge: Boydell & Brewer

Grey, W, 1649 *Chorographia, or a Survey of Newcastle upon Tyne*. Repr 1813. Newcastle: Antiq Soc of Newcastle upon Tyne

Griffiths, M, 1979 *Penmark and Porthkerry: Families and Farms in 17th-century Vale of Glamorgan*. Cardiff: University College Cardiff

Grove, J, 2004 *The Little Ice Ages*. 2nd edn. 2 vols. London: Routledge

Guillery, P, 2004 *The Small House in 18th-Century London*. London: Yale University Press

Guillery, P, & Herman, B, 1999 Deptford Houses 1650 to 1800, *Vernacular Archit* **30**, 58–84

Hall, E (ed), 1986 *Michael Warton of Beverley: An Inventory of his Possessions*. Hull: Centre for Regional and Local Hist, University of Hull

Hall, L J, 1983 *The Rural Houses of North Avon and South Gloucestershire, 1400–1720*. Bristol: City of Bristol Museum & Art Gallery

Hall, L J, 2005 *Period House Fixtures and Fittings 1300–1900*. Newbury: Countryside Books

Harding, V, 2001 City, Capital, and Metropolis: The Changing Shape of 17th-century London, in J F Merritt (ed), *Imagining Early Modern London: Perceptions and Portrayals of the City from Stow to Strype, 1598–1720*. Cambridge: Cambridge University Press, 117–43

Harrington, D, Pearson, S, & Rose, S, 2000 *Kent Hearth Tax Assessment Lady Day 1664*. British Record Soc Hearth Tax Ser **2**. Kent Archaeol Soc Kent Records **29**. London: British Record Soc

Harrison, B, 1991 Longhouses in the Vale of York, *Vernacular Archit*, **22**, 31–39

Harrison, B, & Hutton, B, 1984 *Vernacular Houses in North Yorkshire and Cleveland*. Edinburgh: John Donald

Harrison, W, 1587 *A Description of England*. G Edelen (ed), 1994. New York: Dover Publications

Hartley, M, and Ingilby, J, 1990 *Life and Tradition in the Moorlands of North-East Yorkshire*. 2nd edn. Otley: Smith Settle

Harvey, P D A, 1993 *Maps in Tudor England*. London: Public Record Office

Hasted, E, 1797–1801 *The History and Topographical Survey of the County of Kent*. 2nd edn repr 1972. 12 vols. Wakefield: EP Publishing

Hatcher, M J, 1993 *The History of the British Coal Industry. Volume 1. Before 1700: Towards the Age of Coal*. Oxford: Clarendon Press

Havinden, M A, 1965, *Household and Farm Inventories in Oxfordshire, 1550–1590*. Hist Manuscripts Comm Joint Publication **10**. Oxford Record Soc **44**. London: HMSO

Heesom, A, 1988 The Enfranchisement of Durham, *Durham University J*, **80**, 265–85

Heslop, D H, & McCombie, G, 1996 Alderman Fenwick's House, a Late 17th-Century House in Pilgrim Street, Newcastle upon Tyne, *Archaeologia Aeliana*, 5th ser **24**, 129–69

Hey, D, and Redmonds, G, 2002 *Yorkshire Surnames and the Hearth Tax Returns of 1672–3*. Borthwick Paper **102**. York: University of York

Hicks, J D (ed), 1978 *A Victorian Boyhood on the Wolds*. East Yorks Local Hist Ser, **34**. Beverley: East Yorks Local Hist Soc

Hindle, S, 2004 *On the Parish? The Micro-Politics of Poor Relief in Rural England, c 1550–1750*. Oxford: Clarendon Press

Hodgson, J, 1820–58 *History of Northumberland*. 3 vols. Newcastle: E Walker

Holderness, B A, 1984 East Anglia and the Fens: Norfolk, Suffolk, Cambridgeshire, Ely, Huntingdonshire, Esssex, and the Lincolnshire Fens, in Thirsk 1984a, **1**, 197–238

Hoskins, W G, 1953 The Rebuilding of Rural England 1570–1640, *Past & Present*, **4**, 44–59

Hoskins, W G, 1957 *Exeter in the 17th Century: Tax and Rate Assessments 1602–1699*. Devon & Cornwall Record Soc, new ser **2**. Torquay: Devon & Cornwall Record Soc

Hoskins, W G, 1959 *Local History in England*. Repr 1984. London: Longman

Hoskins, W G, 1965 *The Midland Peasant: The Economic and Social History of a Leicestershire Village*. London: Macmillan

Howard, M, 1987 *The Early Tudor Country House: Architecture and Politics 1490–1550*. London: George Philip

Hughes, E, & White, P, 1991 *The Hampshire Hearth Tax Assessment 1665*. Southampton: Hampshire Record Office

Hull, C H (ed), 1899 *The Economic Writings of William Petty*. 2 vols. Cambridge: Cambridge University Press

Hunneyball, P M, 2004 *Architecture and Image-Building in 17th-Century Hertfordshire*. Oxford: Clarendon Press

Husbands, C, 1992 Hearths, Wealth and Occupa-

tions: An Exploration of the Hearth Tax in the Later 17th Century, in Schürer and Arkell 1992, 65–77
Hutton, R, 1986 *The Restoration: A Political and Religious History of England and Wales, 1658–1667*. Oxford: Oxford University Press
Hyde, R, 1992 Introductory Notes, in *The A to Z of Restoration London (The City of London, 1676)*. London Topographical Soc Publication **145**. London: London Topographical Soc
James, M E, 1974 *Family, Lineage and Civil Society: A Study of Society, Politics and Mentality in the Durham Region 1500–1640*. Oxford: Clarendon Press
Johnson, M, 1993 *Housing Culture: Traditional Architecture in an English Landscape*. London: UCL Press
Jones, P D, Ogilvie, A E J, Davies, T D, & Biffa, K R (eds), 2001 *History and Climate: Memories of the Future*. New York: Plenum Publishers
Keene, D, 1985 *Winchester Studies 2. Survey of Medieval Winchester, Parts 1 and 2*. Oxford: Clarendon Press
Kent, J, 1986 *The English Village Constable, 1580–1642: A Social and Administrative Study*. Oxford: Clarendon Press.
Kirby, T, & Oosthuizen, S (eds), 2000 *An Atlas of Cambridgeshire and Huntingdonshire History*. Cambridge: Centre for Regional Studies, Anglia Polytechnic University
Lapsley, G T, 1900 *The County Palatine of Durham: A Study in Constitutional History*. New York: Longmans
Larminie, V, 1995 *Wealth, Kinship and Culture: The 17th-Century Newdigates of Arbury and their World*. Studies in History, **72**. Woodbridge: Royal Historical Soc
Leech, R H, 1996 The Prospect from Rugman's Row: The Row House in Late 16th and Early 17th-Century London, *Archaeol J*, **153**, 201–42
Leech, R H, 1997 The Topography of Medieval and Early Modern Bristol. Part 1: Property Holdings in the Early Walled Town and Marsh Suburb North of the Avon, *Bristol Record Soc*, **48**, i–xxvii, 1–220
Leech, R H, 1999 The Processional City: Some Issues for Historical Archaeology, in S Tarlow & S West (eds), *The Familiar Past? Archaeologies of Later Historical Britain*. London: Routledge, 19–34
Leech, R H, 2000a The Topography of Medieval and Early Modern Bristol. Part 2: The St Michael's Hill Precinct of the University of Bristol, *Bristol Record Soc*, **52**, 1–133
Leech, R H, 2000b The Symbolic Hall: Historical Context and Merchant Culture in the Early Modern City, *Vernacular Archit*, **30**, 1–10
Leech, R H, 2003 The Garden House: Merchant Culture and Identity in the Early Modern City, in S Lawrence (ed), *Archaeologies of the British, Explorations of identity in Great Britain and its colonies 1600–1945*, One World Archaeology, **46**. London: Routledge, 76–86
Leech, R H, 2004 The Atlantic World and Industrialisation: Contexts for the Structures of Everyday Life in Early Modern Bristol, in D Barker & D Cranstone (eds), *The Archaeology of Industrialisation*. Soc for Post-Medieval Archaeol Monograph **1**. Leeds: Maney, 157–64
Leech, R H, forthcoming, *Town Houses: Capitalism, Slavery and the Streets of Bristol*
Levine, D, & Wrightson, K, 1991 *The Making of an Industrial Society: Whickham 1560–1765*. Oxford: Clarendon Press
Loder, R, 1610–20 *Robert Loder's Farm Accounts, 1610–20*. G E Fussell (ed), 1936. Camden Soc, 3rd series **53**
Lomas, R, 1996 *County of Conflict: Northumberland from Conquest to Civil War*. East Linton: Tuckwell Press
Longcroft, A, 1998 The Development and Survival of Post-Medieval Vernacular Houses: A Case Study from Norfolk. Unpubl PhD thesis, University of East Anglia
Machell, T, 1692 *Antiquary on Horseback... Towards a History of the Barony of Kendal*. J M Ewbank (trans & ed), 1963. Cumberland & Westmorland Antiq and Archaeol Soc, Extra Series **19**. Kendal: Titus Wilson & Son
Machin, R, 1977 The Great Rebuilding: A Reassessment, *Past & Present*, **77**, 33–56
Machin, R, 1978 *The Houses of Yetminster*. Bristol: Bristol University Dept of Extra-Mural Studs
Machin, R, 1994 *Rural Housing: An Historical Approach*. London: Hist Assoc
McCord, N, & Thompson, R, 2004 *The Northern Counties from AD 1000*. Harlow: Longman
McGrath, P, 1968 *Merchants and Merchandise on 17th-Century Bristol*. Bristol Record Soc **19**. Bristol: Bristol Record Soc
McIntosh, M, 1998 *Controlling Misbehaviour in England, 1370–1600*. Cambridge: Cambridge University Press
McKellar, E, 1999 *The Birth of Modern London: The Development and Design of the City 1660–1720*. Manchester: Manchester University Press
Meekings, C A F (ed), 1940 *Surrey Hearth Tax 1664*. Surrey Record Soc **17**, nos 41 and 42. Frome & London: Surrey Record Soc
Meekings, C A F (ed), 1951 *Dorset Hearth Tax Assessments 1662–1664*. Dorchester: Dorset Natural Hist & Archaeol Soc
Meekings, C A F, 1962 *The Hearth Tax 1662–89: Exhibition of Records*. London: Public Record Office
Meikle, M, 2004 *A British Frontier? Lairds and Gentlemen in the Eastern Borders, 1540–1603*. East Linton: Tuckwell Press
Mercer, E, 1975 *English Vernacular Houses: A Study of Traditional Farmhouses and Cottages*. London: HMSO
Miller, G, 2002 *Historic Houses in Lancashire: The Douglas Valley 1300–1770*. Pendle: Heritage Trust for the North West
Moorhouse, S A, 1981 Rural Houses, in M I Faull

and S A Moorhouse, *West Yorkshire: An Archaeological Survey to A D 1500*. Wakefield: West Yorkshire Metropolitan County Council

Morgan, K, 2000 *Slavery, Atlantic Trade and the British Economy 1660–1800*. Cambridge: Cambridge University Press

Mussett, P, with Woodward P G, 1988 *Estates and Money at Durham Cathedral 1660–1985*. Durham: Dean & Chapter of Durham Cathedral

Neave, D, 1996 Artisan Mannerism in North Lincolnshire and East Yorkshire: The Work of William Catlyn (1628–1709) of Hull, in C Sturman (ed), *Lincolnshire People and Places*. Lincoln: Soc for Lincs Hist & Archaeol, 18–25

Neave, D, 1998 The identity of the East Riding of Yorkshire, in E Royle (ed), *Issues of Regional Identity*. Manchester: Manchester University Press, 184–200

Neave, D, 2000 *Port, Resort and Market Town: A History of Bridlington*. Howden: Hull Academic Press

Neave, D, & Neave, S, 1996 Population Density: 1672 and 1743, in S Neave & S Ellis (eds), *An Historical Atlas of East Yorkshire*. Hull: University of Hull Press, 44–45

Neave, S, 1990 Settlement Contraction in the East Riding of Yorkshire *c* 1660–1760. Unpubl PhD thesis, University of Hull

Newton, R, 1972 *The Northumberland Landscape*. London: Hodder & Stoughton

Nicolson, J, & Burn, R, 1777 *The History and Antiquities of the Counties of Westmorland and Cumberland*. Repr 1976. 2 vols. Wakefield: EP Publishing

O'Neil, B H St J, 1949 North Street, Folkestone, Kent, *Antiq J*, **29**, 8–12

O'Neil, B H St J, 1953 Some 17th-Century Houses in Great Yarmouth, *Archaeologia*, **95**, 141–80

Osmond, P, 1913 *A Life of John Cosin Bishop of Durham 1660–1672*, London: Mowbray

Overton, M, Whittle, J, Dean, D, & Hann, A (eds), 2004 *Production and Consumption in English Households, 1600–1750*. London: Routledge

Pallister, A, and Wrathmell, S, 1990 The Deserted Village of West Hartburn, Third Report, B Vyner (ed), *Medieval Rural Settlement in North East England*. Durham: Archit & Archaeol Soc of Durham & Northumberland

Parkinson, E, 1990 Glamorgan Hearth Tax Records 1664–1673. Unpubl MA thesis, University of Wales, College of Cardiff

Parkinson, E, 1994 *The Glamorgan Hearth Tax Assessment of 1670*. South Wales Record Soc, **10**. Cardiff: South Wales Record Soc

Parkinson, E, 2001 The Administration of the Hearth Tax, 1662–1666. Unpubl PhD thesis, University of Surrey, Roehampton

Pearson, S, 1994 *The Medieval Houses of Kent: An Historical Analysis*. RCHME. London: HMSO

Pearson, S, 2001 Boughton Monchelsea: The Pattern of Building in a Central Kent Parish, *Architectural Hist*, **44**, 386–93

Perlin, J, 1989 *Forest Journey: The Role of Wood in the Development of Civilization*. New York: W W Norton

Pettit, P A J, 1968 *The Royal Forests of Northamptonshire: A Study in their Economy, 1558–1714*. Northamptonshire Record Soc, **23**. Northampton: Northampton Record Soc

Pevsner, N, 1967 *The Buildings of England: Cumberland and Westmorland*. Harmondsworth: Penguin

Pevsner, N, 1968 *The Buildings of England: Bedfordshire and the County of Huntingdon and Peterborough*. Harmondsworth: Penguin

Pevsner, N, & Neave, D, 1995 *The Buildings of England: Yorkshire. York and the East Riding*. Harmondsworth: Penguin

Pevsner, N, & Richmond, I, 2001 *The Buildings of England: Northumberland*. 2nd edn, revised by J Grundy, G McCombie, P Ryer and H Welfare. Harmondsworth: Penguin

Phillips, C B, 1973 The Gentry in Cumberland and Westmorland 1600–1665. Unpubl PhD thesis, Lancaster University

Phillips, C B (ed), 1979 *Lowther Family Estate Books 1617–1675*. Surtees Soc Publications, **191**. Gateshead: Northumberland Press Ltd

Phillips, C B, 1981 Town and country: economic change in Kendal *c* 1550–1700, in P. Clark (ed), *The Transformation of English Provincial Towns 1600–1800*. London: Hutchinson, 99–132

Phillips, C B, & Gibson, J S W (eds), 1985 *Stockport Probate Records 1578–1619*. Record Soc of Lancs and Chesh, **124**. Chester: Record Soc of Lancs and Chesh

Plot, R, 1686 *The Natural History of Staffordshire*. Oxford: The Theatre

Porter, S, 1994 *Destruction in the English Civil War*. Stroud: Sutton Publishing

Pound, J, 1988 *Tudor and Stuart Norwich*. Chichester: Phillimore

Power, M J, 1972 East London Housing in the 17th century, in P Clark & P Slack (eds), *Crisis and Order in English Towns 1500–1700: Essays in Urban History*. London: Routledge & Kegan Paul, 237–62

Power, M J, 1978 Shadwell: The Development of a London Suburban Community in the Seventeenth Century, *The London Journal* 4(1), 29–46

Power, M J, 1986 The Social Topography of Restoration London, in Beier & Finlay 1986, 199–224

Purdy, J D, 1991 *The Yorkshire Hearth Tax Returns*. Studies in Regional and Local Hist, **7**. Hull: Centre for Regional and Local Hist, University of Hull

Rackham, O, 2003 *Ancient Woodland: Its History, Vegetation and Uses in England*. 2nd edn. Dalbeattie: Castlepoint

Ramsden, C, 1998 *The Westmorland Hearth Tax for the Year 1674*. Cumbria Family Hist Soc

RCHME 1926 *An Inventory of the Historical*

Monuments in Huntingdonshire. London: HMSO

RCHME 1936 *An Inventory of the Historical Monuments in Westmorland*. London: HMSO

RCHME 1952–75 *An Inventory of the Historical Monuments in Dorset*. 5 vols in 8. London: HMSO

RCHME 1985 *Rural Houses of the Lancashire Pennines, 1560–1760*. By S Pearson. London: HMSO

RCHME 1986 *Rural Houses of West Yorkshire, 1400–1830*. By C Giles. London: HMSO

RCHME 1987 *Houses of the North York Moors*. London: HMSO

Richards, J F, 2003 *The Unending Frontier: An Environmental History of the Early Modern World*. Berkeley: University of California Press

Rigold, S E, 1969 Timber-Framed Buildings in Kent, *Archaeol J*, **126**, 198–200

Roberts, E, 2003 *Hampshire Houses 1250–1700: Their Dating and Development*. Southampton: Hampshire County Council

Rushton, P, 1989 The Poor Law, the Parish and the Community in North-East England, 1600–1800, *Northern Hist*, **25**, 135–52

Sacks, D H, 1991 *The Widening Gate: Bristol and the Atlantic Economy*. Berkeley: University of California Press

Salter, H E, 1960–69 *Survey of Oxford*. 2 vols. Oxford: Oxford Record Soc

Sawrey-Cookson, M, 1979 Newbiggin Hall, *Trans of the Cumberland & Westmorland Antiq & Archaeol Soc*, new ser, **79**, 124–29

Schofield, J (ed), 1987 *The London Surveys of Ralph Treswell*. London Topographical Soc Publication, **135**. London: London Topographical Soc

Schürer, K, & Arkell, T (eds), 1992 *Surveying the People: The Interpretation and Use of Document Sources for the Study of Population in the Later 17th Century*. Oxford: Leopard's Head Press

Seaman, P J (ed), 1988 Norfolk and Norwich Hearth Tax Assessment. Lady Day 1666, *Norfolk Genealogy*, **20**

Seaman, P, Pound, J, & Smith, R, 2001 *Norfolk Hearth Tax Exemption Certificates 1670–1674: Norwich, Great Yarmouth, King's Lynn and Thetford*. British Record Soc Hearth Tax Ser **3**. Norfolk Record Soc **65**. London: British Record Soc

Sheppard, F H W (ed), 1957 *Survey of London, 27: Spitalfields and Mile End New Town*. London County Council. London: The Athlone Press

Sketchley, J, 1775 *Sketchley's Bristol Directory: Including Clifton, Bedminster, and the Out-Parishes of St. James and St. Philip*. Bristol: James Sketchley

Skipp, V, 1979 *The Centre of England*. London: Eyre Methuen

Slack, P, 1988 *Poverty and Policy in Tudor and Stuart England*. London: Longman.

Slater, T, forthcoming, *Historic Atlas of Warwickshire*. Chichester: Phillimore

Slocombe, P M, 1988 *Wiltshire Farm Houses and Cottages*. Devizes: Devizes Books

Smith, J T, 1992 *English Houses: The Hertfordshire Evidence*. London: HMSO

Smith, P, 1975 *Houses of the Welsh Countryside*. London: HMSO

Smith, R, & Carter, A, 1983 Function and Site: Aspects of Norwich Buildings Before 1700, *Vernacular Archit*, **14**, 5–18

Smuts, R M, 1991, The Court and Its Neighbourhood: Royal Policy and Urban Growth in the Early Stuart West End, *J British Studies*, **30**(2), 117–49

Snell, K D M, 1991 Pauper Settlement and the Right to Poor Relief in England and Wales, *Continuity & Change*, **6**(3), 375–415

Spence, C, 2000 *London in the 1690s: A Social Atlas*. London: University of London, Institute of Hist Research, Centre for Metropolitan Hist

Spufford, M, 1962, The Significance of the Cambridgeshire Hearth Tax, *Procs of the Cambs Antiq Soc*, **55**, 53–65 (Repr with original pagination in Spufford 2000b)

Spufford, M, 1974 *Contrasting Communities. English Villagers in the 16th and 17th Centuries*. Cambridge: Cambridge University Press

Spufford, M, 1990 The limitations of the probate inventory, in J Chartres & D Hey (eds), 1990, *English Rural Society 1500–1800*. Cambridge: Cambridge University Press, 139–74 (Repr with original pagination in Spufford 2000a)

Spufford, M, 2000a *Figures in the Landscape: Rural England 1500–1700*. Aldershot: Ashgate

Spufford, M, 2000b The Scope of Local History, and the Potential of the Hearth Tax Returns, *The Local Historian*, **30**(4), 202–21

Spufford, M, 2000c The Scope of the Enquiry, in Spufford, 2000a, 1–20

Spufford, M, & Spufford, P, 1964 *Eccleshall: The Story of a Staffordshire Market Town and its Dependent Villages*. Keele: University of Keele

Spufford, M, & Watt, J, 1995 *Poverty Portrayed: Gregory King and the Parish of Eccleshall*. Keele: University of Keele Press

Statutes of the Realm 1810–28. 9 vols in 10. London: G Eyre and A Strahan

Steer, F W, 1950 *Farm and Cottage Inventories of Mid-Essex, 1639–1749*. Chelmsford: Essex Record Office

Stow, J, 1603 *A Survey of London*. C L Kingsford (ed), 1908. 3 vols. Oxford: Clarendon Press

Strickland, H E, 1812 *A General View of the Agriculture of the East Riding of York*. York: Board of Agriculture

Summerson, J, 1945 *Georgian London*. H Colvin (ed), 2003. London: Yale University Press

Taylor, C, 1979, *Roads and Tracks of Britain*. London: Dent

Thirsk, J (ed), 1967a *The Agrarian History of England and Wales, Volume 4: 1500–1640*, Cambridge: Cambridge University Press

Thirsk, J, 1967b The Farming Regions of England, in Thirsk 1967a, 1–112

Thirsk, J (ed), 1984a *The Agrarian History of England and Wales, Volume 5: 1640–1750*. 2 vols. Cambridge: Cambridge University Press

Thirsk, J, 1984b Industries in the Countryside, in J Thirsk, *The Rural Economy of England: Collected Essays*. London: Hambledon Press, 217–33

Thirsk, J, 1997 *Alternative Agriculture: A History from the Black Death to the Present Day*. Oxford: Oxford University Press

Thirsk, J, & Cooper, J P (eds), 1972 *Seventeenth-Century Economic Documents*. Oxford: Clarendon Press

Thomas, K, 1983 *Man and the Natural World: Changing Attitudes in England 1500–1800*. Harmondsworth: Allen Lane

Tolhurst, P, 1982 The Vernacular Architecture of Norfolk. A Sample Survey. Unpubl MA thesis, University of Manchester

Tolhurst, P, 1993 Brick as an Indicator of Wealth 1450–1750, in Wade Martins 1993, 112–13

Tomalin, C, 2002 *Samuel Pepys the Unequalled Self*. London: Allen Lane

Totman, C, 1989 *The Green Archipelago: Forestry in Preindustrial Japan*. Berkeley: University of California Press

Unwin, J, 2002 Hallamshire Cutlery Trades in the Late 17th Century: A Study of the Hearth Tax Returns and the Records of the Cutlers' Company. Unpubl PhD thesis, University of Sheffield

Urry, W, 1967 *Canterbury under the Angevin Kings*. London: Athlone Press

VCH 1926–36 *The Victoria History of the Counties of England: The History of Huntingdonshire*. W Page & G Proby (eds). 3 vols. London: St Catherine's Press

VCH 1953 *Victoria History of the Counties of England. The History of the County of Essex 4*. R B Pugh (ed). London: Oxford University Press

Veasey, E A, 1984 *Nuneaton in the Making, Part 2: Town growth*. Nuneaton: Nuneaton Library

Vernacular Architecture Group 1998 Vernacular Architecture Group: Northumberland Spring 1998. Unpubl conference brochure

Vernacular Architecture Group 2000 Vernacular Architecture Group: Staffordshire and Cheshire Spring 2000. Unpubl conference brochure

Wade Martins, P, 1993 *An Historical Atlas of Norfolk*. Norwich: Norfolk Museums Service

Wade Martins, S, 1997 *A History of Norfolk*. Chichester: Phillimore

Watts, S J, & Watts, S J, 1975 *From Border to Middle Shire: Northumberland 1586–1625* Leicester: Leicester University Press

Weatherill, L, 1996 *Consumer Behaviour and Material Culture in Britain, 1660–1760*. 2nd edn. London: Routledge

Webster, W F, 1988 *Nottinghamshire Hearth Tax 1664: 1674*. Thoroton Soc Record Series **37**. Nottingham: Thoroton Soc

Willan, T S, 1976 *The Inland Trade: Studies in English Internal Trade in the 16th and 17th Centuries*. Manchester: Manchester University Press

Williams, E, 1944. *Capitalism and Slavery*. Chapel Hill: University of North Carolina Press

Williamson, T M, 1993 *The Origins of Norfolk*. Manchester: Manchester University Press

Wilson, A, 1993 *Rethinking Social History: English Society 1570–1920 and its Interpretation*, Manchester: Manchester University Press.

Winstone, R, 1960. *Bristol in the 1890s*. Bristol: Reece Winstone Publishing

Wood-Jones, R B, 1963 *Traditional Domestic Architecture in the Banbury Region*. Manchester: Manchester University Press

Woodward, D (ed), 1984 *The Farming and Memorandum Books of Henry Best of Elmswell, 1642*. London: British Academy

Woodward, D (ed), 1985 *Descriptions of East Yorkshire: Leland to Defoe*. East Yorks Local Hist Ser, **39**. Beverley: East Yorks Local Hist Soc

Wright, N, 1990 The Gentry and Their Houses in Norfolk and Suffolk c 1550–1850. Unpubl PhD thesis, University of East Anglia

Wrigley, E A, 1990 Urban Growth and Agricultural Change: England and the Continent in the Early Modern Period, in P Borsay (ed), *The Eighteenth-Century Town 1688–1820*. Harlow: Longman, 41–47

Yaxley, D (ed), 1984 *Survey of the Houghton Estate by Joseph Hill, 1801*. Norfolk Record Soc, **50**. Norwich: Norfolk Record Soc

Yaxley, S, 1995 Men of Fakenham versus Big H, 1520, in A Longcroft & R S Joby (eds), *East Anglian Studies. Essays presented to J C Barringer on his Retirement*. Norwich: Marwood Press, 311–14

Index

Page numbers in *italics* denote that the reference is, or includes, an illustration. The letter n following a page number indicates that the reference will be found in a note. Places are located within their 17th-century counties.

Abbots Ripton (Hunts) 102
Abbotts, Ann 115
Abbotts, Thomas 112, 115
Acie, Adam 126
Adamson, John 146
Adlinton, Edmund 171
agricultural economies 180–1
Albemarle, Lord 59
Alconbury (Hunts) 96, 103
Alexander, Lewis 15
Almen, Judeth 136
almshouses 8, 18, 19, 116, 122
Alnwick Castle (Northumb) 158
Amey, Thomas 63–4, 67
Andrews, Margery 87
Appleby (Westmorland) 168, 170
Arbury Hall (Warks) 111, *112, 113*
architecture *see* houses, vernacular
Arlush family 129
Armstrong, Grissell 113
Ash (Kent) 46
Ashbourne, Tobias 131
Ashford (Kent) 52
Ashmanaugh (Norfolk) 63
Ashow (Warks)
   Fir Tree Cottage *117*
   parish 119n
Ashridge (Akerigg), William 171
Atkinson, Henry 170
Atkinson, Robert 173n
Atkinson, William 171
Attwood, Margaret 115
Avon, former county of 67
Aydon Castle (Northumb) 158–9

Bacton (Norfolk) 63
Baddesley Clinton (Warks) 109
Badwell Ash (Suffolk) 64
Baildon (W Yorks) 134, 135
Bainton Beacon (E Yorks) 125, 127
Baker, Ann 115
Baker, Henry 112, 115
Baker, John 87
Baker, Mary 115
Banbury (Oxon) 23–4, 25, 29
Bankes, John 167
Barbon, Nicholas 35
Barford (Wilts) 76
Barham (Kent) 49
Barking (Essex) 30
Barley, M W 3

Barlichway hundred (Warks) *106*, 107, 109
Barrington, Ann 30
Barrow, Alice 171
Barrow, Christopher 171
Barton Turf (Norfolk) 63
bastles 159, *160*
Bates, Isabell 113
Beamish, Lidia 113
Bedlington (Northumb) 160
Bedworth (Warks) 29, 107
Beeleigh Abbey (Essex) 56
Beeston St Lawrence (Norfolk) 63
Belsay Castle (Northumb) *158*
Benenden (Kent) 24, 25
Bennet, Edward 87
Berkshire 7
Berwick upon Tweed (Northumb) 155, 156
Best, Henry 128
Best, John 128
Best, Sarah 128
Bevan, Thomas 90
Beverley (E Yorks) 122, 127, 128–9
Biddenden (Kent) 24
Billers, Alderman 109
Bingley (W Yorks) 137
Birmingham (Warks) 19, 109
Blackbourne hundred (Suffolk) 64
Blackburne, Thomas 10
Blackburne hundred (Lancs), Hearth Tax list *10*
Blackheath hundred (Kent) 49
Blackwell, Capt 91, 92
Blickling (Norfolk) 72
Blofield hundred (Norfolk) 62
Blome, Richard 129
Bodsey Grange (Hunts) 104
Bolt, Tho 113
Borden (Kent) 46
Boreham (Essex) 59
Bothomley, Edmund 137
Boughton Monchelsea (Kent), houses 52
   Bishops Farmhouse 52, *53*
   Fir Tree Cottage 52
   Swallows 50
   White Cottage 50
boundaries, township 4
Bourne hundred (Lincs) 20–1
Bower, John 130
Bowler, Henry 11
Boxted (Essex) 59
Boyle, George 139–40
Boynton family 128

192 Index

Braikenridge, George Weare 84
Bramhope (W Yorks) 136
Brampton (Hunts)
   estate 98
   Pepys house 99, *100*, 101
Brancepeth (Durham) 153
Brandesburton (E Yorks) 125
Brathwaite, Brian 165
braziers 134
Breconshire 17n
Bretton (W Yorks) 133
Brian, Edward 113
brick, use of 24–5, 30, 132, 179, 180, 181
   Essex 30, 56–7, 60, 61
   Hertfordshire 25
   Huntingdonshire 96, 101, 102, 103, 104, 105
   Kent 48, 49–50, 52, 54, 59
   Norfolk 70, 71, 72
   Yorkshire, East Riding 124, 128, 129, 130, 131
   Yorkshire, West Riding 137
Bridge (Kent) 24
Bridlington (E Yorks) 122, 129–30
Brigstock Little Park (Northants) 76
Brimsden, Christopher 93
Brington (Hunts) 102
Bristol
   Arthur's Acre 84
   Broad Quay 92
   Castle Green/Street 86–7, *88–9*, 90, 94
   expansion 93–4
   Hearth Tax records 83–4
   houses 84–5
      garden houses 90, *91–2*, *93*, 94
      hallhouses 85, *86*
      inns 92–3
      redevelopment 87–90
      shophouses 86–7, *88–9*
      sub-tenants 87
   inns
      Bear 93
      Black Boy 92
      Gillows 92
      Great House 93
      Lamb 93
      Red Lion 93
      Three Cranes 92
      White Horse 93
   King Street 87, 94
   Red Lodge 91, 92
   Redcliff Street 84, 90, 93
   St Michael's Hill 84, 90, *91*, *92*, 94
   St Michael's ward/parish 90–2
      Broad Street 84, 90, 92
      Park Lane 90
      Park Row 91, 92
      Upper Church Lane 91, 92
   St Nicholas Street 90
   St Thomas Street 93
   St Thomas ward 92–3
   St Werburgh parish 85, 86
      Corn Street 85
      Small Street 85, *86*, 90
   Tower Street 94
   Tucker Street 84, 93
   Welsh Back 90
   Wine Street 90
Britch, Roger 171
British Academy 182
British Record Society 4, 5
Brooke, Lord 109
Brough, Robert 171
Brough, Roger 171
Broughton (Hunts) 101
Brown, Samuel 112
Browne, Elizabeth 90
Browne, Patrick 87
Brownsword, Revd William 165
Bryant, Richard 87
Buckden (Hunts) 96, 98, 99
Buckinghamshire 20
Buckrose wapentake (E Yorks) 125, 127
building materials 180
   Dorset 75
   Huntingdonshire 96
   Northumberland 155
   Warwickshire 109, *111*
   Yorkshire, East Riding 124, 130
   see also brick
buildings *see* houses, vernacular
Bullock, Mr 91
Bullock Road/Track 96
Burkitt, Miles 173n
Burmarsh (Kent) 24
Burroughs, William 92
Burton Agnes (E Yorks) 128
Burton Constable Hall (E Yorks) 128
Butcher, John 86
Buttsbury (Essex) 59
Byerley family 152–3
   William senior and junior 153
Byers Green (Durham) 153

Calais (France) 26
Calder Valley (W Yorks) 4, 64
Cambridge (Cambs) 23, 30
Cambridgeshire, Hearth Tax returns
   county list 11, *12*
   exemptions 62
   mapping 64, 66, 70–1
   population density *98*
   publication 4
   wealth 67, 74, 179
Canley (Warks), Ivy Farm *117*
Cann, Margaret 85
Cann, Sir Robert 85–6
Canterbury (Kent) 24, 46, 83
   Archbishop of 20
Carlill, Robert 127
Carmarthenshire 17n
Carr, Ralph 156
Cary, Christopher 91
Caston (Norfolk) 63
Catlyn, William 129
cauldrons 25

Cave, Henry, drawing by 124, *125*
Challoner, Robert 90
Charing (Kent)
    medieval houses 46
    Wickens 49, *50*
Charles II 151, 182
Chartham (Kent) 24
Chatham (Kent) 52, 54
Chedgrave (Norfolk) 72
Cheeseman, Stephen 50
Chelmsford (Essex) 59
Cheney, Sir Thomas 48
Chesapeake Bay (Virginia, USA) 79
Chetnole (Dorset)
    Chetnole Farm *80*, 81, 82
    The Laurels 75
Chiddingstone (Kent) 50
Childes, Edward 119n
Chilvers Coton (Warks) 107, 111, *112–15*
chimney men 11, 150, 152
chimneys
    design 24–5, *178*, 179, 180, 181
    discussion by county
        Cheshire *178*, 179
        Dorset 75, 76, 77, 78, 79
        Durham 148, 154
        Essex 30, 56–7, 59, 60–1
        Hertfordshire 24–5, 177
        Huntingdonshire 96, 98, 99, *101*, 102–3, *104–5*, *178*, 179
        Kent 48, 49–50, *51*, 52, 54, *178*
        Norfolk 67, 70, 71, 72
        Northumberland 162
        Westmorland 165, 168, 169–70
        Yorkshire, East Riding 124, *125*, 128, 129, 130–1
        Yorkshire, West Riding 134, 137, 140
    numbers, increase of 23, 132, 177, 180, 181
The Chimney's Scuffle 150
Chipchase Castle (Northumb) *157*, 158
Chippenham (Cambs) 64
Chocke, Robert 87
Christian, William 151
churchwardens 18, 19–20, 144
Cinque Ports 46, 52
Civil War 99, 150, 155, 181–2
Clark, Jo 113
Clark, William 113
Clarke, George 15
Claverdon (Warks) 109
Clements, Mary 113
clergy 18, 19–20
Clerk, Sir Henry 60
Cleveland 3
Clifford (W Yorks) 136
Clifford, Lady 134
Clifton (Glos), list 8, *9*
climate 22–3, 24, 75
coal 23–5, *26*, 27–30, 162, 180
    Durham 148, 149–50
    Essex 59, 61
    Huntingdonshire 102
    Yorkshire, East Riding 127, 130
Coke, Paul 29
Colchester (Essex) 30, 56
Combe Abbey (Warks) 109
commissioners 16
commons, settlement on 153–4
community politics, Durham 144, 150–4
Connington Hall (Hunts) 97–8
constables 5, 8–10, 144, 150, 151–3, 154
Cooper, Elizabeth 99
Corbridge (Northumb) 159
Corfe Castle (Dorset) 75
Corfe Mullen (Dorset) 78–9
Cornwall 15, 25, 62
Cosin, John, Bishop of Durham 150, 152
Cotton family 99
    Sir John 99
Coventry (Warks) 107, 109, 119n
Cox, Mary 91
Crackenthorp, Mrs 170
Cranbrook (Kent) 52–4
Craven, Earl of 109
Cressing (Essex) 56, 59–60
    Appletree Farm Cottage 56, *57*, 60
Creswicke, Sir Henry 85, 87, 90
Creyke, Gregory 128
Croftes, James 85
Cromwell family 99, 104
Cropredy (Oxon) 29
Cropton, William 126
Croxton, Thomas 102
Crush, Thomas 60
Cugley, Elizabeth 90
Cumberland 62, 159, 169, 164, *165*, 166
Curdworth (Warks) 109

Dagle, Jos 113
Danby, Lord Treasurer 15
Darnton (Durham) 153
Dartford (Kent) 46, 52, 54
Davis, Sir Thomas 59–60
Dawson, Nicholas 171
Deal (Kent) 54
Dearden, John 132
Dearden, Joshua 132
Deare, William 15
Defoe, Daniel 103, 122
Dent (W Yorks) 4
Denton, Richard 136
Denton Hall (Northumb) *161*, 162
Deptford (Kent) 46, 52, 54
Derbyshire 62
Dering family 49
Derwentdale Plot 151
Devon, list 15, *16*
Dickering (E Yorks) 125, 127
Dilham (Norfolk) 63
Dinas Powys hundred (Glam), list *13*
Dinckley (Lancs), list *10*
dissenters 150–1
Dixwell, Sir Basil 49
Docking (Norfolk) 68

Doddington (Cambs), list 11, *12*
Dorking (Surrey) 29
Dorset 3, 74–82, 179, 181
Dowell, Ja 113
Downton, Thomas 81–2
Drakford, Richard 113
Drayton, Michael 155
Drew, John, house of 86, 87, *89*
Ducket, Anthony 173n
Duckett, Richard 171
Duffield Firth (Derbys) 29
Dunkirk (France) 26
Durham (city) 144, 146, 153
Durham (county), Hearth Tax returns
 housing 144–6, *147–9*, 150, *151*, 159
 North Durham 160
 politics of 144, 150–4
 publication 4
 social relations 144–6
 terrain types 144, *145*
Dyke (Lincs) 20–1
Dyto, Francis 115–16
Dyto, Katherine 115

Earith (Hunts) 96
Easington (Durham) 151
East Barsham (Norfolk) 72
East Bradenham (Norfolk) 63
East Flegg hundred (Norfolk) 62
East Ham (Essex) 30
East Hanningfield (Essex) 59
East Peckham (Kent) 48, 50
 Old Well House 50, *51*
East Riddlesden Hall (W Yorks) 133, 134
East Sutton (Kent) 50
Eastgate (Durham), Westernhopeburn Farmhouse *149*
Easton (Hunts) 99, 105
Ebony (Kent) 24
Ecclesfield (W Yorks) 4
economy, effect on hearth numbers 180–2
Eden family 150, 152
 John 152
Edingthorpe (Norfolk) 63
Edlingham Castle (Northumb) 156, *157*
Edmondsham (Dorset), two-unit Hart's Cottage type *78*
Elham (Kent) 24
Elloughton (E Yorks) 127
Elmsted (Kent) 24
Elmswell (E Yorks), Old Hall *128*
Elsdon Tower (Northumb) *159*
Elton Hall (Hunts) 98–9
Embleton (Northumb) 159
enclosure 148, 150, 153
Errington family 162
Essex
 assessment list 1671 55–6
 fuel 23, 26, 30, 31, 59
 household density *55*, 56
 houses *56–8*, 59–60
 research topics 60–1

Evans, John 87
Evelyn, John 29
Exchequer 8, 9, 11–13, 14, 16
exemptions 8, 11, 15, 18–21
 Bristol 87
 Dorset 74, 76
 Durham 144, 146, 150, 151, 153–4
 Essex 55
 Glamorgan 13
 Huntingdonshire 62
 Kent 46, 62
 London 35, 37, 43–5
 Norfolk 5, 21, 62–3
 Warwickshire 106, 107, *108*, 112, 114, 115–16
 Westmorland 164, 167
 Yorkshire, East Riding 122, 127, 129–30
 Yorkshire, West Riding 5
Exeter (Devon) 15
Exhall (Warks) 107

farmers 11–14, 15–16, 18, 64, 152, 164
Farrier, Thomas 20
Farrier, William 93
Faversham (Kent) 52
Fell, William 169
Felmingham (Norfolk) 63
Fenery, William 64
Fenton, Roger 170
Fenton, William 165
Fenwick, Alderman, house of *163*
Ferrers, Henry 109
Ferrers, John 109
Fiennes, Celia 125
Filey (E Yorks) 125
Fimber (E Yorks) 127
firehoods *see* smoke bays/firehoods
firewood *22*, 23–4, 25–7, 28, 30, 31
 Essex 59
 Huntingdonshire 102
Flailcroft (W Yorks) 134–5
Fleming, Sir Daniel 164, 170
Fleming, Margaret 173n
Fleming, Thomas 167, 173n
Foleshill (Warks) 107
Folkestone (Kent) 24, 54
Ford (Northumb) 159
Foulden (Norfolk) 63
fuel 22–31, 177, 180
 Durham 148, 149–50
 Essex 59, 61
 Huntingdonshire 102
 Yorkshire, East Riding 127, 130
furnaces 8, 18, 19, 27
Furness (Westmorland) 164, 166

Garveston (Norfolk), Waterloo Farm *69*, 71
Gast, John 81–2
Gateshead (Durham) 151
Gay, Anthony 90
Gibbon, Whittgift, house of *15*
Giles, C 3–4
Glamorgan, county list *13*, *14*, 15

Glatton (Hunts) 102
Gloucester (Glos) 181
Gloucestershire, county list 8, *9*
Godmanchester (Cambs), Ermine Street 101
Godwin, William 85
Gonning, John 90
Goode, Thomas 102
Goodnestone (Kent) 46, 52
Goudhurst (Kent) 24
Gramer, Francis 107
Gravesend (Kent) 46, 52, 54
Graveship of Holme (W Yorks) 4
Grayrigg Hall (Westmorland) 170
Great Bowden (Leics) 29–30
Great Catworth (Hunts), Brook End Farmhouse *101*, 102, 105
Great Gransden (Hunts) 105
Great Leighs (Essex), Willow Farm 56
Great North Road 96
great rebuilding, concept of 4, 183
　Durham 150
　Kent 5
　Westmorland 169
　Yorkshire, East Riding 131
　Yorkshire, West Riding 132–3, 142
Great Staughton (Hunts), Highbury *104*, 105
Greatham (Durham) 153
Green, Edwin 173n
Green, W, etching by 167, *168*
Greenwich (Kent) 46, 49
Gresham (Norfolk) 19, 21
Grey, William 160
Griff (Warks) 111, *112*
Grigg, Edwin 173n
Guildford (Surrey) 29
Gunning, John 85
Gurnell, William and Ann 171
Gwinn, John 85

Hadrian's Wall 155, 162
Haggett, John 90
Hail Weston Farmhouse (Hunts) *105*, *178*, 179
Hale, Richard 87
Hall, Francis 87
Hallamshire Cutlers' Company 5–6
Hallhead, Mabel 167
Hallhead, Nicholas 167
Hamerton (Hunts) 98, 101
Hampshire 11, 48, 77
Hancocke, Leonard 90
Hanson, John 137
Harris, John 87
Harris, Thomas 87
Harrison, B and Hutton, B 3
Harrison, William 23–4, 28, 30, 56–7, 132–3, 134, 142
Harston (Cambs) 63
Harthill Wapentake (E Yorks) 125, 127
Hartlepool (Durham) 146
Harwell (Berks) 75
Hatch, Richard 50
Hawksworth, Sir Richard 133

Haworth (W Yorks) 4, 136
Haynes, Thomas 85
Hazell, William 85
Hazelwood (Derbys) 29
Headcorn (Kent) 24
Hearne, Christopher 15
hearth furniture 23, 25, 29, 30, 180
　Essex 58–9, 60
　Westmorland 169, 170
　Yorkshire, East Riding 126, 127, 128
　Yorkshire, West Riding 136, 137, 140
hearth numbers 177, 180–3
　Bristol 85, 86–7, 90, 91, 92–3
　Dorset 74, 76, 77, 79, 80, 81–2
　Durham 144–6, *147*, 148–9
　Essex 59–60
　Huntingdonshire 98–9, 101, 102
　Kent 46, *48*, 49, 50, 52–4
　London 35, *36*, 37–9, 44, 45
　　Clerkenwell 41–3
　　Spitalfields 40–1
　　Whitechapel 39
　Norfolk 63–4, *65–7*, 68, *69–70*, 71–2
　Northumberland 156, 158–9
　Warwickshire 107, *108*, 109, *110*, 111, 112, 114–18
　Westmorland 164–71
　Yorkshire, East Riding 125, *126*, 127, 128–9, 130–1
　Yorkshire, West Riding 134–40, 142
Hearth Tax
　administrations 7, 8–16
　assessments *see* hearth numbers
　avoidance 5, 10, 11, 64, 81, 131
　duration 3, 7
　exemption *see* exemptions
　frequency 3, 7
　historical summary 7–8
　refusal to pay 8
　study of 3–7
　units of assessment 4, 8
　　Essex 55
　　Huntingdonshire 96
　　Kent 46
　　Northumberland 160
　　Warwickshire *106*, 107
　　Westmorland 164, *165*
　　Yorkshire, East Riding 122
　yield 7, 8
Hearth Tax Act 1662 7, 8, 18, 19
Hearth Tax Act 1663 7, 9, 10
Hearth Tax Act 1664 7, 11, 18
Hearth Tax Act 1689 7
Heath (W Yorks) 133
heating
　cultural factors 182–3
　development of
　　Dorset 75
　　Durham 146–8
　　Essex 56, 57–9
　　Kent 48–9, *51*, 52
hedge breaking 30, 31

Hedon (E Yorks) 122
Hellier, John 91
Hemlingford hundred (Warks) *106*, 107, 109
Hemmingford Grey Manor (Hunts) 104
Henry VIII 26–7
Heptonstall (W Yorks) 136
Herbert, James 48
Herbert, Philip 48–9
Hereford (Herefs) 19
Herefordshire 11, 19, 20
Heritage Lottery Fund 4
Heron, Sir Cuthbert 158
Hertford (Herts) 18, 21
Hertfordshire 20, 21, 24, 25, 31, 177, 179
Hett (Durham), Slashpool Farm *149*
Hexham (Northumb) 152
Higgins, Thomas 109
Hill, Elizabeth 29
Hill, George 90
Hillier, John 90
Hinchingbrooke (Hunts) 96, 98–9
Hinde, John 165
Hinxton (Cambs) 63
Hoare, - 87
Hobbs, Francis 87
Hobson, William 85
Holderness (E Yorks) 127
Hole Bastle (Northumb) 159, *160*
Holkham (Norfolk) 72, 73
Hollister, John 87
Holloway, Moses 109
Holme, Henry 171
Holme, Margaret 171
Holme Beacon (E Yorks) 127
Holme Hale (Norfolk) 63
Holmes Chapel (Ches), The Medicine House *178*, 179
Holmfirth (W Yorks) 4
Holy Island (Northumb) 160
Honing (Norfolk) 63
Hooke, Robert 87
Hopkins, Sir Richard 109
Horning (Norfolk) 63
Horsforth (W Yorks) 138
Hoskins, W G 3, 4–5, 132
hospitals 8, 18, 19
Hough, William 112
Houghton (Hunts) 105
Houghton (Norfolk) 72, 73
houses, vernacular 3–5, 179–80
　Bristol 83, 84–5
　　garden houses 90, *91–2*, 93
　　hallhouses 84, 85, *86*
　　inns 92–3
　　redevelopment 87–90
　　shophouses 84, 86–7, *88–9*
　Dorset 74–5, *76–81*, 82
　Durham 144–6, *148–9*, 150, *151*
　Essex *56–8*, 59–60
　Glamorgan *15*
　Huntingdonshire *99–101*, 102, *103–5*
　Kent

　　17th-century rural 52, *53*
　　medieval legacy 46–8, *49–51*, 52
　　town houses 52–4
　London 35, 39, 45
　　Clerkenwell 41, *43*, *44*
　　Spitalfields 40–1, *42*
　　Whitechapel 39–40, *41*
　Norfolk 62, 65, 66–7, *68–9*, 70–2
　Northumberland 155, 156
　　rural, larger 156, *157–9*
　　rural, smaller 159, *160*
　　urban 160, *161–3*
　Warwickshire 109–11, 112, *113–17*, 118
　Westmorland 171–2
　　multi-hearthed 167–9, *170*, 171
　　single-hearthed 165–7, *168*
　Yorkshire, East Riding 122, *124–5*, 127, *128–30*, 131
　Yorkshire, West Riding 133, 140–2
　　gentry and nobility *132*, 133–4
　　yeomanry and lower ranks 134, *135–6*, 137, *138–9*, 140, *141–2*
Hoveton St John (Norfolk) 63
Hoveton St Peter (Norfolk) 63
Howden (E Yorks) 122
Howdenshire (E Yorks) 127, 128
Huddersfield (W Yorks) 4, 137
Hudson, William 130
Hugh, Christopher 15
Hull (E Yorks) 122, 127, 129
　Wilberforce House *129*
hundreds 8
Hunsley Beacon (E Yorks) 127
Hunstanton (Norfolk) 72
Hunt, Flower, house of 86–7, *88*, 89
Huntingdon (Hunts) 96, 98
Huntingdonshire
　chimneys 102–4, *105*
　Hearth Tax returns 62, 96–7, *98*, 99–102
　houses *99–101*, 102, *103–5*
　landscape and geography 96, *97*
Hurstingstone hundred (Hunts) 96, *97*, 102
Hutton, B *see* Harrison, B and Hutton, B
Hutton Wandesley (W Yorks) 5
Hyne, Widow 173n

Ibstock (Leics) 29
industrial activity, increase in 23, 27–8, 29
Ingatestone (Essex) 30, 56, 59, 60
　Potter Row House *57*
inns 15
　Bristol 92–3
　Essex 60
　Warwickshire 109, 115, 119n
investment cycles 181
Irstead (Norfolk) 63
Irwin, Lord 134
Iwade (Kent) 24

James I 49
James II 130
Jayne, William 93

Jefferies, Thomas 85
Jennings, Mrs 91
Jennings, Thomas, house of 91, *92*
Johnson, Henry 136
Johnson, Margaret 113
Johnson, Robert (of Arbury) 113
Johnson, Robert (of North Newbald) 125–6
Johnson, Sarah 113
Johnson, William 5
Jones, Henry 90
Jopson, Henry 165
Jordan, Richard 90
Justices of the Peace 8, 10, 18, 19, 20
   Durham 144, 151, 152
   Westmorland 164

Kay, John
   house of *151*, 152
   notebook 152, 153
Kendal (Westmorland)
   Hearth Tax documents 164
   housing 165, 168, 170–1
   Sticklandgate 165, 171, *172*
Kent
   exemptions 62
   fuel 23, 24, 25
   geographical regions 46, *47*
   Hearth Tax records 4, 5, 46
   heating, development of 48–9, *51*, 52
   housing 177
      medieval legacy 46–8, *49–50*
      rural, 17th-century 52, *53*
      town houses 52–4
Kent, William 130
Ketteringham (Norfolk), Juniper House *69*, 71
Ketton (Durham) 152
kilns 8, 18, 19
Kimbolton (Hunts) 96, 98, 99, 102, 105
   Bunyan Cottage 102, *103*
Kineton hundred (Warks) *106*, 107
Kineton hundred (Westmorland) 64
King, Gregory 27, 119n, 146, 168, 177
King, Henry 115
King's Lynn (Norfolk) 22, 96
King's Walden (Herefs) 20
Kingsbarton hundred (Glos), list 8, *9*
Kingston (Surrey) 10, 28
Kirkland (Westmorland) 164
Knedlington Old Hall (E Yorks) 129, *130*
Knightlow hundred (Warks) *106*, 107

Lancashire 3, 30, 65, 180
   county list *10*
Lane, George 90
Langtoft (E Yorks) 126
Langton, Thomas 85, 90
Launder, Edward 93
Lax, John 109
Leamon, George 85
Leath (Westmorland) 164, 166
Ledston Hall (W Yorks) 134
Leigh (Dorset), Iles Farm *81*, 82

Leigh, Lord 109, 115
Leigh, Christopher 115
Leighs Priory (Essex) 59
Leightonstone hundred (Hunts) 96, *97*
Lenham (Kent) 24, 25
Leppington (E Yorks) 131
Levens Hall (Westmorland) 170
Lewis, Sir John 134
Lexden hundred (Essex) 56
Lincoln (Lincs), bishops of 99
Lincolnshire 20–1
Lines, James 113
Lionello, Giovanni Battista 155
Lister, Hugh 129
Little Bowden (Leics) 30
Little Ellingham (Norfolk) 63
Loder, Robert 75
London
   Covent Garden 44
   Emanuel Hospital 125
   expansion 93, 94
   fuel 23, 28, 29
   Great Fire 181
   Hearth Tax administration 11
   households and houses 35–9
      Bethnal Green 37, 38, 39
      Clerkenwell 37, 38, 41, *43*, 44
      Limehouse 39
      Ratcliff 37, 38
      Shadwell 38, 39
      Spitalfields 37, 38, 40–1, *42*, 44
      Wapping 38, 39
      Whitechapel 37, 38, 39, *40*, *41*, 44
   markets 181
   rents, exemptions and politics 43–5
   Westminster School, price of fuel *27*, 28
London, Richard 63–4, 67
long houses 77–8, 124, 150
Long Newton (Durham) 153
Lowther, Sir John 169–70
Lowther Hall (Westmorland) 169, *170*
Luke, Sir Nicholas 104
Lysons, William 85

Machell, Thomas 167, 169
Maidstone (Kent) 46, 49, 52
Maldon (Essex) 59
Mancetter Manor (Warks) 107
Manchester, Earl of 99
Market Harborough (Leics) 29
markets, access to 181
Marsden (W Yorks), Green Top *136*, 137
Marshall, Richard 87
Marton Hall (E Yorks) 128
Mathew, Mr 133
Mawson, George 169
Meekings, C A F 3
Melbury Osmund (Dorset), passage house *76*
Merricke, William 85
Methley Hall (W Yorks) 134
Middlesex 17n, 35, 38, 45
Middleton, Thomas 171

Middleton family of Belsay 158
　Sir William 158
Millerd, map by 92
Milner, Anthony 137
Milton (Kent) 24
Minster (Kent) 24
Mirfield (W Yorks) 136
Mitford, Humphrey 158
Mitford Castle (Northumb) 158
Montague family 99
Montgomeryshire 179
Moore, Gilbert, house of 90, 91
Moore, James 171
Moore, John 30
Moore, Sam 113
Morgan, W see Ogilby, J and Morgan, W
Morice, John 118
Morley St Botolph (Norfolk), Fir Grove Cottage 69, 71
Morris, Thomas 11
Morris, William 8
Mortemer, William 112
Mortimer, John Robert 127
Motley, Henry 11
Moulsham (Essex) 59
Mountnessing (Essex) 59
multiple occupation 11
　Bristol 87
　Essex 60
　Huntingdonshire 97–8
　Kent 54
　London 38, 39, 40, 45
　Westmorland 165–7, 171
Murgatroyd family 133

National Archives 4, 5, 7
Natland (Westmorland) 167
Neatishead (Norfolk) 63
Necton (Norfolk) 63
Neithrop (Oxon) 29
Nethercote (Oxon) 23, 29
Nettleton, Christopher 137–8
Nevett, Nathaniel 11
Newbiggin (Westmorland) 170
Newby, Stephen 173n
Newbystones in Morland (Westmorland) 21
Newcastle upon Tyne
　castle 158, 162
　coal 23, 28, 31, 129, 162
　housing 156, 162–3
　map of 161, 162
　riots 152
　status 160, 162
Newdigate, Sir Richard 112, 113
　family and household 112, 113, 119n
Newington (Kent) 24, 50
Nicholson, James 171
Nicholson, John 173n
Noble, William 171
Nobumasa 22
Norfolk
　estates 70, 72

Hearth Tax
　assessments 5, 21, 62–4
　mapping 64, 65–7, 68, 69–71, 72–3
　soil types 65, 66, 72
Norham (Northumb) 160
Norland (W Yorks), Lower Old Hall 140, 141
Norman Cross hundred (Hunts) 96, 97
North Newbald (E Yorks) 125–6
North Pickenham (Norfolk) 63
North Walsham (Norfolk) 62, 63
Northumberland
　housing
　　rural, larger 156, 157–9
　　rural, smaller 159, 160
　　urban 160, 161–3
　instability 181
　research process 160
　topography and character 155, 156
Norwich (Norfolk) 62, 64, 71
Nott, George 113
Nottinghamshire 3, 10, 17n, 65

occupancy, identification of 84
Ogilby, J and Morgan, W, map by 35, 39, 40, 45
Olliffe, Ralph 93
Orlestone (Kent) 24
Ouldstone, Francis 87
Ovenden (W Yorks) 140
ovens 8, 18, 19
overseers of the poor 18, 19–20
Ovington (Norfolk) 63
Oxburgh (Norfolk) 72
Oxford (Oxon) 23, 83
Oxhill (Warks) 21

Pace, Margaret 113
Parker, Ann 115
Parker, Jo 115
Parker, John 112, 115
Parker, Roger 10
Paston (Norfolk) 63
Patton (Westmorland) 169
paupers 18–19
Pearson, S 3, 5
peat 30, 127, 180
peles 159
Penmark (Glam) 15
Pepys, Samuel, house of 99, 100, 101, 102
Perdue, John 92
Perkin, Edward 140
Peterborough (Cambs) 30–1
Petham (Kent), Dormer Cottage 50–2
Petre, Lady 60
Petre, Sir William 56
Petty, Sir William 150
Pilgrimage of Grace 156
Pilson (Pilston), Elizabeth 15
Pittington (Durham) 148
Pleshey (Essex) 56, 60
Plot, Robert 27–8
Plush (Dorset), three-unit house 77
Pocklington (E Yorks) 122

poll tax 1660 18
poor relief 5, 19, 122, 153, 154
Porthkerry (Glam)
   Church Farm 15
   county list 13, 14, 15
Portington, Henry 128
Portington Hall (E Yorks) 128
Powell, Charles 90
Preston (E Yorks) 126
Priestley, Thomas 140
Pritchard, John 93
probate inventories 3–4, 5, 177–9, 182
   discussed by county
      Bristol 84, 85, 86, 87, 90
      Cambridgeshire 179
      Dorset 74–5, 78, 81–2, 179
      Essex 57–9, 60
      Huntingdonshire 99, 101, 102
      Kent 49, 50, 52
      Norfolk 67
      Northumberland 163
      Warwickshire 109, 111, 115, 116–18
      Westmorland 164–7, 168, 169, 170, 171
      Yorkshire, East Riding 124, 125–9
      Yorkshire, West Riding 133, 136, 137–8, 139–40
   fuel, references to 23–4, 25, 29, 30
Proby family 99
   Sir John 99
Pryme, Abraham de la 129
Puckering, Sir Henry 109
Puddletown (Dorset), Tudor Cottage 79
Putney (Surrey) 18, 19, 21

Quarter Sessions 7, 8, 10, 11, 46, 152, 153

Radnorshire 17n
Radwinter (Essex) 23, 30, 56
Ramsey (Hunts) 96, 98, 99, 104
Randle, William 112
Randles, Katherine 115
Randles, William 115
Rawcliffe (W Yorks) 5
Reade, Robert 137
receivers 11, 14, 15, 18, 64, 151
Regill (Westmorland) 165
Restoration 150–1
Richmond (Surrey) 83
Riddlington (Norfolk) 63
Ridgley, John 109
riots 152
Rising of the Northern Earls 156
River (Kent) 24
Robertsbridge (Sussex) 27
Robines, Edith 85
Rochester (Kent) 46, 52
Rockland St Peter (Norfolk) 63
Roehampton (Surrey) 18, 19, 21
Roehampton Project 4, 5, 6
Romney Marsh (Kent) 46
Rougham (Norfolk) 72
Roxwell (Essex) 56, 57, 59, 60

Royal Commission on the Historical Monuments of England 74
Ruckinge (Kent) 24
Rydal (Westmorland) 167
   Hart Head 167, 168
Rye (Sussex) 26

Saffin, John 91
Saffron Walden (Essex) 23, 30, 31
Saham Toney (Norfolk) 63
St Helen Auckland (Durham) 153
St Ives (Hunts) 96
St Neots (Hunts) 96
Salvin family 150
Sandal (W Yorks) 136
Sanders, Mr 126
Sanders, Jane 113
Sandwich (Kent) 23, 25, 31, 52, 54
Sandwich family 99
Saunders, - 87
Savile, Sir John 134
Scala, Gian Tomasso 162
Scampston (E Yorks) 122, 125
Scarborough (N Yorks) 129
Sco Ruston (Norfolk) 63
Scotland, border with 155–6, 160–2, 181
Scott, Mr 113
Searle, Sarah 113
Sedgeford (Norfolk) 68
Selby family 99
   John 99
Sellindge (Kent) 50
Selside (Westmorland) 169, 173n
Sergeant, Francis 112
Sergeant, Robert 113
Sevenoaks (Kent) 52
Sharlston (W Yorks) 137
Sheffield (W Yorks) 5–6
Sheldrich (Kent) 24
Shelf (W Yorks)
   High Bentley 140, 142
   Jackroyd 139–40
Shepherd, Thomas Hosmer, watercolour by 41–3, 44
Shepperd, William 169
Sheppey (Kent), Shurland House 48, 49
sheriffs 8–10, 11, 151
Shewell, Thomas 90, 91
shielings 156
Sidney, Sir William 27
Silbeck, Thomas 23
Simonds, Katherine 87
Simpson, James 171
Singleton, John 171
Sizergh Castle (Westmorland) 170
Skipton Castle (W Yorks) 134
Skircoat (W Yorks) 137, 139
Slaithwaite (W Yorks)
   Birks 135, 136–7
   house of Edmund Bothomley 137
   house of Edward Perkin 140
Sloley (Norfolk) 63

Smallburgh (Norfolk) 63
Smarden (Kent) 24
Smart, - 87
Smith, Daniel 136
Smith, Marmaduke 126
Smith, Thomas 10
smoke bays/firehoods 180
  Essex 56
  Huntingdonshire 102
  Kent 48, 49–50, *51*
  Yorkshire, West Riding 134, 137, 138, 140
Smyth, Edward 115
Smyth, Peter 115
Smythe, John 86
Smythson, Robert 133
Snaith (W Yorks) 5
social status 177, 179
  Bristol 85–6
  Durham 146, 148, 150
  Norfolk 67
  Westmorland 167–8, 169, 170
  Yorkshire, East Riding 130
South Dalton (E Yorks), Oak Cottage *124*
South Pickenham (Norfolk) 63
South Shields (Durham) 146
South Walsham hundred (Norfolk) 62
Southowram (W Yorks) 135–6
Southwark (Surrey) 92
Sowerby (W Yorks)
  house of Daniel Smith 136
  Wood Lane Hall *132*, 133–4
Spaldwick (Hunts)
  Soke of 99
  Spaldwick Manor *99*
Speed, John (of Bristol) 85
Speed, John, map by *161*, 162
Springfield (Essex) 59
Spufford, Margaret 4
Stainland (W Yorks) 136
Standish, Arthur 23–4, 28, 30
Stanhope (Durham) 152
Steeple Bumpstead (Essex), Moyns Park *56*
Stelling (Kent) 24
Stert, Arthur 93
Stiffkey (Norfolk)
  Apple Cottage 67, *68*
  3–5 Bridge Street 67, *68*
  Pip Cottage 67, *68*
  38–40 Wells Road 67, *68*
Stock (Essex) 59
Stockport (Lancs) 30
Stoneleigh (Warks) 111, 114–18
  3 Birmingham Road *117*
  Bridge Cottage *117*
  11–12 Coventry Road 115, *116*
  1–2 Coventry Road *117*
  Manor Farm 115, *116*
Stoneleigh Abbey (Warks) 109, 114
Stones, Jo 113
Stoughton, Nathaniel 119n
Stow, John 39
Stowe Maries (Essex) 56

Stratford-upon-Avon (Warks) 109
Streamer, Richard 85
street directory, Hearth Tax as 83–94
Stubbs, Robert 85
Suffolk 23, 30, 62, 64
Suffolk, Samuel 112
Sunderland (Durham) 28, 129, 146
Sundridge (Kent) 46
surnames 3, 167
Surrey 3, 18, 19, 21, 27, 29, 92
Sussex 23, 27
Sutton, Richard 112
Swafield (Norfolk) 63
Swaine, Samuel 138
Swinburne, Sir John 156

Tacolnston (Norfolk) 72
Tadcaster (N Yorks) 5
Tamworth Castle (Warks) 109
Tandridge (Surrey) 29
Taylor, Alice 29
Taylor, George 140
Taylor, John 23
Taylor, Thomas 29
Temple Newsam (W Yorks) 134
Temple Sowerby (Westmorland) 170
Terling (Essex) 59
Terrington St Clement (Norfolk) 68
Thetford (Norfolk) 63
Thissell, Kath 113
Thompson, Henry 102
Thompson, John 167
Thornton (W Yorks) 136
Thorpe, Daniel 137
Thorpe Audlin (W Yorks) 136
Titus, Susan and Katharine 104
Tiverton (Devon), list 15, *16*
Tivetshall St Mary (Norfolk), Old Ram Inn *69*, 71
Tomson, Tho 113
Tong (W Yorks), Ryecroft 137, *138*
Toseland Hall (Hunts) 104
Toseland hundred (Hunts) 96, *97*
Towers, Ann 171
Trawdon (Lancs) 10
Treswell, Ralph 39
Tudhoe (Durham) 150, 152–3, 154
Tunstead (Norfolk) 63
Twysden family 48
Tyler, Robert 85
Tyly, Edward 90
Tynemouth (Northumb) 162
Tyson, John 171

Ulcombe (Kent) 24
underassessment
  Durham 144, 152–4
  Huntingdonshire 97
  London 45
  Norfolk 67
Urchfont (Wilts) 76

Vernacular Architecture Group 74

Wade, Samuel 140
Wagstaff, Dr 109
Wagster, George junior 112
Wales 75; *see also* Glamorgan
Walgrave, Mr 60
Walker, - 87
Walker, William 167
Walker family, maps by 56, 57, 59, 60
Wall (Northumb) 159
Wallas, Robert 126–7
Wallhead, John 60
Walmer (Kent) 24
Walsgrave (Warks) 107
Walter, Thomas 90
Waltham (Kent) 24
Wansford (Hunts) 96
Waresley (Hunts) 98
Warkworth Castle (Northumb) 158
Warley (W Yorks)
   house of John Hanson 137
   Peel House *139*, 140
Warren, Joyce 93
Warriner, Anthony 171
Warriner, Thomas 173n
Warton, Michael 128–9
Warwick (Warks) 107, 109, 119n
Warwickshire, Hearth Tax returns 7, 106
   individuals and houses 109–11
      Chilvers Coton 111–12, *113–15*
      Stoneleigh 114–15, *116–17*, 118
   statistical analysis 106–7, *108*, 109, *110*
Washingley (Hunts) 98
Watton (E Yorks) 122, *123*
Watton (Norfolk) 63
wealth 3–5, 177–83
   Bristol 83, 84–6, 90, 92
   Dorset 74, 79, 80–2
   Durham 144–6, 148, 150
   Essex 59
   Huntingdonshire 101, 102
   Kent 46, 52, 54
   Norfolk 62–4, 67, 69, 71–2
   Warwickshire 106, 107–9, 111, 116
   Yorkshire, East Riding 120–30
   Yorkshire, West Riding 140–2
   Westmorland 164
Weaverthorpe (E Yorks) 127
Wednesbury (Staffs) 29
Wells, Thomas, house of 91, *92*, *93*
Welton Hall (Northumb) 162
Wendover (Bucks) 20
Wennington (Hunts) 102
Wentworth, Sir Thomas 133
West Auckland (Durham) 146, 150, 152, 153
   East Oakley House *151*, 152
West Bradenham (Norfolk) 63
West Cassop (Durham) 148
West Flegg hundred (Norfolk) 62
West Ham (Essex) 30
West Horndon (Essex) 59
Westbere (Kent) 24, 50
Westmorland *165*

   avoidance 64
   documentary evidence 164
   exemption 18, 21
   houses 171–2
      multi-hearth 167–9, *170*, 171
      single-hearth 164–7, *168*
Wethersfield Hall (Essex) 30
Wheldrake (E Yorks), cottage 124, *125*
Whickham (Durham) 146, 150
Whinfell (Westmorland) 169
Whistons, Jane 113
White, Ann 112, 115
White, Edward 113
Whitehead, Thomas 85
Whithead, Gervas 113
Whitmore, Francis 115
Whitwell (Westmorland) 169
Wigston Magna (Leics) 3, 4–5
Wild, Thomas 29
Williamson, Robert 127
Willoughby, John 93
Wilson, Charles 173n
Wilson, George 171
Wilson, Thomas 130
Wilton (E Yorks) 125, 127
Wiltshire 67
Winchester (Hants) 83
Winchilsea, Earl of 122
Wingham (Kent), 113 High Street 52, *53*
Winship, Thomas 163
Wisbech (Cambs) 30–1, 96
Wisse, Anthony 5
Wisse, Thomas 29
Witchford hundred (Cambs), list 11, *12*
Witton (Norfolk) 63
Wolsingham (Durham), Old Queen's Head
   148
Woodham Walter (Essex), The Bell *58*
Woodland (Warks) 111, *112*
Woodward, Mrs 91
Woolwich (Kent) 46, 49
Worstead (Norfolk) 62, 63
Wrathbone, Gamaliel 60
Wrinehill (Staffs), chimney *178*, 179
Writtle (Essex) 30, 57, 60
   Benedict Otes *58*, 60
Wye (Kent) 24

Yalding (Kent), Nightingale Farm *178*
Yate, Robert 85, 86
Yeamans, Robert 91
Yeomans, William 85, 86
Yetminster (Dorset) 181
York, Archbishop of 20
York (N Yorks) 181
Yorkshire, East Riding 122
   Hearth Tax assessments 122, 127, 131–2
   housing *124–5*, 127, *128–9*
   population decline 122–4
   ports 129–30
   probate inventories 125–7
Yorkshire, North Riding 3, 152, 180, 181

Yorkshire, West Riding
  avoidance 5–6
  housing 3–4
    gentry and nobility *132*, 133–4
    standards 140–2
    yeomanry and lower ranks 134, *135–6*, 137, *138–9*, 140, *141–2*
  themes and sources 132–3